For the Union of Evangelical
CHRISTENDOM

Recipient of
the 1993 Albert C. Outler Prize in Ecumenical Church History
of the American Society of Church History

For the Union of Evangelical
CHRISTENDOM

The Irony of the Reformed Episcopalians

ALLEN C. GUELZO

The Pennsylvania State University Press
University Park, Pennsylvania

Library of Congress Cataloging-in-Publication Data

Guelzo, Allen C.
    For the union of Evangelical Christendom : the irony of the
Reformed Episcopalians / Allen C. Guelzo.

        p.   cm.
    Includes bibliographical references and index.
    ISBN 0-271-01002-9 (alk. paper). — ISBN 0-271-01003-7 (pbk.)
    1. Reformed Episcopal Church—History.   2. Reformed Episcopal
Church—Relations.   3. Episcopal Church—Parties and movements.
4. Evangelicalism—Episcopal Church.   5. Evangelicalism—United
States—History.   6. Anglican Communion—United States—History.
7. Evangelicalism and Christian union.   I. Title.
BX6065.G84   1994
283'.3—dc20   93–2305
                                                                        CIP

Published by The Pennsylvania State University Press,
University Park, PA 16802-1003

It is the policy of The Pennsylvania State University Press to use acid-free paper
for the first printing of all clothbound books. Publications on uncoated stock
satisfy the minimum requirements of American National Standard for Information Sciences—Permanence of Paper for Printed Library Materials, ANSI
Z39.48–1984.

Contents

           Tell Them to Go Forward
           Descent into Confusion
           Remodeling a Church Government
           The Vestments Controversy

VII.   Recovery and Disillusion   269
           They All Ended in Failure
           Miss Benson's Seminary
           The Long Shadow of Robert Livingston Rudolph
           Our Bitter, Mendacious, and Unscrupulous Enemy,
               Dr. Gregg
           The Special Jurisdictions

       Epilogue   311

       Notes   337
       Bibliography   375
       Index   393

List of Illustrations

Acknowledgments

Everyone who ever put pen to paper will admit that all the people they have ever met become a part of what they write. In the case of this book, that Tennysonian truism is not nearly true enough. Some special debts need to be singled out here, not just to acknowledge my personal obligations but also to point out where some very important sources of ideas in this book are located. The book itself began in October of 1982 with a suggestion by Frank Batten, managing editor of the *Norfolk Virginian-Pilot*, and once the active research on the book began in 1986, he and the vestry of Covenant Reformed Episcopal Church of Roanoke, Virginia, supported and encouraged the project all the way to the finish. Another major contributor to the book was Bishop Daniel Gilbert Cox, Assistant Bishop of the New York and Philadelphia Synod of the Reformed Episcopal Church and rector of Bishop Cummins Memorial Church in Catonsville, Maryland. In addition to his personal friendship, Bishop Cox generously gave me access to the only surviving collection of George David Cummins's sermon manuscripts and permitted me to borrow the immense Benjamin B. Leacock Miscellanies Book, both of which belong to Bishop Cummins Memorial Church. The Rev. Walter Truesdell, librarian of Philadelphia Theological Seminary, and his assistant Matthew Thomas also gave me extraordinarily free use of the Reformed Episcopal Church's archival collections at the seminary, especially the Robert Livingston Rudolph papers (which, when I was working on them, were still in the cartons the Rudolph family had used to ship them to the seminary only weeks before). In similar fashion, Gardner Rainey of the Maryland Diocesan Archives freely provided me with access to his substantial collection of Cummins-related material, including printed sermons that had eluded the National Union Catalog's listings; and the Rev. Edwin Schell and his staff at the United Methodist Historical Society in Baltimore exhumed a simply astonishing number of references and clippings concerning Cummins from their collections. Frances Swinford Barr of Lexington, Kentucky, provided me with the results of her research on Cummins in the Diocese of Lexington. I also appreciated the generosity of the C. P. Van Pelt Library of the University of Pennsylvania and the Speer Memorial Library of Princeton Theological Seminary in lending much-needed materials.

I have benefited in many ways from my conversations with a number of scholars who have, like me, found themselves drawn to the peculiar world of Evangelical Episcopalians. The Rev. Canon Richard Fenwick of Guildford Cathedral placed key parts of the puzzle of the Free Church of England and Thomas Huband Gregg into my hands, by way of photocopies and numerous transatlantic telephone conversations. Diana Butler (Westmont College) exchanged notes and a copy of her dissertation on Charles Pettit McIlvaine. Robert Bruce Mullin (North Carolina State University) chimed in at appropriate moments to remind me that there is another side to the Evangelical story. David L. Holmes (College of William and Mary) provided an encouraging comment on an early version of Chapter I. Justus Doenecke (University of South Florida) provided helpful commentary on Charles Edward Cheney. Warren E. Platt of the New York Public Library was especially helpful in providing me with a photograph of Association Hall from the reference collections of the library. The Most Rev. Anthony F. M. Clavier shared his observations on the insular dynamic of small religious groups, and although he had not necessarily intended them as a comment on the Reformed Episcopalians, what he said had clear application to the history of the Reformed Episcopal Church. The Rev. William Deutsch, former diocesan historiographer of the Diocese of Chicago, and Rima Schultz, of the Chicago Area Women's History Project, put me on the trail of several important sources on Charles Edward Cheney; Dr. Schultz also did me the kindness of reading an early version of my account of the Cheney trial. Several other portions of this manuscript were presented in an unusual variety of forums, including the Philadelphia Chapter of the Catholic Clerical Union (an Anglo-Catholic fellowship that listened to my analysis of American Anglo-Catholicism with extraordinary gentleness) on May 18, 1988. Several early versions of parts of the book have appeared as essays in a number of periodicals, including "The Reformed Episcopalians: Restoring Some Old Paths," *The Christian Challenge*, May and September 1990; "The Reformed Episcopalians: The Old Paths Restored," *The Churchman* 104 (Fall 1990); and "A Test of Identity: The Vestments Controversy in the Reformed Episcopal Church, 1873–1897," *Anglican and Episcopal History* 41 (September 1992). Another essay, which extends my exploration of the career of George David Cummins, will appear shortly in the *Filson Club History Quarterly*. Two other parts of this manuscript have been read as papers at the meetings of the American Society of Church History (ASCH): "Ritual, Romanism, and Rebellion: The Destruction of the Evangelical Episcopalians, 1853–1873," at the annual meeting of the ASCH with the American Historical Association in Washington, D.C., on December 29, 1992, subsequently published in *Anglican and Episcopal History* 62 (December 1993); and "The Two Martyrdoms of Charles Edward Cheney: Class, Politics, and Evangelicalism in the Nineteenth-Century Episcopal Church," at the ASCH spring meeting at the College of William and Mary on April 2, 1993. A "semi-paper" entitled "Restoring the Old Paths: The Meaning of the Reformed Episcopal Church" was read by myself along with a paper by the Rev. Canon Daniel Stevick (professor emeritus at the Episcopal Divinity School, Cambridge, Massachusetts) as the preface to a joint Evensong of Episcopalians and Reformed Episcopalians at St. Peter's Church, Philadelphia, Pennsylvania, on April 25, 1993.

In the process of reading papers and exploring manuscripts, I came to treasure the friendship of a wide variety of Anglicans, especially the Rev. Canon Richard K. Bernard of the Chapel of the Cross, Dallas, Texas; the Rev. Dr. Roger Beckwith, the generous and beloved Warden of Latimer House, Oxford; the Rev. Canon Harry Krauss of All Saints' Church, Wynnewood, Pennsylvania; and the Rev. Dr. David Ousley of the church of St. James the Less, Philadelphia, Pennsylvania.

James W. Hankins of Harvard University and Peter J. Potter of the Pennsylvania State University Press had faith in this project even when I didn't, and in the process they became living examples of the meaning of stick and carrot. Debra, my wife, has been a loving, faithful, and true witness and has endured without complaint what almost anyone else would find beyond endurance—the endless litany of fascination with long-dead and rightly-obscure ecclesiastical personages—while Jerusha, Alexandra, and Jonathan managed to walk in the shadow of George David Cummins without once asking who he was.

Thanks alone are, in all these cases, far from a true acknowledgment of the depth of my gratitude, but even if they fall short of satisfying the many obligations I have from this work, perhaps they will better serve as an encouragement and a reminder that no one, not even a historian, needs to be an island.

For David—

who fled from Saul to the mountains

SCHISMATICS AND SECTARIES

There are moments in the unfolding of great controversies when so much anguish becomes packed into certain words that even the whisper of one of them a century later can still set off a reeling series of echoes, like a gong in a dark tunnel. A word like that—the word *schism*—was buried deep in the appendices to the Journal of the 1988 General Convention of the Episcopal Church, and it was used to describe a group of people who, like some obsolete battleship, had once shaken the Episcopal Church to its core, but whom now not one in a hundred in that Convention had ever heard of:

Resolved, the House of Bishops concurring, That this 69th General Convention direct the Standing Commission on Ecumenical Relations to explore the possibilities of dialogue with representatives of the Reformed Episcopal Church looking toward the healing of this particular schism, and direct the Standing Commission on Ecumenical Relations to report to the next General Convention. (P. 499)

The reemergence in 1988 of the Reformed Episcopal Church came as a surprise to virtually every Episcopalian, except the handful of church antiquarians who happened to be serving as convention delegates that year. For most Episcopalians, the Reformed Episcopal Church had disappeared into the mists of Episcopal time nearly a century before, and had been scarcely heard from since. Among the antiquarians, some might have remembered that the Reformed Episcopal Church had come into existence more than a century earlier, in 1873, as the only schismatic split-off the Episcopal Church suffered in nearly 150 years. A few more might have known that the Reformed Episcopal Church was the creation of George David Cummins, then the assistant bishop of the Episcopal Diocese of Kentucky. And perhaps even a few more than that might have known that the Reformed Episcopal Church was the result of a Protestant and Evangelical secession movement led by Cummins to contest the growth and dominance of Anglo-Catholicism in the Episcopal Church in the nineteenth century. But on the whole, the institutional memory of the Episcopal Church is not long, and it is safe to say that no one in the 1988 General Convention would have recognized the Reformed Episcopalians for what they really were in 1873.

And yet simply because the Episcopal Church had ceased to notice them did not mean that they had ceased to exist. Although the membership of the Reformed Episcopal Church in the 1980s and 1990s is not large—approximately 6,000 adult communicant members—it remains an active religious denomination, with outposts in most of the major northeastern United States cities, a flourishing and mostly African-American synod in South Carolina (dating, remarkably, from Reconstruction times), a sprinkling of new parishes in Texas and California, two small theological seminaries (in Pennsylvania and South Carolina), and quite the usual array of auxiliary organizations. More important, it preserved over the years a clear episcopal succession from the founders who left the Episcopal Church, and a sturdy replica of the 1928 Episcopal Book of Common Prayer, mildly vetted and reshaped to suit the evangelical propensities of

Reformed Episcopalians. Reformed Episcopalians look, in fact, so much like old-fashioned, high-button-shoe Episcopalians that why they determined to live a separate denominational life from the Episcopal Church has frequently been cause for some wonder, and the 1988 General Convention resolution was in no small measure a recognition of the family resemblance.

But, as this volume shows, the Reformed Episcopal Church was more than a mere footnote to the history of the American Episcopal Church. It was part of the larger religious and cultural conflicts within American society in the last half of the nineteenth century. On the surface, the Reformed Episcopal schism of 1873 was the culmination of an internecine battle between two factions—the Evangelicals and the Anglo-Catholics—each wanting desperately to direct the future of the Episcopal Church. Beneath that surface, however, the differences that polarized these factions represented deep-seated tensions and anxieties that permeated American culture. The Reformed Episcopalians, as we shall see, were at the center of a fierce struggle between the rationalist impulse of the Evangelical mind in the nineteenth century (so well anatomized by Herman Hovenkamp, Theodore Dwight Bozeman, and James Turner) and the Gothic Romanticism of the Anglo-Catholics, between classical Protestant dogma and gaudy Catholic ritual, and between the symbols of Whig republicanism and the ambiguous antimodernism of an industrial consumer culture.

It is ironic, in that light, that the word in the 1988 General Convention resolution which triggered those nervous echoes was not "republicanism" or "evangelicalism" or "romanticism"—all that would have required precisely the historical consciousness of the 1873 schism that modern Episcopalians seem to lack—but "schism." A substantial part of the irony in this is that schism is a dangerous and difficult concept in Anglican thinking, and likely to blow up in the hands of Episcopalians who resort to it or who attempt to apply it to others. And the echoes set off by this word were all the more violent for being applied to a tiny Episcopal denomination whose history was intimately wrapped up in questions of ecumenicity and church union, ideas that Anglicans have professed great reverence for but have served with surprisingly poor results. Like the concept of schism, the Reformed Episcopalians were, and remain, a nagging question-mark at the heart of Anglican identity, not to mention being an embarrassing blot on the modern Episcopal Church commitment to ecumenical dialogue.

For those reasons, the resolution as it was written never survived to make it to the floor of the 1988 General Convention. Instead, another word was substituted, which substantially toned down the negative ecumenical and theological implications of the word "schism" and set up an ironic contrast that said more than the authors of the resolution probably intended to say:

> *Resolved,* the House of Bishops concurring, That this 69th General Convention direct the Standing Commission on Ecumenical Relations to explore the possibilities of dialogue with representatives of the Reformed Episcopal Church looking toward the healing of this particular division and direct the Standing Commission on Ecumenical Relations to report to the next General Convention. (P. 329)

The substitution of "division" for "schism" helped those few members of the Convention who knew anything about the mysterious history of the Reformed Episcopalians breathe a sigh of relief, since the resolution allowed the Convention to acknowledge, with a little less pain, the existence of the most difficult skeleton in the Episcopal closet.

The desire to dodge pain and embarrassment on this point is indicative of the way modern Episcopalians have cultivated a public image that is free from conflict and dogmatism, "a religion for sophisticates" that avoids the doctrinal troubles that have shivered so many other American religious groups into splinters.[1] Most students who ponder the tensions of ideas, culture, and tradition in American religion turn first for their material to the Puritans, the Methodists, or the Roman Catholics, but not to the Episcopalians. Episcopal Church historiography appears to be free from serious collision and conflict, flat and almost suspiciously featureless, dominated by the mythology of painless synthesis. "Indeed," sighed one of the most recent historians of the Episcopal Church in the nineteenth century, "the standard image of the successful and socially prestigious average Episcopal congregation seems to fly in the face of any talk of the travail of assimilation."[2]

The reasons for this apparent immunity are both theological and historical. To use and to understand the term "schism" assumes that both sides of a schismatic collision have clear and irreconcilable ideas about their group identity. And one major reason that the Episcopal Church, and the larger Anglican Communion of which it is a part, have usually swept the question of schism under the ecclesiastical rug is that modern Anglicanism lacks much coherent sense of its corporate, ecclesiastical, or theological identity as a Christian fellowship. In one sense, the question of Anglican identity is actually an old one, posed for the first time in the sixteenth century by the very Protestant reformers who gave life to the ambidextrous entity forever since known as the Church of England. Although English Protestants of the sixteenth century re-formed what was then only the English province of the Catholic Church around Protestant doctrine, turned it into an independent Protestant Church of England, and wrote its basic creedal document (the Thirty-Nine Articles of Religion) and its worship manual (the Book of Common Prayer) in strongly Protestant terms, they had nevertheless imparted to their English Reformation an ethos quite distinct from, and much less well-defined than, that of the other Protestant churches of Europe. Much as the English Reformers embraced the new Protestant doctrines, they also carried over into the Church of England the episcopal government of the pre-Reformation church, and a good deal of the ceremony and vestments of the old church, and they sought to prove that a national church could indeed reform itself around the Protestant principles of *sola scriptura* and *sola fide* without sloughing off fifteen centuries of the church's history.

This mixing of new and old in the Church of England occurred for three reasons: (1) because the leadership of the English Reformation saw themselves as reformers of catholic Christianity, not revolutionaries against it, (2) because they were tradition-laden Englishmen who derived no small degree of satisfaction from traditional English practices, and who saw no reason to change them merely for the sake of resembling what other European Protestants were doing, and (3) because they did not have much choice. Even if the English reformers had wanted to introduce further reform into the structure of the Church of England, the English government held an absolute veto power over such change, and the monarchs of England preferred to change as little as possible.

On those terms, it is not surprising to find English clergymen in the century following the Reformation at odds with themselves and their church over the real reason for being what they were. At one end of the spectrum of opinion were those whom we have often tagged as the High Churchmen, who rejoiced in their Englishness and in all the trappings of episcopacy, liturgy, and ceremony that went with being part of the Church of England. At the other end were those whom we even more often call Puritans, who viewed their church as parochial, suspecting that all the elaborate justifications of episcopacy they had been raised on were little more than strained efforts to make a religious virtue out of a political necessity. Between these extremes was a large mass of indifferent, government-appointed time-servers, the so-called "dead Dogges who will not Bark," whom the High Churchmen and the Puritans spent considerable amounts of effort blaming each other for.

With the right leadership, the antagonisms of the High Churchmen and the Puritans might have been fused into a healthy, self-correcting tension. Critical though the Puritans were, comparatively few of them before 1625 really intended to abandon the Church of England. But such leadership was not forthcoming. To the contrary, the ham-handed ecclesiastical policies of King James I and his ill-starred son Charles I provoked a civil war in 1642 that arrayed Puritans and members of the Church of England against each other in arms and that came within an ace of destroying the Church of England for good. Previously, Puritans and High Churchmen had at least been bound together by a common loathing for Roman Catholicism, but the civil war dissolved even that bond. By the 1660s, both Puritans and High Churchmen had so mutually exhausted each other that they were forced to yield to the evil that both of them dreaded, as the government now turned to that great indifferent mass in the middle to provide the leadership of the church. This "Latitudinarian" party had learned at least one lesson from the civil war, and that was to ask no questions and rock no boats. With but few exceptions, the church wallowed in weary indifference for almost a century, until the appearance of the Evangelical Revival under the Wesley brothers and George Whitefield, and the emergence in the 1800s of a self-conscious and determined Evangelical churchmanship in William Wilberforce, Charles Simeon, the Earl of Shaftesbury, and a cast of Evangelical bishops from John Bird Sumner to H.C.G. Moule.

And yet, despite this history of conflict within Anglicanism, there still remained to the outside observer several important characteristics shared by all who called themselves Anglican. These common strands, which continued to hold together Anglican identity throughout these crises and until the nineteenth century, were: an unimpeached consensus concerning the authority of Scripture, a generalized Protestantism, and the blunt legal fact of the state establishment of the church—what Paul Avis has called "the erastian paradigm."[3] When Fielding's Parson Thwackum mentioned religion, it was precisely this consensus that he had in mind: "When I mention Religion, I mean the Christian Religion; and not only the Christian Religion, but the Protestant Religion; and not only the Protestant Religion, but the Church of *England*." The need to reconcile the opinions of High Churchmen, Evangelicals, and the assorted vicars of Bray within this "Protestant religion" fairly well guaranteed that theological agreement would be thin at best. But thin or not, the authority of Parliamentary statutes (which imposed the implicit Protestantism of the 1662 Book of Common Prayer as the uniform liturgy of Anglican churches) and the visible governorship of the Crown held the competing voices of the Church of England together in a single Protestant chorus.

But these vital continuities, which had survived reformation in the sixteenth century and revolution in the seventeenth, were themselves shortly to be overtaken by new and unheralded political and ecclesiastical events beginning in the eighteenth century. In the first place, the religious uniformity once guaranteed by the Crown began to be lost as the newly independent American republic, and the remaining English colonies overseas, were gradually permitted to develop their own mostly autonomous versions of Anglicanism, over which the legal establishment of the Church of England no longer had any authority.[4] But a much more dramatic challenge to the "erastian paradigm" of state supremacy was offered before the middle of the nineteenth century by the Oxford Movement.

Beginning in 1833, John Henry Newman, John Keble, and Edward Bouverie Pusey collectively gave birth to what became known as Anglo-Catholicism. Anglo-Catholics soon proved to be very troublesome to the Church of England. Ostensibly, Anglo-Catholicism was only another Puritan-style protest against the interference of the English government in the affairs of the English church, but in fact it erected an utterly different way of understanding Anglican identity. Avis has tagged this as the "apostolic paradigm" because the Anglo-Catholics took as their model not the Puritans but the pre-Reformation English church, which as they supposed had possessed spiritual authority of its own, independent of the state, derived by episcopal succession from the apostolic origins of the early church.[5] Their embrace of the ethos of the Middle Ages led in turn to the embrace of its doctrines, ceremonies, and vestments.

Had the Oxford Movement succeeded entirely in its urge to "convert England in this generation," the Protestant and Erastian identity of the Church of England would simply have been erased and a new ecclesiastical identity substituted for it. But the Oxford Movement only came and saw; it did not conquer the Church of England. At its high-water mark in 1928, it came close to pushing a revision of the prayer book through Parliament that would have effectively established the "apostolic paradigm" as the new norm for the Church of England. But throughout the nineteenth century, the Evangelicals staged a bitter rear-guard action in the parishes and the church courts. Meanwhile, as old High Churchmen, Anglo-Catholics, and Evangelicals were violently grappling with each other, yet another departure from the old identity developed in the German-inspired liberalism of *Essays and Reviews* and F. D. Maurice. The Anglo-Catholic bid to establish a liturgical ascendancy in 1928 died in Parliament—and on the very Erastian principles that the Anglo-Catholics loathed. With at least four different competing identities in its own ranks, the Church of England was left to wallow rudderless, bereft of any star of authority by which to set its course.

Modern Anglicans have attempted to put as good a face on this elephantine dilemma as possible. Some have looked on it as a blessing in disguise, because it leaves Anglicans freer to experiment theologically and spiritually than those who inhabit smaller confessional rooms; others, with a more pragmatic sociology in mind, have simply argued that this is as much as one can expect from a national church in an increasingly pluralistic and multicultural environment. And the late missionary bishop and New Testament scholar Stephen Neill actually suggested that his fellow Anglicans look on the effacement of Anglican identity as an opportunity to practice ecumenical brotherhood with other Christian groups. "The Anglican Churches are sometimes seen to advantage as *par excellence* the ecumenical Churches," Neill declared in his lively *Anglicanism* (1958). "With their own diversity and variety of tradition, they reach out in all directions, can find themselves at home with all manner of Churches, and can to some extent serve as interpreters to one another of widely divided Churches both within and outside the ecumenical fellowship."[6]

At least in theory, Neill had a point, and he was certainly justifed in claiming that Anglicans have been the first off the mark in many of the great ecumenical rushes of the last century. The elegant generosity of the Lambeth Quadrilateral (1886/88), the great "Appeal to All Christian Peoples" issued by the 1920 Lambeth Conference, the Church of South India scheme, and the more recent Anglican–Roman Catholic International Commission (ARCIC) are all ready witnesses for Neill's case. The question, however, is whether there is in fact any real connection at all between the "diversity" he applauded in Anglicanism, and the ecumenicity he spent much of his life promoting. Even Neill had to admit that "comprehensiveness has its drawbacks as well as its advantages." For some, instead of promoting ecumenicity with other Christians, Anglican "diversity" has merely acted to condone the ghettoization of various theological parties *within* Anglicanism—Evangelical, Anglo-Catholic, Liberal, and so on. For others, Neill's idea of comprehension has turned out in practice to mean that Anglicanism's task is either to synthesize opposites somehow or to create gentlemanly strategies for ignoring them. Religious journalist John Whale would only have confirmed Neill's deepest fears about the uses of comprehension when, just before the 1988 Lambeth Conference, he cheerfully declared:

> You are an Anglican if you think you are. The terms are comprehensive. You are most incontrovertibly an Anglican if you have been confirmed by an Anglican bishop and go regularly to an Anglican church. . . . But you are just as much an Anglican if you go regularly to an Anglican church, unconfirmed; or if you go intermittently; or if the church you would go to if you ever went is Anglican; or if it is an Anglican church that you look to for the rites of passage, or that others look to on your behalf. . . . It [the Anglican Church] is already unhostile to departures from doctrinal orthodoxy. Alongside doctrinal authority it will increasingly accommodate the idea of a God who does not act, and a unitarian God at that. It will be explicitly uncertain about an after-life, and unassertive about the exclusive rightness of Christianity as against other faiths. Indeed, before long, it will enter seriously on dialogue with other faiths.[7]

Whale's optimism notwithstanding, this shyness about locating a theological center has produced an atmosphere of malaise and confusion inside Anglican circles.[8] "It must be said bluntly," Bishop Stephen Sykes has written, "that it has served as an open invitation to intellectual laziness and self-deception" and ultimately has led the Church of England to the "illusory self-projection as a Church without any specific doctrinal or confessional position."[9] Even the most recent attempt by the Church of England to feel its way around the theological elephant, the House of Bishops' *Nature of Christian Belief* (1986), was greeted with the derisory comment that it was "a highly self-conscious and ambiguous document, designed to defend their orthodoxy and yet revealing the latitude which some bishops expected for themselves."[10]

The result has been that, outside Anglican circles, the inability to define an Anglican identity has often chilled (instead of promoted, as Neill hoped) ecumenical dialogue. For all of its celebrated gestures in the direction of ecumenicity, the actual sum of ecumenical accomplishment has been comparatively meager in the Anglican Communion. Alongside the Lambeth Quadrilateral, there is the Kikuyu debacle of 1913; alongside the ARCIC there is the ignominious collapse of the Anglican-Methodist accords. Neill himself reluctantly acknowledged that the non-Anglican churches "are sometimes driven to distraction and infuriation by the uncertainties of Anglican action and the indefinable quality of Anglican thought."[11]

In this light, the question of schism takes on uncertain and ominous overtones. Generally speaking, "schism" means a deliberate breaking of ecclesiastical communion and fellowship, most obvious in the repudiation of established ecclesiastical authority and the refusal of eucharistic fellowship.[12] But determining just who is a schismatic and who is the victim of schism usually depends very much upon whose ox is being gored, because ecclesiastical authority is not proof against self-compromise, and eucharistic fellowship can scarcely ignore, or even survive, the emergence of conflicting modes of belief. Furthermore, the meaning of *schism* loses even more force in the Anglican context, where since the mid-nineteenth century it has rarely been possible to judge what the standard for a schismatic to rebel against is.[13]

On those grounds, Anglicans can respond to the breaking of communion by individuals or groups only by two rather peculiar methods. First, they can impute motive. Since the putative schismatic can have no justifiable doctrinal disagreement with a communion that apparently embraces all points of view, the only possible motivation that can explain separation and division is personal. Failing that, they can bury the record, because the fact that schism has occurred in the Anglican world (and more and more frequently in more recent times) can, in this environment, only constitute an embarrassment. And indeed, Anglicans have, while at the same time professing interest in ecumenical dialogues since 1886, done surprisingly little to deal with the separatist movements that have hived off from the Anglican Communion since then, even though some of them (such as the overwhelmingly evangelical Church of England in South Africa) have reasonable legal standing for insisting that they are still loyal members of the Church of England. This is not because of a lack of goodwill in certain quarters. But the Anglican schismatic, by the very action of separation, is suggesting that some theological touchstone does really exist, and any attempt to deal with the claims of such schismatic groups would place an unbearable tension on the already attenuated unity of the Anglican Communion. Someone would have to be acknowledged as right, and someone wrong, and nothing seems to cut so far against the Anglican propensity to insist that all have won and all must have prizes as that deceptively simple but intractable deliberation. Either way, however, the result is that Anglicans prefer to pretend that schism is simply something that doesn't really happen to them, and therefore the Reformed Episcopalians do not exist—did not exist—simply be-

cause, in an Anglican world, they cannot be conceived of as existing.

This only sketches the conceptual problems any historian finds in
laying out the controversies that gave rise to the Reformed Episcopalians. An equally serious problem is logistical—by which I mean,
the simple act of locating sources. Given the visibility of the Episcopal Church as the religious body of choice of upper-class Americans
since the Civil War, that may not seem at first to be a serious disad-
vantage. But the truth is that, in contrast to the lavish and spectacular
attentions showered on the Congregationalists, the Presbyterians, the
Baptists, and the Methodists, few American historians have been
disposed to concede much intellectual or social vitality to Episcopal
history. Instead, it is implicitly understood that the history of the
Episcopal Church is superficial, unintellectual, obsessed with social
status, antidemocratic and not a little racist. Consequently, the number of serious analytical studies of the denomination's history in the
last thirty-five years can almost be counted on one hand, while most
histories of the Episcopal Church rarely rise above the level of the
tepid and self-admiring.

It is difficult to believe that an institution with such an immense
material presence (the most spectacular church buildings in the
United States are usually Episcopal churches, beginning with the
National Cathedral in Washington, D.C., and the Cathedral of St.
John the Divine in New York City) and such impeccable elite social
credentials should suffer from such neglect, but, in spite of it all, the
historiography of the Episcopal Church remains virtually comatose.
That there once existed in the Episcopal Church a militant and powerful Evangelical consensus that plunged the church into an intellec-
tually and theologically complex battle of wits lasting nearly a generation has gone largely unnoticed, both as an event and as a symbol. The
same general Episcopal complacency that today discourages the historian in search of conflict and tension generally slows down even
the most dogged researchers long before they pick up the trail of the
old Evangelicals, and their heirs, the Reformed Episcopalians.

On the other hand, much as the elaborate theology and ritual, not
to mention the denominational exclusiveness, of Episcopalians can
easily put the ambitious historian to sleep, the effort to reintegrate
Episcopalians into the larger matrix of American culture will yield
some rich and complicated results. It can be asked of Episcopalians
why Catholicism, so long a bugbear of American Protestants and so
apparently foreign to the kind of egalitarian republicanism that triumphed in the Civil War, suddenly became so acceptable, and especially to urban elites. Although Anglo-Catholicism gained its great-

est ground among affluent urban white Northerners, their embrace
of a Catholic ethos unavoidably identified them with Roman Catholic immigrants and with white Southerners in their resistance to
modernization, and that calls for a significant rethinking of the image of American Episcopalians as the steady cultural center of American religion.

Similarly, it is important to ask what kind of religious culture the
old Evangelicals codified, as well as to ask what their doctrinal system looked like. The temptation, in the past, has been to resort to a
"myth of synthesis" in Episcopal Church history that seeks to de-
fang the Evangelicals by portraying them as an unusual and remarkable comet, briefly intercepting an Episcopal orbit that is revolving
ineluctably in a Catholic ellipse. But the old Evangelicals and their
Reformed Episcopal protégés challenged fundamental aspects of Anglican and Episcopal order and raised serious questions about nineteenth-century market culture, and the evidence of the Tyng and
Cheney trials shows that the Evangelicals were so threatening and
antithetic a movement that violence was the only answer the Anglo-
Catholics could ultimately provide to them.

Of course, the myth of synthesis, even if it has not encouraged
Episcopal historians to confront these kind of questions or to take
the Evangelicals with sufficient seriousness, does not quite deserve
all the blame. Some of the fault for their historical oblivion must be
laid at the feet of the Evangelicals and the Reformed Episcopalians
themselves. They inscribed much of their discourse in the minutes
and records of societies and conferences, now almost entirely lost,
and in an extensive pamphlet literature that has proved difficult (if
not downright impossible) for archivists and librarians to save or
relocate. They had no great journals. And even though they published numerous magazines and newspapers, it is difficult for modern historians to decode the peculiar language-system of Episcopalians and sort out the trivial from the significant. That problem, in
turn, is further complicated by three fatal Evangelical habits: the
frequent use of anonymous correspondents in Evangelical and Reformed Episcopal publications (which makes it difficult to track important identities and groups), the lack of reliable publishing sched-
ules and systems, and the failure to transmit important material
from weekly or monthly periodicals into the more permanent form
of the book. Only three Reformed Episcopalians in the first generation published books (Cummins, Nicholson, Gallagher), and only
one of those (Gallagher) was actually writing about questions central
to Reformed Episcopal identity.

But the most obvious difficulty in penetrating the ethos of the old Evangelicals and the Reformed Episcopalians has been the undoubted success of the Anglo-Catholics in establishing their own hegemony, and therefore their own version of Episcopal history, as the single reigning view of the history of the Episcopal Church. The Anglo-Catholics and their descendants have, so to speak, taken care of their own through a lengthy series of arid filiopietist biographies of priests and bishops intended almost exclusively for an uncritical Episcopalian audience. The names of Johns, McIlvaine, Sparrow, Eastburn, Tyng, Bedell, Milnor, Clark, Stevens, and of course Cummins have simply been chiseled off the Episcopal monuments. Thus, a reader may be able to read about the history of the Episcopal Church, but the convention of complacency that the Anglo-Catholic hegemony has deposited thickly on the Episcopal past will probably convince the reader that further penetration of that history is probably pointless. Or, to put it another way, the same reader can read *about* George David Cummins, but not without heroic effort can anything *by* Cummins be located or read.[14]

But more than merely losing sight of the Reformed Episcopalians as an institution, the easy acceptance of self-congratulation as the primary mode of Episcopal historical discourse has cost Episcopalians an important theological insight into their history, and that is what Reinhold Niebuhr once defined as the concept of *irony*. Niebuhr offered irony as a paradigm of historical understanding for the benefit of Americans who, as a whole, were too convinced of their own historical innocence; only by seeing that even the most virtuous of actions and clearest of intentions were flawed by sin, only by allowing oneself to hear the laughter of God at human pretentiousness, and only by understanding the sympathy that stood behind that laughter could Americans arrive at a just and moral understanding of themselves and their place in the global community. Martin Marty recently employed this concept of irony as an interpretive device for understanding what happened to American religion at the turn of the twentieth century: rather than describing American religion in that era strictly in terms of conflict, Marty preferred to show how conflict consistently yielded to irony. Religious modernists found their modernisms rendered quickly obsolete and in constant need of updating, or discovered that their struggles to repudiate tradition and formalism contain "surprising revisitations" of what they thought they were abandoning. At the same time, religious conservatives in this era turned out to be far from "merely" conservative; they were, in fact, surprisingly willing to employ the latest technol-

irony:
a subtly
humorous
perception
of
inconsistency

ogy to further their ends and to reconfigure their "old-time religion" in what Marty calls "innovatively reactive" ways.[15]

Marty's "irony thesis" has peculiar and dramatic application to the modern history of both the Episcopal Church and the Reformed Episcopal Church, as this book demonstrates. On the one hand, Anglo-Catholicism plunged the Episcopal Church into a world of medievalism, canon law, and prelacy, but at the same time, it allowed the mind of the church to accommodate itself to modernism far more easily than if it had been ruled by the Evangelicals. Similarly, the Anglo-Catholics came to believe that their construction of Anglicanism was irresistible; they did not foresee the strength of the Evangelical resistance, the willingness of one bishop to provoke schism as a response to Anglo-Catholicism, or the ability of the Evangelicals to survive as a movement outside the official boundaries of the Episcopal hierarchy. By the same token, the Evangelicals who became the Reformed Episcopal Church after 1873 also thought of themselves as a conservative movement (at least in terms of resisting Anglo-Catholic "innovation"), but as the debates over the prayer book and the vestments of the Reformed Episcopal Church amply demonstrate, they were perfectly willing to alter those traditions even as they doggedly announced their intention to preserve them. The Reformed Episcopalians were not New Testament repristinators like Alexander Campbell, something the early Reformed Episcopalians were at pains to point out. They were, however, complex innovators, and what they formulated as an alternative to the Episcopal Church after 1873 combined so many disparate and unlikely elements that it is a wonder they survived Cummins himself.

It would be easy to write these ironies off to the parochialism that invariably attends tiny sectarian movements, especially in the American environment. But this would be to miss the larger connections which the Reformed Episcopalians, as Anglicans and Episcopalians, had to the larger movements of Anglo-American religion and culture in the nineteenth century. It is worth remembering that Anglicanism itself was beginning to be plagued by the same diffusion and dislocation of identity, and has struggled for almost as long as its Reformed Episcopal offspring with the dilemmas of a ruptured sense of the past and a crumbling arrangement of order. Moreover, as much as they embodied a particular set of Anglican questions, the Reformed Episcopalians are also located within the complex history of late nineteenth-century and early twentieth-century American religion. On one level, they represent one more chapter in the Napoleonic retreat of American Protestant evangelicalism into a marginalized and defensive fundamentalism. But on another level, the Reformed Episcopalians also represent a determined if unsuccessful effort to shore up Protestant hegemony in American culture through a primitive but ambitious ecumenicity. Although the American religious environment is overpopulated by separatist movements that advertised themselves as movements toward unity, few such movements started out making greater promises to promote ecumenical unity and evangelical brotherhood, and yet became so ingrown and parochial, as the Reformed Episcopalians, and few ever gained such widespread national notice and yet became so little known. The Reformed Episcopalians became, in fact, virtually a sampler of the ironies Martin Marty found typical of American religion at the turn of the century—of conservatives who manage to destroy past legacies, of integrators who only end up promoting fragmentation, of controversialists whose complaints are ignored by the real objects of complaint (in this case, the Episcopal Church) and who instead devote their controversial energies to destroying each other.

The opening chapters of this book reconstruct the place once occupied in the Episcopal Church of the nineteenth century by its Evangelicals, and move from there to consider the causes and consequences of the Oxford Movement for the Episcopal Church. Because this is not, after all, a book about the Evangelical Episcopalians, but about what happened to them after they left the Episcopal Church in 1873, these chapters are of necessity sketchy, and I can only beg the reader to await the fuller work of David L. Holmes and Diana Butler (which together with this book will form something of a trilogy about the rise and fall of the Evangelical Episcopalians). What I have to say about them, and about the pecularities of such apparently unrelated subjects as William White and the 1785 prayer book, all has a logical place in this story, but only for setting the stage. This is also not a book about the Oxford Movement. John Henry Newman, John Keble, and Edward Bouverie Pusey were men who placed Christian holiness above all things—their careers, for starters, and their lives, if it had come to that—and they restored much that was fundamental to the life of the entire Church of England. But the Evangelicals saw them in quite a different light, and because this is a book about Evangelicals, I have chosen to let the Evangelicals speak for themselves and to put analytical attention on the unhappier aspects of the Anglo-Catholics which provoked Evangelical criticisms. This will not permit the painting of a particularly happy picture of the Anglo-Catholics, but I should say by way of exculpation that the parade of Evangelical criticism that marches forth here is a historical one and is concerned with the perceived behavior of nineteenth-century Anglo-Catholics rather than Anglo-Catholicism as a religious system. This may not make either critics or Anglo-Catholics happy, but space also prevents me from saying everything I want to about the Evangelicals. (Mentioning this allows me to add that, for the sake of establishing distinctions, I have used the upper-case "Evangelical" to refer to those of that allegiance within the Episcopal Church, and the lower-case "evangelical" when I am describing that generic persuasion among other American Protestant denominations.)

This material is followed by the introduction of Charles Edward Cheney and George David Cummins, the principal players in the drama of the Reformed Episcopalians. Here, I pay close attention to the peculiar construction of Cummins's Evangelicalism and the reasons for his break with the Episcopal Church. The narrative then turns to the organization and early years of the Reformed Episcopal Church, when the future seemed especially optimistic and the weight of its unresolved identity had not yet begun to tell on its strength. The next chapters outline how the cracks in the structure of the new church finally opened and threatened collapse in the aftermath of the disastrous Fourteenth General Council in 1897. The final chapter focuses on the institutions and leaders of the early twentieth century—especially Robert Livingston Rudolph—who succeeded in steadying the stricken church, although only at the price of imposing by sheer personality a rigid and frequently self-contradictory identity on what now lapsed into being merely one more small Protestant denomination on the featureless sea of American denominationalism.

Many of the illustrations in this book had to be copied from originals that were not of good quality to begin with. For instance, many of the photographs of turn-of-the-century Reformed Episcopalians were taken from copies of the *Episcopal Recorder* in the 1920s, when the *Recorder* first began to run black-and-white photographs. Those pictures were very grainy when first printed, and the decay that has attacked the highly acidic paper they were printed on seventy years ago made modern reproduction of them something of less than sterling quality. I have chosen to include them anyway, because in some cases they are the only surviving images of places, persons, and things pertinent to this narrative.

Above all, I hope the reader will forgive the fact that this is not always a pleasant story. There are scoundrels as well as saints in this book, and some readers who are familiar with this story will squirm to discover that even some of the saints wore tarnished halos. But the unpleasant surprises are there because I set out to write more than simply a "church history" or a "denominational history." My foremost desire is to show that the Reformed Episcopalians were part of the larger, troubled story of the fall of American Protestantism from its place of cultural hegemony in American life, and that they were one group of Evangelicals who struggled to counteract that fall with an aggressive commitment to Evangelical ecumenical union. And, in a larger context, I want to show how the story of the Reformed Episcopalians is, in the long term, indistinguishable from the fate of Anglican identity. This book is therefore simply a long way of saying that I believe the instinct of the 1988 General Convention was right after all—that what occurred was a division, not a schism.

I

THE EVANGELICAL EPISCOPALIANS

To Revive Spiritual Religion

Sometime during the summer of 1830, the Rev. Dr. James May, an Episcopal clergyman and at that time rector of St. Stephen's Episcopal Church in Wilkes-Barre, Pennsylvania, boarded a Hudson River steamboat on his way to a well-earned rest in the New York mountains. Sharing the same steamboat and the same destination was "a prominent Presbyterian Clergyman of the city of New York," the Rev. Dr. George Washington Bethune. The two divines fell to talking denominational shop, and "in the course of their conversation the Presbyterian spoke most favorably of the Protestant Episcopal Church." May was evidently taken aback; he was not accustomed to unsolicited endorsements from Presbyterian quarters. But Bethune was insistent: "I do not see," said he, "what is to hinder your Church from becoming the dominant Christian body in this country before the close of the next half century."[1]

Bethune could not, in 1830, have been speaking strictly in terms of numerical growth. After four decades of publicly proclaimed religious pluralism, the membership of the Methodist churches in the United States had topped 478,000, followed by some 310,000 Baptists, 173,000 Presbyterians, and 110,000 Congregationalists, while Episcopal Church membership stood at scarcely 50,000; in the 1820s the Presbyterians owned nearly three times as many church buildings as the Episcopalians, and the Methodists and the Baptists each boasted five times as many.[2] And given the fact that the Episcopal Church still represented the unpleasant memories of English domination during the colonial era, and represented as well a stately, formal hierarchy of bishops and read liturgy, there would have been little reason to look for a particularly astounding crescendo of growth by the Episcopalians in a self-consciously republican culture, dominated as it was at almost every point by the interests and energy of pietist evangelicalism.[3]

But Bethune was not talking about numbers. He was instead talking about identity and ethos and purpose. In a little less than two decades, he had seen the Episcopal Church transformed from a denomination tainted with the implications of deadness, formalism, and monarchy to a church that frankly advertised itself as the banner-bearer of "a new era" in American civilization. "She was as nothing in the beginning, doubting of her own ability to rise and stand," wrote Episcopal Church apologist Calvin Colton in *The Genius and Mission of the Protestant Episcopal Church in the United States* (1853), but "now she is eminent." And it was now "her office and her mission, in the providence of God" to become "the fast anchor . . . of the American Protestant world."[4]

But it was particularly the banner under which Bethune saw Episcopalians like May marching as to war that prompted his prophecy of Episcopalian hegemony, for the public face of the Episcopal Church had been regenerated since the turn of the century by the explosive eruption of an Evangelical revival. "There has not [been] a more valuable or remarkable change . . . in the circumstances of the Episcopal Church, in the progress through which it has lately passed," wrote Stephen Tyng in 1835, than the sudden and unanticipated appearance of an Episcopalian Evangelicalism.[5] Virtually without warning or introduction, the Episcopal Church had been wrenched out of the side-ditch to which the aftermath of the American Revolution had consigned it and pushed up into the mainstream of American evangelical life. It suddenly developed prayer meetings, revivals of "religious sensibility," evangelical newspapers, and all the trappings of an evangelical and republican culture, and did it all without the frantic splinterings and divisions that were already cracking apart the Presbyterians, Methodists, and Baptists. "Every day's experience shews us, that [the Episcopal Church] is competent under the divine blessing to produce, to sustain, and, what is more, to *revive* spiritual religion," wrote William Holland Wilmer, a colleague of May's in Alexandria.

> The church in England and America, presents at the present moment, a very unusual phenomenon; "a green old age"; a clergy in many instances, combining the youthful ardour of a sect, with the calm wisdom of a long and temperate course. By a resuscitation of her decayed powers, she has, as it were, broken the bars of the tomb; revived first in one limb, and then in another; and promises, under God, again to advance a favorite child of the reformation, and to bear her share in the dispensation of religion to a perishing world.[6]

To Dr. Bethune, the evangelicalizing of the Episcopal Church had transformed it from what Tyng had described as "an enemy in disguise" to the rest of American Protestantism into what Wilmer called an "ark of the covenant" that "has preserved the law." It had made "a public liturgy" the "remedy" against Unitarianism and New Divinity; it had made episcopal order a refuge from the divisiveness of evangelical sectarianism. It could become, to paraphrase Bethune's oracle, the engine of Christian power in a secular republic.

Some ten years later, May found himself on a similar Hudson River steamboat, and to his amazement once again in the company of the oracular Dr. Bethune. "They naturally referred to their former meeting and conversation, and to the ecclesiastical events that had in the interval interested the Church at large." Bethune remembered the comment he had made to May about the coming dominance of the Episcopal Church, and he asked May if he recalled it. "Yes, perfectly," May replied innocently. "Well," answered Bethune, "I can now tell you why the Protestant Episcopal Church will not be the leading denomination in the next fifty years."

We do not know what must have passed through May's mind as Bethune delivered that sepulchral introduction to the next hour's conversation, but he probably could guess all too well what was coming. Within one generation after Bethune's earlier prophecy, the Evangelical tide in the Episcopal Church was ebbing out as suddenly as it had flowed in, carrying with it into historical forgetfulness the wreckage of the most poisonous controversy in the history of the Episcopal Church. In its wake came an entirely new Episcopal denomination, dedicated to the Evangelical principles—and the religious hegemony—that had once bid so fair to redefine the identity and mission of American Episcopalianism. "The Presbyterian was right," concluded Benjamin B. Leacock, an Evangelical Episcopalian who recorded May's story in 1883. At the time of May's first encounter with Bethune, "a liturgical Church, with an earnest, humble, Gospel-preaching ministry, would have been a rallying point for all the conservative elements in the different, and at that time more or less distracted, Church organizations . . . until eventually, it would have become the head of the sisterhood of Evangelical Churches in this land." But, as Leacock concluded with disgust, "the Protestant Episcopal Church threw away its God-given opportunity." It would, in that process, exchange its opportunity to exercise the national religious hegemony Bethune had predicted for the more well-known role it would play as the religious preserve of the wealthiest of American elites, and trade its Evangelical revival for "a very formal, elaborate, orthodox religion with an extremely worldly, wealthy, and rationalistic congregation."[7]

We have no better idea what Bethune proceeded to lay before the hapless Dr. May as his diagnosis of this startling and incommensurate shift. But it was from precisely the shock of that failure that the Episcopal Church sustained its most significant and embarrassing division, until very recent times, the formation of the Reformed Episcopal Church. Like Bethune, the leaders of the Reformed Episcopal movement were fully confident that an Evangelical episcopacy, sufficiently reformed to avoid the mistakes of the old church, could finally carry American Protestant culture before it as no other movement for evangelical unity had ever done before. And, as Bethune had once predicted, many American Protestants, in the first flush of Reformed Episcopal success, were certain that they would do just that. But they failed, and in the story of the Reformed Episcopalians there was an unpleasant warning for later partisans of Protestant ecumenicalism—that the fissiparous reality of American Protestantism was going to prove more exhausting and intractable than anyone had thought possible.

The Making of a Protestant Episcopal Church

The Evangelical Revival in the Protestant Episcopal Church, not to mention the Reformed Episcopal Church that later sprang up from it, appears abruptly after 1811 as a surprising departure from what had passed for Episcopal practice and belief in the 200 years since the first Church of England services were read on the wilderness shores of the North Atlantic seaboard.[8] Although the "constitucions of the Church of England in all fundamentall pointes" had been planted in the British North American colonies along with the first settlement of Jamestown,[9] its general effectiveness as the official church of all English subjects was hampered, first by the fact that most of the English subjects who could be prevailed on to run the forbidding risks of a colonial plantation were usually dissenters in varying ways from the Church of England, and second by the fact that colonial Anglicanism took the form of two utterly incompatible forms of churchmanship. And neither of these two configurations—the High Churchmen of Connecticut or the state-established Latitudinarians of the middle and southern colonies—had anything at all in common with what was to come in the shape of Evangelicalism.

The development of eighteenth-century Connecticut High Church-manship is probably the best-known and most well-worn story in all of American Episcopal Church history, and largely because it sprang with such dramatic contrariness in 1722 from the unlikely soil of New England Puritanism.[10] Dissatisfied with the Puritan notion that authority in the New England churches belonged to individual con-gregations (rather than to the ordained ministry of those congrega-tions), Timothy Cutler, rector of Yale College, Samuel Johnson (a former tutor at Yale), and five others prepared to abandon Connect-icut and Congregationalism and journey to England to find ordina-tion in the more authoritarian bosom of the Church of England.[11] Cutler and Johnson were both ordained by Thomas Green, the bishop of Norwich, on March 31, 1723, and in September both were back in New England, with Johnson as the Society for the Propagation of the Gospel's missionary at Stratford, Connecticut.[12] The persistent handfuls of practicing Anglicans in New England greeted the return of the "apostates" with something bordering on delirium. But Johnson soon learned what other Anglican mission-aries had learned before him, that Anglicans no matter how de-lerious were a decided minority in New England, and that "it was as much worth a man's life was worth even to talk of 'the Church' in Connecticut without the means of self-defense."[13]

Weighed against this barrage of Puritan hostility, Johnson's achieve-

ment as an apostle of Anglicanism in Connecticut is genuinely remarkable. By 1760, he could report to the Archbishop of Canterbury that "there are now thirty churches in that colony," almost all
of which he had a personal hand in organizing and nurturing.[14] Even
more remarkable, he had also managed to enlist a promising band of
young clergymen, most of them recruited by his own efforts and
most of them, like himself, converts from Congregationalism. But
Johnson's converts possessed little of Johnson's patience with the
shrill denunciations of their erstwhile brethren. Goaded and harassed
on all sides by Puritan spitefulness, they lashed back with ever more
strident claims for the virtue of episcopacy, ratcheting up the case
for episcopal government higher and higher with each new round of
violent debate.

No better example can be found of the sharp temper of these
Connecticut High Churchmen than Samuel Seabury, whom Johnson singled out in 1748 as "a solid, sensible, virtuous youth."[15] Solid
he certainly was, if his portraits tell us anything, but sensible is another matter, for Seabury was also arrogant and self-inflated, and he
did not believe in sparing the rod in controversy. In Seabury's mind,
there was no question that episcopacy, with its threefold ministry of
bishops, presbyters, and deacons, had sprung immediately and full-
grown from the heads of the apostles themselves.[16] To deviate from
that order was to deviate from Christianity itself, and Seabury did
not flinch from telling the Puritans that, by this logic, their congregations were nothing but "Conventicles of Hereticks & Schismatics,
who, whatever they pretend, are really no part of the Catholick
Church."[17]

Whether because of the spitefulness of his enemies, or because of
the counter-spite of his friends, Johnson's Connecticut High Churchmanship never became more than a relatively small fragment of the
overall membership of the Church of England in British America.
The Anglicanism of the middle and southern colonies—fueled by
the official backing of colonial governors and imperial bureaucrats,
and by the aggressive intervention of Anglican mission societies like
the Society for the Propagation of the Gospel—was a much more
successful enterprise than Johnson's missions. In fact, it was much
more of a success than it is often given credit. Six of the thirteen
North American colonies actually established the Church of England
by law, and by 1750 some 167 of the 289 Anglican churches in the
thirteen seaboard colonies were located south of Pennsylvania.[18] But
the Anglicanism that prevailed south and west of the Hudson River
noticeably lacked the passion of the Connecticut High Churchmen
for episcopacy. And that may seem strange, because the colonial

South was a structured, hierarchical society of great gentrymen, vast gangs of slaves, and poor white planters who minded, and were reminded of, their place—just the atmosphere, we may suppose, where a structured, hierarchical church ought to flourish. But in the colonial South, the same wealth that made the gentry great also guaranteed that they controlled the vestries. And so long as there was actually no bishop resident in America, the vestries controlled the churches and the clergy, and, unlike Seabury and Johnson, were understandably happy to see matters stay that way.[19]

And then came the American Revolution, which not only destroyed any hopes for the settlement of an Anglican bishop in America but almost destroyed American Anglicanism itself. The Church of England was too closely linked to the policies of Great Britain not to become a target for elimination by American patriots. As for the Anglican clergy, their emotional identification with English values and society was too important an aspect of their lives to allow them to duck the stones hurled at them.[20] By the time the Revolution ended, 131 of the 286 Anglican clergymen resident in America in 1774 had disappeared into exile, and most were from the most critical areas in the Northern states.[21] The Church might well have perished by common consent had it not been for the unlikely and ingenious proposals of the Rev. William White of Philadelphia.

The key to understanding William White and his astounding rescue of American Anglicanism lies mostly in appreciating how much plain geographical distance lay between him and Samuel Seabury. William White was born, lived, and died in the quiet, tolerant atmosphere of Philadelphia and, unlike Seabury, spent sixty untroubled years as the rector of Philadelphia's United Parish of Christ Church and St. Peter's. Philadelphia Episcopalianism had a distinct flavor of genteel Latitudinarianism to it and found most prominent expression in William Smith, the semi-Arian provost of the College of Philadelphia, and the frankly deistical artisan, Benjamin Franklin. Far from the polemical battlefields of New England, White was never beset by the need to defend episcopal order in the extravagant terms of Johnson or Seabury. Little wonder, then, that White took a more indulgent view of Anglicanism and episcopacy than the Connecticut High Churchmen, and when White surveyed the wreckage of Anglicanism in America at the end of the Revolution, he unhesitatingly proposed as a solution a plan utterly unthinkable to the likes of Samuel Seabury.[22]

On at least one basic point, White agreed with Seabury and the Connecticut High Churchmen: the American Anglicans had to have a bishop—and have one *now* to rally the bleeding remains of Anglicanism in America—or the whole enterprise was finished. However, White also knew that no English bishop was legally able to consecrate an American without first administering an oath of loyalty to the royal supremacy, while no American could now conscientiously swear it. Therefore, White decided to move off in a typically Latitudinarian direction. In 1782, he published his proposals in *The Case of the Episcopal Churches in the United States Considered*, where he acknowledged that "the succession cannot at present be obtained."[23] But rather than wait indefinitely until a regular consecration could be pried loose from an English bishop, White suggested that the time had come for the Americans to take matters into their own hands. In the terms White sketched out, this meant holding a convention, selecting one of the remaining presbyters by popular vote, and having his fellow presbyters "consecrate" him as a bishop in the new church. In White's so-called "federal plan," the proposed convention would take on itself the authority to constitute the new church, and the bishops it "elected" would be nothing more than its officers, not its rulers.[24]

White's proposal was greeted with horror by all High Churchmen who read it. They had spent a generation in the hostile environment of New England proving, at least to their satisfaction, that no church could be valid apart from properly consecrated bishops, and they were not about to surrender that point merely at William White's urging. "In our opinion," the Connecticut High Churchmen warned in June 1784, "the first regular step is, to have the American Church completed in her officers; prior to that we conceive all our proceedings will be unprecedented and unsanctioned by any authoritative example in the Christian Church."[25] The fatal flaw in this logic was that it reeked of divine-right monarchy, and monarchy was precisely what the Americans had fought in the Revolution to overthrow. On the other hand, White's plan for electing bishops had a republican flavor that appealed to American tastes. The notion of church government by convention, with the bishops as executives and administrators rather than monarchs, fit neatly with the ideas of a representative legislature and limited government for which the American Revolution had been fought. Counting on the practical appeal of his "federal plan," White moved at once to organize a local convention of episcopal churches in Philadelphia in 1784, which in turn issued invitations to churches in eight other states to send delegates to an organizing convention in New York City later that year. The organizing convention met in October 1784, with delegates from nine state conventions attending, and drew up recommendations for a general ecclesiastical constitution and called for "a general convention of the Episcopal Church in the United States of America."[26] The General Convention met in Philadelphia on September 27, 1785, and moved to ratify the recommendations of the preliminary convention and to call into being the Protestant Episcopal Church in the United States of America.[27]

White's easygoing notion of episcopal government was matched by an equally undemanding but consistently Latitudinarian approach toward theology.[28] His sacramental ideas rose no higher than the bare minimum, and he denied flatly that the Lord's Supper was the occasion of a "sacrifice" of any sort. "The offering to God of the bread and the wine is representative of the body and blood of Christ, but . . . is no more a sacrifice, than the offering either of alms or praise." The Communion is simply "an edifying act," a memorial that involved only "the due contemplation of the subject with suitable affections."[29] Similarly, White agreed with the prayer book's declaration that baptism secured regeneration, but he understood that it meant "not a moral change" but only "a putting into a state of grace or covenant with God."[30] The clergy of the Episcopal Church might be officially described as priests, but in White's hands "the word 'priest' is 'presbuteros' with an English termination," and any suggestion that "priest" implied "affirming a proper sacrifice in the eucharist" was dismissed by White as "unauthorized either by Scripture or by our Church, or rather in violation of the authority of both."[31] White called his new church a "Protestant Episcopal Church," yet he denied the central tenet of Protestant theology, justification by the imputed righteousness of Christ; he spoke of the Bible as "merely . . . containing credible history, transmitted, like other histories, by those who were the subjects of them respectively"; and he even suggested in 1823 that the heresy of Arius, the fourth-century forerunner of unitarianism, was only a little worse than the "minute distinctions" of Arius's opponents and freely suggested that the Nicene Creed and the other anti-Arian documents in the prayer book were "calculated rather to obscure than to elucidate the truths of Scripture."[32]

The place where these theological heterodoxies took their most unmistakable form was in the new revision of the Book of Common Prayer authorized by the 1785 General Convention. Some revision of the prayer book was inevitable, if only to delete the references to King George. But the final product of the Convention's revision committee showed that White was not the only one in the Convention whose mind wandered in some unexpected directions. What became known as the "Proposed Book" called for significant, and not always prudent, changes:

Complete elimination of the Nicene Creed, as well as the other great anti-Arian symbol, the Athanasian Creed

Elimination of the phrase *he descended into hell* from the Apostles' Creed

Routine substitution of the word *minister* for *priest* at all points in the prayer book, and elimination of any reference to "regeneration" in the Baptismal Office

In the excising of the Nicene and Athanasian creeds, White's Latitudinarian proclivities come to the front most decidedly, for nothing else could justify so decisive a repudiation of the theology of those creeds except the customary Latitudinarian discomfort for trinitarian language about God. This is underscored by the number of other, even more drastic, revisions that were debated on the floor of the Convention but never actually made it into the Proposed Book (such as John Page's call for suppressing the Invocations in the Litany on the grounds that the invocation of the Trinity was "inappropriate" in divine worship).[33]

Yet, the only audible protest against the plans of White and the Philadelphia Convention was the muttering sent up by Samuel Seabury and the High Churchmen of Connecticut. Without much likelihood of getting a hearing from White, the Connecticut clergy decided in the spring of 1783 to circumvent White by sending one of their own—Samuel Seabury—to England to shake loose a consecration from an English bishop before White's convention could elect one.[34] Predictably, Seabury got nowhere. The Bishop of London and the Archbishop of Canterbury treated Seabury as an uninvited nuisance who spoke for no one in America except a band of truculent malcontents, and they firmly repeated their unwillingness to consecrate anyone from America without also administering the oath of royal supremacy.[35] Seabury blustered, argued, and pled for more than a year, to no avail. Finally, unable to persuade the archbishops, and unwilling to return to Connecticut in disgrace, Seabury resolved to get the episcopate—*any* episcopate—and by any means possible. This determination drove him, in November 1784, into the arms of a poignant band of Anglican outcasts known as the Scottish Episcopal Church.[36]

The Scottish Episcopalians had, until 1689, actually been the established Anglican Church of Scotland. In 1689, King William III, to please his Presbyterian subjects in Scotland, as well as to stick another thorn into English High Church flesh, disestablished the

Scottish Episcopal Church and replaced it with the Presbyterian Kirk. The Scottish Episcopalians had developed too high a notion of episcopal grandeur to accept being shut down by a mere king, and so they clung to a forlorn existence of their own as the so-called Non-Jurors. Disowned by the Anglican establishment in England, they had nevertheless maintained a clear line of succession in their bishops, and when in 1784 the Scottish *primus*, Robert Kilgour, learned of the plight of Samuel Seabury, Kilgour concluded that the opportunity to strike a bargain was at hand.[37]

Consequently, on November 14, 1784, Samuel Seabury was consecrated a bishop according to the ordinal of the Scottish Prayer Book (the Non-Juror's reworked version of the Book of Common Prayer) by three Scottish bishops in the second-floor rooms of a back-alley house-chapel in Aberdeen. Having been given what he wanted, Seabury was required the next day to give the Scottish Episcopalians what they wanted: recognition of their legitimacy as a church from the new American bishop. Seabury signed a concordat affirming the validity of ordination in the Scottish church and including an assertion that the church was independent of royal authority. The most controversial article of the concordat, and the one that would come back one hundred years later to haunt Evangelical Episcopalians, was article 5, which committed Seabury to introducing into American use the communion service of the Scottish Prayer Book.[38]

The significance of this is lost unless we realize that Seabury was pledging himself in this agreement to march contrary to William White, not only on church organization but on the new prayer book as well, for the Scottish communion service faced in exactly the opposite direction from the Proposed Book. The Proposed Book organized the communion service as a series of petitions to God culminating in a fairly modest consecration prayer in which the bread and wine in the Eucharist became "body and blood" only in a metaphorical sense. The prayer asked that

> we receiving these creatures of bread and wine, according to thy Son our Saviour Jesus Christ's holy institution, in remembrance of his death and passion, may be partakers of his most blessed body and blood.

Not so in the Scottish service. Although the Scots preferred the term "presbyter" to "priest," they had inserted into the service in 1764 two entirely new prayers—the Oblation (the offering of the communion bread and wine) and the Invocation (calling on God to transform the bread and wine)—*after* the usual consecration prayer, which subtly altered the meaning of the communion service:[39]

> Wherefore, O Lord, and heavenly Father, according to the institution of thy dearly beloved Son our Saviour Jesus Christ, we, thy humble servants, do celebrate and make here before thy divine majesty, with these thy holy gifts, WHICH WE NOW OFFER UNTO THEE, the memorial thy Son hath commanded us to make; having in remembrance his blessed passion and precious death, his mighty resurrection, and glorious ascension; rendering unto thee most hearty thanks for the innumerable benefits procured unto us by the same.
>
> And we most humbly beseech thee, O merciful Father, to hear us; and of thy almighty goodness vouchsafe to bless and sanctify, with the word and Holy Spirit, these thy gifts and creatures of bread and wine, that they may become the body and blood of thy most dearly beloved Son.

Here are two new ideas, at least for Americans. First, in the oblation prayer, there is a shift toward ideas of a propitiatory offering, "celebrated" and "made" as what could be termed a "sacrifice." Second, the Invocation specifies that the bread and wine must "become" the "body and blood" of Christ, suggesting in faintly un-Protestant terms that Christ must be made physically present in the sacrament as an oblation to offer up to God.[40] None of this was necessarily overt, and it would be difficult to make a case for "popery" from the oblation prayer and the Invocation, but it certainly pointed in a different direction from the Proposed Book and encouraged those inclined to move as far in that direction as they could.

Was Seabury aware of the full implications of his bargain with the Scots? Probably not, for his main preoccupation was with church organization, and to that end he set sail as soon as possible for New England.[41] But he got no welcome from William White, who (with the urging of the Archbishop of Canterbury) dismissed Seabury's consecration as invalid and closed the churches associated with White's convention to any of Seabury's ordinands.[42] Seabury was pointedly not invited to attend the General Convention when it met again in 1786, and White proceeded with his own plans as though Seabury had never existed.

So, by 1786, there were two rival Episcopal churches in America: one headed by Seabury in Connecticut, the other by White and the

General Convention in Philadelphia, each representing two very different ideas of churchmanship and each incapable of doing anything that would not, at least in theory, destroy the other. Something had to give, and of course it did.

White and the General Convention began to give second thoughts to both the Proposed Book and the wisdom of a self-made episcopate. In 1786, Parliament permitted the English bishops to dispense with the supremacy oath when consecrating bishops for foreign jurisdictions. This eliminated the need for White's convention to create its own bishops. At the urging of the General Convention, White and Samuel Provoost journeyed to England to be consecrated by the Archbishop of Canterbury on February 4, 1787.[43] At the same time, the Convention moved to reconsider the Proposed Book when it reconvened in Wilmington, Delaware, later in 1786. The Archbishop of Canterbury had expressed strong disapproval of the deletion of the Nicene Creed and the *descensus* ("He descended into Hell") and the Convention was too eager to see White's consecration go through not to want to please the Archbishop at any cost.[44] The result was that the Proposed Book never became more than a proposal, and in 1789 the revision committee was compelled to return to the drawing board to prepare a more conservative prayer book for the American church.

Then Samuel Seabury began to make conciliatory noises about White and the Convention. By all the standards Seabury held dear, White's consecration was incontestably valid, whereas Seabury's was at best irregular and at worst fraudulent. Therefore, unable any longer to beat White in the race for a valid episcopate, Seabury concluded that he should join him. Seabury even expressed his willingness to swallow the Proposed Book if that was what was required, but the pressure exerted on White and the Convention to rescind the Proposed Book made the task of reconciliation considerably easier for Seabury.[45] White, for his part, sensed that he could not go on ignoring the Connecticut "diocese" forever. Besides, tradition dictated that three bishops were necessary to provide further consecrations, and White was going to need Seabury to make up his threesome if he hoped to consecrate more bishops in America. When at last the Archbishop of Canterbury qualified his objections to Seabury's consecration, White saw to it that Seabury and his High Church followers were invited to a place in the climactic General Convention of 1789.[46]

The General Convention of 1789 was, in many respects, the real beginning of the Protestant Episcopal Church, because it finally brought together under a single united episcopate all the former Anglicans in the United States. But the other results of the Convention were a mixed bag. In the first place, the new prayer book that was adopted included the Scottish Oblation prayer and the Invocation, the Nicene Creed, the *descensus*, and a few references to "priests." But the oblation prayer was toned down, the Athanasian Creed was not restored, the rubric before the Apostles' Creed rendered the *descensus* optional, and the term "priest" was used with "minister" so interchangeably that it lacked any discernible meaning of its own.[47] The 1789 Convention then proceeded to address the problem of episcopal authority. By sending White and Provoost to Canterbury, the American church at last had a duly consecrated episcopate from England. But that only raised the question of where authority in the new church now lay—in the Convention, with the representatives of the parishes and dioceses, as White had originally planned, or in their bishops, as the representatives of the Church of England, and behind them, in the apostles?[48] The question was never really resolved, largely because of White's personal unwillingness to press the issue. Consecration or not, White intended to act merely as the president of the presbyters, not the successor of the apostles, and the only concession he made was to Seabury's insistence that the three bishops meet separately as a house of their own during the convention sessions. However, this meant that the new church would begin its life containing within itself two antithetical principles of government thinly papered over by William White's sense of restraint. It was not a hopeful formula for growth.

The Principles of Evangelicals

In 1797, an Englishman named William Wilberforce published a short, pungent critique of the quality of religious life in the Church of England. Entitled *A Practical View of the Prevailing Religious System of Professed Christians in the Higher and Middle Classes in this Country Contrasted with Real Christianity*, it tolled the death knell of Latitudinarianism:

> It is not an occasional invocation of the name of Christ, or a transient recognition of his authority, that fills up the measure of the terms, *believing in Jesus*. This we shall find no such easy talk; and if we trust that we do believe, we should all perhaps do well to cry out in the words of an imploring supplicant . . . "Lord, help thou our unbelief." We must be deeply con-

scious of our guilt and misery, heartily repenting of our sins, and firmly resolving to forsake them: and thus penitently "fleeing for refuge to the hope set before us," we must found altogether on the merit of the crucified Redeemer our hopes of escape from their deserved punishment, and of deliverance from their enslaving power. This must be our first, our last, our only plea. We are to surrender ourselves up to him to be "washed in his blood," to be sanctified by his Spirit, resolving to receive him for our Lord and Master, to learn in his school, to obey all his commandments.[49]

These words did more than just signal the end of the Latitudinarian church—they effectively launched the great Evangelical Revival in the Church of England. That revival really began in the 1730s with George Whitefield and the brothers John and Charles Wesley. Even though many of the Wesleys' devoted "methodists" eventually left the Church of England, the Evangelicals had, by the end of the eighteenth century, secured a small but definite niche in the Church of England, and Wilberforce's book, which went through five editions in five months, and forty editions over the following twenty-seven years, was a manifesto that galvanized them into a vigorous mission of preaching and conversion.[50] Within three decades, they had become a major force in the church, and within four decades the Archbishop of Canterbury was an Evangelical.[51]

Charles Simeon, who became the bright and shining light of Evangelical Anglicanism, once defined "Evangelical" in terms of an attitude rather than a specific set of dogmatic premises. To be truly "Evangelical," "Christ must be set forth as the only foundation of a sinner's hope," and with such tenacity "as to make us determine never to know any thing else, either for the salvation of our own souls, or for the subject of our public ministrations." That, in turn, would reveal to the Christian soul that "holiness in all its branches must be enforced . . . as the main-spring and motive of all our obedience." And not "our obedience" only—Simeon fully expected that the Evangelical would turn from the sanctified life within to sanctifying the lives of others outside. "We must call upon our hearers to rejoice and glory in it, and to display its sanctifying effects in the whole of their life and conversation." To preach this, but even more "thus to live, would characterize a person, and his ministry, as evangelical."[52] But that fundamental attitude which Simeon regarded as the spirit of Evangelicalism never existed far from some very explicit and often quite dogmatic theology. In an influential essay entitled "Evangelical Religion," a later nineteenth-century Evangelical

bishop of Liverpool, John Charles Ryle, looked back on the heyday
of the Evangelical Revival in England and summed up its theological principles under five points:

1. The "absolute supremacy" of the Bible "as the only rule of faith
   and practice, the only test of truth, the only judge of controversy"
2. The corruption of human nature by sin
3. The centrality of the Atonement of Christ as the theological remedy for this condition
4. The necessity of an "experimental knowledge of Christ crucified
   and interceding," to be applied by "the inward work of the Holy
   Spirit in the heart of men"
5. The requirement of a serious, holy life as "the only certain evidence of a man's spiritual condition"

This was not to say that the Evangelicals were the first ever to discover these things in the Church of England. Rather, Ryle insisted,
it was the place of supremacy that the Evangelicals gave to these
doctrines over all others which made these points unique in Evangelical hands. "We say boldly that they are first, foremost, chief,
and principal things in Christianity, and that want of attention to
their position mars and spoils the teaching of many well-meaning
Churchmen."[53]

But even within these five points, pride of place unquestionably
went in Evangelical minds to *conversion*—the "real experimental
business within a man," as Ryle put it, "the great change" (as Wilberforce described it) in which "relying on the promises to repenting
sinners of acceptance through the Redeemer, they have renounced
and abjured all other masters and have cordially and unreservedly
devoted themselves to God."[54] Simeon was a spiritually careless undergraduate at Cambridge in 1779 when his crisis came in the form
of the university requirement of Easter Communion. Turning for
preparation to Bishop Thomas Wilson's *Instruction for the Lord's Supper*, Simeon was panicked by the thought of his own unworthiness
and made himself ill with fasting and praying. But then he came on
Wilson's description of the Old Testament sacrifices of atonement—
"The Jews knew what they did when they transferred their sin to
the head of their offering"—and at that moment Simeon was over-
whelmed by the realization "I can transfer all my guilt to Another"
and at once determined: "I will not bear them [my sins] on my soul
a moment longer."

Accordingly I sought to lay my sins upon the sacred head of Jesus; and on Wednesday began to have a hope of mercy; on the Thursday that hope increased; on the Friday and Saturday it became more strong; and on the Sunday morning, Easter Day, April 4th, I awoke early with those words upon my heart and lips, "Jesus Christ is risen today! Hallelujah! Hallelujah!" From that hour peace flowed in rich abundance into my soul, and at the Lord's Table in our Chapel I had the sweetest access to God through my blessed Saviour.[55]

Simeon is also a good measure of the extent to which the Evangelical Revival was at the same time a "churchman's revival." In his fifty-three years as rector of Holy Trinity Church, Cambridge, Simeon turned a half-empty, indifferent church into a vital center of serious Christianity that needed an additional six galleries to accommodate its congregation.[56] Although the Evangelicals often grew frustrated with the Church of England when it failed to live up to their expectations and demands, they remained remarkably loyal to it and to its institutions. No one had more fault to find with the Church of England than John Charles Ryle, but Ryle rejected any suggestion that Evangelicals should secede, either literally or metaphorically, from the church. "Evangelical Religion *does not undervalue the Church*," Ryle insisted. "In sincere and loyal attachment to the Church of England we give place to none."[57] And in testimony to that loyalty, by 1853, Evangelicalism had contributed 6,500 clergy to the church (more than one-third the number of Church of England clergy).[58]

The work of Wilberforce and Simeon in England did not escape the attention of American Episcopalians for long. As in England, the foundations for an American "churchman's revival" had been laid a half-century earlier by George Whitefield, who toured the American colonies repeatedly from 1739 until 1770 and set off shockwaves of revival with each visit. But Whitefield's converts were greeted with pursed lips by the likes of both William White and Samuel Seabury, and the largest part of them ended up with the Methodists. The most direct route American Episcopalians took into the Evangelical Revival was through the reading of Wilberforce's *Practical View*, which if it slew its thousands in Britain it slew its tens of thousands in America. William Meade, later Bishop of Virginia, recalled vividly seeing Wilberforce's book in the hands of his family as a boy, and he marked "the blessed change" in Virginia from a Latitudinarian to an Evangelical diocese from the time the *Practical View* appeared.[59]

Another source, oddly enough, was the Methodists. The White-Seabury détente of 1789 produced union in the Episcopal Church, but not growth. Dour old Samuel Provoost glumly expected the Episcopal Church to die out as the last colonial families passed from the American scene, and the church statistics did little to refute him. The General Convention of 1789 was attended by two bishops and twenty clergymen; in 1811 the Convention was still attended by only two bishops and by twenty-five clergymen. In an effort to recruit more clergy, both White and Seabury reluctantly turned to the Methodists, who were, at least in terms of structure and liturgy, still close enough to Anglicanism for crossovers to take place.[60] What they got for their efforts must have surprised them. Samuel Seabury had "heard a good account" of Joseph Pilmore, a Methodist preacher, and on little more than the strength of that, Seabury ordained Pilmore a deacon on November 27, 1785, and a priest two days later. Pilmore promptly broke every rule in Seabury's book and packed St. Paul's Church in Philadelphia with 700 communicants, who marveled at the novelty of an Episcopalian with fervor.

> The two most remarkable characteristics of his preaching [recalled one of Pilmore's parishioners in the 1850's] were evangelical fervor and simplicity. As for the matter of his discourses, he never wandered far away from the Cross; he delighted to dwell upon the character and work of Christ, and the grace of the Holy Spirit; he was especially at home on all topics connected immediately with experimental religion.[61]

But the decisive moment in the transition of the Evangelical Revival to American Episcopalianism came in 1810–11 with the conversion to Evangelical principles of Alexander Viets Griswold, and his consecration as the twelfth American bishop. Although the circumstance in Griswold's case was his consecration rather than an undergraduate communion service, Griswold's description of his conversion is an uncanny echo of Simeon's. Ordained in 1795 by Seabury, Griswold played the role of the ultra High Churchman, "regarding the Church more than religion and the Prayer Book more than the Bible," and by his own admission he was "destitute of true piety and renovation of heart."[62] But in 1810, the handful of Episcopal congregations that had been scattered over Massachusetts, Maine, Vermont, Rhode Island, and New Hampshire were united into one sloppily constructed diocese, and Griswold was given the nod as bishop. Whatever he had been before his consecration on

May 29, 1811, the solemnity of being set apart as a shepherd over such a pitifully scattered flock impressed him deeply, and the consecration service proved to be "the means of the awakening of my own mind to more serious thoughts of duty as a minister of Christ; and in consequence I . . . with more earnest zeal preached 'Jesus Christ and him crucified.'"[63]

A discreet revival infected Griswold's parish in Bristol, Rhode Island, and by the summer of 1812 it had spread throughout his diocese. By September, he could report 1,212 confirmations of new church members, three ordinations, and five more candidates for orders.[64] Thirty-one years later, at his death, Griswold had built his ramshackle diocese into five fully organized dioceses and had overseen construction of fifty-five new church buildings, not to mention bringing four future bishops into the ministry of the church.

Griswold's conversion was soon followed, like firecrackers on a string, by a rapid flurry of further Evangelical conversions and consecrations. Richard Channing Moore, sitting in a New York City barbershop, glanced carelessly through a Bible and was struck by words he found there: "Saul, Saul, why persecutest thou me?"

The circumstance was apparently a trifling and accidental one. But it startled him. It appeared to him, doubtless, as a message from God, though it had come at an unexpected time, and under unwonted circumstances. . . . An arrow of conviction had pierced his heart which could be extracted only by the hand of pardoning mercy. Let him go where he would: and whether engaged in the cares of professional business, or whirling in the giddy circles of worldly pleasure, the awful appeal of his neglected and injured Master would be still ringing in his ears: "*Why persecutest thou me?*" It would interrupt his enjoyments by day and disturb his slumbers by night; so that he could find neither rest nor peace, till, bowing in the spirit of penitence and submission at the foot of the cross, he inquired, like the subdued and converted Apostle, "*Lord, what wilt thou have me to do?*"[65]

Moore entered the ministry and in 1814 carried Evangelical fire to Virginia as bishop of that diocese. Thoroughgoing churchman though he was, Moore urged his Virginians to adopt a variety of departures from the exclusive use of the Book of Common Prayer, such as free prayer meetings and preaching missions, in order to spread the gospel as far across Virginia as possible. Over the course of twenty-seven years as Bishop of Virginia, Moore watched his diocese grow from 7 clergymen to 100, and from 14 churches to 170.[66]

Assisting and then succeeding Moore as Bishop of Virginia was William Meade, the Ezra to Moore's Nehemiah, who "never wavered in his adherence to that system of evangelical teaching and practice to which his earliest religious convictions were due, and under the preaching of which he had seen the Church in Virginia rise as though from the dead."[67] Meade was followed as Bishop of Virginia by John Johns, of whom it was said, "Whatever his particular subject, it always proceeded from or revolved around the same theme, Christ and the Cross."[68] Johns's classmate at Princeton Theological Seminary was Charles Pettit McIlvaine, who began his ministry as chaplain at West Point, and promptly turned the military academy into a uniformed prayer meeting. In 1853, McIlvaine was elected Bishop of Ohio, where he "preached with unwonted faithfulness the unsearchable riches of Christ."[69] McIlvaine was only the second Bishop of Ohio, his predecessor being the most energetic Evangelical missionary bishop of them all, Philander Chase, who almost single-handedly founded and built not only the Diocese of Ohio, but, after that, the Diocese of Illinois and Kenyon College in Gambier, Ohio.[70]

This hardly touches the other Evangelical worthies in the church. James Milnor, a Philadelphia Quaker, encountered the preaching of Joseph Pilmore in 1810, entered the ministry in 1814, and turned St. George's Church in New York City into an Evangelical hothouse.[71] Milnor was succeeded at St. George's by Stephen H. Tyng, who had been converted under Bishop Griswold and who, before coming to St. George's, had also served at Pilmore's old church in Philadelphia, St. Paul's. Preaching three times on Sundays and again on Wednesdays, Tyng had packed St. Paul's so densely that the church was known as "Tyng's Theatre," and it was once said that Tyng could have walked from the pulpit to the street over the heads of the congregation.[72]

During the same years that Tyng held forth at St. Paul's, Gregory Townsend Bedell preached to immense crowds of his own across town at St. Andrew's Church. Ordained in 1814 and a nephew of Bishop Moore, Bedell's outstanding talents as a preacher, together with "his peculiar vivacity of spirit and cheerful pleasantry in conversations," won him early popularity. In 1822, during a preaching mission at St. Paul's, Philadelphia, Bedell was approached by thirty-four Episcopalians who wanted to organize a new version of St. Paul's in their own neighborhood on Fifteenth Street. Bedell hesitatingly agreed, but over the next eleven years his hesitations vanished, as the communicant membership, lured by Bedell's "language of affectionate and earnest expostulation," swelled to 334 individuals, who built for him "the most beautiful house of worship then erected in Philadelphia."[73] St. Andrew's became a center of weekday prayer meetings and lectures, revivals of "religious sensibility," and so many other events that "nearly every day in the year there was some religious meeting in connection with St. Andrew's Church." And far from feeling even the hint of rivalry, Tyng wrote of Bedell what may serve as a summary of all the Evangelical Episcopalians:

> He habitually dwelt in his sermons, upon those great truths of the gospel which are revealed in the redemption of sinners through the obedience and death of the Lord Jesus Christ, and which were given to make men "wise unto salvation." These truths he exhibited in a singularly clear, intelligible, and faithful manner. . . . This was the chief peculiarity of his preaching. He ceased not, in the most direct and simple manner "to teach and to preach Jesus Christ"; the peculiar intelligence of God's redeeming love for sinners; as the appointed instrument in the divine hand of everlasting good to their souls. The necessity and danger of man as a lost being; the wonderful grace and power of "God manifest in the flesh," as the sinner's glorious substitute and Saviour; the glorious work of the Spirit in forming men anew for God; were his theme in public, and from house to house. He was never wearied in the consideration of these truths himself, and he feared not the wearying of others by their repeated declaration. Christ was "all in all" in his addresses to the souls of men.[74]

Like the English Evangelicals, their American counterparts had a strong tinge of Calvinism to their theology, although it was by no means either uniform or ultra in nature.[75] On the one hand, the young William Bacon Stevens, Bedell's successor at St. Andrew's, Philadelphia, defined Evangelical theology in strongly Calvinistic terms during a series of anniversary sermons celebrating the mission of St. Andrew's Church in 1858. The "foundation-stones which underlie the Gospel structure" could be nothing less than "man's total depravity, his utter inability to save himself, the complete worthlessness of his so-called goodness, the alone sufficiency of Christ's atoning blood, the imputed righteousness of Christ made ours by faith," and, above all, "the sovereignty of God in man's salvation," with its natural concomitant, "election by grace."[76] On the other hand, William Sparrow, dean of the Virginia theological seminary and "the profoundest theological mind of the party," was simply an eclectic Arminian who "seems to have swept the field from Origen, Swedenborg and Schliermacher to Channing, Parker and Socinus."[77] But even Sparrow's Evangelicalism had enough of a Calvinistic tinge that he could preach: "It is an infinite consolation to all considerate men, that, though our nature is so corrupt, and human passion is so strong and lawless, it is not taken from under all control, but that God still rules and reigns and overrules . . . and in every case is either restrained altogether, or made conducive to God's glory."[78]

It would not be their Calvinism, or lack thereof, that would become the great issue for the Evangelicals. Instead, it was their notions of church order and sacraments, and as with the English Evangelicals, a natural logic in their priorities invited them to set both sacraments and order further down the scale from faith and repentance. Episcopal order, for the Evangelicals, was simply one way among many that Protestants might construct a church organization, and none of these ways was to be regarded as having any greater biblical or divine sanction than another. Manton Eastburn, Bishop of Massachusetts and Griswold's handpicked successor, argued that the Episcopal Church, by promoting the episcopal scheme of church government, "merely claims to say, with every other Christian body, what is the constitution of the ministry which, among ourselves, is deemed to be after the scriptural and apostolical pattern."[79] What was important to the Evangelicals was the harmony of common belief, not a subordination to a common discipline. The church, Eastburn confidently asserted, "fulminates no ban of excommunication against that uncounted host, who within other pales, are dispensing to famishing millions the bread of life."[80]

What was less easily apparent in the Evangelicals' intercession for other Protestant ministries was the implication it contained for their own, for on those terms the Episcopal ministry could only be one ministry among many, not an exclusive caste. At this point, the Evangelicals happily fell back on the logic promoted by William White in the 1780s, for although the structure of their ideas on order sprang from sources that were radically different from White's Latitudinarian tolerance, the Evangelicals were happy to deploy the conclusions of the Episcopal Church's first presiding bishop as a rationalization for their own brand of Evangelical comprehensiveness. Hence, as William Sparrow insisted in 1869, the Evangelicals uniformly proclaimed that their ministry was, like other Protestant ministries, simply that of service of the gospel, not the extension of Episcopal territory, "not a *sacerdotium*, but a *ministerium*."[81] It was not the administration of sacraments, but the "direct presentation to the mind, and conscience, and heart, of the simple truth of God, as revealed in, and peculiar to the Gospel" which Charles Pettit McIlvaine held up as "the great instrument of sanctification, of awakening and converting the sinner, of leading him to Christ."[82]

And this, in turn, encouraged the Episcopalian Evangelicals to take greater liberties in defining the sacraments than did the English Evangelicals, for in many cases the Americans were so intent on promoting the work of preaching that they often made the sacraments into little more than acted exhortations—only (in the words of John Johns, successor of Meade and Moore as Bishop of Virginia) "Sacred Symbolical" events, designed as outward stimulations to the Christian's pious imagination.[83] "Eating and drinking," said William Sparrow in a sermon on the Last Supper, "are figurative expressions for coming to Christ, and believing on him." As far as Sparrow believed, "Eating his flesh and drinking his blood clearly stand for the exercise of faith; faith, trust, dependence on his atoning death."[84] The same basic argument applied to baptism. Because "the sacraments are not channels, through which life from Christ flows, without reference to any thing but the divine ordinance," James May warned the Virginia diocesan convention in 1847 that without "the repentance and faith of those who believe them . . . the baptized man may be, to all intents, a pagan, having no more than a mere name in the Church, shut out from the kingdom of God as truly as a carnally-minded Jew, or even a heathen."[85] Never mind that the baptismal order in the Book of Common Prayer had, since 1789, required all Episcopal clergy to declare that a baptized child "is regenerate." Manton Eastburn merely replied that this declaration was "simply *hypothetical* in its character."[86]

The common denominator of these conceptions of the sacraments and church order was the priority they gave to the inwardness of religion rather than to the externalities. "We need," declared Henry Washington Lee to the Iowa diocesan convention in 1857, "a kind and a tone of *Churchmanship* that shall never exalt the form above the spirit, that shall regard all external order as subservient to the promotion of true spiritual religion." And anything that usurped that relationship, or attempted to confuse the subordination of the outward to the inward, and the material to the spiritual, aroused all their thoroughly Protestant hackles. To exalt baptism over faith, or church order over revival, complained Lee, "seems almost to ignore spiritual religion, and yet joins, with apparent and commendable interest, in the outward part of an eminently spiritual service."[87]

For the Evangelicals, the Atonement, not the Incarnation, was their commanding doctrine, and repentance, not baptism, was the mark of their identity. "He is not a member of the Church, who is one outwardly, neither is that regeneration which is outward by water," explained James May, "but he is a member of the Church who is one inwardly, and regeneration is that of the heart, in the Spirit, and not in the letter, whose praise is not of men but of God." And it was precisely this "error of confounding the outward and the inward, the Church in visible organization, and the spiritual Church, in unseen living union with Christ" which led to the even more dreadful "error of unduly exalting the prerogatives of the Church."[88]

It is ironic that, for all the downplaying of episcopal order by the American Evangelicals, the voice that persistently and overwhelmingly emerges from the record is that of ordained clergy. In fact, if there was any obvious point at which the American Evangelicals differed from their English brethren, it was the surprising invisibility of the laypeople. Although William Sparrow warned his students at the Virginia Theological Seminary that "it is an evil day for true religion always, when the laity are supplanted and their part in legislation, administration and especially their control of Church property, is infringed upon," the truth was that the Episcopalian Evangelicals produced nothing that compared in scope to the outsized role played by the laity in the Evangelical Revival in the Church of England. Against the example of Wilberforce, Shaftesbury, and the Clapham sect, the Americans could point only to John Jay of New York and Francis Scott Key of Baltimore as their best-known spokesmen among the laity, and they certainly seem to have had no Hannah More.

Despite that ominous failing, the growth of Evangelical Episcopalianism was, as it had been in England, nothing short of breathtaking. McIlvaine recalled that at the General Convention of 1820, only "three clergymen, with the Chairman, constituted the whole evangelical force in the Lower House," and that, among the lay deputies, "Key was the only one who was allowed to stand up in defence of evangelical truth."[89] But within thirty years of Griswold's consecration, the Evangelicals had colleges, like Kenyon, and two theological seminaries—one under the auspices of the Diocese of Virginia at Alexandria, the other attached to the Diocese of Ohio at Gambier. They also had newspapers and magazines, principally the *Gambier Observer* in the West, the *Southern Churchman* in the South, and the *Episcopal Recorder* in the East, and they had three major societies for promoting Evangelical interests: the Protestant Episcopal Evangelical Society, the Society for the Promotion of Evangelical Knowledge, and the Evangelical Education Society.[90] It was the

Evangelicals who first carried the Episcopal banner over the Appalachians into what became the Evangelical bastion of Ohio in 1817, and by 1830 the Evangelicals had blazed the trail into Kentucky (led by William Kavanaugh, a former Methodist), Louisiana (where Philander Chase was the first Protestant minister to work in President Jefferson's famous purchase), Indiana, Illinois, and Iowa.[91] All this Evangelical growth took place even though, from 1835 onward, "there was a tacit understanding which amounted to a moral obligation . . . in the division of the world into two fields," in which "the domestic department was committed substantially, and practically, to the High Church party" and in which foreign missions were committed to the Evangelicals.[92] And yet, far from regarding that cartel as a political dead end, the American Evangelicals threw themselves into foreign missions work with fully as much energy (though with little of the success) of their Church of England counterparts, planting Episcopal missions in Greece, in South America, in Japan, and in the deadly and ill-starred station at Cape Palmas in Liberia.[93] From next to nothing in 1811, the Evangelicals claimed the allegiance of two-thirds of the clergy of the church at the General Convention of 1844.[94]

Thus it was that, on the wings of the transplanted Evangelical Revival, the Protestant Episcopal Church embarked on a spiral of growth that took it beyond the Mississippi River and made it the odds-on favorite to become America's almost-established church. "However imperfectly Evangelical men have carried out their principles," claimed William Sparrow in 1854, "they have done nearly all that has been done in that way; and if I know anything about the secret workings of their minds and hearts in this matter, the great absorbing motive with them, in what they do, is a regard to Christ's command, a love for His name, a jealousy for His honor, a desire to see all men blessed with the Gospel."[95]

The Evangelicals and the Republican Ideology

Before the relentless energy of the Evangelicals, the old Latitudinarians virtually melted away. But the High Churchmen did not, and this was due in large measure to the tireless labors of the bishop who was consecrated on the same day as Griswold—the redoubtable and energetic John Henry Hobart.

Ordained one year after the death of Seabury, Hobart became Bishop of New York fourteen years later, and with that emerged as the most splenetic and provocative spokesman for High Church principles in the nineteenth century.[96] It was a task he was fitted for almost perfectly, for Hobart had all of Seabury's pugnacity and more than Seabury's allotment of native intelligence, and he was dedicated to the quintessential High Church principle that the Episcopal Church should be a middle ground between "reducing the Gospel to a cold, unfruitful, and comfortless system of heathen morals" (which was his general judgment of Latitudinarianism) and the "wild spirit of enthusiasm" (which was his particular judgment of American evangelicals). As a High Churchman, Hobart believed that this middle ground consisted primarily "in the devout and humble participation of the ordinances of the Church, administered by a priesthood, who derive their authority by regular transmission from Christ."[97] He prized orthodoxy, orderliness, and the liturgy as the substance of his religion, and he took the Episcopal Evangelicals' affection for prayer meetings and other nonliturgical services as evidence of a secret distate for the Book of Common Prayer.

Hobart was also suspicious that the Evangelicals were something less than heart-and-soul believers in the episcopal system of church government. He complained vehemently and publicly that Evangelical Episcopalians "made no distinction as to authority between episcopally ordained, whom the Episcopal church considers alone 'lawful ministers,' and those who had not received Episcopal ordination," and, just to make sure that his point was lost on no one, he made a public habit of refusing to cooperate with ministers of other denominations in the work of interdenominational Bible societies. As for the hapless Evangelical Episcopalians within his jurisdiction as Bishop of New York, Hobart put them on quick notice that he regarded as inadmissible any "indifference or laxity of opinion" within his diocese "which threatened destruction to the distinctive principles of the Episcopal Church."[98] It was not an idle threat. Hobart was a tremendous organizer and propagandizer and ceaselessly crisscrossed New York on visitations to preach, exhort, and finally found the General Theological Seminary as a beacon of High Church principles. Thus was the Diocese of New York made into a stronghold of High Churchmanship and a bed of nails for Evangelicals.

But noisy as Hobart's demands became for submission to High Churchmanship, none of them might have gotten him much more than irritated complaints outside his diocese, and ecclesiastical courts-martial within it, had it not been for the backdrop against which Hobart played. The decades of the 1820s and 1830s witnessed the political triumph of an egalitarian brand of American republicanism, carrying its hero, Andrew Jackson, into the White House in 1828. At the same time, the old hierarchy of Congregationalists and Presbyterians, which had tacitly governed the life of American Protestantism throughout the colonial era, collapsed before a rush of Methodists, Baptists, and a host of come-outer revivalists who swept everything before them in the 1820s in a whirlwind of camp meetings, "new measures," and emotional riot. Not all Americans were pleased with what they took to be the violence of Jacksonian politics and the slouchiness of Jacksonian culture. Old-fashioned conservatives of rank and traditional station who had been forced down on their hands and knees before the new political and religious democracy cast around for associations and alternatives to soothe their frustration and alienation.

They found such an alternative in Hobart's High Churchmanship, for Hobart was able to convert the aristocratic flavor of High Churchmanship, which had been such a political liability in the clumsy hands of Samuel Seabury, into a social asset of considerable value. He had no hope of seeing the old colonial establishment returned to literal power, but then again he did not need to hope for that, so long as he could reconstitute its attitudes and ethos within his parishes, and the descendants of the old colonial families, whose word had been law a century before, turned to Hobart's High Churchmanship as a dignified and orderly refuge from the passionate barbarism that was fast becoming a trademark of American life. To join the Episcopal Church, especially in the Diocese of New York, was to re-join an aristocracy of sorts, this time one that claimed an aristocracy of souls in organic unity with the apostolic church. One convert explained his reverence for the church in precisely these terms in the year of Hobart's death:

> It is the glory of our Church that she maintains and seeks to perpetuate a reverence for order. The reality and nature of her divine constitution is, theoretically, a question of theology. . . . Practically however, it is a question of social order; and every individual may judge for himself, whether her system is not the most conducive to the interests of society. The great practical feature of that system is subordination—a subordination based on principle and not convenience—existing in virtue and divine command, and not of human suggestion. . . . This subordination involving *right*, or authority, as its conservative principle, is the grand characteristic of heaven, and to the violation of it may be traced the origin and all the subsequent developments of evil.[99]

Evangelical Episcopalians responded to Hobart's proclamations with a mixture of annoyance and embarrassment. If High Churchmanship carried within itself an aristocratic and Old Worldish sense of distaste for American culture, the Evangelicals represented the attempt of Episcopalians to come to terms with their American identity. Whatever the Americans owed to the English Evangelicals in terms of dogmatics, they entertained no illusions about the practicality or even the desirability of re-creating the kind of hierarchical demi-world imagined by John Henry Hobart. If the Evangelicals owed their theology to the Wilberforces and the Simeons, they owed their polity to a happy embrace of republicanism.

The republican ideology of the eighteenth and early nineteenth centuries in the United States was an interesting compound of secular political philosophy, classical rhetoric, and religious moralism, and its chief attraction was the balance it offered between the unappetizing patriarchal politics of monarchy and the rampant individualism of Locke's *Two Treatises on Government*. Republicanism preached the supremacy of personal rights; but because the uncontained exercise of personal rights could easily lead to inequality, luxury, and finally corruption, the republicans corralled the anarchy of rights with an obligation to "virtue." Transferred to religious structures, republicanism offered the possibility of holding individual religious interests in tension with the fear of corruption and luxury, and if we can regard the 1789 General Convention as the Glorious Revolution of the Episcopal Church, then the balance struck by the Evangelicals between the religious individualism of conversion and the obligation to the larger community of the prayer book and the episcopate seemed to be as close to the republican ideal of "mixed government" as a church order was likely to get. This also explains the ambiguity the Evangelicals felt toward the episcopate: on the one hand, it was the symbol of the most ancient monarchy in Christendom; on the other hand, it could be used to diminish and restrain corruption, luxury, and individual religious self-interest. Like government itself in the republican ideology, the episcopate had to be constrained and exalted at the same time.

The problem of choice for the Evangelicals in the 1820s, however, was that there were multiple brands of republicanism on offer in the United States. The most politically successful (at least in terms of winning the American presidency) was the radicalized republicanism that emerged under the banner of Andrew Jackson and the Democratic Republicans. The Democrats, however, recruited comparatively few of the Evangelical Episcopalians, who occupied instead the same political and cultural middle ground that was forming in the 1830s around the National Republicans (or Whigs). The Whigs were attempting to pour the new wine of protectionism, industrialism, and nationalism into the old wineskins of republican virtue and independence. Charles Sellers, George Thomas, and Daniel Howe have all shown how closely the moralist concerns of "moderate Light" Protestant evangelicals fitted Whig republicanism, and the Evangelical Episcopalians were no exception to that affinity.[100] Their fervent Evangelical gospel message, their passionate devotion to evangelical ecumenism, their plain, undecorated churches with central pulpits and well-nigh invisible altars and fonts, their clergy in don's gown, surplice, and scarf[101]—all these match the small-producer ethic of national unity and the sturdy republican simplicity that was at the core of the nineteenth-century Whig agenda.

It comes as no surprise, then, to find the leadership of the Evangelical Episcopalians turning to the Whigs (and later to the Republicans of the 1850s) for political identity, and the Whigs finding a congenial ally among the Evangelical Episcopalians. Henry Clay, the patriarch of the Whigs, turned Episcopalian in 1847 and was confirmed by the Evangelical Bishop of Kentucky, Benjamin Bosworth Smith, and at the height of the debates over the Compromise of 1850, Clay turned to the Evangelical Episcopalian chaplain of the Senate, C. M. Butler, as his spiritual counselor (Butler also happened to be a Whig).[102] The political "brains" of the Republicans in the 1850s was Salmon Portland Chase, an Evangelical Episcopalian and nephew of Philander Chase, the pioneering Evangelical bishop of Ohio and Illinois, who went to an Evangelical Episcopal parish while he was secretary of the treasury to hear a "good plain sermon" and deny himself Communion for feeling "too subject to temptation to sin."[103] Anna Pierpont, Charles McIlvaine's "spiritual friend," cheered on Whig electors in New York City, and McIlvaine himself went to England during the Civil War as President Lincoln's goodwill ambassador to the Church of England.[104] The Episcopal missionaries who sacrificed themselves on the altar of the Episcopal Church's Liberia mission were all Evangelicals, in a cause that was widely understood to be the preparation for that great Whig solution to the slavery question—West African colonization.[105] In some cases, they even looked like Whigs: Jefferson Davis thought that John Johns's pulpit mannerisms bore a singular "resemblance to Mr. Clay," but he reminded himself that the resemblance was "probably accidental."[106] Perhaps so, but Johns and the Evangelicals certainly resembled the Whigs in their promotion of "simplicity" over "luxury." In addition, their distaste for concentrating church power in the hands of an apostolic episcopate dovetailed finely with the Whig resistance to Jackson's "imperial" presidency; their affection for pan-evangelical unity echoed the Whig call for national unity against the specter of state democracy (and the egalitarian localism of the Baptists); and, above all, like the Whigs, they were happy to welcome the rewards of commercial and mercantile prosperity into their fellowship.

And so in distinction to Hobart on the one hand, and Andrew Jackson on the other, the American Evangelicals sought to cultivate "republican" Whig attitudes and to advertise their church as the embodiment of what Charles Grandison Finney called "Church Republicanism."[107] "The genius of the American Church is not like the genius of the Church of England, not at all," warned the Whig Episcopalian Calvin Colton in 1853:

> The greatest obstacle in the way of the extension and prosperity of the American Episcopal Church, down to this time, has been the erroneous assumption, that she is a type of the English Church—the same thing. She is not the same thing, far from it, as we shall yet have occasion largely to show; but in this place, we have only to do with that radical, fundamental, vital, and most important difference, the republican character of the American Episcopal Church. . . . The Church of England is not so. There is not a single feature of republicanism in her polity. . . . None can deny, on the contrary, all must see, that the genius of the American Episcopal Church is republican.[108]

It was for this reason that, from the 1820s onward, the Evangelicals came to adopt William White as the figurehead of their movement—not because they had much sympathy for White's doctrinal Latitudinarianism (which they conveniently ignored) but because his urge to tailor episcopal order to revolutionary reality dovetailed so neatly with the elitist brand of republican virtue the Whigs sought to cultivate. Hobart, by contrast, would have choked if he had read John Alonzo Clark's happy declaration "Every one now begins to see that the principles of our church are in most delightful harmony with republican government."[109]

For that very reason, however, the Evangelicals balked just as much at Hobart's commitment to Episcopal monarchicalism. And so the Evangelicals and the High Churchmen found themselves at odds, not simply over theories of episcopal order but also over the question of the fundamental cultural identity of the Episcopal Church. "The one claimed piety, simplicity, and scriptural authority as its distinguishing notes," remembered Henry Codman Potter, "and the other glorified order, reverence, and apostolic tradition as its pre-eminent distinctions; and neither willingly lost an opportunity of disparaging brethren of the same household of faith, with whom they were proud to disagree." Good Whigs that they were, the Evangelicals wanted to make episcopacy easy and accessible for all Americans; Hobart, good aristocrat, wanted to make it as exclusive as possible.[110] Consequently, it was crucial for the Evangelicals to distance themselves as much as they dared from the High Churchmen and to persuade others that the High Churchmen did not speak for the church as a whole.

It would be wrong, however, to overdraw the differences that separated the High Churchmen from the Evangelical Episcopalians.[111] Despite Hobart's suspicions, the Evangelicals' republicanism was genuinely reluctant to abandon such highly authoritarian symbols of cultural discipline as the Book of Common Prayer and the episcopate for the value they had as symbols of restraint, virtue, and balanced government. Alfred Lee, the Evangelical bishop of Delaware, was eulogized as "holding very decidedly and intelligently the views of Divine Truth held by what is called the Evangelical School," but his fellow bishop, William Bacon Stevens, also knew that Lee's "Church views were based on the Bible and the Prayer-Book, and never did he show the slightest disloyalty to either, but was an uncompromising defender of the faith of the Church as set forth in the Creed, the Catechism, the Offices, and Articles of the Book of Common Prayer."[112] And Stevens insisted that Evangelicalism in general "has maintained, inviolate, a strict attachment to our devout liturgy; it has cherished, decidedly, the distinctive features of our holy catholic Church."[113] The Evangelicals knew as well as Hobart how easy it was to abuse Evangelical principles, and how vulnerable Evangelicals were to many of the criticisms Hobart and the High Churchmen leveled at them, and they were no more eager than Hobart to take up the excesses of the revivalists into the Episcopal Church with no questions. John Cotton Smith, one of the most prominent Evangelical rectors in the nineteenth-century church, candidly admitted that Evangelicalism was not a perfect system:

> I know that the evangelical system, in the hands of fallible men, is attended with many and great dangers. Its indifference to the external and formal leads sometimes to the undervaluing of historic institutions, and of the body, so to speak, of historic Christianity. Its dependence upon the teaching of the Holy Spirit is sometimes accompanied by a

confounding of the impulses and conclusions of the individual with the promptings of the Holy Ghost. Its strong, high view of the relation of Christ to the believer, and the substitution of the one for the other, sometimes leads to such an identification in idea of the two, that the believer comes to regard himself, not only as forgiven and accepted, but as sinless in Christ. . . . What is there in it, then, that constitutes its inestimable value? It is this. It tells me, and this interprets the deepest wants and most ardent longings of my spirit, that when my soul understands that Christ is a Saviour from sin, and rests on him for salvation, I am saved. I may have been under a gracious covenant before, which has sheltered my infancy, and early youth; or I may have been a wanderer all my days from God; but this trust in Christ has made me now, once for all, a child of God. . . . I have a power in the consciousness of this which moves me, as nothing else could, to a consecration of myself, body, soul, and spirit, to the Saviour.[114]

Some of the same qualifications must be applied concerning the High Churchmen. Although John Henry Hobart made many a New York parish too hot to hold Evangelicals, Hobart was far more willing to incorporate the Evangelical ethos into his ministry than Samuel Seabury would ever have been. He took as his motto the strikingly un-Seabury-like slogan "Evangelical Truth and Apostolic Order," and he despised the antics of the revivalists while at the same time preaching fire and brimstone with all the fervor of the best of them.[115] Justification by faith occupied as high a place in Bishop Hobart's preaching as it had in the mind of any of the Evangelicals, for "pardon, justification, eternal life as the free gifts of God the Father, through the merits and intercession of his eternal Son, and through the renovating and sanctifying agency of the Holy Spirit . . . are the great Evangelical truths which alone render of value or of efficiency the ministrations and ordinances for which the High Churchman contends."[116] Although the 1789 prayer book had retained the title "priest" for the clergy, Hobart denied that this had anything to do with any sort of eucharistic sacrifice, and as routinely as he talked about "altars" he insisted that nothing happened on those "altars" but a simple memorial communion service involving "lively symbols."[117] Whatever superiority the High Churchmen believed could be found in episcopal order, few were willing to push it so far as to unchurch all other nonepiscopal denominations. "It is our sacred privilege to know that we stand in the line of that apostolic succession, that we have the complete and formal title to all its benefits," wrote John Henry Hopkins, Bishop of Vermont and the inheritor of Hobart's High Church mantle. All the same, however, Hopkins strongly disapproved of "the systematic refusal of the term Church to the various orthodox communities of our non-episcopal brethren, on the alleged ground, that since episcopacy is manifestly of divine institution, there can be no Church where there are no bishops."[118]

Nor did the Hobartian High Churchmen show much inclination toward overindulgence in ceremony and vestments. Hobart was notorious for often forgetting to bring his episcopal robes with him on visitations, and the use of the surplice by his clergy had by 1838 so completely disappeared that a resolution restoring its use had to be introduced into the General Convention—only to fail.[119] Even in Connecticut, the ancestral home of High Churchmanship, the clergy generally wore the surplice only during Communion, and otherwise preached and prayed in a black Geneva gown and cassock indistinguishable from that of Presbyterians or Baptists.[120] Indeed, taken as a whole, Evangelicals and High Churchman were separated not so much by theology or even style as by vocabulary: Evangelicals "administered" Communion, while High Churchmen "celebrated" it, but both thought of it basically as a symbolic spiritual occasion; Evangelicals loved the interdenominational Bible societies, while High Churchmen loved only the Episcopal Bible societies, but both reverenced the Bible; Evangelicals resorted to prayer meetings, while High Churchmen would use only the Book of Common Prayer, but both prayed; Evangelicals disliked the use of the term "priest" in the prayer book, but both Evangelicals and High Churchmen agreed that it was only the English contraction of the New Testament term "presbyter," not a synonym for a sacrificial order of celibate clergy.

And on those terms, there was no reason Evangelicals and High Churchmen could not have worked out, or at least tolerated, their differences and worked in tandem to make the Episcopal Church into the grand national church that its Presbyterian admirer, Dr. Bethune, was sure would inherit the land. But it was not to be. Instead, the only inheritance the Episcopalians would confront in the middle decades of the nineteenth century was an increasing crescendo of strife, culminating in a single, shattering explosion.

II

AN EMBARRASSMENT OF RITUAL

The Offense of the Anglo-Catholics

The impetus behind the Evangelical Revival in the Episcopal Church came from England, and in particular from the long-term influence of the Wesleys and Whitefield and the near-term example of Wilberforce and Simeon. As it turned out, the undoing of the Episcopal Evangelicals also came from English sources, and it began in a most unlikely and unecclesiastical place—Parliament. It is one of the curiosities of English life that, ever since the Reformation, Parliament has retained the right to oversee, restrain, and generally meddle in the most basic spiritual, liturgical, and pastoral affairs of the Church of England.

This might not have been all that odd so long as voting rights in Parliamentary elections and the right to sit in Parliament were restricted to good Anglican churchmen, and all kinds of non-Anglican "Dissenters" and Roman Catholics kept out. But in the first half of the nineteenth century, the winds of democratic revolution blew open the turreted casements of Europe's doddering monarchies, and in England those winds forced the haphazard electoral system of England's Parliament to yield to fuller and freer voting rights. In 1829, that pressure for democratic reform compelled Parliament to pass the Catholic Emancipation Act, giving Roman Catholics for the first moment since the Reformation the right to vote and hold public office. This was followed in 1832 by the First Reform Bill, which reorganized voting apportionments to give more adequate representation in Parliament to the new industrial districts where the Baptists, Methodists, and other brands of Dissenters were the overwhelming majority.[1]

All this naturally gave Parliament a religious complexion completely different from what it had ever enjoyed before. But much as this prospect rejoiced the hearts of previously disenfranchised Catholics, Dissenters, and even atheists, the prospect of demonstrably non-Anglican (and perhaps even wickedly anti-Anglican) members of Parliament sitting at Westminster and controlling the funds, personnel, and ultimate direction of Anglicanism filled English churchmen with foreboding. It did not take long for their forebodings to be amply justified. In June 1833, Parliament passed (as a sop to Irish Catholic political feelings) the Irish Church Temporalities Bill, which suppressed two of the four Anglican archbishoprics, and eight more of the lesser Anglican bishoprics, it had maintained in Ireland since the sixteenth century. The bill outraged the Church of England, which now had to remember in the starkest and most unpleasant way that its destiny was not in its own hands. Frightened and angered voices within the Church of England now began to demand to know by what right a secular legislature presumed to imperil a church whose bishops could, after all, boast apostolic descent for their office and apostolic doctrine for their authority. The most principled statement of that outrage came from a poet and Fellow of Oriel College, Oxford, named John Keble, who delivered on July 14, 1833, the sermon most have regarded as the opening gun of the Oxford Movement. Keble took as the title for his sermon "National Apostasy" and posed a powerful and provocative question:

> Disrespect to the successors of the apostles, as such, is an unquestionable symptom of enmity to him who gave them

their commission at first, and has pledged himself to be with
them for ever. Suppose such disrespect general and national,
suppose it also avowedly grounded not on any fancied tenet
of religion, but on mere human reasons of popularity and
expediency . . . [then] that nation, how highly soever she
may think of her own religion and morality, stands convicted
in his sight of a direct disavowal of [Jesus Christ's] sovereignty. . . . And, if it be true anywhere, that such enactments
are forced on the legislature by public opinion, is APOSTASY
too hard a word to describe the temper of that nation?[2]

Behind Keble at Oxford were two other Oriel Fellows, John
Henry Newman and Richard Hurrell Froude, and further behind
them were two others, Hugh James Rose (the vicar of Hadleigh in
Essex) and William Palmer of Worcester College. They had already
begun meeting in the Oriel common room during the summer
Keble preached his sermon; in August they agreed to the principles
of a new movement and planned to announce those principles in a
series of *Tracts for the Times*.[3] Within a year, forty-six such tracts had
been published, calling for renewed recognition of the authority of
the Church of England, for stricter discipline, for the defense of the
Book of Common Prayer, and for paying more attention to what
Newman called "the real ground on which our authority is built—
OUR APOSTOLICAL DESCENT."[4]

On the surface, these Tractarians, as they were known, seemed to
share some of the same disenchantments nursed by Simeon and the
other Evangelicals. Like the Evangelicals, the Tractarians were bitterly critical of Latitudinarianism and "high and dry" churchmanship, and yearned for the renewal of spiritual devotion and vitality
in the church.[5] But it became apparent, as the tracts continued to
come out, that the tracts concealed a very different substance beneath that surface. If, as Keble had asserted, the authority and independence of the English church depended on the connection its
bishops enjoyed with the apostles, then likewise the doctrine of the
English church had better find some earlier resting-place than the
sixteenth-century Reformation. Edward Bouverie Pusey's *Tract No.
67*, on baptism, invoked the church fathers as witnesses that baptism
imparts a "principle of life" and an "infusion of grace," while Robert
Isaac Wilberforce's *Doctrine of the Incarnation* (1848) insisted that the
communion service must necessarily "be allowed to be as truly a
sacrifice as any of those ancient rites to which that term was commonly applied either in Scripture or by men."[6] W.J.E. Bennett simply and frankly declared that he would "adore and teach the people

to adore Christ present in the Sacrament under the form of bread and wine, believing that under their veil is the Sacred Body and Blood of my Lord and Saviour Jesus Christ." All this was moving considerably far from anything anyone had previously thought of as Anglican. Finally recognizing that, Newman eventually urged Anglicans in *The Prophetical Office of the Church* (1837) to think of themselves as an alternative both to Protestantism and to Roman Catholicism (which he called "Anglo-Catholicism") with the mission "of representing a theology, Catholic but not Roman."[7]

Tractarianism, however, represented only the first phase of Newman's "Anglo-Catholicism." By 1839, the Tractarian phase of the Oxford Movement had begun to yield to a Ritualist movement, the goal of which was to shift the attention of Anglo-Catholicism away from patristic literature and toward medieval ritual, striving in the process to accomplish as great a revolution in church architecture, liturgics, and vestments as the Tractarians had accomplished in the more abstract regions of patristics and ecclesiology. Beginning with the founding of the Cambridge Camden Society by E. J. Boyce, J. M. Neale, and Benjamin Webb, the Ritualists promoted an extraordinary revival of medieval Gothic architecture, ritual, and spirituality.[8] Chancels were cleaned out and replaced with surpliced choirs and sanctuary lamps; communion tables were shoved against the back wall to become altars topped with crosses and candles;[9] the communion service itself became the Mass, complete with incense, bowing, crossing, and genuflecting; and elaborate vestments (surplice, cope, alb, chasuble, cincture, cassock) were introduced as proper Anglican dress.[10] Neale, who feared no controversy and brooked no opposition, provoked riots when he began "reserving the Host" after the communion service in 1857. Undismayed by the threat of violence, he followed in 1858 with the institution of the Benediction of the Blessed Sacrament.[11]

The outcry in the church against the Anglo-Catholics made the fury against the Reform Bill pale by comparison. Hugh Nicholas Pearson, the dean of Salisbury Cathedral, denounced Anglo-Catholicism for being "derived essentially from Romanism, and consistent with its intolerant and exclusive principles, but abhorrent from those of genuine Christianity, and of our Reformed Church." Anglo-Catholicism, predicted Pearson, "would, ere long, degenerate into mere ritual and superstitious observance, and cold and barren orthodoxy."[12] These complaints were fanned still hotter by three sensational events. The first was the posthumous publication of Richard Hurrell Froude's literary *Remains* in 1838, which allowed horrified Protestant Englishmen to read what a Tractarian leader *really* thought about their church: "Really I hate the Reformation and the Reformers more and more and have almost made up my mind that the rationalist spirit they set afloat is the *pseudoprophetes* of the Revelations."[13] Then, in February 1841, Newman published the ninetieth in the series of *Tracts*, a half-serious, half-contemptuous effort to confront the Protestantism embedded in the Thirty-Nine Articles of Religion by insisting, with the most desperate twists of interpretation, that the Articles really said nothing to prevent anyone from holding Roman Catholic doctrine.[14] The bishops could stand no more, and the Bishop of Oxford forbade Newman from publishing any more *Tracts*. Newman withdrew from Oxford and in 1845 renounced the Church of England and became a Roman Catholic, thus confirming in the public mind what the real intent of the Tractarians had been all along.

Finally, in 1848, a judicial confrontation became unavoidable. An Evangelical, George Cornelius Gorham, was offered the parish of Brampford Speke, in the diocese of Exeter, by the Lord Chancellor; Henry Philpotts, Bishop of Exeter, disliked Evangelicals in general and Gorham in particular, whom he wanted nothing to do with in his diocese. Gorham and Philpotts, both obstinate men of detail, had already clashed over the subject of baptism, Gorham insisting that it was no doctrine of the Church of England that baptism "regenerated" anyone, and Philpotts using Tractarian arguments to insist otherwise. Philpotts saw Brampford Speke parish as an opportunity to chastise Gorham publicly, and on March 11, 1848, Philpotts announced that he would refuse to institute Gorham as rector of Brampford Speke because of Gorham's "unsoundness" concerning baptismal regeneration. Gorham responded first by denying that his views on baptism were a violation of Anglican doctrine, and second by challenging Philpotts's jurisdiction over Brampford Speke, because the appointment had, after all, come from the Lord Chancellor. On those grounds, he proceeded to appeal the case over Philpotts's head to the Court of Arches, the chief ecclesiastical court of the Church of England.[15]

On both counts, Gorham became the bogeyman of the Anglo-Catholics. A decision by the Court of Arches in Gorham's favor would obviously discredit all their efforts to revive "Catholic" doctrine in the church, and to their relief the Court of Arches found against Gorham in August 1849. But Gorham then appealed further to the Judicial Committee of the Privy Council. This move was even more threatening to the image of the Church of England, which the Anglo-Catholics were laboring to construct, because the Judicial Committee was the government's creature, established in the same year as Keble's Assize sermon. The committee had the final authority in determining doctrinal and liturgical matters in the Church of England, so the very existence of such a committee was, for the Anglo-Catholics, an outrageous reminder that the last legal word on the faith of the Church of England was still uttered by the state. And to their horror, in 1850, the committee overturned the Court of Arches judgment and ordered Philpotts to institute Gorham. The damage done to Tractarian hopes was enormous. In despair, Archdeacon Henry Manning, Robert Isaac Wilberforce, and a number of the other Tractarians concluded that the Church of England was hopelessly secularized and Protestantized, and submitted to Rome. The first great epoch of Anglo-Catholicism came to an end.

For many contemporaries, however, Anglo-Catholicism was anything but a spent force. Some of this attraction was surely that Anglo-Catholicism possessed a deep appeal to the elite of a nation who found themselves threatened with political and cultural dispossession by the first tides of an Industrial Revolution that was turning England into a nation of shopkeepers and mill owners who owed no deference to the old Tory gentry and who swarmed after evangelical preachers. Anglo-Catholicism simultaneously reasserted the virtues of hierarchical, divinely ordered authority, before which obedient peasants tugged at their forelocks, and breathed the spirit of a premodern society in which money-grubbing commercialism was unknown. Much more potent but also much more subtle was Anglo-Catholicism's appeal to, and place within, the overarching mentality of Romanticism.[16] The Romantics found their starting point not in intellectual symmetry and consistency but in the intuitive response of feelings to the sublime, and Anglo-Catholicism had an undeniable and powerful affinity with this spirit. Anglo-Catholic vestments promoted a visual sense of continuity with an aristocratic past; Anglo-Catholic piety, patterned as it was on medieval models, seemed to offer its devotees a passion and an intensity that easily surpassed bourgeois Evangelical respectability or sterile High Churchmanship.[17] They offered the Church what the Evangelicals could not—an awesome religious aesthetic of vestments, colors, and candles, surrounded by the "dim religious light" of Gothic Revival architecture.

The most obvious difficulty with this awe was that it often permitted the Anglo-Catholic to wave away the intellectual doubts of the nineteenth century with acts of religious will and sensibility. In that sense, what Newman said in *Tract No. 90* really was of far less significance than what Keble said in *Tract No. 89*, that the Anglo-Catholics manifested "the studied preference of *poetical* forms of thought and language, as the channel of supernatural knowledge to mankind."[18] Their common ground was not with the church fathers but, ironically, with their own contemporaries—Schleiermacher, Bushnell, Emerson—who likewise hoped to sustain religion by trading in its dogmatic discourse for poetic sensibilities. But a far larger difficulty was that the antimodern poses of the Anglo-Catholics might actually threaten to debase the piety that the authors of the *Tracts* had hoped to revive, turning the movement instead into a therapy to drive away cultural anomie, and turning the self-denying celibacy of its clergy into an exercise in narcissism.[19] In the end, like so many other antimodern movements in the nineteenth century, Anglo-Catholicism was easily converted into a means of accommodation with the modern world of rationalized markets and rationalized mentality, while still granting its adherents the illusion of protest against it. And it was this potent mixture of Romantic authoritarianism and antimodernism that was now prepared, in the 1840s, to make its transit to the Episcopalians of America.

Catholic Challenge, Evangelical Response

The *Tracts* were not published in collected form in the United States until 1839, although extracts and copies of Newman and Pusey had been circulating through Episcopalian hands before.[20] Initially, both Episcopalian High Churchmen and Episcopalian Evangelicals treated the Anglo-Catholics with irritation and contempt. The contempt came first. "As to the propriety of 'increased ritualism' in our Protestant Church," wrote one incredulous American Evangelical,

> We ask . . . what there is, that is imposing in the spectacle of men, of supposed sense and professional education, dressing themselves up in attire, strange and ludicrous, as well from its fantastic shape, as from its flimsy material . . . and increased yet more in its absurdity by posture and grimace, and little boys dressed up in gay or sad garb, as the feast day or fast day may demand. . . . Nor can I understand how two such pretended priests, arrayed like mountebanks, when they look at each other in the vestry, and form their little cortege with their boys to go into church, before the people, can keep their countenances, in the solemn sham, and go through

their parade without crimson cheeks, for the very effeminacy. No—if ever device deserved to be driven from the temple with a whip of small cords, it is this presumptuous folly of stage performance by ministers in a Protestant Church—nor can it be denounced, ever, in terms too severe.[21]

But other Evangelicals were not so cocksure or so dismissive of the Oxford Movement. Bishop Charles Pettit McIlvaine of Ohio, who had seen the impact of Anglo-Catholicism firsthand while visiting Oxford in 1835, took the Anglo-Catholics much more seriously. The debate over the *Tracts* was "about the very life of Christianity,"[22] McIlvaine told his Ohio presbyters, and so in 1841 he published a weighty 546-page attack on the *Tracts*, entitled *Oxford Divinity*. In it, McIlvaine struck savagely at Anglo-Catholicism as "a lamentable departure from the true doctrines of the Gospel, and of the Church of England . . . to those doctrinal corruptions of the Church of Rome of which the Temple of God, in England, was cleansed, at the blessed era of the Protestant Reformation."[23]

American High Churchmen proved to be at least as annoyed as the Evangelicals by the Anglo-Catholics' exhumation of medieval religion. John Henry Hopkins, Bishop of Vermont, had never found any reason to swerve from the "*really Catholic principle*" of "faithful adherence to the Holy Scriptures as THE SUPREME RULE, and to the primitive Church as THE BEST INTERPRETER," and far from sympathizing with Newman, "as soon as that melancholy proof of perversion, Tract No. 90, appeared, I was compelled to see the perilous consequence of their course, and promptly contributed my own poor share in denouncing the delusion."[24] Bishop Thomas Church Brownell, the heir of Connecticut High Churchmanship, understood clearly that the real allure of Anglo-Catholicism lay in the subtle appeal of the Anglo-Catholic aesthetic for the Romantic temperament. "Those in our Church who would carry us back again to the showy ceremonial of the Romish Ritual," declared Brownell to his diocesan convention in 1850, have been moved by little more than "the promptings of a fanciful temperament."[25]

But before long, Anglo-Catholic agitation proved to be an apple of discord thrown between the Evangelicals and the High Churchmen. The principal problem was that no matter how united they might be in their distaste for the Anglo-Catholics, neither Evangelicals nor High Churchmen could agree on a method to deal with Anglo-Catholicism that would not tread on the other's toes. Eventually, because most of the initiative for dealing with the Anglo-

Catholics came from the Evangelicals, and most of the resistance to those plans came from the High Churchmen, the Evangelicals began to perceive the High Churchmen as little better than truculent fellow-travelers of ritualism, while High Churchmen began to view the Evangelicals as false and untrustworthy friends who were as bent on weird innovations of their own kind as the Anglo-Catholics. The Anglo-Catholics, for their own safety, were quick to take advantage of this suspicion by exhorting the High Churchmen into ever more stubborn resistance to change and by taunting them with accusations of disloyalty to their own principles should they ever concede anything to the Evangelicals. By stiffening the backs of the High Churchmen against their erstwhile allies, the Anglo-Catholics successfully played one party off against each other.

Between 1840 and 1873, Evangelical Episcopalians grappled with this two-horned dilemma by proposing three methods for sealing off the doors of the church to ritualism, and each method did more to antagonize the High Churchmen than to discourage the Anglo-Catholics. The Evangelicals' most controversial and repellent strategy was *canonical*: they began to press for changes in the canon law of the church that would forbid the liturgical innovations (especially in vestments and ceremony) of the Anglo-Catholics. More of them favored *liturgical* strategies instead, which in practical terms meant changes in the Book of Common Prayer to exclude the doctrinal innovations of the Anglo-Catholics. The most ingenious strategy, however, was an *ecumenical* one, for the strongest ground the Evangelicals held in the American Republic was their quasi-republican fellow-feeling for other evangelical denominations, and it was possible to use that (at least in terms of public rhetoric) as a stick with which to beat Anglo-Catholic exclusivism.

This last method was also the least successful, even though it was predicated on the apparently equitable notion of broadening the appeal of the Episcopal Church to other evangelical American denominations. But unsuccessful as it might have been in the event, the ecumenical gambit started out with two tremendous advantages. First, this way of dealing with the problem avoided the acrimony and embarrassment of a direct confrontation with the Anglo-Catholics and merely suggested that if the church meant to be so open as to tolerate the eccentricities of the ritualists, then it ought to be equally open and permit the Evangelicals liberty to welcome non-Episcopalians into their folds and to work with non-Episcopalians in their own endeavors. Second, this proposal had as its chief spokesman the venerable figure of William Augustus Muhlenberg, rector of the Church of the Holy Communion in New York City and in many respects almost the last man anyone expected to hear speaking for the Evangelicals.

Born in 1796 in Philadelphia, Muhlenberg had been ordained by William White in 1817.[26] He made his name in the church as the founder of the Flushing Institute, a boys' boarding school that quickly became the basic model for the creation of the Episcopal Church's famous chain of church-related preparatory schools. His concern for the spiritual life of his boys, as well as a "poetic and imaginative spirit," led him to resort to increased experimentation in ritual and ceremony. By the time he left Flushing Institute, he had built the devotional life of the school around an elaborate observation of the church year, together with a surpliced boys' choir in the chapel and an altar with flowers and pictures of the Nativity and the Resurrection. In 1846, when he became the rector of the Church of the Holy Communion in New York City, Muhlenberg introduced weekly communion services, organized a sisterhood for social service, put away his preaching gown in favor of exclusive use of the surplice, and erected an altar with crosses, candles, flowers, and incense. To young seminary students enchanted with the *Tracts*, the Church of the Holy Communion appeared as "the extremest height possible, and its extremes consisted of a proper altar with a cross and flowers, and a choir of unvested boys who chanted the Psalter."[27]

But Muhlenberg was neither High Churchman nor Anglo-Catholic. Whatever his dress and the peculiar decorations of his church, his theology and his spirit were firmly Evangelical. His ceremonial innovations, often his own ad hoc inventions, were part of his private campaign for an "Evangelical Catholicism" that would harness the fervency of "practical Christianity" to the discipline of "Catholic" church order, a subject on which Muhlenberg and Newman shared not even the slightest common ground. At first he had been intrigued by the *Tracts*, and he visited England in 1843 principally to interview Newman and Pusey. But what he found there, and in Newman's writings, worked in him a profound revulsion against Anglo-Catholicism.[28] By the time he came to the Church of the Holy Communion, he had concluded that Anglo-Catholicism was a "delusion," and those in New York who mistook his penchant for ceremony there as sympathy with the Anglo-Catholics were about to receive the surprise of their lives.[29]

On October 18, 1853, during the sessions of the General Convention of the church, Muhlenberg and eleven other presbyters put before the House of Bishops a "Memorial" that in effect called on the bishops to set the church on a direction decisively away from the

Tracts and more toward the pan-Protestant ecumenism so beloved by the Evangelicals.[30] Muhlenberg declared in the Memorial that "the divided and distracted state of our American Protestant Christianity" and "the utter ignorance of the Gospel among so large a portion of the lower classes of our population" had forced him to question whether the Protestant Episcopal Church, "with only her present canonical means and appliances, her fixed and invariable modes of public worship, her traditional customs and usages, is competent to the work of preaching and dispensing the Gospel to all sorts and conditions of men." But Muhlenberg did not propose to dismantle any of those means and appliances. To the contrary, hardly anyone could have loved Episcopal government, liturgical worship, and traditional "customs and usages" more. The problem lay not in the "means and appliances" but in the narrowness with which the Episcopal Church guarded them, a narrowness that the Anglo-Catholics now threatened to narrow still further. The solution, not only to the general problem of the church's mission but also to the specific problem of the Anglo-Catholics, was to make the "means and appliances" more available and less restrictive to other Christian churches. Hence, the Memorial made three basic recommendations:

1. The extension of episcopal ordination to non-episcopal clergy; or to put it in plainer terms, the free offer of the episcopal principle and the blessing of an apostolic ministry to any ministers who wanted it, even if they were and remained Presbyterians, Methodists, or Baptists
2. The loosening of restrictions on "opinion, discipline and worship" for those presently within the Episcopal Church in order to create a new ecclesiastical system "broader and more comprehensive than that which you now administer"
3. Stronger ecumenical ties with other Protestant denominations to effect "a Church unity in the Protestant Christendom of our land."[31]

Underlying the demands of the Memorial was Muhlenberg's contention that the essential doctrines of the Episcopal Church had nothing to do with ordination or ritual and could be satisfied if any non-Episcopalian were willing to agree to three basic conditions:

1. That "they declare their belief in the Holy Scriptures and the word of God, in the Apostles' and Nicene creeds, in the divine

Institution of the two sacraments, and in the 'doctrines of grace,' substantially as they are set forth in the Thirty-Nine Articles"

2. That they would use certain parts of the liturgy including the essential parts of the administration of the Holy Sacraments

3. That "they will make report of their ministry once, at least, in every three years to the bishop or some approved ecclesiastical tribunal."[32]

The nature of these conditions made it clear that Muhlenberg believed that episcopacy existed simply as the best way of preaching those facts to the world, not as an end in itself. If the church would begin to give away its blessings to other Protestants instead of clutching its prerogatives closer and closer, it would find that the gifts would eventually bring the recipients back to the Episcopal fold and create a new superchurch that would embrace all American Protestants.

But the Memorial was greeted coldly by the House of Bishops, for the High Church bishops seated there were aghast at Muhlenberg's proposals. George Washington Freeman of Arkansas protested incredulously the suggestion that he ordain any willing Protestant without making him an Episcopalian at the same time:

> An ordained minister of *the Church* not bound to conformity to the "worship, discipline, &c." of the Church! How could it have entered into the mind of man to conceive of such a thing? And to impart holy orders to one who is not *of* the Church, and is *not to be amenable to her authority*, what is gained to the cause of truth and Christ? . . . On the contrary, the usual indications are of a contempt for what we call Apostolic ordination and authority, and an entire satisfaction with their own orders and authority.[33]

By contrast, William Meade of Virgina and Alonzo Potter of Pennsylvania pleaded for the Memorial, admitting that "it might be more just" for the church "to wait till they who have gone out from her, return and sue for readmittance," but countering that "it would be more Christ-like, more in the genius of her mission as the Lord's representative among men to go out to them and offer the gifts where with she is entrusted." It made no difference. Potter's pleas were snarled down by the reply that "the Presbyterians, Congregationalists, Methodists and Baptists" who might be interested in the Memorial's proposals were really only "mere drones or idlers, restless, contentious, and desirous of a change only with the hope of improving their condition."[34] In Muhlenberg's Memorial, the old High Churchmen saw only what amounted to a watering-down of episcopal prerogatives and a loosening of episcopal government, and the only end for that was a steady hemorrhaging of the Episcopal Church's unique identity. And so, in 1856, when the House of Bishops reported on its investigation of Muhlenberg's proposals, it granted only minor concessions on liturgical freedom and halfheartedly offered to create a committee on church union.[35] None of the major proposals was adopted, and it was made quite clear that the High Churchmen had begun to wonder who was worse: the Anglo-Catholics, pushing episcopacy to one extravagance, or the Evangelicals, pushing to the opposite extravagance. Forced to a choice, it was apparent which extravagance the High Churchmen would prefer.

The failure of the Muhlenberg Memorial compelled the Evangelicals to look in a different direction for safeguards from the Anglo-Catholics, and the direction in which the majority found themselves looking toward was revision of the Book of Common Prayer. Before the 1840s, the Evangelicals had few objections to any aspect of the prayer book. They might have been troubled by the continued use of the word "priest" in the rubrics and the ordinal to describe the clergy, or the declaration that baptized children were "now regenerate." But the unspoken consensus of both Evangelical and High Church was content that "priest" was merely the English contraction of "presbyter" (elder), not a synonym for the Latin word *sacerdos* (a sacrificial order of clergy).[36] As for "regenerate," it was again generally understood that the term yielded a number of possible interpretations, most of which were compatible with Evangelicals' insistence on the critical importance of faith for salvation.[37] Charles Wesley Andrews, a Virginia Evangelical, suggested in 1869 that there were as many as seven ways of interpreting what was meant when the prayer book declared "this child now regenerate," six of which reduced baptism to a "charitable hope" or a "covenant sign."[38] Not all these possibilities were logically coherent, or even mutually exclusive, but they were understood and recognized by the body of Evangelical opinion in the Episcopal Church to be legitimate alternatives, and few really believed that, with these interpretive options available, the words of the baptismal service could be turned against their Evangelical principles.

They were, to their dismay, proven wrong. When Evangelicals confronted Anglo-Catholics with the Protestant (and erastian) doctrines of the Thirty-Nine Articles of Religion, the new American converts to the *Tracts* smilingly opened the Book of Common

Prayer and insisted that "now regenerate" could only mean *moral* regeneration; that "priest" could only mean a full-fledged sacrificing priest after the Roman model; and that these "priests" at their ordinations received "the Holy Ghost" from the hands of the bishop, denying thereby that the Holy Ghost was available to any other than those ordained by bishops in regular succession from the apostles. Baffled and amazed, the Evangelicals recoiled from their own prayer book.[39] And so the Evangelicals now began angrily demanding unheard-of changes in the liturgy, and signing petitions begging for relief from the use of "regenerate" in baptism, "priest" in ordination, and other changes. The cries for revision reached their crescendo with the publication in 1868 of Franklin S. Rising's manifesto, *Are There Romanizing Germs in the Prayer Book?* Rising impatiently dismissed as an elaborate etymological game the customary Evangelical attempt to prove that "priest" and "regenerate" really meant something Protestant. Rather than viewing the offending terms as Protestant vocabulary twisted out of shape by Anglo-Catholic chicanery, Rising insisted that these terms were really "romanizing germs," little Trojan horses left embedded in the liturgy since the Reformation and now opening up to unleash a terrible vengeance.[40] Rising warned that Evangelicals must not fool themselves into thinking that the prayer book was their friend; Anglo-Catholicism was no exotic or abnormal growth, and it was pure folly for Evangelicals to think that they could "stay the tide of High-Churchmanship by quoting the Prayer-Book."[41]

Rising's solution was to "*agitate, agitate, AGITATE*" for wholesale revision—"a purely evangelical Liturgy"[42]—but that was a course liable to incur the wrath of the High Churchmen and drive them further into the arms of the Anglo-Catholics. Alteration of the prayer book was precisely what no High Churchman was prepared to grant, even in the direst straits and even for the goal of silencing the Anglo-Catholic annoyance. High Churchmen prized their prayer book almost as much as their Bibles, and they could not see why the Anglo-Catholic effort to reinterpret the Book of Common Prayer gave any grounds for the Evangelicals to mutilate it. What the High Churchmen did not understand was the imbalance of that comparison, and Evangelicals were left to wonder why High Church bishops should be so indignant when Evangelicals wanted to *remove* some words from the liturgy and so complacent when the Anglo-Catholics *added* candles, altars, and vestments and tantalizing elements of the Roman Missal.

The last option open to the Evangelicals, after the failure to open up the church and to open up the Book of Common Prayer, was to close down the canons of the church, and to obtain legislation in the General Convention which would ban the ritual innovations, if not the theological innovations, of the Anglo-Catholics once and for all. The Evangelical campaign against ritualism had actually been going on almost from the beginning of the Anglo-Catholic movement, starting with Alexander Viets Griswold's public criticism of St. Stephen's Church, Providence, Rhode Island, in his 1841 diocesan convention address.[43] But it reached its high-water mark in the General Convention of 1868, when the Evangelicals submitted for debate nearly twenty memorials calling for new canons that would restrict specifically Anglo-Catholic ritual practice. The Convention's Committee on Constitution and Canons timidly proposed the "avoidance of unseemly disputes and contradictory practices"; that only served to set the stage for Judge John N. Conyngham of Pennsylvania to rise and offer a substitute "Canon on the Manner of Conducting Divine Worship." Conyngham's canon, which represented a minority report of the Committee on Constitution and Canons, called for elimination of any vestments beyond "surplice, stole, bands or gown," the suppression of "candlesticks, crucifixes, super-altars," and the prevention of "bowing at the name of Jesus, except in repeating the Creed" (which would indicate veneration of the physical body and blood of Jesus on the altar), the elevation of the bread and wine during the Prayer of Consecration (which might symbolize the offering of a sacrifice) or "the use of Incense."[44]

Judge Conyngham's canon aimed purely and nakedly at restriction, but unhappily for the Evangelicals, the whole ethos of American Episcopacy, from William White onward, had pointed in precisely the opposite direction. And it certainly seemed strange that Evangelicals who had supported the open-ended and comprehensive proposals of the Muhlenberg Memorial with such gusto should, fifteen years later, be calling now for restriction. The confusion and impasse resulting from Conyngham's canon was resolved only by referring it to the House of Bishops for a ruling at the next General Convention in 1871. The bishops formed a committee, chaired by Alfred Lee of Delaware, and under Lee's Evangelical eye the committee issued a report that endorsed virtually all of the proposed canon.[45] But the House of Bishops as a whole was too badly divided to come to an agreement on its own committee's report, and when the General Convention assembled in Baltimore in October 1871, the bishops simply handed the committee report back to the lay delegates and waited for them to take the first action. The result was predictable. If the Convention had not approved the canon outright in 1868, there was even less chance it would do so in 1871, especially after the halfhearted response of the bishops. The Evangelicals fought a long and tenacious rear-guard action in defense of the canon, but after twenty days of nearly continuous debate the canon was finally put to the question; it perished in a narrowly divided vote taken by dioceses and orders. In its place, a joint committee of bishops and laymen chaired by Bishop William R. Whittingham of Maryland substituted a watered-down resolution on ritual that left all determinations concerning ceremony and vestments in the hands of each diocesan bishop.[46] This action was so plainly calculated to do nothing that the foremost of the Anglo-Catholics, James DeKoven, now stood and confidently quoted to the Convention W.J.E. Bennett's provocative declaration: "I believe in 'the Real, Actual Presence of our Lord under the form of bread and wine upon the altars of our churches.' I 'myself adore' and would if it were necessary or my duty 'teach my people to adore Christ present in the elements under the form of bread and wine.'"[47]

On all three counts—ecumenical, liturgical, and canonical—the Evangelicals had failed either to exclude Anglo-Catholic influence from their "Protestant and Reformed" Church, or obtain guarantees to protect themselves within it. Some, like Bishop McIlvaine, put as good a face on matters as they could and insisted that even though the canon against ritualism had failed, "the exposure of it was so thorough and crushing, as well by High Churchmen and Low, and the defense was so exposing, that its doom in our Church has been pronounced." But McIlvaine was whistling in the dark. "*No liberty to Protestant principles*—and *no restraint on Ritualistic fooleries*—this was the spirit of the Convention," wrote one embittered delegate.

> As Evangelical men we have no relief, no help or comfort to expect from the legislation of the Church. We have nothing to look for from the action of our General Convention but oppression, such as has now been inaugurated, increased and intensified, till conscience and loyalty to God and his truth can bear it no longer.[48]

For some, that breaking point had been passed even before the 1871 Convention had assembled. The first surreptitious gathering of Evangelical dissidents had already taken place, talking of secession and the establishment of "a new Episcopal Church."[49]

The failure of the Evangelicals to quash the Anglo-Catholics produced two bitter legacies. For one thing, the failure of the High Churchmen to rally against the Anglo-Catholics destroyed the fragile trust Evangelicals and High Churchmen had once shared, for neither Evangelical nor High Churchman ever fully comprehended the motives for each other's actions. "The High Church men will vote with the Ritualists rather than with the Evangelical men," one Evangelical complained. "These two parties have united; and this union gives them control of the Church."[50]

This left the Anglo-Catholics free to antagonize the Evangelicals as much as they pleased. And antagonize they did, for Anglo-Catholics possessed a significant tactical advantage over their Evangelical brethren in the influence they quickly acquired over church education. General Theological Seminary in New York City was the Oxford Movement's port of entry into American Episcopalianism, and its prominence as the most important of the three then-existing Episcopal seminaries (the other two were the Evangelical seminaries at Alexandria, Virginia, and Gambier, Ohio) gave the Anglo-Catholic influence a substantial foothold in the Episcopal Church. A fourth seminary, Nashotah House, was organized in Wisconsin in 1842 entirely on Anglo-Catholic principles, thus giving the Anglo-Catholics an influence over Episcopal theological education far larger than their actual numbers in the church.

Perhaps because so much of American Anglo-Catholicism would rest on its appeal to a generation of seminary students, American Anglo-Catholicism developed a reputation for novelties and practical liturgical jokes that looked downright flippant beside the austere discipline of saints like Newman and Pusey. American Anglo-Catholics, rather than publishing the *Tracts*, concentrated on ritual, the more provocative the better, and their general response to Evangelical sensitivities was to trample on them. Clarence Walworth, who came under the sway of Anglo-Catholicism while a student at General Theological Seminary, later described how he and several of his comrades reacted to Evangelicals:

> Hewit Baker and some others . . . would gladly have pushed their imitation of Roman observances much farther. This they could not very well do at St. Paul's where they attended, for Dr. Wyatt was omnipotent there and clung to the more Protestant practices in which he had been brought up. There, they contented themselves with kneeling with their faces toward the altar though the rest of the congregation faced the other way. Providence soon opened another way to play Catholic. They came to know a well-disposed rector of a rather small brick church in a poor district of Baltimore. He warmly sympathized with Hewit and Baker in their Catholic tendencies and allowed them to remodel the interior of the

church and to imitate Catholic ceremonies according to the full desires of their heart. This liberty they carried so far that the congregation became alarmed and remonstrated; and as the bishop seemed indisposed to interfere, they began to forsake the services. The parish was threatened with ruin both spiritual and financial. At this juncture a power more effectual than that of a bishop interposed. This was the rector's wife. With her, it was a matter of bread and butter and she interposed her authority so effectually that all the innovations were brought to a stop. The obnoxious symbols on the window curtains were banished out of sight. The chancel was restored to its former simplicity, containing no longer anything bearing resemblance to an altar but revealing as before the old marble-topped communion table which, like so many others, would have served as well for a washstand.[51]

The Evangelicals, already angered at Anglo-Catholic doctrinal curiosities, were reduced to gibbering fury by such liturgical naughtiness. One apoplectic Evangelical clergyman warned in the columns of *The Episcopalian* in 1869 that the policy of the Anglo-Catholics "is to crush out the Evangelical party, to drive them to the sects, to get possession of their churches, to crush their braver spirits singly, and to annoy and harass as far as practicable where they cannot cajole, and bring into line."[52] And so the 1850s and 1860s began to see conflicts between Evangelical parishes and new, young Anglo-Catholic curates, in which High Church bishops occasionally took the opportunity to even up some old scores by giving the curates free rein.

The most sensational conflicts occurred in the cities, especially New York City and Chicago. In 1865, Bishop Horatio Potter of New York issued a pastoral letter to his clergy, informing them that he intended to take a strict view of the church's exclusionary canon (Title 1, Canon 11, Section I), which forbade nonordained people from ministry in Episcopal churches:

> No person shall be permitted to officiate in any congregation of this Church without first producing the evidence of his being a minister thereof to the Minister, or in case of vacancy or absence, to the Church Wardens, Vestrymen, or Trustees of the Congregation.[53]

In Potter's terms, "no person" meant no clergyman lacking episcopal ordination was to be allowed to preach or administer the sacraments in his jurisdiction. "The Church requires of all who minister to her congregations two things," Potter declared. "*First*, that they be *Episcopally ordained*, and *second*, that they be Episcopally ordained *ministers of this Church*." Consequently, "Non-Episcopal divines are, therefore, doubly excluded . . . not only from administering the Sacraments, but also from teaching within her fold."[54]

The Evangelical clergy of his diocese were dumbfounded, because Potter had made it quite clear that his interpretation of the canon included cases in which "ministers of this Church are understood to have united with ministers of non-Episcopal bodies in holding services in Churches of this Diocese; or else ministers of this Church went to non-Episcopal places of worship and preached, without the due performance of the devotional services enjoined by the law of the Church."[55] Eli Hawley Canfield, the rector of Christ Church, Brooklyn, immediately assumed that he was the target of Potter's letter and pointed out to Potter that the bishop's interpretation of the canon was unheard-of in New York, even in Hobart's days. "It is generally conceded that the section under consideration was originally designed to apply to *imposters*" and "very properly forbids, not ministers [of other denominations], but 'persons' falsely claiming to be ministers of this Church, officiating in any congregation of the same."[56] John Cotton Smith, yet another of Potter's Evangelical clergy, assumed that *he* was the object of Potter's ire for having held a joint Easter service with William Augustus Muhlenberg and noted New York Presbyterian Dr. William Adams. "The history of the Canon shows indeed that it was originally designed to protect our congregations from imposters," Smith angrily declared. "There was no intention to make it exclusive in the sense now attributed to it."[57]

But no one had more defiant words to utter than Stephen H. Tyng, son-in-law of Alexander Viets Griswold and rector of St. George's Church, New York City. Tyng protested that "neither the spotless Griswold, nor the patriarchal White" had ever interpreted the canon in such a fashion. To the contrary, "in invitations to ministers of other churches to preach in his church, in a free and friendly union in religious exercises with all who loved the Lord Jesus, Bishop Griswold set me the example and gave me my direction. . . . But these High Church principles I never heard, or heard of, in my youth." Likewise assuming that *he* was the quarry Potter was hunting in his letter, Tyng replied:

A reasonable and free interpretation of the canon, and not what you call a "severe" and excluding one, has been the habit of my work and the rule of my ministry. I have neither the ability nor the intention to change it. If this be a violation

of my oath, I must bear the penalty and endure the guilt. . . .
To change this practice and silence this universal freedom is
beyond the power or the right of Episcopal authority.[58]

Both Potter and Tyng were as good as their word. In the summer
of 1867, Tyng's son, Stephen H. Tyng Jr., who was the rector of
the Church of the Holy Trinity in the same diocese with his father,
accepted an invitation to preach at St. James's Methodist Church in
New Brunswick, New Jersey. As soon as notice of the younger
Tyng's intention became known, two of the local Episcopal clergy
in New Brunswick, Alfred Stubbs and Edward Boggs, warned
Tyng not to preach within "their parochial cure" on the authority
of the exclusionary canon. Tyng ignored the warning, and Stubbs
and Boggs filed charges against him with the bishop of New
Jersey, who then referred the case to Bishop Potter as Tyng's
diocesan.[59]

It was obvious at first glance that this was intended to be the test
case of Potter's attempt to extend the scope of the exclusionary
canon to control both non-Episcopalians in Episcopal pulpits as well
as Episcopalians in non-Episcopal pulpits. When Potter convened a
board of inquiry at St. Peter's Church, New York, on January 10,
1868, packed audiences and high-powered legal counsel were very
much in evidence on both sides. In addition to the lawyers' briefs,
the Evangelical clergy of the diocese put themselves on record with
a "Declaration of Certain Clergy and Laity of the Protestant Episcopal Church" (and signed by John Cotton Smith, Eli Canfield, Marshall B. Smith, William Wilberforce Newton, the elder Tyng, and
"many other clergymen and laymen"), which not only repudiated
Potter's interpretation of the canons, but also accused him of using
the canons as a stalking horse for setting up Anglo-Catholic notions
of the ministry.[60] "Let not rubrical irregularities or canonical infrac-
tions be punished, while practices involving doctrinal enormities
pass unnoticed," William Augustus Muhlenberg warned Potter.
"Let not one be held up to the world as violating his ordination
vows because of a sermon from a non-episcopal brother in his
pulpit, or because of his putting up a prayer not in the Book while
the author of the accusation quietly allows the Communion Office
to be transformed as far as possible into the Roman Mass, Sunday
after Sunday, in churches under his own jurisdiction."[61]

Potter could ill afford to lose such a contest, and he was careful
not to. When the board rendered its judgment on February 24, the
younger Tyng was duly condemned for breach of the canons, and
he was summoned to appear for sentencing before Bishop Potter at

the Church of the Transfiguration on March 14. Potter prudently
limited the sentence to "admonition" to avoid further aggravating
Evangelical opinion.[62] Tyng was neither grateful nor repentant.
"That organization which presumes to interpose its man-made law
between the burden of the salvation of the world and the full liberty
of preaching must either prove itself infallible or confess itself im-
pertinent," Tyng told the congregation of Holy Trinity Church,
with appropriate republican flourishes. "No American, worthy of
the name, could enter a ministry which so violences human freedom."[63] However, nothing could erase the mortification the judgment brought the Evangelicals, and the elder Tyng made the occasion of the sentencing the stage for one last, mute protest against
Potter's ruling. Standing among the crowds that gathered at the
Church of the Transfiguration to watch his son humiliated, Tyng
waited until Potter had concluded the reading of the sentence to
advance to the chancel of the church and place in Potter's hands a
protest against "this whole proceeding . . . as false in its allegations,
unjust in its principle, uncanonical in its form, illegal in its transac-
tions, iniquitous in its purpose, and voluntarily and persistently per-
secuting in its spirit process and development."[64]
   With the successes of each one of the Anglo-Catholic "policies,"
Evangelical frustration became increasingly more strident, more futile, and more despairing. At first, there were only the individual
acts of defiance. In 1843, Arthur Carey, another graduate of General
Theological Seminary, was ordained by Bishop Benjamin Onderdonck over the vigorous protests of the two Evangelical presbyters,
John Cotton Smith and Henry Anthon, who had sat on Carey's
ordination exam and who had heard Carey make no secret of his
respect and admiration for Roman Catholic doctrine. Smith and Anthon were so alarmed at Carey's theology and Onderdonck's indifference that in the middle of Carey's ordination at St. Stephen's
Church, New York, on July 2, 1843, both stood up to read a protest. Onderdonck listened, waited until Smith and Anthon had
walked out, and then proceeded with Carey's ordination as though
nothing had happened. Further confrontation was avoided only because of the premature death of Carey less than a year later and the
suspension of Onderdonck from the episcopate in 1845 on charges
of drunkenness and womanizing. Then there came the corporate ta-
ble-poundings in the form of the Evangelical conventions. In November 1867, a convention of Evangelicals met at the Church of the
Epiphany in Philadelphia to reiterate the demands of the Muhlenberg Memorial and complain that Anglo-Catholicism meant nothing less than "an entire subversion of the Protestant and Evangelical

character of our Reformed Church."[65] Yet another Evangelical convention assembled in Chicago in June 1869 around the proposition that "a scheme exists to undermine the Scriptural foundation of these Churches, on the specious plea of a 'revived catholicity.' "[66] But the conventions had no authority to do anything more than pass resolutions and further agitate their participants.

That left open to the Evangelicals only two last-ditch alternatives. The first alternative—and this was chiefly for those consigned to marginal parishes or hostile bishops—was simply to concede the game to the Anglo-Catholic "policy" of "drive them to the sects," and leave the Episcopal Church. For Evangelicals with large, wealthy parishes, or with friendly or unobtrusive bishops, the other alternative was to resist being forced out and to take such matters as prayer book revision into one's own hands in the privacy of one's own parish. And that was the path that led to the sensational affair of Charles Edward Cheney.

The Trial and Deposition of Charles Edward Cheney

Charles Edward Cheney was born and bred to the Episcopal manner, the third generation of an Upstate New York Episcopal family. He had the look and feel of a good old Hobartian, with a ramrod-stiff back (to compensate for his diminutive stature) and an enormous pair of powder-puff side-whiskers (subtly attracting attention away from the baldness that crept over him in his twenties). "Rev. Mr. Cheney is a robust, handsome man, with side whiskers of the best English cut, which alone would admit him to the first circle of Montreal society," a Berkshire newspaper said admiringly when Cheney was vacationing there in 1871. "He has a full, rich voice, his pronunciation is distinct, and his delivery admirable."[67] He was even a graduate (in 1857) of what was then known as Hobart College (now Hobart and Smith) in Geneva, New York. But whatever his roots in Hobart's soil, Cheney was not actually an Episcopal aristocrat at all (his father was a country doctor in Canandaigua, New York), and his convictions were all over on the Evangelical side. And so it was to the great Evangelical seminary at Alexandria, Virginia that he went for training for the Episcopal ministry.

For long after Cheney's student days, the Virginia seminary was one of the most thoroughgoing Evangelical seminaries in the Episcopal Church, and the formidable Evangelical bishop of Virginia, John Johns, had selected the seminary as his residence in 1854. There, Cheney sat at the feet not only of Bishop Johns but also of the great teachers of Evangelical Episcopalianism—William Sparrow, James May, and Joseph Packard. In his senior year, he was invited to become the assistant at St. Luke's, Rochester, New York, and was duly ordained deacon on November 21, 1858, by Bishop William Heathcote DeLancey, a bleak, Hobartian High Churchman. He served briefly as minister-in-charge of St. Paul's Church in the tiny hamlet of Havana, New York, and was then advanced to the priesthood by DeLancey on March 4, 1860, in Rochester. From there he went in April to answer a new call from the infant parish of Christ Church, Chicago.[68] When Cheney stepped off the train to meet his new flock, he found "a membership of but seven, a Sabbath-school numbering 30 members, a congregation of 50, and a frame building worth about $1,000 and no lot."[69] His ministry was only one year old when the Civil War broke out, draining men, money, and interest out of churches and into the war effort; and in 1864, the church building burned down. It was half-rebuilt by a contractor who soon went bankrupt, and was finally completed by fits and starts at almost five times the original cost.[70] But Cheney was not easily bent or discouraged. His first sermon in Chicago was preached from Philippians 1:27—"That ye stand fast in the Spirit"— and he spent the next nine years living that sermon out.

At the center of his preaching was the unremitting demand for Evangelical conversion.[71] He was impatient with those who only "admire the beautiful moral precepts of the New Testament" and who "never will be led to make them the guiding principle" of their lives.[72] And he had no use for "any essential doctrine which does not find its basis and ultimate authority in the Bible."[73] In his mind, that limitation excluded any notions of church order that made claims to apostolic succession or that implied the "unchurching" of other evangelical denominations. "Surely nothing can be clearer than this fact that a bishop and a presbyter in the view of the New Testament are one," Cheney argued, and the Episcopalian has no real right to vaunt episcopal orders over nonepiscopal orders.[74] His Evangelical principles also excluded any exaggerated views of the efficacy of baptism. Although Cheney, from the very beginning of his career, had accepted the responsibility laid on him by the prayer book to baptize infants and then declare "this child now regenerate," he had done so in the customary Evangelical fashion of attaching several mental reservations to the words he was uttering.

I tried to accept what was called "the hypothetical view," which taught that when the minister said the child or the adult was "regenerate" the moment that the water of baptism had been applied, he was simply looking down the future of the baptized person, and upon the theory that the candidate *would be* converted and become a Christian, the officiating clergyman was justified in assuming hypothetically that he was already regenerate.[75]

And yet, Cheney resists being cataloged merely as a party-line Evangelical who regarded his Episcopalian identity more as a duty to bear than a banner to flaunt. "I am an Episcopalian of the Episcopalians," Cheney declared, and he never ceased insisting that "we ought to love our own Church as a true man loves his home."[76] He was suspicious of letting the Evangelical penchant for open-armed fraternalism run too far, and he sharply criticized those of his fellows who "have been so captivated with the idea of consolidation of all the various divisions of Christendom into one vast body."[77] He was also as reluctant to have Evangelicals depreciate the sacraments as he was to hear the Anglo-Catholics inflate them. "The Bible clearly declares it the duty of every believer to confess his faith by a baptism with water in the name of the Holy Trinity," Cheney warned. "Such a fact lifts the baptismal washing out of the realm of mere optional ceremonial."[78] There was still enough of the old New York Hobartian in Cheney to make him an extremely well-starched Evangelical.

Few of his parishioners who left recollections of Cheney's ministry describe him as a power in the pulpit. What does come through well-nigh unanimously is that Cheney was, for all his forbidding public manner, an enormously skillful and even "lovable" pastor. "He was a faithful pastor and we knew him as such," recalled Samuel Gibson, Cheney's last assistant at Christ Church, in 1916. "He told me many times that he could not preach unless he visited people in their homes. It was his invariable rule, in pastoral visiting, to have prayer with the families, and the benediction not only of his presence but of his prayer in many homes, will be a treasured memory." He was, in his parish, remarkable for valuing the "little opportunity" in people's lives, and he "realized that in such little opportunities lay his field of influence."[79] Precisely because he was so secure in his own knowledge of himself and his powers, people troubled by the doubts and insecurities of post–Civil War America found in him an unruffled certainty that calmed their fears. And so, by 1869, Cheney had built up Christ Church not only into a new

stone church building worth more than $100,000 but also into a
congregation with 300 communicants, a "congregation numbering
600 or 700 ordinarily" on Sunday mornings, and a Sunday School of
"600 or 700 members."[80]

With such an institution around him, Cheney could easily have
afforded to ignore the mounting conflicts between Evangelicals and
Anglo-Catholics in the Episcopal Church. But he could not deny a
definite distaste for the Anglo-Catholics, and he once remarked in
no uncertain terms that "two systems, the exact opposite of each
other, have been struggling for supremacy within" the Episcopal
Church. "If the doctrine of justification by faith in the blood of Jesus
is the truth of God, then justification by sacraments is a lie, whose
author is the Father of lies," Cheney declared. "There is no possible
ground on which to stand between the two."[81] But there was no
compelling reason why Cheney should have risked his hard-won
eminence at Christ Church by entering directly into the lists against
the Anglo-Catholics, and between 1860 and 1868, Cheney stayed
pretty much out of the ecclesiastical fray.

And then, sometime in 1867 or 1868, something in the quality of
Cheney's patience snapped. The element that snapped it was the old
Evangelical bogeyman, the declarations in the baptismal office that
baptized adults or infants were now "regenerate." In the usual Evangelical fashion, "I satisfied my conscience, through many years of
ministry in the Protestant Episcopal Church, by trying to *explain
away* the language of the service," Cheney recalled. But "there came
a day when conscience told me that I was juggling with plain words
to torture them from that which they did not mean."[82] A question
began to nag at Cheney: "When I got down on my knees and began
to thank God—what was I thanking him for?"

> "We thank thee that it hath pleased thee to regenerate this
> person *by thy Holy Spirit.*" Then it was precisely the same
> regeneration about which our Lord talked to Nicodemus
> [i.e., a moral change]. Suddenly I found that my conscience
> was troubled beyond endurance and without a word to any
> human being, not even to my beloved wife, I dropped that
> expression quietly from both the exhortation and the thanks-
> giving itself.[83]

Cheney never specified what, exactly, caused him to "suddenly"
find his conscience troubled about the baptismal service, although it
may have been the realization that "his own labored explanations of
the baptismal office were of no avail to root out from the minds,

especially of the young and uneducated, the notion that the sacrament of baptism was a magical charm possessed of inherent saving power." Whatever it was, it meant that, rather than appeal for liturgical or canonical relief or for permission to dispense, Cheney proposed to take the risky and unquestionably illegal path of performing his own private revision of the Book of Common Prayer.

Cheney's decision to take the prayer book into his own hands runs very much against his grain, both before and after this incident. Perhaps he seriously believed that it would never be noticed, since Cheney clearly seems to have had evidence that Evangelicals in other dioceses were performing similar quiet alterations while their bishops looked the other way. In 1871, he claimed he did not believe "that he was, in so doing, committing any offense against the law of the Protestant Episcopal Church"; he had observed clergymen making omissions from almost all the offices of the prayer book at some point or other, "yet, from all these, omissions are made without notice or rebuke."[84] Cheney certainly took little trouble to advertise his innovation, and none of his congregation or vestry betrayed him to higher diocesan authorities. He might, in fact, have gotten away with it for a lot longer had he not, one day in the spring of 1869, blurted out his little secret to an indiscreet Baptist:

> One day in a Church bookstore, I fell into conversation with a Baptist clergyman of Chicago, whom I knew very well, and who was an exceptionally prominent man. It so happened that we drifted into a little controversy about Infant Baptism, and turning upon me, my Baptist friend said, "Mr. Cheney, I do not see how you can conscientiously use your Baptismal service while holding your views about spiritual regeneration." "Well," I said, "I do not use it; that is, I do not use the part of it that asserts spiritual regeneration as infallibly tied to baptism."[85]

In his "Journal of Services," Cheney identifies this "Baptist clergyman" only as the "Rev. Dr. Goodspeed,"* and though the date of this fatal encounter was not recorded, it seems fair to speculate that it took place sometime in mid-April 1869. If so, it took only six

---

*This was, in all likelihood, Thomas Wakefield Goodspeed (b. 1842) who was at that time pastor of the Vermont Street Baptist Church in Quincy, Illinois, but who moved in 1877 to Chicago to become pastor of the Morgan Street Baptist Church (1877–1880); he served as Secretary of the Baptist Theological Union Seminary from 1876 until 1889, and was prominent in the founding of the University of Chicago, raising an estimated $1,000,000 for the new university between 1889 and 1890.

weeks for the damaging news to circulate up the diocesan grape-
vines, for on May 31, 1869, Cheney was interrupted in his study by
a messenger bearing the calling card of the Rt. Rev. Henry John
Whitehouse, Bishop of Illinois.

Henry John Whitehouse was the second Bishop of Illinois, the
successor of the florid and Evangelical pioneer bishop Philander
Chase. Amazingly, Whitehouse too was a product of St. Luke's,
Rochester, having served as rector there in the 1830s. Even more
amazing was that he had been heavily involved in those years with a
number of Evangelical societies and mission agencies, including the
promotion of the revival campaigns of Charles Grandison Finney in
Rochester.[86] But by the time he was elected Bishop of Illinois in
1851, he had begun to move in directions that were significantly
different from those of either Chase or Finney. For one thing,
Whitehouse had developed his own notions of what constituted appropriate episcopal dignity and refused to take up residence in the
Diocese of Illinois for nine years after his election until the diocese
agreed to meet his demands for an annual salary of $2,500, a new
cathedral in Chicago, and an episcopal residence. He was, as James
DeWitt Clinton Locke observed (and Clinton Locke, who arrived in
Illinois only four years before Cheney, was not unsympathetic to
Whitehouse), a "thorough aristocrat by birth and training and accustomed to every luxury." In fact Whitehouse was independently
wealthy and in no personal need of the stipend that had been promised. Unfortunately, Whitehouse, in addition to being an aristocrat,
was (as Clinton Locke also observed) "one of the poorest judges of
human nature I ever met" and seemed "to lack completely the
power of seeing the effect certain positions taken would have on the
public, how men would estimate them, what would be the public
judgement of them, whether a wise and eminently proper expediency did not counsel another course."[87] The result was that Whitehouse mismanaged the land and money that were obtained for the
Cathedral; and when the laypeople of the diocese began to question
Whitehouse, his irritable dismissals of their questions only height-
ened suspicions that Whitehouse was either an arrogant fool or a
thief, or some combination of both.[88]

The ensuing diocesan convention of 1860 was not a pretty event
to behold. Whitehouse was charged with dereliction of his episcopal
duties, and one lay delegate attacked him for "his peculiar turn of
mind—the tendency to close framing of bargains and contracts—the
mind at all times leaning towards the accumulation of money. . . to
shrewd management—to financial scheming, to skill in baffling, to
concentrating in himself power and control, to exercising judgement

in every thing, save in that one glorious line, which seems to engage the heart and soul of every other Bishop of the Church, namely, the winning of souls to Christ."[89] Whitehouse responded by accusing the diocese and the Standing Committee of miserliness and lack of cooperation in managing the mission work of the diocese, and by ruling out of order any effort from the floor of the convention to call for an investigation of episcopal finances. In protest, nine of Whitehouse's clergy circulated a document, refuting Whitehouse's charges and ominously suggesting that "if the Bishop's statements are erroneous in these relations, may they not be in other particulars?"[90] One of signatories of the circular was Charles Edward Cheney.[91]

Whitehouse's handling of diocesan money was not improved by his responses to the Civil War in Illinois, for Whitehouse was an old-line Democrat, and he made little secret during the war of his Copperhead sympathies. These sympathies became a matter of public notice in the abrasive case of John Wesley Cracraft, an Evangelical Episcopal priest who was canonically resident in the Diocese of Ohio but who had moved to Galesburg, Illinois, in 1864. Grace Church, Galesburg, was then without a rector, and the congregation happily turned to Cracraft as a likely candidate and invited him to preach and read services. On October 1, 1864, however, Whitehouse forbade Cracraft from officiating at Grace Church, ostensibly on the grounds that Cracraft had neither obtained not presented appropriate letters dimissory from Charles Pettit McIlvaine, Bishop of Ohio. But both Cracraft and McIlvaine accused Whitehouse of prejudice against Cracraft's Evangelicalism and Cracraft's sermons on "the questions involved in the then existing war" and "the duty of sustaining the Government." In the end, Cracraft was forced to back down, but not before Whitehouse had been loudly denounced as a Copperhead. And this, once again, would have boded no good for Charles Edward Cheney, since Cheney and the Illinois Evangelicals went solidly for the Union, even to the point (in the case of John Wesley Cracraft) of defying Whitehouse's attempt to stifle "political sermons" on emancipation and the war effort.[92] The war, and Whitehouse's lack of enthusiasm for it, only created another ground of provocation for Cheney, who liked to remind people that he once had a Springfield lawyer named Lincoln in his congregation as a curious visitor.[93]

Whitehouse was at his most provocative, however, as he began to shift closer and closer into the Anglo-Catholic orbit. He shocked the diocese's convention in 1868 by asserting that "in the *Regeneration by Holy Baptism*, in the spiritual and *ineffable* presence of our Lord in the Eucharist, with the *Mystical Nutriment* through His Body and Blood, as well as in the definition of the Sacraments, generally there is VIRTUAL CONCURRENCE in the accepted standards of the historical Churches, Eastern, Western [i.e., Roman], and Anglican."[94] No sentiments like those would sit easily with a convention still populated with Philander Chase's old fellows, and on February 18, 1869, six of Whitehouse's clergy and seventeen of his laypeople issued a dramatic declaration, attacking Whitehouse's convention address as a device for "*unprotestantizing* this Protestant Episcopal Church, corrupting her doctrine, debasing her worship, and over-turning her long-established rites, ceremonies, and usages," and calling for the assembly of an Evangelical Convention in June in Chicago to determine further policy.[95] Among the six clergy signers was Charles Edward Cheney.

On all these scores, Cheney and Whitehouse had found more than enough disagreements to make them irreconcilable opponents. Cheney was the product of the middling American classes who voted for the Whigs and then the Republicans, and who believed sublimely in the "harmony of interests" of labor and capital; and his Evangelical convictions ran straight in the line of Whig public moralism. Whitehouse stood, both in style and in substance, with the old elites whom Lee Benson, Joel Silbey, and Edward Pessen have found in the backbone of the Democratic party, and his increasing affection for Anglo-Catholicism (which in the Episcopal Church had a solid attraction for Democratic elites) only reinforced his suspicion of the nettlesome Evangelicalism of Charles Edward Cheney.[96] Thus, in the spring of 1869, when Whitehouse learned of Cheney's unilateral deletions from the baptismal office, it was suddenly clear that Cheney had unwittingly presented Whitehouse with an opportunity to even up a few theological and personal scores with a troublesome and annoying priest.

Whitehouse's interview with Cheney on that fateful last day of May 1869 was brief and undramatic. Whitehouse (as Cheney remembered it) "told me that from the lips of this Baptist minister he had heard that which he could not believe, namely that I had made this omission in the Baptismal service."[97] Cheney frankly told Whitehouse that not only was what he had heard the truth but, moreover, that Cheney could in conscience never use the full baptismal office again.

> I cannot . . . nor do I wish to deny that I do not use the baptismal office for infants as it is. What you have heard is a fact, and it is true that I do omit the clause which declares the

child to be "regenerate," from the service. I cannot conscientiously say so for myself or my congregation.[98]

Whitehouse then drew himself up and announced that, in the face of Cheney's refusal, he intended to have Cheney tried and deposed from the ministry. "But Bishop," Cheney replied, "how can you tell beforehand that I will be found guilty or that I will be deposed from the ministry?" "Because," answered Whitehouse, "I shall not allow any man to be on the court who has signed his name to a certain document [i.e., the February protest]."[99] Shaken by Whitehouse's threat, Cheney begged for a week to review the matter, and Whitehouse, solemnly placing the episcopal hat upon the episcopal head, granted his request and drove off in his carriage. Whitehouse received his final communication from Cheney on June 8:

> Right Rev. and Dear Sir — I regret that circumstances compelled me to delay for a few hours the answer which I promised to send you in one week from our conversation on Monday, the 21st ult. After the most serious and prayerful deliberation, I can only say that I have been able to arrive at no other conclusion than that already expressed to you.
>
> Very truly yours,
> *Charles Edward Cheney*[100]

A confrontation was now unavoidable. On June 12, 1869, Whitehouse appointed a committee of three to investigate the matter and recommend the proper proceedings. Predictably, the committee found that the evidence warranted a presentment, and on June 21 a citation was issued to Cheney to await trial.

The Cheney trial proved to be another cause célèbre on the order of the Tyng trial of the year before, but magnified several times greater. William Sparrow, Cheney's old teacher at Alexandria, anxiously awaiting the trial, wrote with remarkable prescience to one his former students:

> If he is acquitted, it will help deliver us from that rubrical marinetism which has of late been in a course of imposition on our Church while latitudinarianism is allowed in the infinitely more important matter of doctrine. If he is condemned, it will lead to the establishment of independent Episcopal Churches, till at length they get a Bishop at their head, and so we shall have another Episcopal Church in these United States![101]

Arrayed before Cheney were Whitehouse as judge and five hand-picked clergyman as assessors, Samuel Chase (as president of the diocesan court), T. W. Benedict, John Benson, Henry Niles Pierce, and A. W. Snyder, all of whom could be counted on to stand behind their bishop. Cheney had been given a list of eight from which to choose but had refused to choose any, on the grounds that all of them were equally hostile. On his side of the bench, Cheney had behind him the full resources and support of Christ Church and the legal talents of a team of lawyers headed by Melville Weston Fuller, a prominent Illinois Democrat (destined to become the most reactionary Chief Justice of the U.S. Supreme Court since Roger Taney). Cheney had originally hoped to make his defense on the very words of the baptismal office itself and wanted to bring in Richard Newton and Stephen Tyng as witnesses that other clergy in other dioceses were making the same omissions as Cheney, without episcopal inhibition. But Fuller pointed out that Whitehouse was bringing his charges against Cheney not on the basis of the truth or untruth of the service, or the practice of other clergymen in other dioceses, but strictly on the canonical question of whether Cheney was rendering due obedience to his diocesan bishop by refusing to use the prayer book as stated.[102] The only way to confront Whitehouse's determination to hang Cheney on technicalities was to find technicalities in Cheney's favor with which to hang Whitehouse.

Fuller proved a smarter lawyer than Whitehouse. The trial opened on July 21, 1869, in the Chapel of Whitehouse's hard-won Cathedral of Sts. Peter and Paul, with two hundred spectators crowded into the airless room. Two specifications were lodged against Cheney: one, that he had made unlawful alterations in the prayer book in his services, and two, that these alterations consisted chiefly in the intentional omission of any affirmation of "regeneration" in the baptismal office. Cheney could deny little in the specifications, so Fuller at once swept into action with a series of time-killing exceptions: that the assessors had no jurisdiction, that Cheney was denied the right of challenge, that the court was prejudiced in its membership, that it was in the pocket of the bishop, that Cheney was being denied employment and the pursuit of the only vocation he had ever followed, and so forth. "Everything," reported one newspaper, "relating to the origination of the trial, in regard to the irregularity of the Court, and of the acts of the Bishop and his advisers was searched, and exposed." And, to Fuller's amazement, everything was overruled on every point without any effort at explanation.[103] "Can the Court assign us any reasons for this decision?" asked a baffled member of Fuller's legal team when yet another objection was handily dismissed. "Lawyers ought not to ask an ecclesiastical court to assign reasons for a decision," came the airy reply of the court proctor.[104]

Giving Cheney's secular lawyers such a comeuppance may have provided Whitehouse with a momentary thrill, but it was a red flag to Fuller. The next day, Fuller came back to ask for a postponement of thirty days, and when this was preemptorily refused by the diocesan court, Fuller whipped out a surprise of his own:

> Mr. President, the assessors have overruled our objections as they have been severally presented. They have persistently, and without cause, declined to recognize the plain letter of their own law. This has been the invariable course pursued by the board of which you are the presiding officer, until we think we have reached a point at which we shall go no farther. I have applied to the Superior Court of Chicago for an injunction, which has been granted, against further proceedings.[105]

As the chapel resounded with applause (the spectators had made no secret of their sympathy for Cheney as the underdog), Fuller called in the sheriff of Cook County to deliver the injunction, and the confused court adjourned itself to figure out what to do next.[106] When the court collected its wits and reassembled on July 23, it had little choice but to concede the injunction and suspend proceedings.[107]

This put Whitehouse on dangerous ground. Reconstruction of the defeated Confederacy was still in full swing in 1869, and a Republican Congress was giving serious consideration to major new civil rights legislation that would extend federal civil rights jurisidiction even into church affairs. Much as it rankled his Catholicism and his self-image to have a secular court interfere in Cheney's prosecution, Whitehouse had even more to lose if Cheney's case should provide an alarming precedent for civil action in religious cases. Whitehouse cautiously appealed the injunction, but it was not until early in 1871 that the injunction was finally dissolved by the State Supreme Court and the diocesan court was left free to proceed where it had left off two years earlier. And they would have eagerly made quick work of their job, but the original court could no longer be assembled. In the interim, Henry Niles Pierce had been elected and consecrated Bishop of Arkansas, which made him canonically ineligible to serve on an Illinois diocesan court. Because this immediately rendered the original court one less its specified number, Cheney and Fuller were quick to seize on this as a serious legal obstacle to any further proceedings.[108] Whitehouse, fuming and impatient at another obstruction, ordered what remained of the original court to move ahead anyway, and on February 7, 1871, Cheney was found in violation of the original specifications and "suspended" from the ministry.[109]

When Cheney, on Fuller's advice, ignored the findings as null and void, Whitehouse charged Cheney with "contumacy." A second court was assembled in March to pass judgment on this new charge; he was found guilty, and on June 2, 1871, Whitehouse duly pronounced Cheney deposed from the priesthood.[110] When Whitehouse arrived at Christ Church for his next episcopal visit on September 10, he was greeted in the vestry room by the churchwardens and Cheney, in surplice and tippet, and when Cheney greeted Whitehouse, the bishop only replied, "I cannot recognize you in those robes." After "a short discussion," Whitehouse drove off, never to darken the door of Christ Church again.[111] Cheney was now, in every ecclesiastical sense of the word, alone.

Amid these grim clouds, it was still possible to discover a few silver linings. Christ Church loyally rallied behind Cheney and refused to hear any suggestion that he resign as rector to unburden them. Because the property of Christ Church was technically registered in the name of one of the members of the vestry, the congregation handily rejected every demand from Whitehouse that they dismiss Cheney and successfully resisted a suit brought by Whitehouse in 1872 to seize the church buildings and rectory.[112] Cheney was less happy, however, with the response of his fellow Evangelical clergy. A few rallied loyally to his side. Two days after Cheney's deposition, Stephen Tyng Jr. boldly appeared to preach for Cheney at Christ Church and to administer communion beside him to crowds that filled "every inch of space in the Church . . . even thronging the chancel and blocking up the street."[113] And in May 1871, as his deposition loomed, he received a circular of support from sixty-three of his Evangelical colleagues (including Tyng, John Cotton Smith, William Tufnell Sabine, and Benjamin Leacock) that supported his "right to such decision and action as that for which you have been punished by an ecclesiastical sentence [i.e., the omission of "regenerate"], as a right which many others of the clergy of the Protestant Episcopal Church, experiencing similar difficulties, have habitually exercised."[114]

But hardly any of the Evangelical priests were willing to do more than mail out circulars. The Evangelical Convention that was to meet in June 1869 convened under the cloud of Cheney's first citation, and at some points it threatened to develop into a referendum on Cheney's actions. For two days 200 lay and clerical delegates debated and struggled to achieve consensus, only to come away with no better result for their efforts than another dreary set of resolutions, reaffirming their opposition to "unsound and unprotestant" teachings in the church and calling yet once again for the removal of "all words and phrases seeming to teach that the Christian ministry is a priesthood, or the Lord's Supper a Sacrifice, or that Regeneration is inseparable from Baptism" from the prayer book.[115] Of Bishop Whitehouse, whose remarks to his diocesan convention had triggered this meeting in the first place, nary a word was said. That stunning display of impotence, together with the weight of the proceedings against him and the disgrace of a deposition hanging over his head, nearly pressed Cheney to the breaking point. "In one word, the whole Evangelical party deserted me," Cheney recalled bitterly.[116]

More telling still was the deafening silence Cheney met from the Evangelical bishops. In May 1871, three weeks before his deposition by Whitehouse, Cheney was quietly visited by Henry Washington Lee of Iowa, together with Henry Benjamin Whipple, Bishop of Minnesota. Lee pleaded with Cheney not to allow himself to be thrust out of the church and urged the Gorham judgment on him as proof that the words of the baptismal office need not force an Anglo-Catholic conclusion. But Cheney pleaded in return that his decision had been motivated by conscience, not notoriety, and that he had been malevolently singled out by Whitehouse for "the first trial in the history of the Church for any omission of parts of the service, while it was well known that such offenses had been common." Whipple was deeply moved by Cheney's sincerity—"we were all in tears during most of the interview"—and even attempted to intercede with Whitehouse on Cheney's behalf. But Whitehouse brushed Whipple's offer of negotiation away; and Lee, who had far closer connections to Cheney than Whipple, did nothing further to help him.[117] For the next two years, Cheney would be an outcast, a man privately sympathized-with but publicly shunned as a controversial character with whom it was not wise to be seen. There was, in the end, only one bishop out of the entire House of Bishops willing to offer Cheney what little comfort could be offered a man compelled to carry the brand of a defrocked clergyman in his hand. That one bishop was George David Cummins, Assistant Bishop of Kentucky.

III

THE EDUCATION
OF GEORGE DAVID CUMMINS

The Impetuous Preacher

On the morning of November 15, 1866, the sun rose grudgingly
over Louisville behind a curtain of gray November clouds, giving a plain, severe cast to the Kentucky countryside and the flat,
monotonous farmland across the Ohio River in Indiana. But below the spire of Louisville's forty-four-year-old Christ Church, a
very different morning began. Lined up outside was a colorful
procession of clergy and bishops, while within the diminutive
church a choir of fifty voices ungracefully but heroically boomed
out Mozart. The new assistant bishop of the Episcopal Diocese
of Kentucky was to be consecrated this day, the first bishop so

consecrated in Kentucky since the first and original Kentucky bishop, Benjamin Bosworth Smith, had been consecrated within the same walls more than thirty years before.

As the organ shuddered into life, twenty-three Kentucky clergy led the procession into the church, followed by representatives from seven other dioceses, and no less than seven bishops, the cream of the episcopal crop—John Henry Hopkins of Vermont, the Presiding Bishop and the doyen of the High Churchmen; representing the neighboring dioceses were Kerfoot of Pittsburgh, Quintard of Tennessee, and Talbot of Indiana; and then there were the Evangelical bishops, Benjamin Bosworth Smith himself and Henry Washington Lee of Iowa, plus the presenter of the new bishop, Robert Harper Clarkson of Nebraska (who himself had been consecrated as Nebraska's first bishop exactly one year before, to the day). The Communion office and the Ordinal were the services appointed, and the sermon fell to Lee of Iowa.

The new bishop-elect sat facing the chancel, an erect, big-shouldered man of forty-four with a strong, jutting chin and a balding, intellectual forehead. His remarkably clear, grayish eyes and his face, which looked as though it had been formed for the purpose of smiling, were circled by a mane of reddish-brown hair that descended in two great sidewhiskers to his jaw. "He is quite a young man; tall, thin, and with dark auburn hair that falls over his shoulders," reported the *Christian Advocate*. "He has marked pulpit ability."[1] At length, as the sermon ended and the climax of the consecration service approached, the nervous bishop-elect rose from the congregation to be presented, to have his testimonials read, and to be vested in his new rochet and chimere. The seven bishops in the chancel advanced to lay their consecrating hands on him, and while he knelt there for a moment "in private devotion before the altar," the clouds outside momentarily broke, and a broad shaft of sunlight through the church windows transfixed the new bishop in a golden tableau.[2]

Under such auspicious circumstances was George David Cummins consecrated Assistant Bishop of Kentucky and the eighty-first bishop in the American Episcopal succession. Little did anyone imagine, least of all Cummins, that in seven years he would become the leader of the greatest ecclesiastical disruption in the history of the Protestant Episcopal Church.

The figure of George David Cummins must necessarily play an oversized role in this history, for it was Cummins who not only founded and organized the Reformed Episcopal Church, but also brought to it the invaluable legitimacy of his episcopal rank and status. But for many Reformed Episcopalians, Cummins has been little more than a figurehead, revered in a rather remote fashion but largely unquoted and unknown. Part of that must certainly be due to his early death in 1876, which robbed him of the opportunity to impress his own personal influence more deeply on the infant Reformed Episcopal Church. But some measure of this anonymity also must be attributed to the fact that it was Cummins as a *bishop* who was important to many of the first Reformed Episcopalians, and not Cummins himself. While he lived, he was hailed as "our Luther." But in the generation after his death, his sermons and writings dropped out of sight and out of print, and Cummins became merely a name to be invoked from time to time as proof that the Reformed Episcopalians had really been called into being by a fully articled Episcopal bishop. To this day, he is more of a mystery than a man to his Reformed Episcopal heirs.

But there is little mystery about Cummins's life and his career in the Episcopal Church before his consecration in 1866. Born on December 11, 1822, to an old Delaware family, Cummins had Episcopalianism in his blood from his father's side. His mother, however, was partial to the Methodists; her grandfather had been "Church of England of the straightest sort" but had opened the family's parlors, and then their barns, for Francis Asbury to preach in, and her father, John Durborow, became one of the earliest Methodist itinerants on the Eastern Shore.[3] When George David Cummins's Episcopalian father died during the boy's fourth year, his mother married a Baltimore Methodist preacher, Joseph Farrow. At age fourteen, he was packed off to Dickinson College in Carlisle, Pennsylvania, to listen attentively to Methodist professors and graduate, in 1841, as the class valedictorian. His original plans had been to practice law, but in April 1839 an evangelical revival swept through the students at Dickinson, and "it was at this time he gave his heart to God, and joined the Methodist Episcopal Church, entering on a life of earnest love and faithful labor for Christ."[4]

Cummins discovered something else at college, and that was heart disease. During his senior year, his health collapsed, and the Philadelphia doctor he consulted diagnosed an enlarged heart. That, on its own terms, might have been enough to put an end to the enthusiasm of anyone for the itinerant labors of the Methodist ministry, but he took a nine-month leave of absence from Dickinson, returning in December 1840 to finish his studies and then go on to take his M.A. from Dickinson in 1844. Meanwhile, on March 2, 1843, he was received into the "itinerant communion" of the Methodist Episcopal Church, under license from the Baltimore Conference of the

Methodist Episcopal Church.[5] In 1843, he began riding the Bladens-
burg (Maryland) circuit under presiding elder Noriate Wilson,
preaching by day from tree stumps and fence rails and sleeping by
night in the rain and heat, throughout eastern Maryland and northern Virginia. The next year, he was transferred to Jefferson's Circuit, in Jefferson County, Virginia (now West Virginia) and worked
the entire county with only the assistance of senior pastor John A.
Gere.[6] It might easily have killed him, but remarkably the exertion
seems to have strengthened him, and even though "many hours of
the day were passed in severe pain," Cummins emerged from his
two-year stint on the circuit with energy and stamina that would
carry him through the next thirty-four years.[7]

Cummins might well have been content to stay with the Methodist Episcopal Church. Outstripping every other American church in
growth, and tightly organized and disciplined, American Methodism was open to anyone with ambition and merit, and the twenty-
two-year-old Cummins had both in considerable quantities. But in
1844, the unity and discipline of the Methodists was shattered by a
disastrous debate within its General Conference over slavery. Anti-
slavery sentiment had long been part of the warp and woof of Methodism (John Wesley had opposed the American Revolution precisely
on the grounds that it was hypocritical for Americans to cry for
liberty from England while they were buying slaves from Africa).
But it reached its peak in May 1844, when Northern Methodists
forced the resignation of a Southern slaveholder from the office of
bishop in the church. Taking this as a calculated insult, southern
Methodists marched out of the General Conference to organize the
Methodist Episcopal Church, South.[8] With them went most of the
Methodist clergy of the slaveholding states, which at this point included both Maryland and Delaware.

As the son of a slaveholder, and both a native of Delaware and
now a resident of Maryland, it might have been expected that Cummins would join the Southern Methodists. And indeed, Cummins
never betrayed any particular opposition to slavery. To the contrary, he insisted, "Every allusion to it by the inspired apostle recognizes it as a part of the social system established by law, and enjoins
fidelity in the discharge of the duties arising out of it, and no where,
in a single instance, is it declared to be of itself sinful." As Cummins
read the Bible, it "never, directly or indirectly, by precept or practice, taught that slaveholding was a sin against God and a crime
against man." Cummins tempered that somewhat by insisting that
the African-American slave was "of one blood with ourselves, a
sharer in a common humanity, a partaker of our hopes and fears,"

but this only meant for Cummins that the proper attitude of the Christian slaveholder was paternalism, not emancipation. "The Anglo-American" is "the tutelar guardian of the African," Cummins wrote, and it is the white man's responsibility "to regard the African race in bondage (and in freedom, too) as a solemn trust committed to this people from God, and that He has given us the great mission of working out His purposes of mercy and love towards them." If there was a future for African-Americans beyond slavery, it would be found not in America but in recolonizing Africa with free blacks as missionaries. "It is a sublime trust, a stupendous work, worthy of the genius of this Christian nation," Cummins said, "to train, to discipline a race," but the real purpose of this training was "to prepare them to work out the destiny of a continent of one hundred and fifty millions of the same race."[9]

But even if Cummins had no objection to being carried off with the proslavery Methodists of the Southern Methodist Church, the instability the schism symbolized may have unsettled him in ways that the precise cause of the schism had not. Cummins, with a college degree, was something of an anomaly among the Methodist itinerants, who counted less than 50 among more than 4,000 itinerant preachers with more than what Peter Cartwright called "a common English education." Whether it was fear of future disruption or a yearning for greater status, Cummins gave neither warning nor explanation, then or later, of his next move, which was simply to abandon the Methodists. He had been on the eve of his first year's examination for study on the circuit, but as the Methodist bishop and missionary William Taylor recalled, "When our class appeared before the examining committee, Mr. Cummings [sic], No. 2 in the class, failed to put in an appearance, but sent a notification of his withdrawal from the Methodist Episcopal Church."[10] That winter, Cummins's mind began to gravitate back to the church of his fathers, and in March 1845 he returned to Delaware to present himself to Alfred Lee, the Evangelical Bishop of Delaware, as a candidate for orders in the Protestant Episcopal Church.

Cummins stayed under Alfred Lee's tutelage in Wilmington, Delaware, for six months. On April 20, 1845, Cummins was confirmed by Bishop Lee at St. Andrew's Church, Wilmington, and was ordained there as a deacon on October 26. His enthusiasm for his readopted church grew. "The bishop and his family are my kind friends," Cummins eagerly wrote to his sister. "I am becoming more and more attracted to the Protestant Episcopal Church, and love its Liturgy." He toyed with the idea of volunteering as a missionary to China. But Bishop Lee had other plans, and Cummins was sent instead to Christ Church, Baltimore, as a parish assistant to the powerful Evangelical preacher Henry Van Dyke Johns, whom Cummins would afterward refer to only as "dear Dr. Johns."[11] The brother of Virginia bishop John Johns, Henry Van Dyke Johns had been designated to fill Christ Church, Baltimore, when his brother resigned the parish to become Bishop of Virginia. In so doing, he had already run afoul of Maryland's High Church bishop, William Rollinson Whittingham. On November 6, 1842, as Whittingham installed Johns at Christ Church as his brother's successor, Whittingham proceeded to preach a sermon that offhandedly dropped several explosive assertions concerning the apostolicity of bishops and the priesthood of his clergy. Henry Johns immediately construed Whittingham's sermon as a slur on his brother's opinions and on his own preaching, and that same evening he took the pulpit of Christ Church to deliver a resounding slap at Whittingham's sermon.[12] Under Johns's direction, bishops like Whittingham gradually became poison to Cummins's mind. But with Johns's blessing resting on him, he scarcely needed to fear them, and Cummins quickly made his mark around the parishes of Baltimore and the Chesapeake Bay. On June 17, 1847, the congregation of Christ Church, Norfolk (Virginia), voted to extend him their call to be rector. One week later, the new rector-elect married Alexandrine Macomb Balch, the daughter of a western Virginia justice of the peace. Then, on July 6, Cummins was ordained priest by a delighted Bishop Lee, with Cummins's new brother-in-law, the Rev. L.P.W. Balch (of St. Bartholomew's Church in New York City) preaching the sermon from Psalm 19. The next day, Cummins was in Norfolk.

There is no easy way to make a transition from circuit-riding preacher to rector of a parish, and yet Cummins seems to have moved from prophet to parson without any noticeable commotion. If the tendency of the Methodists was to take the world as their parish, then the temptation of the Anglican Evangelicals was to take their parishes as the world. Like them, Cummins threw himself into parish work with a self-denying seriousness, full of an unrelenting labor and activity among the members of his new parish.[13] Cummins himself struggled to describe that spirit of seriousness in a sermon in 1848, when he said:

> It is the spirit that drives far from it all bitterness & wrath & clamor & evil speaking & malice—& that is kind & tender-hearted, forgiving others even as Christ hath forgiven it. It meets evil with good, cursing with blessing, railing with prayer. It is that disposition without which, though we have

all knowledge & all faith & speak with angel's tongues & give all our goods to feed the poor & our bodies to be burned—we are worse than nothing in the eyes of the Lord.[14]

And more than describing it, Cummins worked to internalize that ideal of Evangelical self-sacrifice. In the summer of 1849, when cholera ravaged Norfolk, Cummins stayed "at his post of duty through all those terrible months, visiting night and day, and ministering not only to his own people but to many poor colored persons, who suffered most from the dread pestilence."[15] It was this in Cummins that made Charles Edward Cheney remember Cummins's "sweet and beautiful spirit of sunshine" and that made Benjamin Leacock describe him as "one of the loveliest Christian men I ever knew," with "the nature of a gentle, refined woman."[16]

If in his parish Cummins was the model of the Evangelical parson, then in the pulpit he was still very much the Evangelical prophet. "The pulpit was his throne," Cheney recalled, "There he was a king of men. . . . His was the nearest approach that I ever knew to that high ideal of eloquence in which the power of speech becomes only a mirror to reflect the deepest workings of a noble heart."[17] Thomas Dudley recollected how "crowds ever thronged the place where he had been announced to preach and were held spellbound by the thrilling tones, the graceful diction and the vivid word-painting of the orator."[18] Leacock also remembered Cummins as a "prince" in the pulpit. "He had no superior, if an equal in the P.E.C. His expositions of divine truth were simple and clear, and his earnest impassioned utterance was to me irresistible." Leacock put his finger especially on Cummins's "impetuousness" as the quality that "helped largely in crowning him with success."[19] And yet, for all the "impetuousness" Leacock saw in Cummins, his surviving sermons and manuscripts reveal a surprisingly disciplined mind behind the passion, for his sermons were invariably written out, word-for-word, in an elegant longhand, with hardly any erasures or additions. Cummins's thoughts flowed naturally onto paper, and his sermons moved rapidly from point to point with a fastidious economy of words and a constant direct appeal for a passion in his hearers to match his own.

And he had his hearers, and not in Norfolk only. In June 1853, the prestigious parish of St. James's, Richmond (Virginia), unanimously called him as rector, and partly to ease his wife's ill health in the humid lowlands of Norfolk he accepted. There "his congregation increased until there were no longer seats for more; and extra benches and chairs were provided to be placed in the aisles every

Sunday."[20] Then, in little more than a year, the vestry of Trinity Church, Washington, D.C. (where Henry Clay had attended before his death in 1852 and where Salmon Chase would later come to hear a "good, plain sermon"), extended yet another unanimous call. Because Washington then fell within the diocesan boundaries of the Diocese of Maryland, this amounted to an invitation to run Bishop Whittingham's gauntlet once again. Unabashed, Cummins accepted, and not without the expectation that he would exercise some of the same restraint on Whittingham's High Churchmanship that his mentor, Henry Johns, had tried to exercise. "Although St. James was full, & he extremely popular & apparently useful," wrote the Rev. Robert Croes to Bishop Whittingham. "He thought he could do more good in Bp. Whittingham's Diocese by setting himself against Puseyism & Romanism!"[21] Once again, his congregation prospered, as Trinity Church added to its numbers everything from senators to theological students from the seminary across the Potomac in Alexandria. "He gives all glory to the grace of God for the good done," wrote one of Cummins's admirers at Trinity Church in 1855:

> He has introduced four collections annually for missions; has a missionary meeting once a month when reports and letters are read from missionaries; he has two lectures a week, and a Sunday-school teachers' meeting once a month. There are four schools attached to the church, and over six hundred scholars; Bible-classes for gentlemen and ladies, the questions for which he prepares himself. Besides this, he has two sermons each Sunday, and the Wednesday evening lectures are prepared with as great care as a sermon. They are delivered in courses, and are most interesting.[22]

He managed to avoid any ugly confrontations with Whittingham, and the two maintained a polite but somewhat aloof correspondence. After all, not even Whittingham could argue with a rector whose congregation had discovered so "much religious interest" that he had to importune the bishop for repeated visits for confirmations.[23] Even with the halls of Congress and the boarding rooms of Georgetown ringing with the ugly threats of secession and civil war in the 1850s, Cummins was never at a loss for hearers, and one senator advised Alexandrine Cummins, "Mr. Cummins ought never to leave Washington. No other man can take his place. His power as a preacher surpasses that of any man I know, and his influence is felt throughout the country."[24]

Now the demands for Cummins's services began to come in thick and fast: to address the students at Alexandria in April 1854; to address the anniversary meeting of the Evangelical Knowledge Society in May 1854; to address the annual meeting of the Evangelical Knowledge Society in May 1855; to lecture on "Christian Evidences" at the Washington Young Men's Christian Association in the spring of 1856; and to receive an honorary doctor of divinity degree from Princeton College in May 1857. And then there were the pleas of vestries and bishops. In November 1856, Cummins received the unanimous call of St. Thomas's Church, New York City, a position that would have put Cummins as close as a clergyman could get to the top of the Social Register. And in 1862, William Ingraham Kip, the new Bishop of California, invited Cummins to come west to San Francisco as the dean of Kip's new cathedral. Cummins resisted both of these calls. Instead, in 1858, he yielded to the petition of St. Peter's Church, Baltimore, to return to his first neighborhood and serve as rector. "Here he drew crowds, and gave the old parish a prosperity it had not known for half a century," reported the *Christian Advocate*.[25]

Finally, in 1863, Cummins made his last parish change, moving to Chicago to become rector of his largest congregation yet, Trinity Church. He had been the rector of Trinity Church for only eight days when he met, for the first time, Charles Edward Cheney.

The Cross of Jesus Is the Fulcrum

Cummins and Cheney were unalike in many ways, not the least of which was the simple matter of temperament. Cummins was relaxed, easy, stirred quickly by emotion, a man who moved easily among men; Cheney was short, stiff, and formal, lavishing all his interest and care on his one and only parish, Christ Church. But the traits they shared, which were not spotted nearly so easily by the casual eye, went deeper than any apparent dissimilarities, and Cummins's letters from Chicago quickly began to fill up with references to the side-whiskered rector of Christ Church. "At 7.30 pm we had service, and Mr. Cheney read for me," Cummins recorded during his second week at Trinity Church. And so it went on from there: "Rev. Mr. Cheney read again for me last night," "This morning I breakfasted with Dr. Bishop, Mr. Cheney, and Dr. S[chenck]."[26] Cheney, in turn, was slightly awed by Cummins's power and grace in the pulpit. In less than a year as rector of Trinity Church, Cummins was able to float off a debt of $17,500 that had plagued the parish from its organization and that allowed the church finally to be consecrated (a service Cheney attended).[27] Cummins "had been side by side with me in the city of Chicago, as the rector in a great, powerful church," Cheney wrote half a century later. "It used to be said that every Sunday night, if one wanted to find the way to Trinity Church, he had only to follow the crowd. The magnetic eloquence characteristic of that great man drew other men like a magnet."[28]

Both Cummins and Cheney shared in equal measure the Evangelical commitment to vital religion. First place in Cummins's preaching at Trinity Church went (as it did for Cheney at Christ Church) to the preaching of conversion. Cheney recalled:

> Fidelity to one theme—Christ the sinner's Savior—was more than a duty, more than a privilege; it was a passion. He loved his work with a kind of chivalrous devotion. He inscribed the name of Christ on every public act of his ministry. . . . He preached Christ because his own soul could feed on no other manna. He had found for himself the bread of life; he could not feed other starving souls with husks.[29]

Over and over in Cummins's preaching there appears the demand for change of heart, the dread of judgment for sin, the ever-present consciousness of sinfulness and the need for redemption. The sinner, declared Cummins in 1865, "is to be saved by trust in the Good Shepherd, by simple reliance on the infinite sacrifice of Jesus—by committing his soul to Him who loved him and gave himself for him."[30] This commitment, simple as it was in principle, was no "mere cold act of the intellect" or the "simple assent of the mind to certain propositions." It was simple only in its one object and one overwhelming result, "the whole being surrendered to another, the soul of the sinner committed to the Savior to be possessed, dwelt in, moulded and transformed by Him."[31] Cummins described the cathartic power of humiliation and submission in a sermon in Baltimore in 1861 that comes as near as anything else to a testimony of his own experience of conversion:

> There comes a time in the mercy of God to many . . . when the soul awakens to a sense of its danger, or to speak more correctly, is awakened by the spirit of God. The slumber of spiritual death is broken. The heart is convinced of its guilt. The conscience is filled with keenest self-inflicted suffering.

The soul is alive to its danger. On every side it beholds tokens of wrath. The muttering thunder of Sinai appals it & its
vivid lightning flashes before & around it. The tempest rolls
& thickens over the head. . . . Just then the Cross is revealed,
& on it the bleeding victim . . . & there is a great calm—
peace to the troubled heart, peace to the wounded conscience.[32]

For Cummins, the preaching of Evangelical religion was the only
preaching worthy of the name. "Let me tell you what it is to live
before God," he told Trinity Church in 1864. "It is to recognize
God as the only true foundation of the soul's life & without Him all
is desolation & death . . . to feel the dawning within the soul of a
new life—a life not of nature, but of grace, a life begotten of the
Spirit of the Lord."[33] He was, accordingly, skeptical of social reform, or at least of social reform that paid insufficient attention to
reforming the individual by grace beforehand. If he was an optimist
about the human condition at any point, it was only a spiritual optimism with a faint whiff of postmillennialism. *How will Christ's kingdom come?* he asked:

Not by political reforms! Oh how long before men learn that
these leave untouched the source of all evil—the hearts of
men. Not by the triumphs of civilization alone. . . . But one
power alone is enough to effect that—it is the Gospel of
Christ, the power of God unto salvation to every one that
believeth! It is the truth as it is in Jesus—it is the doctrine of
the Cross—it is redemption through the blood of Jesus. Oh!
here is the mighty lever for the recovery of a world back to
God. Archimedes asked but a fulcrum for his machine & he
would move the world. But the Cross of Jesus is the fulcrum, mighty enough to lift the world out of its ruin & Misery into the light and smile of God.[34]

Cummins was not a theologian. He had no formal theological
education apart from what he might have derived from the Dickinson College curriculum, and most of the rest of his learning had
come by way of his Methodist classes and Bishop Lee's parlor. That
partly explains Cummins's satisfaction with the Episcopal Church;
the great virtue of the Episcopal Church was that it had avoided the
brand of any single school of speculative or dogmatic theology.
"The Church has avoided human definitions of Scripture doctrines,
while she has set forth every Scripture doctrine itself in all its fulness

and all its glory. This is the boast, this is the honor of the Church to which we belong."[35] The unadorned preaching of evangelical conversion could assume so large a place in Cummins's preaching that it almost seemed that he had no theology beyond a plea for the sinner to be saved. On the other hand, it does look as though he had picked up, from his years in Maryland and Virginia, a weak coloring of the Calvinism that dominated Virginia Episcopalianism in one form or another. The volumes of Cummins's personal library (which ended up in the Reformed Episcopal seminary in the 1890s) show that he was a reasonably close reader of the standard Calvinistic divines of the day and a subscriber to the two major Calvinist theological journals, the *Biblical Repertory and Theological Review* from Presbyterian Princeton, and *Bibliotheca Sacra* from Congregationalist New England. But if he reflected any certain Calvinistic influences, they were surely those of the moderate Calvinism of New England rather than the arch-Calvinism of Princeton. To the extent that Cummins believed grace was a divine quality, divinely given, he can be called a Calvinist, but "in all this," he quickly added, "the human soul loses none of its own individuality; no violence is done to a single faculty; only a new power is present to energize & exalt the whole being."[36] And Cummins's insistence that the human will acts without any natural compulsion (as that which is born "free to elect the good or evil," but then "by its own self-determination . . . has impressed a character upon itself" that gives it a "bias" or "habit" toward evil) is hardly a very stiff-necked version of Calvinism.[37]

He would have been more at home with the Princeton divines when he settled onto the position and authority the Bible occupied. Unlike the Tractarians, Cummins fully shared the standard Evangelical confidence that the Bible was sufficient on its own terms to speak to all questions of faith. "There is everywhere in the New Testament . . . a straightforwardness, a total absence of all appearance of understatement, overstatement, and concealment, a disinterestedness, an honest truthfulness, which almost conceal belief." These qualities sufficed for Cummins to demonstrate that the Bible need not, and should not, be questioned as the rule of life: "These traits witness at once to all men that they who wrote were not designing men . . . but honest men whose sole object was to set forth the facts of a veritable history."[38] He was serenely content with the Bible alone as his guide, and he was persuaded that any other spiritual weapon was doomed to break in the user's hand. "If we would be firm in the day of assault from the Evil One," Cummins warned in Chicago in 1865, then "like our Blessed Master this must be our weapon, 'the sword of the Spirit, which is the Word of God.'"[39] It was, however, a sword that he used sparingly within his own ecclesiastical house. Cummins may have been, in Leacock's words, "impetuous" in the pulpit, but in the early parts of his career in the Episcopal Church he steered clear of confrontation and controversy. In large measure, Cummins owed his election to the Kentucky episcopate in 1866 precisely to the reputation he won at the General Convention of 1865 as a reconciler. The 1865 General Convention, coming hard on the close of the Civil War, had been fraught with potential conflict over the questionable status of the delegates and clergy from the former Confederate states. At the outbreak of the war, the Episcopal dioceses in the Confederacy had organized themselves as a separate national province, and in some dioceses had even proceeded to the election of new bishops without the consent of their quondam brethren to the North (one southern bishop, Leonidas Polk of Louisiana, had even accepted a commission from the Confederate government and commanded a Confederate army corps until his death in battle in 1864). The defeat of the Confederacy brought delegates from Tennessee, Texas, and North Carolina back to the General Convention, but there was no guarantee that the aggrieved Northerners would be in any mood to accept them. On the third day of the 1865 Convention, however, Cummins rose to ask:

> That this House offer its profound gratitude to God that we have among us our brethren, the Clerical and Lay Deputies from the Dioceses of Texas, North Carolina, and Tennessee, and that we recognize their presence in our midst as a token and pledge of the future and entire restoration of the union of the Church throughout the length and breadth of the land.[40]

It was one of Cummins's greatest moments, and he defended his resolution with a fiery eloquence that not only won the day for his motion but also won the admiration of the Southern delegates. That admiration was not forgotten nine months later when Cummins was nominated for the assistant bishopric of Kentucky.

Cummins also struggled to be a reconciler over churchmanship. From his Maryland years onward it is evident that he had grown deeply loyal to the prayer book and the principle of episcopacy, even to the point where he resolved to "work side by side with those who held entirely opposite views," an amiableness that passed its own tests during his years under Whittingham's episcopate in

Washington. Even though Whittingham represented a good deal of what Cummins professed to reprobate, "he found his work lay among those chiefly who were then classed as High Churchmen" and "he felt he could consistently with his views of truth work with others who thought differently, as long as he was permitted to promulgate his views from the pulpit unreservedly, and with all the force and ability he possessed."[41] By 1861, Cummins was able to applaud the Episcopal Church precisely because "it is committed to no human system of theology, but is broad enough and comprehensive enough to embrace men who differ widely in their interpretations of Scriptural truth."[42] It was probably this that caused Benjamin Leacock to suppose in the 1860s that Cummins's "affiliations had brought him more in contact with men of a different school of theology, and it was the general impression that he had grown more churchy."[43]

But what Leacock mistook for "churchiness" on Cummins's part was not High Churchmanship, but rather the "Evangelical Catholicism—Reformed—Protestant—Free" of William Augustus Muhlenberg.[44] It is difficult to pinpoint when Cummins first came under Muhlenberg's spell, but it was evident that Cummins held the old Memorialist in high esteem. (In later years, when Cummins lived in New York, he was Muhlenberg's frequent visitor, and in 1873 Cummins would propose Muhlenberg for election as the third bishop of the Reformed Episcopal Church.) Like Muhlenberg, Cummins held back from the demands for radical dissection of the Book of Common Prayer. "I can use, and have ever used, the Prayer Book without conscientious scruples," Cummins declared in 1869. And in fact he recommended the use of the Book of Common Prayer as the great treasury of Evangelical and Catholic doctrine, for "it embodies, as no other uninspired volume does, the ancient and primitive Catholic faith of Christ's Church." Moreover, the Book of Common Prayer was the great ecumenical hope: "This is the work of the Prayer Book, to turn a theological mystery into a precious heart-truth of deepest experience." The task of Episcopalians, in that light, ought to be "to exhibit the adaptation of the prayer book to be the manual of worship for all the confessions which divide the Protestant Christian family and thus to be a bond of union and communion in one visible Church of the living God."[45]

> The Prayer Book is fitted to unite all reformed Communions, because it enshrines most faithfully the true spirit of the Reformation. . . . May we not safely challenge any portion of reformed Christendom to produce in any confession

or symbol, or formulary of devotion, that which represents
so faithfully the spirit of that great movement? . . . Whilst
this Liturgy remains intact, it will prove a mighty breakwater
to save the Church of Christ from ever again being devas-
tated by the floods of superstition and idolatry.[46]

Cummins's confidence that the Episcopal Church Book of Common Prayer was "fitted to unite" the scattered and divided denominations of American evangelicalism leads us to an even more striking, Muhlenbergesque, theme in Cummins's thinking. Beyond just
the prayer book, Cummins rejoiced in the beauty of the Episcopal
Church, and he fully shared Muhlenberg's enthusiastic dream of seeing the whole American Republic united under the ecumenical aegis
of the Protestant Episcopal Church. As it was, Cummins (in common with most of the other Evangelicals) saw his country as a sort
of political miracle—"this union of states . . . and yet blended into
one country; all bearing one name, all sharing in common glory"—
and he saw no reason why a Protestant Episcopacy could not achieve
the same miracle among the plethora of American denominations
and sects.[47] Like the Whig Republicans, Cummins placed union and
unity first among both the political and the ecclesiastical virtues. "I
believe most firmly that a Protestant Episcopal Church . . . would
be a mighty power, and by God's blessing a great success in this
land," Cummins wrote in 1869, "and it may be that God designs
that such a Church shall be."[48]

I have indulged a dream [he told the American Church Missionary Society in November, 1869] of the future of our dear
Church. It is not a reunion with Unreformed Churches, not
an absorption, into a grand system of Ecclesiasticism. Nay, it
has been one far different; it is the hope that this Church
should prove a center, a rallying point for all Protestant
Christendom in this age and nation; that adapting herself to
the mighty mass of humanity around us, with her pure faith,
simple yet majestic worship, conservative spirit, venerable
history and apostolic order, she should gather around her the
divided Protestantism of our day, and holding the post of
honor and responsibility near to the ark of God, go forward
as did the Tribes of Israel, with all her sister churches arrayed
in compact order to the help of the Lord against the mighty,
to the work of Evangelizing and saving souls for whom
Christ died, the work of making this Emmanuel's land, the
joy of the whole earth.[49]

In that light, Anglo-Catholicism appeared to Cummins as an ec-clesiastical dog-in-the-manger. There was no way Cummins could square either his Evangelical loyalty to the Bible alone or his Evan-gelical Catholic loyalty to prayer book and church with the doc-trines and rituals emerging from General Theological Seminary or Nashotah House. "*Superstition* is its name," Cummins announced. "A religion more of form than of spirit. A religion that substitutes penance for penitence—that rends the garments and not the heart."[50] But superstition or not, it was achieving legitimacy in the Episcopal Church, and it forced him (as it was forcing other Evangelicals) into some delicate and sometimes intolerable intellectual balancing acts. Much as he might protest in 1869 that he had no particular objection to the declaration of "regeneration" in the baptismal office, he pleaded that "the regeneration for which we thank God in baptism is not to be taken in any sense as descriptive of the renewing work of the Holy Spirit upon the heart, but only a term equivalent to bap-tism, a sacramental change, a change of covenant relation."[51] And whatever the ritualists might want to make the communion service into, Cummins insisted to the contrary that "Christ's presence at the Supper is not a presence in the elements, not on the table, not re-ceived in the hand or by the mouth."[52] To his congregation at Trin-ity Church, Cummins declared in 1865:

> By giving his flesh for the life of the world, Jesus means his death on the Cross, the giving His body to the agony of crucifixion as a stupendous sacrifice for the sin of the world . . . not in any gross & carnal sense that He would give His fleshly body to be our food. Far from us be any approach to such a thought.[53]

Even the title received by him at his ordination—"priest"—was in Cummins's mind only the title given to every Evangelical believer. In no sense did it suggest to Cummins that he had been granted some peculiar sacrificial or mediatorial status. "Though in the Chris-tian Church there is an order consecrated and ordained to minister in holy things," he told the people of Trinity Church in 1864, "every Christian is a priest to God."[54] He rejected out of hand the Anglo-Catholic claim to a special priesthood and an "apostolic" episcopate, and insisted instead, in his most-often-preached sermon, that "reli-gion is an individual concern" which required the intervention of neither priest nor church. It is "a personal transaction between each soul & God. Nay, as much an individual transaction as though every human being trod the earth alone."[55]

More than anything else, it was the debate over the episcopate which grated on Cummins's sensitivities, since the Anglo-Catholic claim to an exclusive apostolic succession, reserved only to the "catholic" succession of bishops, promised to alienate forever the broad spectrum of American evangelicalism which Cummins had hoped to unite under the banner of the Episcopal Church. "The mightiest barrier today in the way of the reunion of the Protestant Churches," Cummins complained, "is the unchurching dogma which demands the submission of all other Christian bodies to its *jure divino* claim."[56]

The problem for Cummins was explaining how—if the Anglo-Catholics were indeed so far from the mark—their opinions had managed to gain such a hold on his church. He understood clearly enough that one part of Anglo-Catholicism's appeal lay in the fact that it offered to people a vision of a living, tangible Christ, as opposed to the polite, rational deity of the High Churchmen or the fire-ànd-brimstone Judge of the revivalists. "There is a feeling in the breasts of many that it would be an unspeakable privilege, an inestimable blessing to have Christ ever bodily & visibly present with his Church," Cummins admitted in 1863, and it was just this yearning that the high sacramentalism of the Anglo-Catholics was fulfilling.[57] Cummins also saw that another element that made Anglo-Catholicism so attractive was the appeal of its ritualism to the Victorian weakness for Romantic display. This "is a luxurious age," Cummins warned, "an age that seeks to gratify the eye by elaborate ornament, . . . the same spirit craves a more ornate & showy ritual."[58] In Cummins's eyes, the Oxford Movement, no matter what its pious intentions, had gained the ground it had only by invoking a "delusive sentimentalism."

There is no form of this perverted religiousness of our nature more dangerous than that of *sentimentalism*—the outcome of a highly wrought temperament or of an uncurbed imagination. It is a temperament like this that is the first to fall a victim to the wiles of superstition. It pauses not to ask of any system that claims its allegiance—is it true? is it a reality? But it surrenders itself unthinkingly to the ceremonial that can stir and impress the imagination. It is awed by a pompous worship; it is excited to reverence under sublime architecture; it is hushed into silence by sculptured stone and storied lights of Cathedral windows; it is wrapt to the third heaven of intense feeling by the cadences of music. What wonder is it if such temperaments yielded a continuous harvest to superstition![59]

Cummins, by contrast, was baffled by the need for such display. The United States was not England, and tinselly medievalism struck Cummins as noticeably out-of-place against a republican landscape. "If the history of this land is marked by any one feature more strongly than all the others," Cummins declared, it was in the fact that "it was a land free from the fetters of the old traditions. It had no past history to give shape and coloring to the future. It was destitute of hallowed places and local shrines" and "needed not to break away from the bonds of hoary superstition."[60] The only authentic spiritual landscape Cummins would recognize was the more modest inner world of the Evangelical affections; indeed, rather than surrender to Anglo-Catholic "sentimentalism" at any point, Cummins actually found himself talking not about Evangelical affections but about the need for "a *rational* religion."[61] What he meant by that was both the various forms of evangelicalized natural religion that had sprung up in the transatlantic Evangelical community as evangelicalism's strategy for co-opting the Enlightenment, and the "reasonable enthusiasm" of the Edwardseans and the Wesleyans, "the inner life of religion, the living fountain of piety within the soul, feeding the lamp & keeping its flame ever pure and bright." And the real goal toward which his talk of "a *rational* religion" was driving was the same Evangelicalism that looked not to the sacraments or to the faith of the church, but to "the grace of God within the heart, quickening, renewing, sanctifying."[62] To offer "spiritual life through physical media" was merely to set forth a "false gospel."[63]

Still, "sentimentalism" explained only why certain individuals were attracted to Anglo-Catholicism. It really did nothing to explain why the Anglo-Catholics had become the force they were in the church as a whole. But explaining that part would have required Cummins to look more critically both at his church and at his beloved prayer book. So long as his confidence in Muhlenberg's "Evangelical Catholicism" remained strong, and so long as he was only in parish ministry, Cummins had neither the need nor the willingness to take that kind of critical stance. In Maryland, Virginia, and now in Chicago, Anglo-Catholicism had been little more than an "ism," a vague and controversial cloud still only just over the horizon, and easily pushed out of the mind by the work-a-day round of parish duties. But on June 1, 1866, all that changed for George David Cummins. The diocesan convention of Kentucky, meeting at St. John's Church in Louisville, elected Cummins to fill the post of assistant bishop of the diocese, and on November 15, 1866, Cummins was consecrated with all the pomp Louisville could summon. Now Cummins would have no choice but to look the question directly in the face.

Ritualism and Romanism in Kentucky

The Diocese of Kentucky, to which Cummins came as assistant bishop in 1866, comprised only thirty-five parishes and missions and about 2,400 communicants, with twenty-four full-time clergy in parochial or mission work.[64] In terms of churchmanship, it leaned a fair way toward the High Churchmen, though not without an important Evangelical presence; there was as yet no noticeable Anglo-Catholic faction. The Bishop of Kentucky, Benjamin Bosworth Smith, was an Evangelical, "a man of peace, gentle, tolerant, forbearing"[65] who had once been editor of the *Philadelphia Recorder* (forerunner of the *Episcopal Recorder*) and had been elected Kentucky's first bishop as long ago as 1832. Smith had no more love for Anglo-Catholic ritual than Cummins, and he repeatedly warned his diocesan conventions "not to make any, even the slightest innovations upon its established usages and those of the parishes round about."

> [The Book of Common Prayer] disdains the meretricious aid of tinsel ornaments, and groans under the burden of a gorgeous ceremonial. These too often drew attention away from the wants and longings of the soul, and rivet every sense on things to be seen, attitudes to be observed, and words to be repeated, leaving the whole man in the condition of a dead formalist.[66]

However, Smith also had, by 1866, long since lost the confidence of his diocese. Ordained by Griswold, trained under the watchful Evangelical eye of Richard Channing Moore, and consecrated by the aged William White along with John Henry Hopkins and Charles Pettit McIlvaine, Smith had arrived in Kentucky with the full intention of establishing the reign of Evangelical principles there. But in the autumn of 1835, Smith collided with John Esten Cooke, the most formidable layman in his diocese and a straight-up High Churchman. Disagreements over church order quickly evolved into charges and countercharges about Smith's handling of diocesan finances and Smith's high-handed attempt to handpick a new rector for Christ Church, Lexington, where Cooke was senior warden.

Finally, at the 1837 diocesan convention, Smith was forced to ask for a trial to clear his name. The court, chaired by McIlvaine, found Smith not guilty on each of the six charges against him. But Smith was never fully in command of his diocese again, and from the 1840s on, it was John Esten Cooke, and the new rector of Christ Church, Louisville, James Craik, who held the real political control of the diocese in their hands.[67] Moreover, by 1866, Smith was further enfeebled by age, and his health was becoming unreliable (as it was, Benjamin Leacock remembered him as "always weak" and "indecisive").[68] He was thus only too happy to welcome Cummins "to my side in the near and sacred relation which Timothy sustained to St. Paul."[69]

Cummin's election was all the happier for the peace of the Diocese of Kentucky because Cummins had been a compromise candidate, elected on the fourth ballot as the candidate most satisfactory to both High Churchmen and Evangelicals.[70] In fact, Cummins had been the favorite of Craik, who had been favorably impressed both with Cummins's call for reconciliation with the Southern Episcopalians the year before, and with Cummins's potential for rallying and energizing the moribund diocese. "The condition of things in Kentucky was not promising," reported the *Christian Advocate*, "and the Episcopalians, attracted by the popular gifts of Dr. Cummins, elected him assistant bishop."[71] Thus, there was no exaggeration in the claim of George D. E. Mortimer to Cummins that "All . . . united *upon you*." And Mortimer's confident expectation was that "by the blessing of God you can *harmonize* these conflicting interests."[72]

And at least at the beginning of his episcopate, that unity and blessing seemed evident. Cummins began his first round of visitations in Kentucky in January 1867, and by June he had succeeded in visiting every parish in the diocese. "All are impressed with the record of my work for the past six months, and we have now entire harmony," Cummins wrote on the eve of his first diocesan convention. And, he added, he fully desired to rebuild the bridges Smith's unhappy episcopate had pulled down. "I desire to cultivate a spirit of unity and harmony among the congregations. I shall strive to bring the whole diocese into perfect harmony in our great work of extending the Church throughout the State."[73] The diocese responded in kind. In the autumn of 1867, the vestries of Christ Church and St. Paul's Church in Louisville pooled their resources to buy him a country home, Oak Lea, sixteen miles outside Louisville, and there Cummins spent one of the happiest and most contented years of his life.[74]

But that little cloud, which had been only on the distant horizons of Cummins's consciousness in Chicago, now began to assume full and inescapable proportions. In the spring of 1868, by Cummins's recollection, "a Ritualistic service was introduced for the first time into the Diocese of Kentucky, and the unspeakable trial was placed upon me of being compelled to discharge my official duty in visiting this church and taking part in its services."[75] The new ritualism had been introduced into Grace Church, Louisville, a former mission of Christ Church, Louisville, which had taken up a Nashotah House graduate, Louis P. Tshiffely, as its first rector in August 1869. This placed the new outpost of Anglo-Catholicism virtually under Cummins's nose.[76] He did not find the experience pleasant:

> I was compelled to stand in the presence of altar and super-altar, of brazen cross and candlestick, and to behold priest and people turning again and again toward that altar, and bowing in profound adoration toward it, while to my own soul such acts were idolatrous, dishonoring and insulting to Jesus, the Church's only Altar, Priest, and Sacrifice.[77]

And yet there was little he could do about it. His first inclination probably would have been to suppress or curb the more elaborate ritual goings-on, but "as the assistant bishop," Benjamin Leacock remarked, "he was only an episcopal machine. Any word of remonstrance would have been met with the request to keep his place and to attend to his duties."[78] He might have turned to Bishop Smith for support, but Smith was eager to retire gracefully and unwilling to rock any boats. So Cummins had no choice but to suffer in silence, especially when "within a year or two, a second service of the same order was established in the city of Louisville, and this time by one who had been a youth in my first parish in Virginia."[79] Cummins recalled later:

> Bitter has been the trial, terrible the bondage to be compelled by official duty to stand by the side of an altar in God's House—to witness acts of reverence and adoration toward it—to see priest and communicants receiving the elements with a holy reverence as if truly receiving God into their hands.[80]

"Now as never before," observed Leacock, "he began to learn [Anglo-Catholicism's] real meaning, and to understand its aggressive, dictatorial and unscrupulous spirit."[81]

This was only to be Cummins's first lesson. In early October 1868, Cummins headed the Kentucky delegation to the General Convention in New York City, and what he saw there gave him an even greater shock than what he had seen in Kentucky:

> You may judge of my feelings [Cummins wrote to his wife] when, upon entering the church [Church of the Transfiguration], I saw before me in the chancel an altar, with a super-altar, and on it in the centre a brass cross three feet high, and two brass candlesticks of the same height but unlighted. And just in front of the altar was the venerable Bishop McIlvaine, within a few feet of what he had all his life so earnestly protested against. The feeling of indignation in general is very great among all evangelical men, and some will not again attend the meetings if they are held in that church.[82]

But more unsettling than the unconcealed parade of ritual bric-a-brac was the Convention's out-of-hand rejection of the plea of the elder Stephen Tyng that Horatio Potter's reprimand of his son be overturned, and the chilly reception given to the proposed canon on ritual uniformity. "When the Convention of 1868 closed, the Ritualists, so far at least as the Lower House was concerned, felt themselves stronger than ever," recalled Charles Wesley Andrews, an old Virginia Evangelical.[83] And echoing that, Cummins wrote, "We have refused to make any changes in the Prayer Book; we have refused to change the Canon which brought about the Tyng trial, and it stands as it did before; we have refused to alter the Canon concerning the officiating of other than our own ministers in our churches."[84]

Although all these proceedings dismayed and disappointed Cummins, he watched and choked back any protests of his own on the floor of the Convention. But on October 21, after the Convention adjourned, he issued his first major condemnation of the rise of Anglo-Catholic influence in the church:

> Three memorable attempts have been made within the last three hundred years to subvert the work of the Anglican Reformers. The first was in the sixteenth century; the second in the seventeenth; the third in the nineteenth. The first was an attempt by force, the second by fraud, the third by treachery. . . . The simple majestic service of our Church in many places has been transformed into a ritual which the fathers of

the Reformation would not recognize as the service of their deepest love. Altars erected, with super-altars, with burning candles, gorgeous vestments, and floating clouds of incense; the communion service set in a Roman framework; the voice of Jacob put into the hands of Esau; eucharistic services at the burial of the dead, with ceremonies that actually surpass those of Rome, . . . these are but a part of the drapery of false doctrine which has succeeded so sadly in corrupting the faith of a Reformed communion. . . . The evil is not so much in them as in that which they represent. Far below all these surface manifestations, where none of them are to be seen as yet, there is a departure from the doctrinal basis of the Reformation.[85]

Cummins returned to Louisville shaken by what he had seen and heard at the Convention. "This Convention will prove an era in my life," Cummins wrote later in the month, "and may decide the whole future of my career." Still, he was not without hope that Anglo-Catholicism could somehow be contained, and he continued to assure himself that "we can . . . plant ourselves upon the Prayer Book as it is, for thus we can save any movement *Romeward* or *Greekward* by any changes in the Prayer Book."[86] But sometime before the end of 1868, even that ground sank from under him when one of the newly published copies of Franklin Rising's *Are There Romanizing Germs in the Prayer Book?* came into his hands. He recalled:

The Prayer Book of the Protestant Episcopal Church was very precious to me, and I longed to see it become the heritage of all Protestant Christendom. . . . This was my position toward the Prayer Book up through the year 1868. That year brought with it a thorough change in my views. . . . How then, were mine eyes opened? . . . A copy of Mr. Rising's tract reached me by mail, and I well remember the repugnance which the very title awakened, and with which I began its perusal. That simple agent was the first instrument for awakening my mind . . . to the facts of history, into the investigation of which I had shrunk from entering.[87]

Rising's argument that Anglo-Catholicism arose not from sources outside the church but from "Romanizing germs" left inside the prayer book since the sixteenth century at once explained to Cummins how Anglo-Catholics had obtained such a hold, and so quickly, on the Protestant Episcopal Church. "I had watched the rise and spread of the Oxford tract movement until it had leavened, to a vast extent, the whole English-American Episcopal Churches," Cummins wrote in 1876, "but I firmly believed that this school was not a growth developing from seeds within the system, but a parasite fastening upon it from without and threatening its very life."[88] He could believe that no longer, and from 1868 onward Cummins gradually swung further and further toward advocating a root-and-branch approach to both the prayer book and the canons of the church.

In the process, he began losing friends among both Evangelicals and High Churchmen. In May 1869, Gregory Thurston Bedell, assistant bishop to McIlvaine of Ohio, invited Cummins to contribute a letter to the Ohio diocesan paper, *Standard of the Cross*, which would endorse McIlvaine's opposition to "rash movements among our brethren" and reiterate "the inexpediency of attempting to revise the Prayer Book at the present time."[89] Cummins's response, which was printed on the front page of *Standard of the Cross*, obediently rebuked the Evangelicals who wanted "to leave the Church of their fathers and of their first love." But Cummins then turned on McIlvaine and asked, "*Has the Church no duty to fulfill towards the men whom I have described?*" And he dared to suggest that perhaps, after all, the church "should grant them such liberty of action in the omission of words from the Baptismal office as were omitted in the first Prayer Book adopted by the first General Convention of the Church in 1785."[90] McIlvaine was outraged and tried, too late, to have Cummins's endorsement of such "liberty" suppressed. From that point on, his relations with the rest of the Evangelical leadership began to go down hill.[91]

Cummins lost even greater ground with the High Churchmen. In October 1869, Cummins signed a "Proposition of the Nine Bishops" that begged the General Convention to find some way of accommodating Evangelical consciences over the baptismal office. Within forty-eight hours of the appearance of the "Proposition," Horatio Potter of New York issued a violent rebuttal, attacking the signers of the "Proposition" as the promoters of "an absolute impossibility." At the same time, Cummins was also involving himself in extremely hot water with Henry J. Whitehouse of Illinois. On June 3, 1869, Cummins received an urgent and agonized letter from Cheney, breaking to Cummins the news that he "was to be tried, and—as the bishop assures me—*deposed*, for omitting the phrase in the

Prayer Book office for infant baptism which ascribes regeneration to the act of baptism."[92] But as Cheney explained, it was not White-house who had caused him the greatest grief, but rather Cheney's amazed discovery that his citation for trial had been the signal for the Evangelical bishops all with one consent to make excuse. Cheney plaintively wrote at the end of June, "There seems to have been on the part of most of the evangelical bishops . . . a strong impression that those who were desirous of liturgical revision only made it a cloak of their complete alienation from the whole system of our Church. *Such is not the case.*" And he appealed to Cummins to "understand us, and to give us credit for a sincere, honest desire for such a measure of relief as would enable us, without sacrifice of loyalty to God and the Bible, and the supremacy of an enlightened conscience, to be equally loyal to the Church of our Fathers."[93]

Cummins had known nothing of Cheney's private decision to rewrite the baptismal office at Christ Church, and it is doubtful whether he entirely approved of Cheney's actions. But he had already come to the conclusion that Cheney was at least right in principle, and he was too close to being of one mind with Cheney on this issue to refuse him at least some measure of moral support. Cheney was conscious that Cummins "did not sympathize with the more radical wing of the Evangelical Party." Nevertheless, Cheney soon found himself "in frequent receipt of letters" from Cummins "which expressed the tenderest sympathy with me, assuring me that I was constantly in his prayers, and that the time would come when we should be enabled to carry the views that we both held in regard to the revision of the Prayer Book into something like success."[94] Then, in July 1869, Cummins accepted an invitation from his old congregation in Chicago, Trinity Church, to fill the pulpit during the rector's vacation. Cummins was only too happy to accept, but at this point, Bishop Whitehouse, fearing that Cummins would turn any such services into rallies for Cheney, decided to ban Cummins from the Diocese of Illinois. But Cummins was getting beyond the reach of the anger of Whitehouse or anyone else, and he defiantly appeared at Trinity Church not once but twice that July, just as Cheney was being sent to the wall.[95] Years later, Cheney reminded the people of Christ Church what the mere fact of Cummins's presence in Chicago had meant to him:

You in this congregation knew him best in those dreary five years when you and your pastor were under the ban of eccle-

siastical law. He was through all those dark days our only
friend in the house of bishops.[96]

But Cummins paid a tremendous price for his friendship with Cheney, and the animosity of High Church bishops like Whitehouse and
Potter was due to enjoy long innings.

Cummins's new views of the church situation also cost him
dearly within Kentucky. A large part of the trouble Cummins began
to experience there was directly related to the support he had begun
to throw behind the controversial tactics of the American Church
Missionary Society (ACMS). The complicated story of the ACMS
has its roots in the fatal decision of the 1835 General Convention to
leave domestic missions to the High Churchmen, and foreign missions to the Evangelicals. This unwritten agreement had seemed relatively harmless when it was struck, and Cummins himself had
joined vigorously in promoting Evangelical foreign missions. But
by the 1860s it was not the High Churchmen who were pursuing
domestic missions, but the Anglo-Catholics, and as one new ritualistic parish after another sprang up unchallenged in the new western dioceses, the Evangelicals began to look fearfully over their
shoulders. The old Evangelical societies, such as the Protestant Episcopal Society for the Promotion of Evangelical Knowledge and the
Evangelical Education Society (of which Cummins was a vice-president), were unprepared to turn their belated attention to recovering
the ground lost since 1835.[97] So in May 1860, John Stone, Heman
Dyer, Stephen Tyng, Eli Canfield, and Henry Anthon organized the
American Church Missionary Society as an independent missions
organization that took as its frank object to "advance the mission
work agreeably to the views of religious truth and obligation which
distinguish our Evangelical Church, and occupy still more extended
fields of labor."[98] Patterned on the English Evangelical Church Pastoral Aid Society, the ACMS hoped to provide for a supply of
Evangelical curates who could be inserted into new parishes or who
could find a niche in the older ones. That would of course depend
on the cooperation of the Evangelical bishops and how willing they
were to risk the ire of their dioceses at pushing ACMS candidates
down parish throats.

Not many were, and it went virtually without saying that the
High Church bishops would have neither part nor lot with the
ACMS. William Heathcote Delancey, the High Church bishop of
the Diocese of Western New York, attacked the ACMS in the most
ominous terms he could summon in 1862 as "a most dangerous
step toward breaking down the Episcopal Church." The ACMS

"might be Presbyterian or Methodist, but it certainly was not an organ of the Episcopal Church," Delancey complained; it "had within it the essence of *secession*."[99] Cummins, however, embraced the cause of the ACMS eagerly. Not only did he agree to serve as an ACMS spokesman, but he left no doubt that he expected to beat the Anglo-Catholics at their own game by flooding Kentucky with ACMS curates. "Bishop Cummins, they say, is stocking the diocese with radicals," warned Henry C. Lay in December 1869, and "is himself anxious to revolutionize the diocese."[100] In 1867, Cummins had asked the Kentucky diocesan convention to create a diocesan missions board for the purpose of planting new churches across Kentucky. At first, Cummins had enjoyed broad support from the diocese, including the powerful High Church rector of Christ Church, Louisville, James Craik. But after the 1868 General Convention, Cummins began claiming exclusive control over clergy appointments to new mission works and promptly began filling them exclusively with young Evangelical men. Craik protested. Cummins announced that he intended to go further still and affiliate the diocesan missions board with the American Church Missionary Society as an auxiliary of the ACMS. On January 2, 1869, Craik confronted Cummins and accused him of partiality in his appointments; Cummins replied that he "would appoint the very persons he pleased" and strongly implied that "he was on one side and some of us on the other."[101] Craik accepted Cummins's challenge and moved to tie up the diocese's funding for the missions board. "The assistant Bp. of Ky. is not in good odor here," wrote one Kentucky clergyman to Cummins's old bishop, William Whittingham. "His demands touch the pocket idol too much."[102] Nevertheless, even with Craik's opposition, by 1873 the Kentucky diocese was sponsoring seven ACMS missionaries; only Kansas (with eight) and Virginia (with eleven) sponsored more.[103]

Although it cost Cummins dearly in political terms to push the ACMS missionaries into Kentucky, the personal costs of his anti-ritualist campaign were even more painful. Many of the High Churchmen who had welcomed his election in 1866 turned on him as a pariah, "and he was personally made to feel that he could no longer expect sympathy or kindness from those who only two years before had so warmly welcomed him to Kentucky."[104] His salary was allowed to lapse into arrears, and the two parishes that had purchased the mortgage on his home, Oak Lea, stopped payments and allowed the property to be foreclosed in 1870.[105] Then, in 1872, when Bishop Smith finally retired and moved to Hoboken, New Jersey, the diocesan convention, at the prompting of James Craik, administered a further irritant by refusing Smith's resignation as titular bishop and granting him permission to reside outside the diocese—all of which was plainly calculated to keep Cummins from succeeding Smith as Bishop of Kentucky, because (as one of the delegates unwisely said in Alexandrine Cummins's hearing) "Ritualism would be dead in twenty-four hours if Bishop Cummins be allowed to exercise any power in the diocese."[106]

But far from being intimidated by the host of detractors who had risen up around him, Cummins only proceeded to turn up the volume of his criticisms. In November 1869, Cummins used an invitation to address the American Church Missionary Society and declare, "We are in the midst of a reactionary movement that would undo the work of the Reformers, and bring back into our Reformed Church the errors and corruptions that defiled the Medieval Church."[107] Invited to address the anniversary meeting of the Evangelical Knowledge Society at the Church of the Ascension in New York City in 1870, Cummins threw off all hesitations and directly attacked the leading lights of American Anglo-Catholicism as traitors to the Protestant Episcopal Church. Benjamin Leacock, who was in the audience that night, remembered:

> What a grand speech it was!! He came forward holding in his hand a catechism, the joint work of Drs. Morgan Dix and James DeKoven. He denounced it as undisguised Romanism. Its teachings, he said, carried the Church back to ante-Reformation times. He took the little book to pieces. He exposed its Romanism. He asked if such doctrines should be taught in the Protestant Episcopal Church without prompt and crushing rebuke. There was no mistaking where he stood, and for the moment he carried with him the heart of his large audience.

To the Evangelical Educational Society in 1871, Cummins unhesitatingly proposed that "we ought to have united years ago with one of our venerable Bishops, and refused to consecrate a Church having an altar and not an honest communion table."[108]

Cummins proceeded to take his own advice within the bounds of the Diocese of Kentucky. During 1871 and 1872, he conducted visitations to fifty parishes in Kentucky, preaching two and three times in every church and mission in the diocese; the next year, he conducted another 54 visitations, confirmed 366 persons, and preached 170 times at cornerstone-layings, baptisms, ordinations, and confirmations.[109] In each case, he carried his antiritualist message with

him. In September 1873, while preaching at the reopening of St.
Paul's Church, Louisville, Cummins hammered back at "the assaults
. . . of superstition . . . as it seeks to defile the Reformed Church of
Christ by the revival of medieval corruptions of doctrine and practice."[110] He condemned "that great reactionary movement which had
begun in the University of Oxford, . . . a movement whose tendency is to undo and overturn the work of the Reformers of the
sixteenth century, and to bring back among us corruptions in doctrine and practice from which our fathers cleansed the church by a
cost of untold sacrifice, suffering, and blood." And he warned the
congregation of St. Paul's:

> The true glory of the house of God [is] that its courts are
> thronged by those who are seeking to be saved; that within
> its walls human hearts are convinced of sin; that the tear of
> penitence falls unseen by man, and angels, who wait upon its
> assemblies, hear the soul cry "what must I do to be saved?" It
> is the glory of a church that men and women are converted
> to God under its shadow, . . . not merely cold and lifeless
> conformists to church ordinances, but souls that have felt the
> terrible burden of sin, . . . have grasped the cross with the
> hold of a mighty faith, and have tasted the sweetness of par-
> doning grace, and looked up into the face of a reconciled
> Father and God.[111]

But Cummins made his point in the most dramatic fashion in May
1873 when the diocesan convention met in Christ Church, Lexington,
where Jacob Shaw Shipman, a New York-born High Churchman and
a particular favorite of James Craik, was the rector. Cummins
opened the convention on May 27, discovering as he did that Shipman had covered the altar "with a scarlet cloth" and planted upon it
"a magnificent floral cross, the base of which was one mass of
flowers, the shaft and arms dotted with white roses." Cummins immediately objected to what he interpreted as a provocative glorification of the altar, and, this time with the consent of the convention,
"the beautiful floral cross was removed out of sight."[112]

It was evident from all this that, by 1873, Cummins was growing
both more defiant and more desperate. When Cheney was at length
deposed from the priesthood in 1871, Cummins wrote to him, urging him to ignore Bishop Whitehouse's sentence and to "continue
your ministry as before." He added ominously, "You will not be
long without brethren to join you."[113] When the General Convention
of 1871 met in Baltimore and took no more than token action to

placate the Evangelicals, Cummins confessed: "I return to my work with a heavy heart, knowing that every effort to suppress the Sacerdotal system by legislation had failed, and that I was more powerless than ever to resist its influence."[114] Cummins morosely confided to Cheney in January 1872 that he had lost his once-bright faith in the church and the Book of Common Prayer. "I am more deeply convinced than ever that the root of all our evils lies in the sanction which our Prayer Book gives to the Sacerdotal system," Cummins admitted. "I am therefore a most earnest advocate for a thorough revision, . . . but I confess that the effort seems to be utterly vain and idle and hopeless."[115]

All the ties that had bound George David Cummins, as a bishop and a man, to his church were snapping one by one, and at last he began to contemplate what for the dutiful Episcopalian, not to mention a bishop, has always seemed the worst and most unthinkable of sins. In his mind, the church he had served for almost thirty years had shifted decisively off its axis, from being a church that thought of itself as Protestant, and frequently behaved itself as Evangelical, to a church that was busily repudiating both Protestantism and Evangelicalism. And it was all being done by means Cummins found so unconscionable that he could scarcely recognize it as his church any longer—even though, ironically, he had become fully reconciled to using some of the same methods in Kentucky in order to bring the un-Protestantizing of his diocese to an end. Cummins "was unquestionably using the money of his party to stock the diocese with a sufficient number of radical men to change the representation of the [diocesan] convention," Hall Harrison wrote to Bishop Whittingham in 1871, and it did nothing to change that impression that Cummins had successfully twisted the arm of the convention in order to get two of his own nominees elected to the diocesan Standing Committee.[116]

But in his mind, it was the Anglo-Catholics who had committed the greater violence, and, what was more, Cummins believed that the fatal paralysis of Evangelical leadership in the Episcopal Church as a whole justified whatever measures he required to rule his house in Kentucky. He had once dreamt of a great church, the national church envisioned by the Muhlenberg Memorial, and he had lived to see it instead wrap itself into what he could only understand as a cocoon of Romantic medievalism. And now that recovery and reform seemed beyond hope, there appeared to be but one way forward. So, on December 5, 1870, Cummins took his episcopal life in his own hands and quietly met with Stephen Tyng Jr., John Cotton Smith, and thirty-five other clergymen at the New York home of

Colonel George T. M. Davis to discuss, in the most delicate of terms, the "prospect of establishing a new Episcopal Church."[117] Nothing came of it for the moment, but it was evident that only one more spark was now needed to set off an explosion. That spark would fly in less than three years, and the man who would provide it would be no one less than Horatio Potter, Bishop of New York.

The Evangelical Alliance

It is one of the great ironies of Anglican history that, side by side with the Anglo-Catholic effort to return the Church of England to its ancient Catholic shape, the Church of England was being pushed in quite another and more modern direction by both liberals and Evangelicals. Three years before Keble's Assize sermon, Samuel Taylor Coleridge, quondam poet and sometime philosopher, surveyed the lackluster state of the Church of England and, unlike Keble, concluded that Parliamentary intervention might in fact be the only way to save the church for England and from itself. Coleridge's prescriptions were, to be sure, fully as formed by Romantic idealism as Keble's and Newman's, but whereas Keble and Newman sought to satisfy the Romantic yearning for unity by seeking historical unities with the Christian past, Coleridge found his answers in the search for a national unity of parish and nation, rather than what it was in effect—merely the state religion of England. That meant redefining the church, not as a sacrosanct capsule of apostolic truth, lying within the nation and yet not of it, but rather as a national property whose "clerisy" could be any educated man, whose temporal head was the monarch, whose parishes ran both the churches and the schools, and whose boundaries were broad enough to include virtually every English subject, no matter what their precise religious opinions might be.[118]

Coleridge's *On the Constitution of the Church and State According to the Idea of Each* was an idea of the church as a national trust, rather than an apostolic deposit, but in Coleridge's hands it was never more than a vision. The task of distilling Coleridge's ideas into comprehensible details fell to Thomas Arnold. This celebrated headmaster of the Rugby School had, in the same year as the Assize sermon, published a volume on *Principles of Church Reform* that turned the notions of the still-nascent Tractarians on their ears. Contrary to the *Tracts*, Arnold gloried in the unity of Church and Parliament and, following Coleridge's logic to the nethermost, frankly declared that only Parliament was a capable engine of reform and redirection for the church. If, as Arnold believed, the chief end of Christianity is to confront and conquer moral evil and to bring in the rule of the kingdom of God, then a more inappropriate instrument for that end never existed in England than in its dull and slothful church, with its ungainly mechanisms of rule, its absentee clergy, and its witless and unwitting bishops. "I cannot understand what is the good of a National Church," protested Arnold, "if it be not to Christianize the nation and introduce the principles of Christianity into men's social and civil relations." To Arnold, "the true and grand idea of a Church" is "a society for the purpose of making men like Christ, earth like heaven, the kingdoms of the world the kingdom of Christ." The "Scripture notion of the Church," Arnold wrote, "is that religious society should help a man to become himself better and holier, just as civil society helps us in civilization." But the present condition and mental torpor of the Church of England had instead turned it into "an affair of the clergy, not of the people, of preaching and ceremonies, not of living, of Sundays and synagogues, instead of one of all days and all places, houses, streets, towns and country."[119]

But no hope of so thoroughly Christianizing English society had much chance unless Parliament took the church in hand and made it a genuinely national church. And there was no hope of creating such a national church unless the Church of England was willing to let down the bars of liturgy and order that had excluded Dissenters from official English religious life since 1662. "My favorite principle," Arnold announced, is "that the world is made up of Christians and non-Christians; with all the former we should be one, with none of the latter."[120] That was, as Arnold knew, much more easily said than done. The Dissenters, no less than the church, nursed deep suspicions of such wholesale reconciliation. On the one hand, "Episcopalians require that [church government] should be *episcopal*," but equally, on the other hand, "dissenters of almost every denomination insist that it should not be *prelatical*." But, Arnold asked, was it not possible that a scheme for a truly national Church of England could manage to "be the first without being the last"? To that end, Arnold proposed the multiplication of the existing number of English dioceses (to make them more localized and manageable), the creation of diocesan synods, the opening of the universities (and with them, theological education) to "persons of a class much too poor to support the expense of a university education," placing the authority for appointment of parish clergy back into the hands of the parishes and in general broadening the role of the laity in parish "superintendence." By these means, "dissenting ministers might at once become ministers of the establishment, and as such would of course have their share in its government."[121] That would, in turn, compel the Church of England to open its doors and its practices to "allow great varieties of opinion, and of ceremonies, and forms of worship, according to the various knowledge, habits, and tempers of its members, while it truly held one common faith, and trusted in one common Saviour and worshipped one common God."[122] In practical terms, this would include everyone in England but Jews, Unitarians, Quakers, and Roman Catholics and would have required precisely the attitude toward liturgical matters espoused by the Muhlenberg Memorial twenty years later. "There seems to be no reason at all," Arnold conceded, "why the National Church should not enjoy a sufficient variety in its ritual, to satisfy the opinions and feelings of all."[123]

Nothing cheered Arnold more than to see, in 1841, the creation of just such a trial scheme for unity in the creation of the "Jerusalem bishopric." Acting on proposals drawn up by the Prussian diplomat (and fervent Lutheran) Carl Jonas von Bunsen, the British government established an Anglican bishopric in Jerusalem with the avowed purpose of converting the Jews. The bishop of this new diocese would be alternately nominated by the monarchs of England and Prussia and would be free to ordain any Anglican or Lutheran alike who could subscribe to the Thirty-Nine Articles of Religion and the Augsburg Confession.[124] Predictably, the Anglo-Catholics blanched at the Jerusalem bishopric proposal, seeing at once that it would establish de facto intercommunion with the Lutherans and thus sully the "catholicity" of the Church of England. They also protested a new bishopric on the grounds that Jerusalem technically fell within the jurisdiction of the Greek Orthodox Church, which in Anglo-Catholic minds possessed a validity that the Lutherans did not.[125]

But the protests of the Anglo-Catholics meant nothing to Arnold. "It is clear to me that Newman and his party are idolaters," Arnold wrote in a letter in 1836. "They put Christ's Church and Christ's Sacraments, and Christ's ministers, in the place of Christ Himself."[126] In a famous diatribe in the *Edinburgh Review* in April 1836, Arnold attacked the Tractarians as "The Oxford Malignants," a coterie of "formalist Judaizing fanatics . . . who have been the peculiar disgrace of the Church of England."[127] Grant their principles, Arnold warned, and the Church of England would become a church that would have no choice but to withdraw from English society into an apostolic ghetto, leaving society as a whole to drift unresistingly into raw secularism. As for questions of validity and succession, Arnold believed that "what is called Succession, is exactly pedigree," and there was, he added, something "monstrously profane in making our heavenly inheritance like an earthly estate, to which our pedigree is our title."[128] His perfect idea of a national church was the comprehensive Protestantism "of the Edward the Sixth Reformers" of the sixteenth century, whom he lauded for "constructing a truly national and Christian church, and a truly national and Christian system of education."[129]

The difficulty with Arnold's broad-mindedness was that it was hard to know where it ought to stop, or if it could be stopped at all. "I believe that Arianism involves in it some very erroneous notions as to the object of religious worship," Arnold wrote in the *Principles of Church Reform*, "but if an Arian will join in our worship of Christ, and will call him Lord and God, there is neither wisdom nor charity in insisting that he shall explain what he means by these terms."[130] Arnold thus stands (along with Coleridge) at the head of a school of "broad-churchmanship" that included personalities as quixotic as F. D. Maurice, Charles Kingsley, and A. P. Stanley. It was a school (if it can actually be called that) that came to sit as loose by all other notions of theological dogma as it did by episcopal order. No better or more sensational example of where Arnold's ideas were heading can be found than in Arthur Penrhyn Stanley himself, one of Arnold's pupils, the son of one of Arnold's few friends among the clergy, and ultimately Arnold's admiring biographer. Appointed Dean of Westminster Abbey in 1863, Stanley pushed comprehensiveness as far as he dared and as often as he dared. He invited a Lutheran layman to lecture from the reading desk of the Abbey, put up a Scottish Presbyterian to do likewise, and, evenhanded to a fault, also invited Pusey to preach.[131] But nothing quite approached the uproar he created on June 23, 1870, when he invited the entire team of scholars who had been assembled to begin work on the proposed Revised Standard Version of the Bible to a joint communion service in Westminster Abbey. The translation team numbered seven non-Anglicans among them, all unconfirmed and comprising a mixed bag of Presbyterians, Methodists, Baptists, Congregationalists, and even one Unitarian, Dr. Vance Smith. The Anglo-Catholics were horrified at the "Westminster Scandal" and talked of leaving the Church of England "lest they should be involved in the guilt of this sacrilegious Communion." But the Archbishop of Canterbury, Archibald Campbell Tait, defended the Revisers' Communion, as did Bishops B. F. Westcott and J. B. Lightfoot, while the great New Testament scholar F.J.A. Hort demanded to know of the Anglo-Catholics "what is really lost to any great interest by the union once and for all of all English Christians round the altar of the Church."[132]

The Evangelicals looked on the shapeless theology of Arnold and Stanley with a thoroughly Tractarian despair; and Arnold, for his part, regarded with contempt their "foolish fondness for their particular phraseology, and from their want of ability to recognize the real features of any movement of opinion."[133] But all the same, they shared the enthusiasm of the Broad Churchmen for loosening the bonds of episcopal order. They were not nearly as interested in structural reformation of the church as Arnold—or perhaps, more truthfully, they were more candid about the unlikelihood that Arnold's proposals would attract serious support among dissenters— and were less entranced by visions of a national church. But they were no less energetic in their determination to Christianize England and to unite with any willing dissenter in the interests of achieving that end. They were more dogmatic than Stanley, but only in certain select areas (the Bible, the Atonement, and so forth); otherwise, not even Arnold threw the Jonah of episcopal polity overboard with more glee.

This evangelical urge toward confessional boundary-jumping eventually took on a life of its own, and in London in 1846 it took on institutional shape with the creation of the Evangelical Alliance. "The members of this Conference," declared the Alliance's organizing resolution, "are deeply convinced of the desirableness of forming a confederation on the basis of the great Evangelical principles held in common by them, which may afford opportunity to members of the Church of Christ cultivating brotherly love." Its doctrinal platform had only nine articles, beginning with the inspiration and authority of the Scriptures, passing through the Trinity and the Incarnation, affirming "the justification of the sinner by faith alone," and ending with a glance at "the obligation and perpetuity of the ordinances of Baptism and the Lord's Supper."[134] On that basis, the Evangelical Alliance attracted intense public interest from the start, and in 1851 the Alliance sponsored its first International Conference in London, with clergy and representatives from sixteen nations. Successive conferences in Paris (1856), Berlin (1857), Geneva (1861), and Amsterdam (1867) only grew bigger and better, until at the close of the Amsterdam conference Dr. S. Ireneus Prime, one of the American delegates, rose and invited the next conference to meet in New York City.

Prime's invitation to the Alliance to bring its assembly to the United States was at once a symbolic and a highly ironic gesture. On the one hand, nineteenth-century American Protestantism was crisscrossed and entangled with the growths and offshoots of the dozens of radical Protestant sects that had emigrated from Europe during the colonial period. Whether they owed their present existence to New England Puritans or Pietist Lutherans or Anabaptist Mennonites, American Protestants were mostly the children of the Radical Reformation, and the individual legacies of those sects had proven both tenacious and fecund. Despite the large-scale involvement of American Protestants in the upheavals of the Great Awakening of the 1740s, few groups involved in the Awakening were moved by that experience to loosen their grip on their sectarian identities. Although some prominent individuals, such as George Whitefield, Jonathan Edwards, and David Brainerd, seemed to offer an example of how evangelical revivalism could efface formal confessional boundaries in the common task of spreading the gospel, the examples were isolated and sometimes illusory. In fact, the Awakening often succeeded in further multiplying sectarian divisions (as in western Massachusetts and New Jersey); and once the revivalistic dust had settled, the intricate sectarian loyalties and identities reappeared, unmoved and (if anything) stronger for having been injected with a measure of revivalistic fervor.

In that sense, evangelical revival often condoned the persistence of American sectarianism, rather than sinking ecclesiastical differences in the fires of spiritual awakening. Although the revivals of the 1740s encouraged the children of the Awakening to see themselves as part of a great national evangelical Protestant consensus, still, for laypeople and clergy alike, the experience of revival was more likely to confirm them in their confessional or sectarian pigeonhole and increase their confidence in it as the place where they had seen grace come down in divine torrents. And much as they would respect the evangelicalism of other denominations (as Robert Baird's *Religion in the United States of America* showed in 1844), the revivals and awakenings only made people happier to cultivate their own gardens.

This is not to say that none of the American Protestant denominations surveyed by Baird's pioneering volume ever manifested an interest in church union beyond their own confessional circle, or experienced an embarrassment over their rampant and confusing divisions. Alexander Campbell's restoration movement, the "Presbygational" Plan of Union of 1801, Samuel Schmucker's "Apostolic, Protestant Confession" proposal, and even the Muhlenberg Memorial were all notable exceptions to sectarian complacency, and all of them were driven by evangelical convictions. The problem all of them shared, however, was that these convictions were fueled by a mix of pragmatism and fear, rather than serious theological concern over the prospect of a divided Christianity. Schmucker, Muhlenberg, and the "Presbygationalists" were more concerned about the efficiency of missions rather than church union, and there was more than a little touch of disingenuous nativism in plans that often looked like an effort to circle the Protestant wagons against the putative threat of hordes of immigrant Roman Catholics from Ireland and Germany. "Strength to the Protestant cause," declared William Augustus Muhlenberg, "is one of the objects of this movement [i.e., the Muhlenberg Memorial]." Those "who are true to the Reformation standards" needed to present "a united phalanx against Rome," Muhlenberg explained. "And who," he added, with a nativistic flourish, "in view of the advances of Rome upon our shores, will deem this a minor object?"[135]

For those reasons, each of these plans and platforms for unity treated questions of polity and order as obstacles to be nudged aside by genteel compromises, rather than seeing them as issues with a legitimacy of their own. Nor were the compromises consistent: Campbell really wanted church union, but he offered it only on the condition that all other Christians destroy their own polities and join him in practicing his own bizarre brand of congregationalism. Schmucker and Muhlenberg quietly surrendered any hope of achieving actual church union; they called instead for degrees of confederated effort that would leave other individual denominational identities unchallenged and unoffended.

The only other important concept of unity that antebellum American Protestants expended much effort in exploring was the "catholic unity" described and defended by John Williamson Nevin in the 1840s and 1850s and the Anglo-Catholics. Unfortunately, Nevin's "Mercersburg Theology" was never more than a temporary eruption on the small denominational horizon of the German Reformed Church, but Nevin had the virtue of looking the "church question" square in the face, and he insisted that neither the Campbellites nor the Schmuckerites had much to offer American Protestantism until it settled and defined its doctrine of the church. Struggling with that doctrine nearly sent Nevin to Rome, but the seriousness with which Nevin undertook that struggle is a good measure of the power of the "church question" when it was adequately posed, and that attraction explains a good deal of the fascination of Anglo-Catholicism to Episcopalian converts like Clarence Walworth. Unhappily for them, both Nevin and the Anglo-Catholics were moved by the attraction of Romantic ideology at a time when American theological life was still dominated by the prevalence of Scottish realism. Moreover, they chose to experiment in schemes of "catholic unity" at a time when American church life was still too frightened by the specter of immigrant Romanism to find much comfort in anything smacking of "catholicity."

American Protestantism in the first half of the nineteenth century therefore appears on the surface to be full of fraternal affection, ecumenical goodwill, and evangelistic purpose. Beneath that surface, however, the old denominational boundaries and identities, drawn in some cases upon the most extreme principles of the Radical Reformation, still persisted. And in a Republic where religious questions had been placed out of the hands of political settlements by the federal constitution, and where political localism was still very much the climate of opinion, there was little incentive in the air for change.

Little incentive, perhaps, but the very fact that Muhlenberg, Schmucker, Campbell, and Nevin had raised the question of church unity at all meant that there was certainly interest and maybe even hope that the smug sectarianism and cheap confederation could be transformed into the glittering carriage of union. Had not the United States only just fought a savage civil war that wrestled political localism into permanent submission to national sovereignty? In such an atmosphere of reasserted political union, perhaps the American churches could at last find their way to unions of their own; just as the Methodists, Baptists, and Presbyterians had presaged the breakup of the federal union in the 1830s and 1840s, the restoration of the union could signal the need for a similar process amongst the churches. And so it was that the great assemblage of the Evangelical Alliance arrived in New York City, waiting for the spark from heaven to fall on the most remarkable and propitious religious gathering on the North American continent.

The Alliance's New York conference was originally scheduled to meet in the autumn of 1870. But the outbreak of the Franco-Prussian War that year disrupted all the careful plans of the conference's hosts, and not until 1873 was the conference back on its tracks. When it finally opened on October 2, 1873, in the cavernous assembly hall of the Young Men's Christian Association of New York City, it was apparent that the planners had made good use of their extra time. The *New York Times* hailed the conference as "the most remarkable and important religious council which has ever been convened on this continent"; the *Philadelphia North American* marveled that "there is so much common to all of the communions named that it is wonderful they did not recognize the utility of this sort of federation earlier."[136] The crowds evidently agreed. For the sessions on October 5, "the galleries [of Association Hall] were thronged with the public, and such crowds were outside the doors, unable to gain admission, that another meeting was organized impromptu for Dr. Crosby's Church in Twenty-fourth Street."[137] A reporter for the *Hartford Courant* even noticed that some quiet ticket-scalping was going on.[138]

Considering the gilded roster of ecclesiastical worthies who had been recruited to preside over the convention, it is no wonder that the demand for seats to hear them far exceeded supply. More than one hundred speakers had been assembled to read papers for the ten days of the conference under the gilt-lettered banner "In necessitas unitas, in dubiis libertas, in omnibus caritas" (In essentials, unity; in nonessentials, liberty; in all things, charity).[139] They included the great names of Victorian Protestantism: Charles Hodge, the white-haired champion of Presbyterian Calvinism; James McCosh, the Calvinist philosopher and president of Princeton College; Charles Porterfield Krauth, the archconservative Lutheran; John Williamson Nevin and his famed associate Philip Schaff; Noah Porter, yet another Calvinist philosopher and president of Yale; Yale historian George Park Fisher; Canon W. H. Freemantle of the Church of England; William Augustus Muhlenberg and Bishop Gregory Thurston Bedell from the Protestant Episcopal Church; and, bearing a letter of greeting from the Archbishop of Canterbury, no less than the Very Rev. Robert Payne Smith, the Dean of Canterbury. Also scheduled to address the conference, on October 8, on the subject of "Roman and Reformed Doctrines of Justification Contrasted" was the Assistant Bishop of Kentucky, George David Cummins.

It is not clear why Cummins was invited to play such a prominent role in the Evangelical Alliance conference. He was, after all, only the assistant bishop of a comparatively small diocese in the Episcopal Church, and the names of Tyng, Eastburn, Johns, and Alfred Lee enjoyed greater prominence among Evangelical Episcopalianism. But among Cummins's few scattered publications had been a number of articles and addresses on the subject of justification by faith that had earned him some degree of notice on the subject. Moreover, the presence of William Augustus Muhlenberg among the movers and shakers of the conference may explain why not only Cummins but also Gregory Bedell were invited to be speakers. Whatever the reason, the invitation came to Cummins in 1871 and was continued over until the actual meeting of the conference in 1873.

Cummins left Louisville for New York on September 15, 1873, making a leisurely detour through Ohio, New York, and New England, and arrived in New York as the guest of Stephen Tyng Jr.

There is no record of Cummins's activities during the opening days of the conference, although he may have pricked up his ears with pleasure to hear the Dean of Canterbury read Archbishop Tait's letter bestowing good wishes on the Alliance and praying "that God may hasten the time . . . when all who love the Lord Jesus Christ sincerely may be able without compromise of principle to unite both outwardly and in spirit."[140] It is more likely that Cummins was present at the Madison Square Presbyterian Church on Sunday, October 5, where the pastor, Dr. William Adams, presided at the conference's joint communion service, for it was there that Cummins would have seen the Dean of Canterbury, who represented the highest tribunals of Anglicanism, come forward at Adams's invitation to assist in the celebration and receive the eucharistic elements from the Presbyterian Adams's own hands. It could only have consoled Cummins to behold at last tangible evidence that the "Evangelical Catholic" spirit was far from dead in Anglicanism. And beyond the dean's actions, what the dean had to say at that moment could have been taken right out of Cummins's mouth: "The Dean of Canterbury argued that as variety is a divine law, there should be a denominational unity that made allowance for diversity in non-essentials; and that this might be achieved, as no denomination could claim to have monopolized all truth."[141] To put point on his comments, Dean Smith added that "he knew no way in which the communion of saints could better be shown than in this partaking together of the sacramental bread and wine. . . . Each might have his own way of celebrating the divine ordinance, but when they met together from various climes they showed the reality of the unity that bound them together by partaking, in union with believers of every creed, of the emblems of their dead and risen Lord."[142]

In this heady ecumenical atmosphere, Cummins shook off whatever depression and disappointments he had experienced over the previous five years, and on October 8, he advanced to the pulpit of the Fourth Avenue Presbyterian Church (where the "third section" of the conference was to meet) to read his paper on the "Roman and Reformed Doctrines of Justification Contrasted." Ostensibly, his task was to set out the terms by which "the Romish and the Reformed Churches differ as to the *nature* of *justification*," and he fell to this task with a will. "Justification," Cummins declared in purely and classically Protestant terms, "is the office of God, and not the work of man"; it is "the act of God *accounting* us righteous, not making us so." In contrast to Roman Catholic definitions, justification "is the forgiveness of the sinner, the acceptance of the penitent believer, as righteous, into Divine Favor."[143] But his real target was not Roman Catholicism. Indeed, Cummins was willing to allow that "the Reformation was not a sudden outgrowth" of the sixteenth century and that the Reformation emerged out of the life of the Catholic Church "by slow processes, and by many and oftentimes unseen agencies."[144] Read between the lines, the true target of Cummins's address was Anglo-Catholicism. Not only did he smite the "Romish" view expressly with the Anglican Articles of Religion, but he ended his paper with a stirring call for evangelical Protestants to find, in the Protestant doctrine of justification, the philosopher's stone of church union:

> Fellow-Protestants of every name and nationality! children of the Reformation! this is the very citadel of our faith, the very heart of the Gospel. *This truth made the Reformation.* And, under God, this truth alone can preserve it; revive it where it has become sickly and feeble; purify it where it has fallen from its first estate. In the reception, maintenance, and personal experience of this "truth as it is in Jesus," we are to find the real unity of all Protestant Christendom. United to Christ by a saving faith, I am one with every other believer.[145]

And then, as if to give public proof of the second wind of confidence given him by the conference, Cummins accepted the invitation of Dr. John Hall of the Fifth Avenue Presbyterian Church to imitate the example of the Dean of Canterbury and preside at the final communion service of the conference on October 12. It was a warm autumnal afternoon, with a standing-room-only crowd on the floor and in the galleries of the church. Behind a large table in the chancel stood Hall, with Cummins on the left and the Scottish Free Presbyterian William Arnot on the right. Administration of the cup had fallen to Cummins, and before the administration, he made a brief address:

> Tenderly he told of his joy [recalled Alexandrine Cummins] on being permitted the privilege of uniting with them at such a service; of his delight in being allowed to partake of the precious feast of remembrance with those who were children of One Father; of that greater gathering thereafter with all who love the Lord Jesus in the many mansions prepared for them; and that this was but a foretaste of that eternal union in the House not made with hands.[146]

Old Dr. Arnot confessed "to a thrill of joy as I received the cup from [Cummins's] hands," and afterward the aged Presbyterian stopped Cummins to say plainly, "Ah my dear brother, if all Episcopalians were like you, and thought as you do, I would be one of them."[147] And perhaps for that moment, Cummins once again believed that such a union could be possible.

C H A P T E R

IV

THE OLD PATHS RESTORED

A Bishop Resigns

If the Evangelical Alliance had given Cummins new hopes for "evangelical catholicity," the consolation he drew from that probably lasted no more than twenty-four hours. Cummins and the rest of New York City arose the next morning to read, in the letters column of the *New York Tribune*, a slap directed at Dean Smith for daring to give non-Episcopalians any hope that they were welcome within the Anglican world. The letter was dated October 6 and was addressed to Horatio Potter as Bishop of New York, but the author clearly expected a much wider audience for his little broadside:

My Lord Bishop: I have just read with deep concern, in this morning's papers, that an eminent person, now staying in New York, on the occasion of a meeting of the Evangelical Alliance, has so far forgotten what, in my humble judgement, is due you, as the Bishop of this Diocese, and what is due to himself as a dignitary of the English Church, as to officiate with ministers of various denominations in a communion service which differed materially from that of the English and American Prayer Books. . . . I am glad to assure you that, amid various causes of anxiety in the Church of England, we have never had occasion as yet to lament a breach of ecclesiastical order so grave as this which the Dean of Canterbury has committed in your diocese. . . . It is by no means improbable that restless and unstable persons in England will seize upon this act of what I must presume to call open hostility to the discipline of the Church as an excuse, and apology, for attending, from time to time, the attractive services of the Church of Rome.[1]

The letter bore the signature of William George Tozer, "Late Missionary Bishop of Zanzibar."

Tozer was indeed the retired bishop of the Church of England's missionary diocese of Zanzibar. In fact, he was a pioneer of the Universities' Mission to Central Africa, "that most Anglo-Catholic of societies," and had gone out to East Africa in 1863 to meet the challenge of David Livingstone to civilize Africa, abolish the slave trade, and promote the gospel.[2] He had retired from his work in Zanzibar due to poor health in April 1873, and paid an extended visit to New York City, where he was enjoying the best of Anglo-Catholic society. "His Lordship is genial and cultivated," wrote Anglo-Catholic New York layman George Templeton Strong. "His talk is of hippopotami; he enjoys a joke and seems a thoroughly nice person."[3]

Some of the readers of Tozer's letter were inclined to treat it as a joke, as well. Phillips Brooks, the rector of Trinity Church, Boston, and a former classmate of Charles Edward Cheney at Alexandria, dismissed Tozer's broadside with wave of the hand:

What do you think of [Tozer] turning up in New York and writing a letter to Bishop Potter, complaining that the Dean of Canterbury had insulted the Archbishop of Canterbury? There is a roundabout confession and ingenuous intricacy about it all which is nuts to the ecclesiastical mind. One may count upon no end of dreary controversy about whether

Christ is willing that Dean Payne Smith should eat the Lord's Supper in an Episcopal Church, but not in Dr. Adams's Presbyterian Meeting House. As if all the great questions of faith and morals were settled, and that one minute squabble was the last thing left. Surely not till then will it begin to be of consequence.[4]

But Tozer did not seem to be joking in his letter, and its attack on Dean Smith was so slashing and so immediate that the real attention shifted from Tozer and onto Bishop Potter. No one had ever thought to ask Potter's permission to hold the Evangelical Alliance convention within the bounds of his diocese, and it probably would have done no good to ask anyway. But for precisely that reason, it was difficult for many observers not to believe that Potter had put Tozer up to writing the letter. The Evangelical newspaper, *Church and State*, edited by John Cotton Smith, frankly stated its suspicion that the real purpose of the letter was to satisfy Potter's injured episcopal vanity: "The Bishop of New York, it would seem from this letter, does not approve of the Evangelical Alliance." And none of these suspicions was allayed by Potter's disingenuous explanation of *how* the letter wound up in the hands of the *Tribune*—that it had fallen from Tozer's pocket onto a New York sidewalk, where a *Tribune* reporter happened to pick it up.[5]

When Cummins read Tozer's letter that Monday morning, it immediately appeared to him that there was yet another agenda under the cloak of the retired bishop's signature. Cummins had performed identically the same "breach of ecclesiastical order" as Dean Smith only the day before, and there was no way he could avoid concluding that Tozer had meant to hit him with the same stone. At once, Cummins sat down and wrote a feverish reply to Tozer that appeared on Thursday, October 16, in the *Tribune*:

Sir: In common with a vast number of Christian people, and especially of Episcopalians, I have been exceedingly pained to read in your columns this morning a communication from the "late missionary bishop of Zanzibar" to Bishop Horatio Potter, of this city severely censuring the Dean of Canterbury for his participation in a communion service at the Rev. Dr. [William] Adams's Church on the afternoon of October 5th. The eminent and profound scholar, the Dean of Canterbury, is able to defend himself from this attack. But I too am a bishop of the Protestant Episcopal Church, and one of three bishops of the Church who have participated in the work of the Evangelical Alliance. On last Sunday afternoon, October 12th, I sat at the table of the Lord in the church of the Rev. Dr. John Hall, and partook of the Lord's Supper with him and Rev. Dr. Arnot of Edinburgh, and administered the cup to the elders of Dr. Hall's church. I deny most emphatically that the Dean of Canterbury or myself have violated "the ecclesiastical order of the Church of England or of the Protestant Episcopal Church in this country," or have been guilty of an act of open hostility to the discipline of the said churches. There is nothing in the "ecclesiastical order" or "discipline" of the Church of England, or of the Protestant Episcopal Church in this country, forbidding such an act of intercommunion among Christian people, who are one in faith and love, one in Christ their great head.[6]

In hindsight, Cummins was probably correct to insist that neither the English nor the American canons actually forbade an "act of intercommunion"—largely because it was not clear in English or American canon law what an "act of intercommunion" constituted. The real question, however, was whether Smith and Cummins, by their acts at the Alliance communion services, had done more than merely function as parties to a canonical anomaly. Cummins had not preached at the service or otherwise given it supervision than by administering the chalice, but the trial of Stephen Tyng in 1869 had shown that what was really at stake was whether by *any* action (or even by his mere presence), Cummins had implied that the status of ordained Presbyterians was a matter of indifference to ordained Episcopalians. Similarly, Cummins had entered into a communion event that simply happened to be housed under a non-Episcopal roof, not into the stated service of another denomination. Otherwise, without Bishop Potter's prior permission, Cummins would have been in identically the same position as Tyng in 1869. But the October 12 communion service was, after all, only held under the auspices of the Evangelical Alliance, and held in the Fifth Avenue Presbyterian Church merely as a convenient venue. The Alliance was no rival, sectarian denomination, possessing orders to be recognized or not recognized, and its services fell neatly into the cracks in the customary arguments about jurisdiction and validity of orders. Yet, the question still remained whether Potter's episcopate was so utterly exclusive in its claims that *any* ministerial function of *any* clergyman in New York City was a matter of his business as "Bishop of New York." There were so many legal vagaries involved in Tozer's (and Potter's) charges that it is no surprise that

Potter preferred to let Tozer make them in a newspaper letter, rather than issue an ecclesiastical inhibition on his own authority as bishop. Cummins was hardly inclined to endorse the notion of Potter as the supreme prelate of New York City (where Tozer's letter addressed Potter as "Bishop of New York," Cummins's reply deliberately described Potter as being only "of this city"). But he wisely did not try to reopen the question of the extent of Horatio Potter's jurisdiction and whether it included the Evangelical Alliance's meetings. Instead, Cummins freely accepted the more threatening implication that his action gave tacit recognition to the validity of non-episcopal ministries. Remember, Cummins asserted, "the Church of England does not deny the validity of the orders of ministers of the non-Episcopal Churches" (on which point Cummins was at least legally correct), because "for many years after the beginning of the Reformation, Presbyterian divines were received in England and admitted to parishes without reordination, as Peter Martyr and Martin Bucer, who held seats as professors of theology in the universities of Oxford and Cambridge."

But Cummins's deepest resentment was reserved for Tozer's thinly veiled insinuation that this "act of intercommunion" was an act of practical treason because it would remove any incentive for Americans to come over into the Episcopal fold. If anything, Cummins replied, it was "the deadly evil of Ritualism, whose development is the revival of the Confessional," that was discouraging Americans from embracing the Episcopal Church as a "haven of rest." Only when that, and all the mighty pretensions of such men as Horatio Potter, were rooted out of the Episcopal Church would "many souls rejoice to see her the common center and bond of organic unity to all Protestant Christendom."[7]

Horatio Potter was no Bucer or Peter Martyr, and Anglo-Catholicism could not have been less interested in seeing the Episcopal Church become the center of a unified Protestant church. The publication of Cummins's letter in the *Tribune* brought down a hail of abuse, printed and otherwise, onto Cummins's unrepentant head. "As far as is possible, we gladly draw a veil over the vast number of abusive letters which at that time filled the many columns of the daily papers," Alexandrine Cummins wrote five years later. "Other prominent clergymen of the Church of England had acted in like manner, and nothing was said about it, or at best, only a passing sentence of disapproval; but threatened trial—deposition from the Episcopate—and bitter words were only a part of what he endured for joining fellowship [with] believers around the Table of the Lord."[8] Nor was she indulging a mild paranoia. Louis Tschiffely, the rector of Grace Church, Louisville, the Anglo-Catholic parish whose services had so galled Cummins during episcopal visits, gave the *Louisville Courier Journal* his "candid opinion" that it might be necessary to talk of "presenting the Bishop for trial for breaking his consecration vows."[9]

The first of these letters must have been written as early as the morning Cummins's reply appeared in the *Tribune*. In it, the Rev. John H. Drumm (rector of Trinity Church, Bristol, Pennsylvania) opened up a lengthy barrage in the *Tribune* on Cummins's claim that the Church of England had ever taken non-episcopally-ordained clergy into its ranks, characterizing Cummins's claim as a "silly and sinful" idea.[10] From that point, the correspondence went only downhill, with Cummins attacked as an "apostate," a "perjurer," a "fallen bishop," and for lacking either "courage or honesty."[11] On November 1, Potter himself directly joined the attack by publishing, this time in the *New York Evening Post*, a letter justifying all of Tozer's charges and adding a few of his own. Tozer's letter, Potter declared, "was well-considered," and he sneered at the Alliance communion services as "unnatural ecclesiastical unions which compel a sacrifice of truth and a violation of sacred obligations that have been deliberately assumed." This had at last climaxed in outright "undutifulness towards one's spiritual household."[12] Of course, these words were only part of a letter, not an ecclesiastical presentment, and Potter carefully avoided the actual use of Cummins's name anywhere in his comments. But the message was clear: Cummins had confessed, and only time would tell how he would be officially called to account for it.

Or would he? Potter must surely have realized that he was on much more slippery canonical ground in condemning Cummins's actions than he had been with Stephen Tyng, or Potter would have gone directly with his complaint to the Presiding Bishop, Benjamin Bosworth Smith. Moreover, Potter's attack rallied the support of a wide spectrum of Evangelicals for Cummins, and when the three Evangelical societies met at the Church of the Epiphany in Philadelphia on October 23, it was Cummins they invited to address them.

But the savagery of the attacks leveled at him in the public press had shaken Cummins's self-confidence down to its foundations. Alexandrine Cummins met one newspaperman who remarked, "I have never thought such bitterness possible towards any man who has done no wrong. I am old in journalistic work, but I confess this is beyond anything I have known among those calling themselves Christians."[13] Cummins's great expectations stood revealed as a

cruel hoax; the future of the Episcopal Church belonged securely in
the hands of bishops like Potter, not foreign deans like Smith or the
old presbyters like Muhlenberg. Moreover, there was really no
guarantee that wounded feelings and isolation would be the end of it
for Cummins. It was entirely possible, as Cummins saw things, that
Potter might eventually grow confident enough to call for a trial
before the House of Bishops, and what more assurance did Cummins have, canons or no canons, that he might not be sliced up the
same way as Tyng as yet another object lesson to the Evangelical
party? Degradation, suspension, deposition—all these could be visited upon Cummins's head whether he was actually guilty of anything or not. And then what recourse? Drag the affair into the civil
courts, like Cheney? Cummins could only have shuddered at the
prospect.

And even if an actual ecclesiastical trial never materialized, there
was already the considerable damage done by the grilling he had
endured in the newspapers. It takes some effort of the imagination
to remember that in 1873 the notion of Episcopal bishops pillorying
one another in the letters columns of major metropolitan newspapers was almost too unspeakable to discuss; and the spectacle of
one Episcopal bishop holding another up on toasting prongs must
have seemed, if anything, the very ultimate in the unspeakable, a
thing simply not done in polite society. After this sort of humiliation, it would be difficult to imagine how Cummins could return
to his already divided diocese in Kentucky and expect to exert
any meaningful direction or control. Was not his reputation as well,
and his expectations and principles, in hopeless tatters? Was it any
wonder, as Alexandrine Cummins put it, that Cummins "felt deeply
that his position in the Protestant Episcopal Church was indeed
changed"?[14]

So, when Cummins appeared in Philadelphia on October 23 before the fourteenth annual meeting of the American Church Missionary Society at the Church of the Epiphany, he was very much
an angrier and more reckless man. Flanked on the platform by Stephen Tyng and William Rufus Nicholson, the General Secretary of
the ACMS, Cummins railed "strongly against ritualism." There
were no more protests of loyalty, mixed with protests of dismay.
The *Philadelphia Inquirer* reported that Cummins "had visited a
church at Providence the other day, and it looked so much like a
Romish Church that if all the Protestant Episcopal Churches were
like it, he would never worship in one of them." Although Cummins "also touched upon confession, and showed how many people
in the Protestant Episcopal Church had been led to believe that it

was well to confess to a man," it was unquestionably the prayer book that, in Cummins's mind, was the chief problem. "There is but one remedy for all this," Cummins announced, "and that is to revise the prayer book," beginning with the word "priest."[15] Benjamin Leacock, who was at the Church of the Epiphany to hear Cummins's address, remembered Cummins holding up a copy of Morgan Dix's catechism and "an English Ritualistic Manual of devotion," and on this occasion "there was no mincing of matters." Cummins now believed he had nothing left to lose.

> He called attention [wrote Leacock] to the undisguised Romanism taught in the books—he affirmed that these teachings had been on the increase in the Church for the last ten years—that in each succeeding year they were more pronounced and distinct in their Romanism—that nothing had been done by the Church authorities to arrest the progress of these errors—that there was no disposition to do anything— that even where these unprotestant views were not looked upon with favor, there was a spirit of apathy concerning their growth—that the Church was not alive to the danger—that much of the Prayer Book was calculated to foster the growth of these doctrines and to unprotestantize the Church—that so long as this language was allowed to remain in the Prayer Book the Romanizing of the Church would go on—that only a thorough revision of the Prayer Book could arrest the error—that all attempts in this direction had thus far been a failure—that he was fully convinced that all further effort was useless—that there was no hope in the Church for revision. Then he concluded with these memorable words: "What next? It is as the Lord ordereth.
> Only Thou, our leader be
> And we still shall follow Thee."

The radical import of Cummins's words was clear, and the address provoked an uproar that John Cotton Smith vainly tried to silence with his gavel. Heman Dyer, sitting near Leacock in the church, "turned and said, with one of his peculiar laughs, 'That means a new Church, don't it?'"[16]

It is certainly possible that by October 23 Cummins had already concluded that the only way left open to him was to lead some form of Evangelical secession from the Episcopal Church to reconstitute American Episcopalianism on a new and more Evangelical foundation. Three years before, he had met with Stephen Tyng to contemplate a similar possibility, only to reject it. And in the midst of his present crisis, Charles Edward Cheney had written to him to hope "that this may pave the way to the organization of a free Episcopal Church."[17] But it was by no means clear to Cummins that "a new church" was his only, or even his best, option. Even in the anger that permeated his address to the American Church Missionary Society, his only suggestion was for prayer book revision, even though he was sure that the way to such revision was probably hopelessly blocked. Returning to New York City on October 30 (where he found waiting for him a letter of thanks from Dean Smith "for your letter in my defense against the attacks of Bishop Tozer"), Cummins called a meeting of his friends and other interested parties at the home of Colonel John Dake, on East Fifty-Seventh Street, to consider what direction he should take.

Few of those who attended this gathering were sure what advice to give. In addition to the Dakes, the "conference" included four other prominent New York laypeople (James L. Morgan, Dr. Gustavus Sabine, G. M. Tibbetts, and Benjamin Wetmore); two serving clergymen, the colorful William Tufnell Sabine of the Church of the Atonement, and Benjamin Leacock; an exotic missionary named William Riley, who had organized an Episcopal missionary jurisdiction in Mexico called "The Church of Jesus" which enjoyed the sponsorship of the American Church Missionary Society; and even one former clergyman, Mason Gallagher, formerly of the Diocese of Kentucky (though he had left it before Cummins's arrival) who had resigned from the Episcopal Church in 1871. The options they discussed were almost as numerous as the individuals present. Cummins might leave the Episcopal Church and return to the Methodists, but that he seems never to have seriously considered. He might wait for the next General Convention, then only seven months away, "to rally the discontented element around him, to determine the rubrical relaxations and liturgical changes that were wanted, to go to the General Convention with these, and there, if they were not granted, to secede in a body." This was Leacock's advice, but Cummins rejected that too. A still more strange proposal emerged from William Riley, who proposed that Cummins join him in Mexico and bring his episcopate with him for "The Church of Jesus." Cummins himself remained anxious and unsure. "I have formed no plans," Cummins confessed to his wife before entering the meeting. "God, I believe, will lead me—I wish only to do his will." But by the end of the "conference," only one conclusion seemed to have emerged with any clarity: no matter where he might go, go he must. His resignation from the Episcopal Church was inevitable,

Cummins told Leacock at the conclusion of the meeting. "He could never return to his Diocese and distress his conscience as he had been doing. That question was therefore settled."[18]

For nine days thereafter, Cummins agonized in a last indecision before finally putting his pen to the fatal paper. "He was frequently engaged in prayer," recalled Alexandrine Cummins. "It was his custom to pray three times a day."[19] He also visited frequently with the elderly William Augustus Muhlenberg in Muhlenberg's rooms at St. Luke's Hospital, and Muhlenberg punctually returned Cummins's visits at Cummins's temporary residence with the Dakes on East Fifty-Seventh Street.[20] But by November 10, Cummins could put off his final action no longer. He sat down to address to Presiding Bishop Smith his last and most painful official letter:

> RIGHT REVEREND AND DEAR BISHOP: Under a solemn sense of duty, and in the fear of God, I have to tell you that I am about to retire from the work in which I have been engaged for the last seven years in the diocese of Kentucky, and thus to sever the relations which have existed so happily and harmoniously between us during that time. . . .
>
> First, then, you well know how heavy has been the trial of having to exercise my office in certain churches in the diocese of Kentucky, where the services are conducted so as to symbolize and to teach the people doctrines subversive of the "truth as it is in Jesus," and as it was maintained and defended by the Reformers of the sixteenth century. . . . I have lost all hope that this system of error, now prevailing so extensively in the Church of England and in the Protestant Episcopal Church in this country, can be or will be eradicated by any action of the authorities of the Church, legislative or executive. The only true remedy, in my judgment, is the judicious yet thorough revision of the Prayer Book, eliminating from it all that gives countenance, directly or indirectly, to the whole system of Sacerdotalism and Ritualism. . . .
>
> One other reason for my present action remains to be given. . . . On the last day of the late conference of the Evangelical Alliance, I participated in the celebration of the Lord's Supper, by invitation, in the Rev. Dr. John Hall's church. . . . It was a practical manifestation of the real unity of "the blessed company of all faithful people" whom "God hath knit together in one communion and fellowship in the mystical body of his Son, Jesus Christ." The results of that partici-

pation have been such as to prove to my mind that such a
step cannot be taken by one occupying the position I now
hold without sadly disturbing the peace and harmony of this
Church, and without impairing my influence for good over a
large portion of the same Church, very many of whom are
within our own diocese. . . .

I therefore leave the Communion in which I have labored
in the sacred ministry for over twenty-eight years, and transfer my work and office to another sphere of labor. I have an
earnest hope and confidence that a basis for the union of all
Evangelical Christendom can be found in a communion
which shall retain or restore a primitive Episcopacy and a
pure scriptural liturgy, with a fidelity to the doctrine of justification by faith only. . . .

I am, dear bishop, faithfully yours in Christ,

GEORGE DAVID CUMMINS[21]

Three days later, the aged Bishop Smith wrote Cummins an agonized and fatherly reply, begging Cummins to reconsider before the
matter became public. If Smith's few years of association with Cummins as a bishop had taught him anything about Cummins, it was
Cummins's habit of making abrupt and emotional decisions, and he
posed to Cummins a question that would haunt him for the next
two-and-a-half years: "Can it be possible that you have formed such
a determination after duly weighing the gravity and the magnitude
of the consequences of a step without precedent in the history of our
beloved Church?" At least, Smith hoped, "this painful subject will
not be brought before the public."[22] But Cummins was beyond re-
call. In Cummins's mind, it was clearly Horatio Potter who had
already made the whole affair public, and Cummins ignored Smith's
plea in the certainty that there was no point to remaining silent
about his own determinations.

Cummins was probably right, since the newspapers quickly picked
up the news of Cummins's letter from their own sources in Louisville.
On November 14, an unidentified Louisville stringer filed a story
with the New York and the Philadelphia newspapers, announcing
the news of the resignation and citing "private letters" from Cummins that "intimate his intention to continue the Episcopal office on
the basis of Bishop White's prayer-book."[23] The next day, the *New
York Times* broke the news of Cummins's resignation on its Sunday
editorial page, noting that "his resignation has been brought about
by a series of severe criticisms on the part of his High Church brethren, based upon his conduct when a delegate to the Evangelical Alli-

ance meeting in New York." The editorial knowingly added that the premier cause "of the offending of Bishop Cummins was his participation in a Communion service at Dr. Hall's Church in the City." As a result, Cummins "objects to remain in fellowship with those who consider his fraternizing with Christians of other denominations at the Lord's Supper to be an act calling for censure."[24]

The Louisville reporter, whose coup was published in the *Times* side by side with the *Times* editorial (and also on the front page of the *Philadelphia Inquirer*) went on to observe that Cummins's letter "has created a profound sensation among Episcopalians here." Cummins's resignation, "it is thought, will create some complications between the two phases of theology in the Kentucky Episcopal Church."[25] More important, it would create complications for George David Cummins. On November 22, Smith wrote again to Cummins, this time in his formal capacity as Presiding Bishop, informing Cummins that, in accordance with the canons of the Church, unless Cummins recanted or withdrew his action within six months, "you will be deposed from the ministry of this Church."[26]

We Have Laid Down Our Course

For almost an entire month, since the close of the Alliance convention, Cummins had been under the severest of mental and emotional strains. But once his letter of withdrawal had been signed and sealed, the tension broke, and now Cummins wanted only a little peace and quiet away from the charged atmosphere of New York City. The opportunity for such a retreat came in the form of an invitation from Marshall B. Smith, former editor of *The Protestant Churchman* and until 1869 rector of St. John's Church in Passaic, New Jersey. A graduate of Virginia Theological Seminary in the same class with Charles Edward Cheney, Smith had been ordained by the same Alfred Lee who had ordained Cummins. However, the treatment meted out to Cheney in 1869 was sufficient provocation for Smith to hand in his resignation from the priesthood, and he instead entered the ministry of the Reformed Church of America, in the Classis of Paramus, New Jersey. All the while, though, he continued to keep his eye on the mounting turbulence in the Episcopal Church, and on November 9 he boldly addressed a letter to Cummins, urging him in the direction of founding a new church. As soon as the news of Cummins's withdrawal became public, Smith offered his own home in Passaic as a refuge for the exhausted bishop, and so on November 11 Cummins gratefully boarded the train to Passaic.

On the way, Cummins found himself thrown together with Mason Gallagher. Gallagher was another exile, like Marshall Smith. A graduate of General Theological Seminary, Gallagher was a pugnacious Orangeman who, even as a seminarian, was remembered for having a penchant for gymnastics and boxing. It is not altogether clear what his previous relationship to Cummins might have been. Gallagher had briefly served in the Diocese of Kentucky in the 1860s, but he had left Kentucky for the diocese of Western New York before Cummins's consecration in Kentucky in 1866. In New York, he had served as rector of the Church of the Evangelists in Oswego, New York, where he had some passing acquaintance with Charles Edward Cheney, and then moved to New York City to become rector of St. Ann's Church in Brooklyn. By 1871, the ever-growing influence of the Anglo-Catholics had been more than he could stomach, so he resigned and moved to Passaic, where he lived comfortably off a private income. All the evidence suggests that Cummins had known Gallagher personally only since meeting him at the Alliance, and afterward at the "conference" at the Dakes'. Nevertheless, it was to Gallagher that Cummins now gave the first glimmer of his plans, suggesting that his purpose was to organize an independent parish in New York City, with himself as rector, and from that vantage point await the outcome of the impending General Convention. (Benjamin Leacock seems to have had the same impression of Cummins's intentions, or at least believed that this was the path Cummins ought to have followed.)[27] Gallagher could not help his own curiosity. Knowing that Cummins was to be staying with Marshall Smith, Gallagher invited himself into Smith's library the next afternoon.

There Gallagher found Smith and Cummins, together with yet another exile, Smith's father-in-law, Colonel Benjamin Aycrigg, who had come by around noon to visit Smith and stayed to talk with Cummins. At age sixty-nine, Aycrigg was the senior of the group, short and gruff with an immense salt-and-pepperish beard. He was also a lifelong Episcopalian and a highly successful civil engineer, and "as an avowed Low-churchman" he had served as chairman of the Finance Committee of the Diocese of New Jersey and had helped found St. John's Church in Passaic, where his son-in-law had been the rector. But Marshall Smith's successor had leanings toward various ritual innovations, and these had come to an unpleasant climax on October 30, 1873, when the rector made several less than complimentary comments from the pulpit of St. John's about the Evangelical Alliance. Aycrigg stormed out of the church, never to return, and now he found himself in the same room with the very man who had made the Evangelical Alliance a matter of debate in the Episcopal Church.[28]

"We were simply spending together a social afternoon and evening," Aycrigg recalled, but none of them could stay for long off the subject of Cummins's future prospects. "I think that there was no definite beginning on this point, but that it grew imperceptibly," wrote Aycrigg in his memoirs, but in short order it became the topic of consuming interest. It kept them up into the night and resumed the next morning after breakfast, until at last, by ten o'clock on the morning of November 13, Cummins instructed Marshall Smith: "Take pen and paper and write as I dictate."[29] Sometime during those eighteen-odd hours in Marshall Smith's library, Cummins was persuaded to raise the stakes of his independent-parish scheme and do what he was in all likelihood already half-persuaded to do anyway—organize a new Episcopal Church.

This was no light decision. Churches, especially in the Anglican family, are not made overnight, for the Episcopalian ethos has built into itself an inertia and an institutional passivity that make any motion (let alone a first motion) slow under the best conditions and almost impossible under normal ones. What was worse, an Episcopal Church could not simply spring up by itself. As a liturgical church, with ingrained liturgical instincts, any new-model Episcopalianism would also need a prayer book to use, and at once. Yet the only prayer book available in common use in the United States was a book that Cummins had already declared unacceptable without serious revision. In this case, however, history and Marshall Smith came to Cummins's rescue. Although Cummins was not a liturgical scholar, he had somewhere learned of the abortive 1785 prayer book, proposed for use under William White as the first American Episcopal liturgy. Copies of the book were exceedingly rare, however, and Cummins did not actually acquire one himself until the October 30 "conference" at the Dakes'. Ironically, that copy had come from the hands of Mason Gallagher, who had in turn borrowed it from the library of Marshall Smith with the expectation that "it would form a desirable basis for the establishment of a new communion."[30] Cummins had been attracted, then, by the 1785 prayer book's elimination of all the offensive sacramental vocabulary of "priest," of "regeneration" in baptism, of "sacrifice" in the Lord's Supper, and he had prevailed on the laypeople at the October 30 "conference"—Morgan, Tibbetts, Wetmore, and Sabine—to underwrite a private reprinting of the book "*verbatim et literatim et punctuatim.*"[31]

But Cummins's interest at that point seemed merely personal (only fifty copies were struck off), and he may have only wanted to distribute the reprints among friends with a view to offering historical precedent for the liturgical revisions in the prayer book for which Evangelicals had been calling for years. Now, however, the 1785 prayer book offered a shortcut to providing an alternative Episcopal liturgy for a new church, and in that light Cummins threw aside his last hesitations and called for Marshall Smith to take up his pen.

The document Cummins dictated to Smith, which became known as the "Call to Organize" (and which still survives as two close-written legal-sized sheets of paper, in Smith's handwriting), began with an unhesitating declaration of theological confidence:

> DEAR BRETHREN: —The Lord has put it into the hearts of some of his servants who are, or who have been, in the Protestant Episcopal Church, the purpose of restoring the old paths of their fathers, and of returning to the use of the Prayer Book of 1785, set forth by the General Convention of that year, under the special guidance of the venerable William White. . . .

To that end, Cummins announced that

> on Tuesday, the second Day of December, 1873, a meeting will be held in Association Hall . . . in the City of New York . . . to organize an Episcopal Church on . . . a basis broad enough to embrace all who hold "the faith once delivered to the saints" as that faith is maintained by the Reformed Churches of Christendom; with no exclusive and unchurching dogmas toward Christian brethren who differ from them in their views of polity and Church order.

And to make utterly clear that he had finally passed over his own personal Rubicon, Cummins added: "The purpose of the meeting is to *organize*, and not to discuss the expediency of organizing."[32]

That last sentence conveys a real sense of emotional relief, as well as a sense of rejuvenated purpose for Cummins. Once jolted into motion, Cummins would now brook no delay. He took the noon train back to New York, and in two days had page proofs of the "Call to Organize" back from the printer. On November 16, the final copies of the "Call to Organize" were printed in the form of mail circulars, and the first batch was put into the New York City mail on the morning of November 17, 1873.[33]

That left Cummins exactly two weeks to prepare for the inauguration of his new movement, and the omens for it were mixed. On November 27, Charles Edward Cheney mounted his pulpit in Chicago to preach a Thanksgiving Day sermon from Psalm 107: "Oh! that men would therefore praise the Lord. . . . "[34] Cheney, according to the Chicago newspapers, praised Cummins's call, "thanking God that there was one Protestant Episcopal bishop in the United States who had the courage to proclaim the truth." It was, Cheney said, "a grand and hopeful thing, that there was a bishop who preferred the path of God's truth to the walks of the world's favor."[35] The next day, Cheney took the train for New York City to be on hand for the Association Hall meeting.[36] Benjamin Leacock, returning to New York City on November 20 from church business, found his copy of the "Call to Organize" in his stack of mail. He thought the matter over for two days, and then, on November 22, certain that he was putting his neck into a noose, Leacock resigned from the Episcopal Church and walked over to East Fifty-Seventh Street to put his "letter of adhesion" personally into Cummins's hands. On November 26, John Cotton Smith's newspaper, *Church and State*, printed the "Call to Organize" in full. The next day, the *New York Tribune* did the same, and then papers all across the country. Stephen Tyng threw open the Church of the Holy Trinity for Cummins's use for a pair of preliminary meetings with a handpicked steering committee on November 28 and December 1. Even the ancient William Augustus Muhlenberg hobbled over from St. Luke's Hospital to call on Cummins and put his personal library at Cummins's disposal, "assuring him that he would always be ready to assist him with his counsel, and in all ways with his powers."[37] Far away, in West Virginia, James Allen Latane, the rector of St. Matthew's Church in Wheeling, had finally reached the point of despair over his future in the Episcopal Church and had set Sunday, November 23, as his last service before going over to "some other Church where I could at least labor with a clear conscience." But that morning his senior warden burst into the vestry room and said, "Mr. Latane, have you heard of the secession?" "No, what secession?" In reply, Latane was told of Cummins's resignation and the "Call to Organize." Latane said later:

> I made no comment. I could not express what I felt. It seemed to me a marvelous thing that in my distress and perplexity the Lord should have provided relief at such a time and in such an unexpected way. . . . From that Sunday

morning, I was in full accord with Bishop Cummins [and] was laboring for the same end.[38]

On the other hand, Cummins's withdrawal and the "Call to Organize" provoked from the Anglo-Catholics howls of outrage tinged with a sense of panic that at last one of the Evangelical bishops intended to carry out what for years had increasingly been treated as mere bluff. The *Church Journal* derided Cummins for "his wretched effort at a wretched sin" and characterized the "Call to Organize" as "a poor, futile, and ridiculous effort on the part of an unbalanced and unlearned man."[39]

> Perhaps nothing in the last few years becomes his episcopate so well as the leaving of it. He has been half-hearted in his position. He has not believed in the Church of which he was a bishop. He has had no faith in her ways or her tendencies. He has made no secret of this. There have been rumors of long standing that Bishop Cummins would, when time was ripe, head a schism. His act in the communion he speaks of was, as he well knew, a deliberate insult to the Church, and a stultification of his office as Bishop. . . . There are few more popular speakers, of the ordinary fluent American type, than he. But no man ever, we believe, considered him a theologian, a man of learning, or a judicious man.[40]

A Baltimore layman, George Andrew Witte, quickly published a leaflet, "Exsurge Domine," in which he accused Cummins of having been led "on the way of perdition by having heresy substituted for Christ's doctrine."[41] *The Nation* simply wrote Cummins off as "not a man of sufficient force, or learning, or eloquence to make his withdrawal of serious importance, or his new undertaking likely to be very successful."[42] And Morgan Dix, whose catechism Cummins had held up for ridicule in Philadelphia a month before, dismissed Cummins and the "Call to Organize" as "a nine days' wonder, and there it would end."[43]

The response in Cummins's own Kentucky diocese was more ambivalent. Cummins had sent a copy of his letter of resignation to the secretary of the diocesan Standing Committee, E. T. Perkins, and on November 18 the Standing Committee called itself together in Christ Church, Louisville, to certify Cummins's abandonment of the episcopate. But even though the action was purely a formality, one of the five members of the committee, the Rev. W. H. Platt, refused to sign the certificate, and the committee as a whole was unwilling to sanction any but the most cautious canonical proceedings against Cummins. But the preponderance of opinion across the diocese was clearly against Cummins, and indeed he had made too many enemies in Kentucky for them not to find his resignation an opportunity for eradicating whatever influence he had exerted in the diocese. J. S. Shipman, who had been humiliated by Cummins's removal of his rose cross from the altar of Christ Church, Lexington, the previous May, now rose to attack Cummins from the pulpit of Christ Church as a hypocrite whose conduct "darkens with guilt the course which he proposes for the future."[44]

But none of these thrusts wounded Cummins nearly as much as the criticisms hastily pitched at him by fellow Evangelicals, who had pleaded for years for a bishop to do precisely what Cummins was now proceeding to do. The *Church Union* marveled that "men who for years have been making our ears ring with their wails against oppression and puseyism" now rose to "publicly proclaim their sorrow when a chance for relief is offered." It was, the *Church Union* editorialized, "something that almost takes our breath away."[45] But all the same, old Stephen Tyng, Sr. (parting company on this point with his son, who sympathized with Cummins) ascended his pulpit at St. George's in New York City on two consecutive Sundays to state emphatically his "entire disapproval" of Cummins's actions. "By seceding," Tyng announced, Cummins "had betrayed the very trust committed to him" and would end up only "more solitary, a monad, a severed branch, a cloud carried to and from with the changes of the wind."[46] "The Bishop acted by himself and against the protest of Evangelical men," claimed a correspondent of the *Louisville Courier Journal*. "Even the most radical oppose his course and will give his movement no support."[47] Bishop Henry Washington Lee of Iowa, who had preached the sermon for Cummins's consecration, urged Cummins on November 28 to renounce his withdrawal from the Episcopal Church as "the great mistake of your life":

> I know full well how hard it is to bear what you and many others have borne in connection with the present condition of our Church; but it does not appear to me that the point has yet been reached, even if it ever can be, when an actual division and separation are justified and demanded by the leadings of God's Providence. I could earnestly desire and pray that a new and distinct organization might not be effected at the proposed meeting. A secession or schismatical movement

at this time would, in my opinion, be a greater evil than those we are now bearing. . . . It were far better for our extreme Ritualistic brethren to finally secede to the Church of Rome, to which they are tending, than for yourself and others of like mind to leave such a church as ours for a new ecclesiastical organization.[48]

The unkindest Evangelical cut of all came on December 1, when a group of Philadelphia Evangelical clergy put their own counter-"Call" into the mail. It consisted of a postcard that the signers urged recipients to have reprinted in their local newspapers. It read:

The undersigned, having heard with profound sorrow of the movement now making by Bishop Cummins for the organization of a new Church on the basis of the Prayer Book of 1785, desire to say that they have no sympathy with this measure, and that it does not represent the feelings of Evangelical men.[49]

Four weeks before, remarked the *Church Union*, most if not all of the same men had made the Church of the Epiphany quake with applause and acclamation for Cummins. "All Evangelical Episcopalians have had and professed the same grievances, and have contemplated the possibility of a secession in consequence," remarked the elderly dean of Virginia Theological Seminary, William Sparrow. "How, then, when one of their number makes the possibility actual, can they, in a moment, reverse the engine and move backward? They might think Cummins' mode of procedure unwise, but the procedure itself is only what their hearts have been craving for a quarter of a century."[50]

Sparrow's incredulity was shared by many later Reformed Episcopalians who eventually dismissed the refusal of Tyng and Lee and the signers of the Philadelphia card simply as the faintheartedness of false friends. But the criticisms like these, coming from Cummins's former allies and well-wishers, really do raise questions about the wisdom of Cummins's entire enterprise in ways that the snarlings of the Anglo-Catholics do not. Not the least of these questions concerned Cummins himself: Was he really (as he saw himself) a martyr for Evangelical principles, or merely the imprudent (or perhaps ambitious) author of a schism so needless that even his own brethren hung back? Beyond that, there was the larger question of what Cummins actually intended by this new movement: Was Cummins about to create a party movement for party Protestants who could not bear up under Anglican theological pluralism, or was he going to somehow succeed in creating a workable vehicle for Muhlenberg's "evangelical catholicity"?

The answer to those questions, in a rather cautious way, is probably *no*. At least two things emerge as reasonable certainties about Cummins's "Call to Organize." First, Cummins genuinely seems never to have betrayed any hint of pursuing a private agenda or conducting a personal vendetta in the plans for his new organization. Much as he was willing in Kentucky to stuff parishes full of American Church Missionary Evangelicals in blatantly political fashion, Cummins never seems to have seen that as an instrument for his own personal advancement (indeed, surprisingly few of his own protégés in Kentucky followed him out of the Episcopal Church). Benjamin Aycrigg later furiously denied charges that Cummins had demanded assurances of anywhere from $40,000 to $100,000 from unnamed backers as the condition for leading a movement, nor did Aycrigg see anything in Cummins that looked like malicious pique. To the contrary, Aycrigg recalled:

> I was present with Bishop Cummins when a gentleman, who was a stranger to both of us, called, gave his name, and requested to withdraw his adhesion which he sent by mail, signed to a copy of the Call, saying that he was so badgered about it that he could find no peace. The Bishop, smiling, said, "Certainly, if you desire it." He expressed his thanks, saying that he could not have received a greater favor.[51]

Even Benjamin Leacock, who privately considered Cummins a poor judge of character and something less than the ideal leader, nevertheless acknowledged that Cummins never displayed the slightest sense of self-interest in his own movement. "He was too honest himself to suppose men any otherwise than what they seemed," Leacock lamented, and continued:

> I have seen him patient and apparently unruffled under the most uncalled for and insulting provocation. On one occasion we left a Committee room together. My own temper had been greatly excited. I put my hand on his shoulder and said: "My dear Bishop, how could you stand it?" "My dear brother, the Lord helped me," was his reply. He dropped the subject. We were together for more than an hour but he never alluded to the unpleasantness again. It was the same in regard to many cruel attacks made upon him by his quondam

friends and fellow bishops. As his ear would catch one of their rasping utterances, his grieved spirit would find relief in the short rapid ejaculation, "Oh." This was all. Never a word of complaint or remonstrance did I ever hear escape his lips.[52]

By the same token, Cummins's movement resists being tagged as simply an anti-Anglo-Catholic schism, although later there would be no shortage of both supporters and critics who would be inclined to see it that way. Cummins's new movement was, in fact, a much more complex affair than even later Reformed Episcopalians have been inclined to admit, because the incident that triggered Cummins's decision to resign from the Episcopal Church had surprisingly little to do with the customary Evangelical debates over baptism, the Lord's Supper, or even "apostolic succession." What really moved Cummins over the brink was the question of ecumenicity— of what defined the Church and how far one was willing to go in bringing others within that definition. That, together with Cummins's attachment to William Augustus Muhlenberg, links Cummins's interests far more closely to the ambitious ecumenical interests of Muhlenberg, Stanley, and Arnold than even to most of Cummins's fellow Evangelicals. The things Cummins had objected to most in Tozer and Potter had little to do with the usual doctrinal or liturgical grievances Evangelicals nursed against the Anglo-Catholics. Cummins had met enough Anglo-Catholics in his time, and even though the meeting revolted him he had refrained from any hue and cry for suppressions, expulsions, and trials simply for holding those notions, and there is no record that Cummins ever specifically hounded the tiny band of Kentucky Anglo-Catholics or sought their trial or expulsion from his diocese. It was, as Cummins saw it, the way in which these gentlemen proposed to use their principles to draw the drapes and close up the Episcopal house to every other American church body that finally drove him out of the church and toward a new organization. In that light, Cummins was clearly more than just a narrow-gauge Protestant reactionary. Ironically, if Cummins was dreaming of anything when he issued his "Call to Organize," he was dreaming of a great pan-Evangelical future under a cloudless Anglican sky.

But that may well have been his undoing as far as gathering Evangelical support was concerned. Had Cummins chosen the sacraments or liturgy as his primary battlefield, he might actually have generated more enthusiasm. In nineteenth-century terms (not to mention Cummins's own terms), however, ecumenicity was simply too vague and airy a principle for most nineteenth-century Evangelicals to grasp, much less to fight for. The choice of the 1785 prayer book probably cost him even more Evangelical support, not so much because other Evangelicals were more perspicacious than Cummins about its contents, but because by 1873 almost all of them had some pet scheme of prayer book revision of their own to promote and saw no reason to abandon theirs to go chasing Cummins's.

That, in turn, suggests a still larger explanation for the sharp edge of Evangelical criticisms of Cummins. Although Cummins necessarily bulks large in the telling of the Reformed Episcopal story, it is still true that he had little of the stature of such Evangelical bishops as Henry Lee or Manton Eastburn, or even presbyters like Muhlenberg or the senior Tyng. In 1873, Cummins was still only a rising figure in the church, and when he decided to withdraw and organize "another sphere" for his episcopal labors, the great men among the Evangelicals displayed little but irritation that they had not been consulted, or that they should be expected to follow a path blazed by a mere assistant bishop of the Diocese of Kentucky. "Bishop Cummins' name alone was not a tower of strength," admitted Benjamin Leacock, and Leacock was given a convincing demonstration of that fact. When one of Leacock's acquaintances inquired of Stephen Tyng Sr. why he did not join Cummins, "the doctor straightened himself up, turned on him with one of his stern expressions, and in sarcastic tones said: 'Who is Bishop George David Cummins, who is the Rev. Mason Gallagher (and so repeating half a dozen of our names), that I should follow them!'" Leacock remarked, "This was characteristic of the man," but it was also characteristic of what the Evangelical party had become by the 1870s.[53]

For the moment, however, it was neither the criticisms of the Anglo-Catholics nor the haltings of the Evangelicals that were the greatest obstacle to the success of Cummins's "Call." It was the threat of canonical, and perhaps civil, action by his erstwhile brethren in the House of Bishops. Presiding Bishop Smith's first response to Cummins's letter of withdrawal was surprisingly mild, and Smith had evidently missed the implication in Cummins's letter about transferring his "office and work to another sphere." The "Call to Organize" jolted Bishop Smith out of his indulgence. It was apparent that Cummins meant to lead a secession movement, and lead it as an Episcopal bishop, but it was also clear that Smith could do nothing to stop him, for the canonical mechanism for dealing with "apostate" bishops had not been constructed with a situation like Cummins's in mind.

Technically speaking, Cummins could be dealt with as being in active violation of the canons, in which case the legal remedy was for Cummins's accusers to obtain a presentment and proceed as quickly as possible. Under Canon 9, Title 2, of the then-existing canons, Cummins could be held to be an apostate to his ordination vows and tried, suspended, and deposed from the episcopate. Unfortunately, a trial was a public and unpleasant affair, and it would be more unpleasant because Cummins could not be found guilty without causing most of the Evangelicals in the church to be outraged and perhaps driving them straight into his arms. Given what had happened with Stephen Tyng and Charles Edward Cheney, it was not clear that a trial would serve any useful purpose beyond giving Cummins, like Cheney, an even better platform on which to advertise his martyrdom. Even more annoying was that the national canons provided that such a sentence would be handed down under the oversight of the diocese where the trial would take place, and if the sentence was to be handed down under the Kentucky diocesan canons, sympathy for Cummins within his own diocese might make the result unpredictable. On the other hand, if a presentment and trial seemed too unappetizing, it was always possible to resort to Canon 8, Title 2, which specifically covered cases in which a bishop would "abandon the Communion of this Church." This canon had the additional advantage of requiring no public trials or hearings. It mandated only that a certificate of abandonment be issued to the Presiding Bishop by the errant bishop's diocesan Standing Committee; the Presiding Bishop could then declare the bishop in question officially deposed. For dealing with Cummins, this method certainly appeared neater and cleaner, but it had one glaring defect: the Presiding Bishop was required to wait six months from the issuance of the certificate before the deposition could take place, ostensibly so that the accused bishop could have the opportunity to clear his name or sort out his second thoughts. That six-month waiting period, even more than the fifteen pages of procedural details in the canons, which accompanied the alternative procedure of presentment and trial of a bishop, made any movement against Cummins a lengthy and difficult business.

Understandably, Benjamin Bosworth Smith wavered hesitantly between proceeding quickly to a presentment and trial, or settling for the slower but less confrontational strategy of deposition.[54] The risks were fairly evenly balanced: a trial could backfire nastily, but if Smith allowed Cummins the canonical six-month waiting period, Cummins's episcopal acts continued to be as canonically valid as any other bishop's. That meant, as Smith realized, that during the next

six months Cummins was able to perform confirmations, ordinations—even consecrations of new bishops for his movement—all of
which would be as canonically valid as any performed by Smith
himself.

Here, ironically, the tidy mechanism of "apostolic succession"
boomeranged on its promoters, for if ordination and consecration
involved only the communication of some intrinsic ministerial
grace, then surely Cummins had it as a bishop and might give it to
anyone he wished, much as the Muhlenberg Memorial had suggested twenty years before. By the same token, Cummins's insistence that he possessed an episcopal *something* that could be transferred without regard to church office placed Cummins in the
quixotic position of affirming what the Anglo-Catholics had all
along defended. "He claimed to be a Bishop, clothed with authority
greater than that of the late presbyters who are associated with him,
so that he can transmit *his orders*," remarked an incredulous James
Craik to Bishop Smith. "He virtually affirmed that these *Orders* are
indelible, so that neither his renunciation of them, nor the Church's
deposition can work any effect."[55] "That, in fact, is the secret of the
alarm and rage of some parties against Bishop Cummins," com-
mented the *Southern Churchman.* "He has gotten a True Episcopacy
from the Church, and has made off with it and intends to give it to
others."[56] Phillips Brooks sarcastically lampooned Bishop Smith's
dilemma in a letter to a friend in Philadelphia on November 20:

> And what do you think about Cummins? What a panic it
> must make among the bishops to know that a stray parson is
> around with a true bit of their genuine succession, perfectly
> and indisputably the thing, which he can give to anybody he
> pleases! Nothing like it since the pow-wow among the gods
> when Prometheus stole the fire. Wouldn't it be queer if
> Cummins actually became a critical event by the discontented
> from ——— to ——— going off and getting the consecration
> of a new church from him.[57]

But Benjamin Bosworth Smith was not about to let this particular
Prometheus make off with the apostolic fire if he could help it. On
November 29, Bishop Smith summoned to New York by telegraph
the four nearest diocesan bishops (Potter of New York, Littlejohn of
Long Island, Odenheimer of New Jersey, and Stevens of Pennsylva-
nia) and met with them in the vestry room of Grace Church, New
York City. Desperate to head off Cummins before the meeting at
Association Hall could convene, Smith decided to swallow the ca-

nonical risks and call for a presentment.[58] He had taken the extraordinary step of wiring the chairman of the Kentucky Standing Committee to request the committee to prepare a presentment under the terms of Canon 9; it was dispatched from Louisville on November 21, and when he finally had it in hand he at last felt he had a weapon with which to stop Cummins.[59] With only one day remaining before Cummins's Association Hall meeting, Smith and the other bishops (minus Potter, who excused himself from attendance due to "engrossing duties") decided to issue a "proclamation," based on the Standing Committee reply, declaring that "any Episcopal act of [Cummins] pending these proceedings will be null and void."[60] Even if the presentment eventually failed, Smith was obviously hoping that the proclamation might catch Cummins sufficiently off guard to force a postponement of the Association Hall meeting, or at least discourage Episcopalians from venturing too close to a bishop whose actions were now stigmatized as "null and void." A Philadelphia reporter with an ear close to the episcopal keyhole confirmed that "it is said that there is a feeling among certain bishops in favor of deposing Dr. Cummins without according him the six months' notice which the canon requires, trusting that the House of Bishops at the next general convention will justify this action."[61]

The "null and void" proclamation was published in the *New York Evening Post* on December 1. (Oddly, Bishop Smith in his haste had sent copies of the proclamation to the Kentucky Diocesan Standing Committee and to the New York papers but forgot to send one to Cummins.) True to Bishop Smith's expectations, it sent a sickening flutter through the handpicked committee of sixteen Episcopalians whom Cummins had summoned to the Church of the Holy Trinity that evening to perfect the plans for the next day's meeting at Association Hall. One of Colonel Aycrigg's friends waved his copy of the *Post* at Aycrigg and announced: "Now, you want the best legal advice that this city can afford." Aycrigg himself grew a little panicky at what the proclamation might lead to:

> It showed that the Bishops were ready to adopt any desperate remedy to prevent the organization proposed for the next day. . . . We also knew that on one occasion a Bishop had surrounded himself with policemen in church. We could not imagine what might be the next act of desperation. Perhaps a Bishop might appear the next day to disperse the meeting, and it was arranged that a layman should be the Temporary President [of the Association Hall meeting] . . . as it would be more seemly for a layman than for a clergyman to send

for the police, and eject any one, whoever he might be, that should attempt to deprive us of our civil rights.[62]

Inevitably, it began to be suggested that perhaps it would be prudent to postpone the meeting, to deal with the charges first, to make careful preparations. Cummins remained silent while his friends and allies expressed their fears and hesitations about proceeding in the face of the "null and void" proclamation. But when everyone had finished speaking, Cummins stood up and, pointing directly at Aycrigg, said, "We have laid down our course, and shall not swerve from it one inch for anything that man can do against us."[63]

And in the end, Cummins was proved right. The usual method of the Episcopal Church, the *New York Times* had warned in a major editorial on November 30, "has been distinguished by a calmly judicious method of dealing," and not by methods chosen by Bishop Smith. Of course, the *Times* evenhandedly added, Cummins was fully as much at fault as his judges. "The appearance of a certain degree of intolerance on both sides of the controversy raised over Bishop Cummins, and of an appearance of injudicious haste by either party to finally sever all connection with the other are phenomena in the history of the Protestant Episcopal Church as novel as they are regrettable." Nevertheless, even

> If Bishop Cummins chose to follow a path in which even those who warmly sympathized with his doctrinal position were unable to follow him that will not justify the Bishops of the Protestant Episcopal Church in deliberately putting themselves in the wrong for the purpose of thwarting the schismatic tendencies of their erring brother. . . . However dreadful the Bishops may regard such a contingency, . . . Bishop Cummins must retain de jure his Episcopal rank and function for six months longer, and all the informal meetings held, or extra-legal proceedings adopted in the interim, cannot change that fact.[64]

Now, having already wagged its editorial finger at both Cummins and Smith on November 30, the *Times* bluntly announced on December 2 that "the authority under which this declaration is made does not very clearly appear from the constitution of the Church, and it will hardly prevent Dr. Cummins from using, at his discretion, the power of ordination of which he must still consider himself to be possessed."[65] But it was not the *New York Times* that offered Bishop Smith his greatest difficulties. In casting around for support for his action, Smith met with serious demurrers from his own legal counsel about proceeding against Cummins under Canon 9. And, worse, James Craik advised Smith that the hastily prepared presentment of the Kentucky Standing Committee would probably fall apart in court. Both Craik and the secretary of the committee had agreed all along that a trial of Cummins would be unwise, and Craik frankly informed Smith, "It is a pity your own better judgement was overruled by some of your brethren in the Episcopate."[66] In any event, no presentment of Cummins for trial under Canon 9 was ever made, and if Smith's "null and void" proclamation accomplished anything, it was to make Smith appear at once both impotent and vindictive.

In fact, far from being intimidated either by criticism or by the threat of presentment, Cummins laid before the steering committee that night the document that would give his proposed movement its confessional foundation as well as its name and identity. Cummins had called it "The Declaration of Principles" (probably borrowing the idea from the model of the Anglican Church of Canada, which prefaced its constitution and canons in 1867 with a "declaration of principles"). Its four articles are a remarkably succinct and restrained statement of the basis on which Evangelical Anglicanism needed to be refounded. It began with the name Cummins had settled on for the new organization—the Reformed Episcopal Church—clinching what was for Cummins the essential claim of the movement, that it was a reform of, not a revolution against, Anglicanism:

I

The Reformed Episcopal Church, holding "the faith once delivered unto the saints," declares its belief in the Holy Scriptures of the Old and New Testaments as the Word of God, and the sole Rule of Faith and Practice; in the Creed "commonly called the Apostles' Creed"; in the Divine institution of the Sacraments of Baptism and the Lord's Supper; and in the doctrines of grace substantially as they are set forth in the Thirty-Nine Articles of Religion.

II

This Church recognizes and adheres to Episcopacy, not as of Divine right, but as a very ancient and desirable form of Church polity.

III

This Church, retaining a Liturgy which shall not be imperative or repressive of freedom in prayer, accepts The Book of

Common Prayer, as it was revised, proposed, and recommended for use by the General Convention of the Protestant Episcopal Church, A.D. 1785, reserving full liberty to alter, abridge, enlarge, and amend the same, as may seem most conducive to the edification of the people, "provided that the substance of the faith be kept entire."

IV

This Church condemns and rejects the following erroneous and strange doctrines as contrary to God's Word:

First, That the Church of Christ exists only in one order or form of ecclesiastical polity:

Second, That Christian Ministers are "priests" in another sense than that in which all believers are "a royal priesthood":

Third, That the LORD's Table is an altar on which the oblation of the Body and Blood of Christ is offered anew to the Father:

Fourth, That the Presence of Christ in the LORD's Supper is a presence in the elements of Bread and Wine:

Fifth, That Regeneration is inseparably connected with Baptism.

Surprisingly little was radical in Cummins's Declaration, in the sense that there was nothing there that Evangelicals, in Britain and America, had not been campaigning for since the Gorham Judgment. Cummins was careful to reaffirm the sacraments as defined in the Thirty-Nine Articles of Religion (not to mention reaffirming the Articles themselves), and his designation of episcopacy as "ancient and desirable" actually pegged Cummins higher on that point than some of his Evangelical brethren were interested in going. Furthermore, even the five negatives Cummins listed in the last article were carefully worded to exclude only the most extreme ultras among the Anglo-Catholics—baptism is not to be understood as "inseparably connected" to moral and spiritual regeneration, but that was by no means the same as saying it had no significance at all. On those terms, the Declaration was an unusually moderate document, inviting broad-based Evangelical assent, and nothing supports this perception of the basic conservatism of the Declaration more than the simple fact of its sources. Although Cummins drew no attention to it at the time, the entire first article was lifted virtually word-for-word, from William Augustus Muhlenberg's "Exposition of the Memorial" of November 1854, while the statement on baptism and regeneration was carefully cribbed from the final text of the Gorham Judgment.[67] All this indicates that the guiding star in Cummins's mind for his new "Reformed Episcopal Church" was clearly Muhlenberg's model of "Catholic Evangelicalism" that had met such a cruel defeat in the 1850s. And it was this that Cummins was now prepared to give institutional life at last as the morning of December 2, 1873, dawned.

The Association Hall Council

Benjamin Leacock awoke on December 2 to find it "one of the most inclement days of a very stormy winter. The wind was at gale force, accompanied by a blinding snow that melted as it fell, covering the pavements with three to four inches of slush."[68] It was the first major winter storm of that season, and in the biting winds and thick snow "pedestrian exercise was rendered well-nigh impossible."[69] But the weather notwithstanding, the foyer and hallway of Association Hall began to fill with people early that morning, until by 10:00 A.M., the hour appointed by Cummins to begin the session, "the rooms were so well-filled that many were standing."[70] Although Cummins had expected he would need only the "inner parlor" of the hall for the meeting, "the outer parlor was crowded by persons who had come to witness the organization of the new church."[71] Nor were the numbers the only surprise. Cummins had also attracted the major newspapers, and as Leacock's eye wandered over the crowd, he also noticed that "many of the New York City clergy were present."[72] Alexandrine Cummins, waiting anxiously for the appointed hour, twisted in her seat to cast her gaze around the hall too:

> At one end of the beautiful room, on the right as you entered, was a large table prepared for the president and secretary. To the left of this was a still larger table, which was filled by seats for the members of the Council. At one end stood a group of students from the General Theological Seminary of the Protestant Episcopal Church, on the other side were a number of the friends of the movement. It was a most impressive scene. No one present could fail to be awed by the quiet dignity, the solemnity and impressiveness of that Council! On the face of each one was impressed the full realization of the responsibility resting on that little band assembled in that upper room.

But the most important people there were the clergy who were now ready to sign their names to the first organized act of secession the Episcopal Church had ever known. Leacock, Gallagher, and Marshall Smith were there, of course, but they were now also joined by Rowland Hill Bourne (the Episcopal chaplain of New York City's municipal hospital) and William V. Feltwell, who was leaving behind thirteen years of ministry in the Episcopal Church. In addition to these five, no one less than Charles Edward Cheney, who had arrived from Chicago on November 29, now also moved through the crowd to find a seat at the front. And then, at the stroke of ten o'clock, Cummins himself appeared, called for prayer and then a hymn, and then another prayer, and then proceeded to the business at hand.

Looking over the hushed crowd, Cummins began to read aloud the "Call to Organize" in its entirety. "The purpose of the meeting is to organize, and not to discuss the expediency of organizing," Cummins repeated, and as soon as he was finished he turned and nominated Colonel Aycrigg as president pro tempore of the meeting. With Aycrigg safely in the chair (Cummins's one concession to Aycrigg's fear about an episcopal disruption), Cummins introduced the text of the Declaration of Principles and called on Aycrigg to appoint a committee of five to review the Declaration. The whole process had obviously been carefully rehearsed, and after Aycrigg quickly tolled off the names of the committee, a twenty-minute recess was called in order to allow the committee to deliberate. The tension in the hall broke for a moment, and Benjamin Leacock found that the standing-room-only situation in the building actually "allowed both freedom of motion, and more or less of mingling and pleasant interchange of friendly greetings." Leacock was relieved to bump into the younger Stephen Tyng and his brother Alexander: "These brethren were most heartily in sympathy with everything that was done."[73]

Then, at the end of the stipulated twenty minutes, the committee trooped back into the meeting, and Aycrigg called the hall back to order. Cummins then rose and read the committee's formal resolution:

> That we whose names are appended to the call for this meeting, as presented by Bishop Cummins, do here and now, in humble reliance upon Almighty God, organize ourselves into a Church, to be known by the style and title of *The Reformed Episcopal Church*, in conformity with the . . . *Declaration of Principles*, and with the Right Reverend George David Cummins, D.D., as our Presiding Bishop. . . . [74]

There could be no doubt about the outcome of a vote in such a resolution. It was passed unanimously and with "a spontaneity and a heartiness about it that was irresistible."[75] Aycrigg then stepped down from his chair to yield it to the new Presiding Bishop of the new church, and Cummins turned to address the entire assembly once more.

"Brethren beloved of the lord," he began, "we have not met to destroy, but to restore; not to pull down, but to reconstruct." Cummins wanted to establish from the very outset that the Reformed Episcopal Church was not a new departure from Anglicanism but a reassertion of its Evangelical principles. "We would repair the breach" made by Anglo-Catholicism, he announced, "and restore the old path to dwell in." The Reformed Episcopalians were not to consider themselves some new sect; they were to be as fully Episcopalians as their fathers before them, and on their fathers' fundamentals. "One in heart, in spirit, and in faith with our fathers, . . . we return to their position and claim to be the old and true Protestant Episcopalians," Cummins declared, "and through these, our ancestors, we claim an unbroken historical connection through the Church of England with the Church of Christ, from the earliest Christian era."[76]

The instrument of this restoration, as Cummins had promised in the "Call to Organize," was to be the 1785 Book of Common Prayer. He swiftly sketched the history of the Proposed Book to establish its historical connections with William White and the founding of the Episcopal Church, and then (holding a copy of the book in his hand) he proceeded to demonstrate how the 1785 prayer book satisfied all the major liturgical objections Evangelicals had been raising within the Episcopal Church for a generation. "The words 'Priest' and 'Altar' are not to be found in the proposed book," Cummins jubilantly noted, and "the difference in the baptismal services is very marked," with the Proposed Book deleting "all allusion to regeneration in baptism."[77]

There were, he admitted, a few other deletions in the Proposed Book which were to be regretted, such as the elimination of the Nicene Creed and the "descent into hell" from the Apostles' Creed, as well as an awkward attempt to condense the Thirty-Nine Articles into twenty.[78] But these, Cummins assured the meeting, were minor difficulties that the Reformed Episcopalians would quickly "amend, alter, enlarge, or abridge." When weighed against the great gains offered by the elimination of the offenses of "priest," "altar," and "regeneration" in baptism, a few easily correctable historical anachronisms were a small price to pay. "Is the Prayer Book of 1785, then, perfect?" Cummins asked. "By no means," he reassuringly replied, but its use does allow the Reformed Episcopal Church to claim genuine roots in Anglican usage in America, rather than being an untried novelty. "We accept it as a precious boon left to us from our fathers," Cummins added, as a document whose use demonstrates that "we are not schismatics," that "we are not disorganizers," that "we are restorers of the old; repairers of the breeches; reformers."[79]

But then, having established the liturgical continuity of the Reformed Episcopalians with "our brethren of the Protestant Episcopal Church," Cummins turned to what was for him the major justification for his actions, an affirmation of the ecumenical brotherhood of Reformed Episcopalians with all other Protestant Christians. "Towards all other Christian people, of like precious faith, our attitude is that only of love, sympathy, and of earnest desire to co-operate with them," said Cummins, deliberately turning his back on the "unchurching dogma" of the Anglo-Catholics. But Cummins had more in mind than simply passive ecumenical cooperation. Along with Muhlenberg and countless other Evangelical churchmen, Cummins confidently believed that an Episcopal Church shorn of Anglo-Catholic excess would be an irresistible magnet for unification of all Evangelicals under a single, Protestant Anglican banner, and he now called on the new Reformed Episcopalians to become that magnet. "We regard our movement only as a step towards the closer union of all Evangelical Christendom," he declared. "For this we shall labor and pray." The Reformed Episcopal Church would be what the Protestant Episcopal Church might have become had it not been paralyzed by the Tractarian virus. And on that high and heady note Cummins concluded, and the meeting burst out with the singing of the "Gloria in excelsis."[80]

It was now time to attend to the business of structuring the new enterprise, and in the half-hour that remained before the lunch recess, a Standing Committee was created, a finance committee (headed by Colonel Aycrigg) was organized, and on the motion of Charles Edward Cheney, an Executive Committee was formed "to frame a constitution and a system of laws for the government of this Church, and to consider all proposed alterations in the Prayer Book of 1785." In addition, the organizing meeting itself took as its designation "the General Council of the Reformed Episcopal Church" and provided for the meeting of a second General Council six months later, in May 1874.[81] With that, the newly styled council rose and adjourned until three o'clock.

Leacock was surprised and gratified that "the business moved on with perfect smoothness, so that there was no waiting or jarring to disturb the prevailing interest."[82] And the excitement was by no means over. When the afternoon session convened (with Cummins

Fig. 1. George David Cummins (1822–1876), founder and organizer of the Reformed Episcopal Church. A native of Delaware, his Episcopalian father died when Cummins was four, and his mother married a Methodist preacher. At age fourteen, Cummins was sent to Dickinson College, where he had a conversion experience in 1839 during an evangelical revival that swept through Carlisle. After a short stint as an itinerant minister in the Methodist Episcopal Church, Cummins rejoined the Protestant Episcopal Church in 1845, and in 1866 he became Assistant Bishop of Kentucky. He died in 1876, from recurring heart problems, less than three years after founding the Reformed Episcopal Church. As a bishop, he gave the church the invaluable legitimacy of his episcopal rank and status.

FIGS. 2–5. LEADING
EVANGELICALS OF THE
PROTESTANT EPISCOPAL
CHURCH IN THE
NINETEENTH CENTURY

Fig. 2. Alfred Lee (1807–1887),
the Evangelical Bishop of Delaware who led Cummins back to
the Episcopal Church in 1845.
While under Lee's tutelage,
Cummins wrote to his sister:
"The bishop and his family are
my kind friends. I am becoming
more and more attracted to the
Protestant Episcopal Church, and
love its Liturgy."

Fig. 3. William Sparrow (1801–
1874), one of the Evangelical
stalwarts of Virginia Theological
Seminary. Sparrow, an elderly
man at the time of Cummins's
secession from the Episcopal
Church, criticized the Evangelicals who had abandoned
Cummins.

Fig. 4. Stephen Higginson Tyng the Elder (1800–1885), son-in-law of Alexander Viets Griswold and rector of St. George's Church, New York City, from 1845 to 1878. Tyng, like many leading Evangelicals, surprised Cummins in 1873 by criticizing him when he left the church.

Fig. 5. Charles Pettit McIlvaine (1799–1873), who began his ministry as chaplain at West Point and later replaced the energetic Evangelical missionary bishop, Philander Chase, as Bishop of Ohio in 1832.

Fig. 7. William Bacon
Stevens (1815–1887),
fourth Bishop of Penn-
sylvania. Despite his
sympathies with the
Evangelicals, he strongly
condemned Cummins's
secession in 1873.

Fig. 6. William Augustus Muhlenberg
(1796–1877), author of the Muhlenberg
Memorial of 1853, which called on the
Episcopal Church to move toward
pan-Protestant ecumenism. Cummins
admired Muhlenberg's "Evangelical
Catholicism."

Fig. 8. Newspaper
sketch of the 1869 cen-
sure of Stephen H. Tyng
Jr. at New York's
Church of the Trans-
figuration. Bishop
Horatio Potter's deter-
mination to punish
Tyng, an Evangelical, for
preaching in a non-
Episcopal pulpit angered
other Evangelicals.

Fig. 9.   Charles Edward Cheney (1836–1916), twenty years after becoming rector of the infant Chicago parish of Christ Church in 1860. Cheney, an Evangelical, was suspended from the ministry in 1871 for making unlawful alterations to the Prayer Book baptismal office. The examples made of Tyng and Cheney led many Evangelicals to question whether they could continue in the Episcopal Church. Two years later, Cheney would become the first Reformed Episcopal bishop created by Cummins.

Fig. 10. The house that Cheney built: Christ Church, Chicago, after its rebuilding following the Great Chicago Fire of 1871.

Fig. 11. Henry John Whitehouse (1803–1874), Bishop of Illinois from 1852 to 1874, who doggedly pursued Cheney and led the proceedings against him. Clinton Locke called Whitehouse "one of the poorest judges of human nature I ever met."

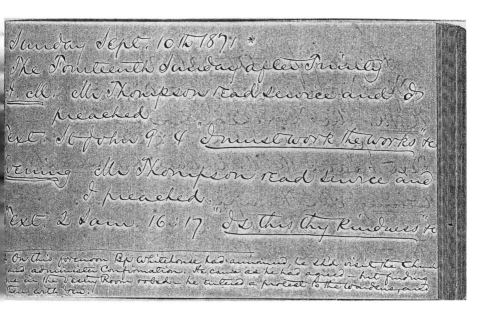

Fig. 12. Page from Charles Edward Cheney's parish register recording Henry John Whitehouse's last visit to Christ Church. When Cheney ignored his suspension, Whitehouse went one step further and deposed him from the priesthood four months later. During his next episcopal visit to Christ Church, three months later, Whitehouse found Cheney in surplice and tippet. He refused to recognize Cheney and left Christ Church, never to return again.

Fig. 13. George David Cummins as a young man of twenty-four at the time of his return to the Episcopal Church. Cummins went home to Delaware, where he presented himself to the Evangelical bishop, Alfred Lee, who prepared him for ordination.

Fig. 14. William Rollinson Whittingham (1805–1879), the High Church Bishop of Maryland from 1840 to 1879 and an early antagonist of Cummins. Before moving to Kentucky, Cummins held two positions in Bishop Whittingham's diocese. Surprisingly, Cummings managed to avoid any ugly confrontations with him, and both later shared an interest in the Old Catholic movement as a basis for Christian unity.

Fig. 15. The Young Men's Christian Association building, New York City (52 East Twenty-Third Street), where the 1873 meeting of the ecumenical Evangelical Alliance was held. Among the attendees were Charles Hodge, James McCosh, John Nevin, Philip Schaff, William Muhlenberg, and the Dean of Canterbury, Robert Payne Smith. Cummins presided over the final ecumenical communion service, an honor for which he was later criticized. Two months later, Cummins met here with the First General Council to organize the Reformed Episcopal Church. Next door is the Fourth Avenue Presbyterian Church. Courtesy, New York Public Library.

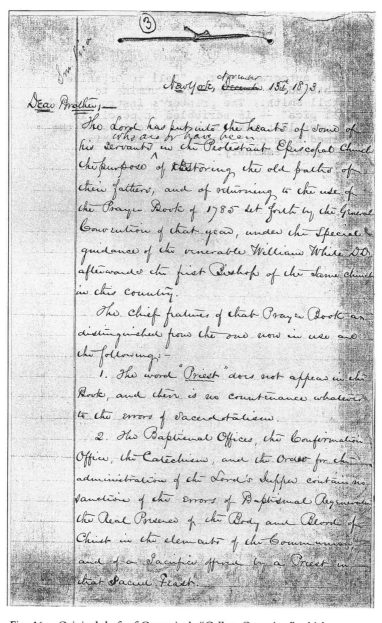

Fig. 16.   Original draft of Cummins's "Call to Organize," which announced a meeting to be held on December 2, 1873, at the YMCA Association Hall "to organize an Episcopal Church on . . . a basis broad enough to embrace all who hold 'the faith once delivered to the saints' as that faith is maintained by the Reformed Churches of Christendom." Cummins dictated the words to Marshall Smith. The printer's instruction—"small pica"—is scribbled in pencil in the upper left-hand corner.

Fig. 17. Newspaper sketch of the Association Hall meeting. Despite inclement weather, "the rooms were so well-filled that many were standing." In attendance were reporters from major newspapers and many of the New York City clergy eager to witness the organization of a new church.

Fig. 18. Six of the seven Evangelical clergy who met to organize the Reformed Episcopal Church. From left to right (standing), Mason Gallagher, William Vessels Feltwell, Marshall B. Smith, Rowland Hill Bourne, and (seated) Charles Edward Cheney and George David Cummins. The photograph was probably taken at the meeting of the Third General Council in Chicago in 1875. Benjamin B. Leacock, the missing member of the group, was prevented by illness from attending the Third General Council. Courtesy, Philadelphia Theological Seminary.

Fig. 19. Cartoon of Cummins consecrating Cheney. Only twelve days after the meeting in New York, Cummins traveled to Chicago, where he consecrated Cheney bishop at Christ Church. This full-page cartoon, which was preserved in Benjamin Leacock's papers, was published the following day in an unidentified newspaper. It depicts Cummins in an Episcopal bishop's miter (which he never wore) and Cheney, with Henry Ward Beecher, the liberal Congregationalist, on the left and Octavius Brooks Frothingham, the Unitarian theologian, on the right. The comment at the top right reads: "If Cheney, why not Beecher and Frothingham?"

Fig. 20. The founders of the Reformed Episcopal Church. This collage of photographs appeared in a supplement to the *Episcopal Recorder* in the 1880s. Under the editorship of Charles W. Quick, the *Recorder* became the voice of the Reformed Episcopal Church.

Fig. 21.   Samuel K. Fallows (1835–1922) preaching to the noonday crowd from a ladder in a Chicago street. Fallows, a former brigadier-general and president of Illinois Wesleyan College, joined the Reformed Episcopalians in 1875 and used his position to work for social and educational reform. He succeeded Cheney as Bishop of Chicago in 1916. If William Rufus Nicholson represented the fundamentalist wing of the church in the New York–Philadelphia Synod, Fallows stood for the "liberal" wing in the Midwest.

Fig. 22. Israel Reformed Episcopal Church, Charleston, South Carolina, one of the African-American congregations in the Reformed Episcopal Church. In the years following the Civil War, African-Americans still could not be ordained in many dioceses of the Episcopal Church, so some black Episcopalians looked to Cummins's church. Frank C. Ferguson, one former slave, brought five black churches and 500 communicants into the Reformed Episcopal Church and started a new mission, Holy Trinity, in the heart of Charleston. Photograph ca. 1900.

Fig. 23. First Reformed Episcopal Church, New York City. After the schism, Cummins organized a parish in New York City that met for morning services in Steinway Hall and for evening services in Lyric Hall. In March 1874 the congregation was duly incorporated with Cummins as its rector. When Cummins's poor health forced him to resign, William Tufnell Sabine, the popular Evangelical, stepped in. The strain of leading the fledgling Reformed Episcopal Church took its toll on Cummins. Poor health in the years before his death in 1876 precipitated a crisis in leadership within the church.

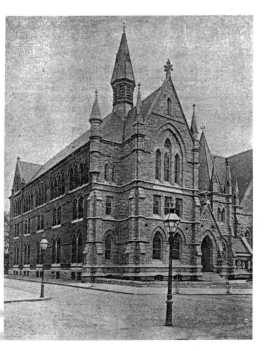

Fig. 25. Harriet Benson, benefactor of Reformed Episcopal Seminary. Benson, one of William Rufus Nicholson's parishioners at St. Paul's, Philadelphia, donated the considerable money needed to build and operate Christ Memorial Church and the seminary in West Philadelphia.

Fig. 24. The theological seminary of the Reformed Episcopal Church, part of the complex of buildings comprising Christ Memorial Church, at Forty-Third and Chestnut Streets in Philadelphia, as it was completed for the first classes in September 1887.

Fig. 26. Christ Memorial Reformed Episcopal Church, Forty-Third and Chestnut, Philadelphia. The complex of buildings includes a chapel (*right*) and the three-story hall of Reformed Episcopal Seminary (*left*). The "Memorial" in the church's name was a remembrance of Harriet Benson's relatives, the Morton family. Although the church was built in a lavish and un-Evangelical Perpendicular Gothic style (by the noted Philadelphia architect and builder Isaac Pursell), the church itself is oriented north-south rather than (in Anglo-Catholic fashion) east-west.

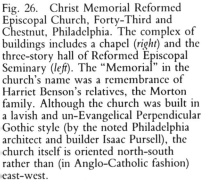

FIGS. 27–30. EVANGELICAL
EPISCOPAL CHURCH
ARCHITECTURE

Fig. 27. St. Paul's, Philadelphia, which Stephen
Tyng the Elder turned into
"Tyng's Theatre" for Evangelical preaching. Note the
classical simplicity of decoration and the supremacy
given to the pulpit.

Fig. 28. Church of the
Epiphany, Philadelphia.
Once again, the pulpit is the
point of focus; the baptismal
font and communion table
are almost unnoticeable.

Fig. 29. St. George's Church, New York City, at the height of Stephen Tyng the Elder's ministry as rector (after St. Paul's) in the mid-1800s. Note the fairly chastened Gothic interior, with the pulpit in the central position and communicants permitted to surround the communion table in the chancel.

Fig. 30. St. George's Church, New York City, after renovation of the interior in 1867. The pulpit remains the central focus, and, even though new elements of Gothic decoration have been added, the architecture continues to promote a close connection between the clergy and people. Anglo-Catholic architecture, with its introduction of pure models of Gothic decoration, preferred to separate clergy and people by means of long, narrow choirs that culminated in raised altars and minuscule pulpits.

Fig. 31. Charles Edward Cheney in his later years. After Cummins's death in 1876, Cheney spoke the loudest for Episcopal traditionalism within the Reformed Episcopal Church. This often set Cheney, and the nine parishes that clustered around him in Chicago, off against Nicholson and the New York–Philadelphia parishes.

Fig. 32. The Jubilee General Council of the Reformed Episcopal Church, on the steps of St. Paul's Reformed Episcopal Church, Broad and Venango Streets, Philadelphia, in May 1924. Sixth from the left on the front row is Bishop Robert Westly Peach, the last ecumenical innovator in the church and Robert Livingston Rudolph's successor as bishop of the New York–Philadelphia Synod. Rudolph is on Peach's left.

Fig. 33.   Brandram B. Ussher, rector of St. Bartholomew's Reformed Episcopal Church in Montreal. Ussher, who was consecrated by Thomas Huband Gregg in 1882, is dressed in his episcopal rochet and chimere. Nothing so divided and tormented the Reformed Episcopalians after Cummins's death as the seemingly incidental matter of vestments. The issue was hotly debated at the 1897 General Council, but the matter was not settled for many years.

Fig. 34.   Bishop Robert Livingston Rudolph (*left of monument*) in some highly unchar-
acteristic dress—surplice and stole—for the reinterment of the remains of Bishop
Fallows in 1927. Rudolph's lifelong friend, William Russell Collins (*right of monument*)
succeeded Fallows as rector of St. Paul's Reformed Episcopal Church, Chicago.
Courtesy, Philadelphia Theological Seminary.

Fig. 35.   Bishop Joseph Kearney as
"superintendent" of the African-
American churches of the Reformed
Episcopal "Missionary Jurisdiction
of the South," with a 105-year-old
parishioner in 1927. Kearney was
later consecrated as missionary
bishop for the South. The South
was not granted its own synodical
organization on a par with Chicago
or Philadelphia for another four decades.

Fig. 36. Robert Livingston Rudolph (1865–1930), the first Reformed Episcopal bishop raised entirely within the Reformed Episcopal Church. His leadership in the early 1900s, by turns autocratic and indulgent, saved the Reformed Episcopal Church from disintegration after the vestments controversy and the deaths of the first generation of Reformed Episcopal leaders. Ironically, the seeds of decline were also sewn during his term of leadership.

reading from 1 Peter and with the singing of "Nearer, My God, to Thee"), Cummins began the session by reviewing the expressions of interest and enthusiasm he had received from all over the country, including no less than "the names of twenty-five clergymen of the Protestant Episcopal Church who were ready to take churches and parishes and congregations in communion with the Reformed Episcopal Church as soon as they could be provided."[83] Cummins himself announced his own intention to start a Reformed Episcopal parish in New York City. But in that case, he observed, he would need assistance in giving oversight to the new church. That meant that another bishop would be called for, preferably one located in the Midwest, and to that end he called for the election of one of the clergy in the meeting as a missionary bishop.

The council at once erupted in applause, and the call went up not for one new bishop but for two. Unprepared for such an unsolicited call for still more bishops, Cummins proceeded to make an ominous misstep. Caught up in the excitement of the process, he unwisely began to propose the nomination of "one who was already a member of the Protestant Episcopal Church," an "old man" whose "high character and standing would be of incalculable advantage to their Church" and "would carry the City of New York as the name of no other man could."[84] Cummins deliberately skirted mention of the name of the "old man," hoping that it would be recognized and offered from the floor of the council, but it was immediately obvious to Leacock that Cummins could mean no one other than William Augustus Muhlenberg.[85]

In one sense, Cummins was right. Muhlenberg's adherence to the Reformed Episcopal Church could easily have pushed many of the waverers among the Evangelicals over into Cummins's fold. And everything in Muhlenberg's behavior toward Cummins in the preceding two weeks had predisposed Cummins to believe that Muhlenberg would welcome such an honor from a church striving to embody his own principles. But Leacock, looking around him, noticed in rising panic that Muhlenberg was nowhere to be seen in the Hall, and in fact, had stayed away from the meeting entirely. Leacock instantly grasped that Muhlenberg's absence was no accident, and that Muhlenberg, whatever his personal interest in Cummins, had no more intention of lining up behind Cummins than had Stephen Tyng Sr. "There was not a shadow of hope for believing that Dr. Muhlenberg would identify himself with us," Leacock recalled, "and his certain declination of the offer would strike us a staggering blow." Hurriedly, Leacock appealed to Mason Gallagher to have Cummins desist from his proposal. A whispered conference took place while other speakers had the floor, and shortly afterward "my request was complied with and the Bishop was induced to drop the subject."[86] (It was just as well, for Leacock had read Muhlenberg aright. Muhlenberg remained friendly to Cummins but not to the point of joining him, and he stayed firmly within the ranks of the Episcopal Church until his death in 1877.)

The proceedings then revolved back to the safer proposition of electing one additional bishop, and with Cummins's stated preference for a midwesterner to take up the episcopal office, it was evident that no better or more obvious candidate could be in Cummins's mind than Charles Edward Cheney. Unlike Muhlenberg, Cheney had been given notice the evening before that Cummins would call for his election, but all the same, he now rose to deprecate the idea. "He said that neither his mental nor physical constitution qualified him for the office," the New York Times reporter noted, "but he chiefly relied upon the fact that the discharge of the duties of a missionary bishop would interfere with those other duties which he owed to the members of his pastorate in Chicago, with whom he had been connected for many years, and whom he could not abandon."[87]

This was no false modesty on Cheney's part. Christ Church had stood by him since his trial in 1869, and for him now to run off after a bishopric on behalf of Cummins and his new church would be small thanks for their loyalty. But at this moment, Marshall Smith rose to save the day by assuring Cheney that "the acceptance of his office was in no way inconsistent with the holding of his pastorate in Chicago," any more than it would be for Cummins, organizing his own new parish in New York. Cummins himself weighed in with the injured protest that "if he now hesitated to accept this ordering of God, it would be the first time he had occasion to be disappointed with him."[88] Cheney was in no better position to slight Cummins's loyalty to him than the loyalty of Christ Church, and reluctantly he agreed to a virtually unanimous election as "missionary bishop for the Northwest."

For all practical purposes, that brought the first General Council to a close. Cheney was to return at once to Chicago to seek the approval of his congregation (they overwhelmingly applauded his election), and Cummins was to undertake arrangements for Cheney's consecration at the earliest possible time—certainly before Cummins's six-month grace period had elapsed—so there would be no question of the validity of Cheney's consecration. The newspaper reporters went away amazed, and Leacock noticed with some satisfaction that even "the High-churchmen present were surprised, and some of them afterward stated that the movement was a more formidable one than they had anticipated."[89] Perhaps so, but its long-term success was going to depend on how swiftly Cummins was going to be able to act in establishing churches, winning adherents, and raising support. However, Cummins was getting used to swift action. It had been only six weeks since William George Tozer's letter had appeared in the *New York Tribune*.

V

TRUE, SIMPLE EPISCOPACY

The Creation of a Republican Communion

In the headlong rush of events that led to the meeting at Association Hall on December 2, 1873, it was easy for the participants
and the antagonists alike to concentrate entirely on the immediate
politics of a church schism and ignore the larger questions about
the significance of this event in American Protestantism, in the
Episcopal Church, and in the troubled intellectual atmosphere of
the American Gilded Age. The historian, however, cannot be
forgiven such an oversight, especially when it was not clear from
the utterances of some of the new Reformed Episcopalians whether
they thought of their movement as the beachhead of a new ecu-

menical or theological era or merely a harried withdrawal into an ecclesiastical cupboard. As his sermon to the Association Hall council reveals, George David Cummins was far from proposing some radical new paradigm of religious understanding as the justification for his secession from the Episcopal Church. Yet, implicitly, his new movement was at least a commentary on other peoples' paradigms. To Cummins, Anglo-Catholicism appeared simply as a throwback to medieval superstition, for even if the Anglo-Catholics could not be directly linked to some unspeakable conspiracy to throw the Episcopal Church back into the arms of Rome, it certainly appeared to Cummins and his fellow Evangelicals as a movement off into a strange and incomprehensible form of nonrational religion. Consequently, Cummins's commitment to a "rational religion" meant more than simply a distaste for liturgical experimentation. Whatever their commitments to supernatural Christianity in terms of spiritual conversion, the Evangelicals of the nineteenth century also present a complementary commitment to the rationalization of God and the reconstruction of belief to make it contiguous with natural science (something that loads Cummins's dismissal of Anglo-Catholicism as "superstition" with as much anxiety as contempt).

The premier Protestant apologists for Christianity in the eighteenth century, Bishop Joseph Butler and Archdeacon William Paley, had attempted to stem the tide of unbelief that they imputed to the new physics of Galileo, Copernicus, and Kepler by converting the mysteries of Christianity into an unassailable rampart of natural facts, and by converting the God of Abraham, Isaac, and Jacob into the God of natural law. It had been amply demonstrated by the discoveries of the seventeenth century that belief was likely to be acted on only if it could be verified in experience, only if it could be exactly and logically formulated, and only if it could be demonstrated to owe nothing to authority or to past wisdom or to anything else the new physics was quickly rendering obsolete. To a large degree, these changes in the legitimacy of ideas were linked to the same instinct for individualism, for hard results, and for predictable rules of action that governed the rise of eighteenth-century commercial capitalism. And taken together, they created a challenge to traditional religion that the theologians could either challenge (and likely lose) or accommodate themselves to.[1] That they chose the latter is not surprising, and by the 1870s even a Calvinist Presbyterian as conservative as Charles Hodge insisted that it was necessary to regard the Bible as being "to the theologian what nature is to the man of science. It is his store-house of facts; and his method of ascertaining what the Bible teaches, is the same as that which the natural philosopher adopts to ascertain what nature teaches."[2]

In American theology, the case for a natural-law God was further reinforced by the influence of Scottish common-sense realism, which obtained a large hold on American thinkers both through the general intellectual connections that bound eighteenth-century Scotland and America together as common borderlands of the British Empire, and through the influence of Scottish Calvinist divines such as Hodge through Princeton College (and later, through Princeton Theological Seminary).[3] Whether it was called Baconian (after the celebrated promoter of empirical methods) or "common sense" or simply "Scottish realism," the rage for a natural-law defense of Christianity pervaded all American Evangelicals at the turn of the nineteenth century, and the Evangelical Episcopalians were no exception. Charles Pettit McIlvaine's *Evidences of Christianity* (1832) was a particularly complacent recital of the natural proofs of Christian truth, and even George David Cummins was inclined to blame the great cholera epidemic in his Norfolk parish on bad habits that violated the natural course of disease, not on sinful behavior that led to divine judgment. In so doing, he and his Evangelical brethren could be pious without making piety look unscientifically ridiculous.

This accommodation laid severe stresses on that piety, not the least of which was the ambivalence it promoted between the premium it set on common-sense rationality and the honor it accorded heart-religion, because Evangelicals could neither bring themselves to choose one nor adequately harmonize both. The uneasiness that arose from this ambivalence was further exacerbated by the rash of anti-natural-law criticism that emerged frank and stark from the pen of David Hume, and then in a more careful (but more influential) tone from Kant and Schleiermacher. In America, the revolt from strict natural rationalism found its first champions in some unusual places: in James Marsh, president of the University of Vermont, who hoped Kant might open a passage around the epistemological impasses of Calvinists and Unitarians; in Edwards Amasa Park, who dared in 1850 to suggest that the theology of the feelings should not play second fiddle to the theology of the intellect; and in Horace Bushnell, who redefined biblical and theological language as poetry rather than sober fact, addressed to the emotions for belief rather than to the mind for analysis. Park and Marsh were scarcely rebels against Evangelicalism, and even Bushnell belongs as much to premodern confessional Calvinism (at least in attitude) as to nineteenth-century Romanticism. But they were read by their Evangelical compatriots as a threat, for in a culture soaked with the material accomplishments of science and technology, the flight from reason and natural law to a religion of the feelings would eventually condemn theology to the margins of modern intellectual enterprise. The profound faith of nineteenth-century Americans in technological enterprise and scientific advancement would, they realized, have little patience with a Bible whose message consisted of poetry rather than fact.

The Evangelicals might have been more successful in shaking off the annoying questions posed by Bushnell and Park if they had not been tripped by the very science they admired. The publication of Sir Charles Lyell's *Principles of Geology* (three volumes, 1830–1833) and then of Charles Darwin's *Origin of Species* in 1859 turned the entire Baconian, empirical, common-sense, natural-law apologetic completely on its head by showing on precisely the same Baconian, empirical, common-sense, natural-law principles as those espoused by Butler, Paley, Hodge, and McIlvaine that the description of the creation and providence of natural world found in the Bible was simply unthinkable.[4] From that point on, the Evangelicals were thrown on the defensive, and a stampede to Romantic escapism in American culture commenced. The natural-law theology stood exposed as incapable of mediating an adjustment of science and religion, and the only alternative (apart from either outright atheism or an unblinking perseverance in the canons of natural-law theology) was a resort to the transcendental epistemology of Romanticism.

Many historians have chronicled this movement into Romantic revolt in terms of individuals or movements, but they have usually missed how perfectly it was embodied in one of the largest, wealthiest, and most influential of American institutions: the Episcopal Church. Anglo-Catholic ritualism served for late Victorian Anglo-American culture the same purpose that the Paley-Butler-Hodge gospel of rationality had once served in the heyday of commercial capitalism, in that the silver plates and rich brocades of Anglo-Catholic ornament reflected the transition of capitalism from the limited horizons of eighteenth-century commercial capitalism to the unprecedented productive power of industrial capitalism and the new patterns of international finance that accompanied it. The sacred symbols of the Anglo-Catholics—such as Ralph Adams Cram's Gothic cathedrals—were also the ultimate symbols of Victorian affluence, and taken together they represent a new attempt to rationalize the aggressive power of the industrial marketkplace without wholly repudiating it. It hardly mattered that, in contrast to the weighty tomes of the Evangelicals, that Anglo-Catholic theology was famished and weightless; its pretend medievalism created the perfect combination of excitement, pleasure, and consumption bound up with doubt that marked off the other major capitalist cultures of northern Europe. Notoriously shy of theology and preaching, Anglo-Catholicism offered its devotees an economy of performance, where the religious product could be consumed or viewed by an self-conscious elite bent on a new ethic of consumption rather than the older natural-law ethic of production. Thus, Anglo-Catholic Episcopalians shunned the old Evangelical urge to examine oneself and exchanged it for what Ann Douglas called the new commandment of the market revolution: display thyself.[5]

It should not be lost on even the casual observer that, on those terms, Victorian Anglo-Catholicism paralleled some of the most acute crises, and some of the most outstanding material triumphs, of Anglo-American culture after the Civil War. It was a profoundly conservative and reactionary movement in an age when the uneasiness of Americans with their new wealth turned them to conservative and reactionary movements.[6] And its preoccupation with the aesthetics of ritual, vestments, and architecture turn on precisely the same hinges (and often involve precisely the same people, such as Isabel Stewart Gardner and Ralph Adams Cram) that the American nouveaux riches turned in its dilettantish obsession with Old Masters. But far from minimizing either the significance or the autonomy of Anglo-Catholicism as a religious movement, the connections actually suggest that Anglo-Catholicism was constitutive (and not merely reflective) of that culture, in that the Anglo-Catholics consciously sought to teach their people a new way of responding to material culture. Anglo-Catholicism and its rituals formed a unique system of communication capable of transmitting meanings that were as potent for the promotion of the material culture of industrial capitalism as they were vastly different from the text-oriented "rational" world of the Evangelicals. No matter, then, that Lyell and Darwin posed an unpleasant series of questions about the authority of Holy Writ. The Anglo-Catholics provided an easy answer, resolving all modern doubt and anxiety into liturgy and acoustics. The sensibilities aroused in the rebellion against Protestant rationalism allowed Anglo-Catholics to easily come to terms both with Darwinian evolution and with German higher criticism. Ritual had made religion acceptable again.

But just as the connection between Anglo-Catholicism and the market revolution has been missed time and again, so also has the significance of Cummins and the Reformed Episcopal Church been missed as a violent rear-guard action against that union. For as small a group as the Reformed Episcopalians eventually became, they embodied a fervent persistence in an older preindustrial mode of cultural explanation that borrowed and lent freely with natural law and republicanism. George David Cummins was, after all, a man of the Age of Jackson, not the Gilded Age. He was born in 1822, not 1852, and three decades made all the difference. Like so many of the Whigs, Cummins was country-bred, made his living in the cities, and fled them as soon as he could, first in Kentucky and then, at the end, in Maryland. He showed only the dimmest sense that evolution (which owed so much of its attractions to the valences it enjoyed with industrial capitalism) posed a problem to nineteenth-century Christianity, and it never seems to have occurred to him that anything but the most rigidly rational apologetic formulas ought to suffice to explain God and the world. His only use for Anglican ritual was, literally, theological rather than aesthetic or poetic—or, to put it another way, he viewed ritual as possessing only the value of production (in that it inculcated the correct relationships and ideas) rather than the value of consumption (which is to be affected or displayed).

Of course, in their suspicion of the mysterious activities of "Romanizing Germs," both Cummins and the Reformed Episcopalians also seem to betray some traces of paranoid American nativism (which would be yet another mark of their connection with Whiggism). Indeed, knowing what we do about the ethnic antagonisms of the Know-Nothings for Roman Catholic immigrants, the temptation is great to explain the Reformed Episcopalians away as simply another species of Know-Nothingism. But tempting as that is in its simplicity, that approach will not bear much weight. Merely to hang the secession of the Reformed Episcopalians on the single peg of nativism overlooks how little the Reformed Episcopalians fit the nativist Know-Nothing rhetoric of the 1840s and 1850s. For one thing, the Reformed Episcopalians said comparatively little about *Roman* Catholics. In fact, Cummins went out of his way to establish parallels between his movement and the post–Vatican Council Old Catholics. Nor do the Reformed Episcopalians show much interest in nativism per se. Little or nothing of the ethnic hostility of the Know-Nothings shows up in the Reformed Episcopalians, and if there were elements of class antagonism, they worked in precisely the opposite direction from classic nativism, because the Reformed Episcopalians came to represent a lower-middle-class brand of Episcopalianism at odds with the ever-more-fashionable brands available at the Church of the Advent or Trinity Church, Wall Street. The

Reformed Episcopalians were arrayed against their fellow white American Episcopalians, not the foreign-born Irish or Germans. It will do the Reformed Episcopalians more justice to concentrate attention on the meaning of their avowed raison d'être, the purification and Evangelicalization of the liturgy. Looked at closely, their contempt for ceremonial is the hallmark of complex preoccupation with a producer (as opposed to a consumer) ethic, rather than a cheap nativism, while their obsession with the right of private judgment established an easy relationship between a Protestant slogan and the tenets of classic eighteenth-century civic republicanism. On those terms, it is no wonder that Cummins and the early Reformed Episcopalians hammered away so relentlessly at the disjuncture between the Anglo-Catholics and the "religion of the Revolutionary patriots," or that the Bishop White prayer book remained an article of Reformed Episcopal pride long after its liturgical awkwardness had caused it to be quietly shelved in favor of a Reformed Episcopal adaption of the then-current Episcopal church prayer book. They saw themselves as guardians of an Evangelical Whiggism, a virtuous republicanism that the goatish greed of postbellum America had all but obliterated. "Is your own communion sufficiently *American*," demanded Mason Gallagher of a Protestant Episcopal bishop in 1893, "while some of its essential principles are feudal and medieval in their character . . . ?" Gallagher wanted to know whether the bishop's principles could be considered "consistent with American ideas" because they embodied "a foreign principle, and one of dangerous character." The "Idea of exclusive Divine Right in the Episcopate" had no place beside "American principles," and to the extent that the Episcopal Church embraced such ideas, it "cast aside the magnificent work of her great Revolutionary, American Founders, and embraced exclusive, Feudal, Anglican principles." Consequently, Gallagher malevolently thundered, "the claim of *Divine Right* of your Episcopate has no substantial basis, is cognate to the asserted Divine Right of Kings, and has no proper place in this land, or age, and is therefore thoroughly un-American."[7]

Cummins's instinctive move to downplay or recast the Book of Common Prayer in favor of the preaching of the Bible was at once an attempt to solidify a Protestant Evangelical identity and to nail the Reformed Episcopalians ever more firmly to the intellectual culture of rational religion. What he and the Reformed Episcopalians missed (and this may have been their downfall) was that the Anglo-Catholics were, in the broadest sense, not the *opponents* of Protestant Evangelicalism (as though they were two incompatibles that could not survive without one killing the other) but its *rivals*. The Evangelicals found the Anglo-Catholics so incomprehensible that they rarely rose far enough above the level of their own anger to realize that the Anglo-Catholics were as much the heirs of Anglicanism as they were, and that the Anglo-Catholics were as fully a coherent and self-contained religious system as they themselves were. Each was seeking to form a viable community of ideas, and each laid claim to offer the true interpretation of American culture. The double liability under which the Reformed Episcopalians operated was that their suspicion of "Romish" garb and vessels set them on a collision course with the culture of capitalist affluence, while their loyalty to rational religion committed them to incessant arguments about the theology of the prayer book at just the moment when American churchgoers wanted only to consume its ethos.

"The New Church Is Fairly Launched"

Three days after the meeting in Association Hall, a flustered and reluctant Bishop Horatio Potter was cajoled out of his sickroom by a *New York Herald* reporter who wanted to know whether the Reformed Episcopal movement "will not seriously affect the Protestant Episcopal Church in this country." No, snapped the irritated bishop, "No more, sir, than a mosquito bite would affect the stone wall of the reservoir in Fifth Avenue."[8]

Other Episcopalians were not so certain. "The Reformed Episcopal Church is an accomplished fact," warned a correspondent for *The Episcopalian*. "It is just as much a regularly constituted Episcopal Church as our own." He continued:

> Whatever virtue there may be, or thought to be, in the Apostolic Succession, this Church has it. It has bishops; it will soon have its two or more bishops. . . . If we say that this new Church has begun in schism, the Church of Rome alleges the same things against us. The real question is, which party is guilty of the schism, the party which separates and goes out? or the party which forces this separation, by making binding on the conscience what Christ has not made binding? . . . To those of us who are already in the ministry of the Protestant Episcopal Church, it is a mixed question. Some of us are not yet entirely hopeless of redeeming our Church from the baneful influences which now control it.

But how much longer can we endure patiently? and all the while here is a harbor of refuge awaiting us, here is a platform presented, having our entire and cordial approval.[9]

The *Church Union* asked, "But will the new church amount to anything?" and answered its own question: "We think it will. . . . They will make the good old hierarchy smell smoke yet."[10] Charles Edward Cheney, of course, was ecstatic. "This is the dawn for which they have watched with eagerness through a long night of persecution," Cheney announced from his pulpit on December 7. "The highest churchman in the land cannot deny the validity of the Episcopate of the Reformed Episcopal Church."

> This is our day of rejoicing and of gladness. You have seen your Rector dishonored and disgraced before the world. You have seen his name cast out as a vile thing. You have heard with pompous dignity the sentence pronounced upon him that consigned him to the uncovenanted mercies outside of the Church of God—and you only twined your arms—God bless you for it!—you only twined your arms around him the more tenderly, you only stood by him with a stronger determination. To-day God is bringing your reward. To-day you have an Episcopal Church; you have the liturgy of your fathers; you have the truth as it is in Jesus, in connection with all that was worth retaining of what is known as the Protestant Episcopal Church. Let us prayerfully and solemnly and decidedly act together.[11]

Even the editorial page of the *Herald*, venturing for once to risk comment on church affairs, declared on December 21: "The new Church is fairly launched."

> Whatever the merits or demerits of the new movement, . . . it affords unmistakable evidence that our Christianity has in it the genuine elements of vitality. . . . In the Episcopal Church, Cummins and Cheney were men of recognized influence, . . . and in so far as they have stood up for principle, fought for conscience, revealed daring and made sacrifices, they have a right to be spoken of with the highest respect and they have a claim on the public for sympathy and support.[12]

Cummins, however, had not stopped to count either his laurels or his critics. As soon as Cheney had obtained the consent of Christ

Church to his consecration, and wired his acceptance to Cummins, the bishop packed himself, his wife, and a small entourage (consisting of Marshall Smith, William Feltwell, Mason Gallagher, Benjamin Leacock, and Colonel Aycrigg) onto the first train to Chicago.[13] In a last-ditch effort to head off Cheney's consecration, Benjamin Bosworth Smith arranged to have a telegram meet Cummins as his train pulled into Chicago on the evening of December 13. It read simply: "I hereby formally and officially withdraw all such Episcopal authority as you have heretofore exercised under Canon thirteenth, Title One. —B. B. Smith, Bishop of Kentucky."[14] But Cummins merely waved it aside. Smith's telegram had no more canonical force than the "null and void" proclamation two weeks before, and Cummins knew it. At the same moment, Cheney's own diocesan nemesis, Henry J. Whitehouse, was also struggling to obtain a court injunction to prevent the use of Christ Church (which Whitehouse still claimed as Episcopal Church property) for Cheney's consecration.[15] But the court refused to grant an injunction without a hearing, and no hearing could be set until the week after the consecration was scheduled to take place. The unhappy Whitehouse discovered that episcopal duties required his presence in Peoria, and Cummins and Cheney were left to enjoy Chicago in peace.[16]

The consecration had been set for Sunday morning, December 14, and by ten o'clock Christ Church "was crowded to suffocation by members of the regular congregation and sightseers representing all religious denominations." The *Chicago Tribune* noted: "Long before services began, not only was every seat taken, but every door and stairway leading to the edifice was thronged."[17] The order of service would be a provisional one, pieced together by Cummins from the Protestant Episcopal Book of Common Prayer as "A Form for the Consecration of a Bishop" (because the 1785 prayer book lacked services for ordination or consecration) and approved by the new Reformed Episcopal Standing Committee on December 7.[18] But even more striking than the new liturgy would be Cummins's sermon, for Cummins intended to take this first fully Reformed Episcopal service as his platform to lay down the fundamental principles of episcopal government as Reformed Episcopalians would see them. "It is meet and right on an occasion so momentous, that we should carefully declare in what estimation the office of a bishop is held in this branch of a Christian Church," Cummins began.[19] And from the first, it was clear that Cummins's notion of a Reformed episcopate was going to be a far cry from that of Horatio Potter.

In the first place, Cummins insisted, there is no such thing as a single divinely ordained method for ordering the Christian church, or at least none discoverable in "the inspired records of the primitive Church of Christ." Not only was it clear to Cummins that "Our blessed Lord Himself . . . *prescribed no form of polity under which it should exist,*" but likewise, "the apostles of our Lord adopted or promulgated no definite code of ordinances and regulations for the Christian Church." The Anglo-Catholic claim to find in the Anglican episcopate either divine sanction or some sort of sacramental succession from the apostles could have no substance. "Succession in the ministry, thus maintained and pressed upon us, as it is, as a vital, constituting principle, is Romish, anti-Protestant, anti-scriptural, anti-Christian, being the very strength of sacerdotalism." This did not mean, Cummins hastened to add, that the principle of episcopal government had no historical substance. It was indisputable that "the word *Episcopos* [bishop] was a familiar word to the Greeks, and was the title chosen by the Gentile Churches to designate him who was set over them as teacher and tutor." But even though episcopacy may have been the ancient and primitive order of the church, its origins still were rational and historical, rather than divine or apostolic. It was, as Cummins put it, an outgrowth of "the synagogue with its pulpit, and Holy Scripture read once every Sabbath day; [and] its ruler, who not only read and expounded God's word, or as we should say, preached to the people."

The episcopate was, therefore, a pragmatic convention, invented for the ease of administration, "*the development of the practice or custom first suggested by the apostles* in delegating to certain of their fellow laborers among the presbyters the oversight or superintendence of the Churches," and not "*an ordinance of apostolic institution.*" And to support his contention that this "*true, simple Episcopacy*" was also the intention of the Church of England prior to the Tractarians, Cummins produced a lengthy catena of Anglican divines—Cranmer, Jewel, Reynolds, Whitgift, Ussher, McIlvaine, and even William Sparrow—all arranged end-on-end to show that "in a Reformed Church" the Anglo-Catholic notion of government by "*pedigree*" was "in a most uncongenial soil, and can be kept alive and active there only by means which tend to the subversion of that church." But the real evil in any theory of "apostolic succession" lay not in its theoretical incompatibility with the standard Anglican divines. It lay, instead, in the practical threat it raised against all hope of brotherhood and charity among Evangelical brethren, and it was this anti-ecumenical side of Anglo-Catholicism that provoked the full tide of Cummins's scorn:

In the eye and light of this [Anglo-Catholic] theory, of what account is a threefold organization of the ministry, both diocesan and missionary; what worship in the use of a matchless liturgy that has received the approving suffrages of all high culture and true seriousness; what an orthodoxy unmistakably ratified by every page of the Bible; what an active and intelligent charity which extends its beneficent arts to the ends of the earth; what a pure deep love to Jesus, such as the Apostle Paul delighted to salute and greet wherever found? Alas, these are nothing without the *pedigree*! . . . Orderly *induction* into office, according to the established usage of the body, all approve and all practice. . . . But while a settled Scriptural system of government, and solemn and regular appointment to all offices in it, . . . are one thing, the very thing meant by the Apostle when he exhorted that all things be done "decently and in order," *pedigree*, . . . ah! this is another thing, a very different thing.

But if the validity of episcopal government did not rest on "pedigree," something had to be said about the criteria for "orderly *induction*." Cummins observed, in the first place, that the fundamental sine qua non of ordination or consecration was spiritual: "No power but that of the Holy Ghost can make an ambassador of Christ," no matter what other credentials a person might enjoy. The second criterion was public recognition or acclamation, so that the actual moment of ordination or consecration was but a ratification of the candidate's election by the people and "their acknowledgement of his call from God to this great work." Cummins was at pains to insist that "*ordination does not confer grace*," but "only authority to execute the offices of the ministry." Thus, Cummins was not making Cheney a bishop through some mysterious powers lying only in his own possession. Cheney was already, de facto, a bishop by virtue of his own sacred calling and the election of the General Council, and Cummins was adding no more to Cheney than (as Cummins put it in thoroughly republican terms) the Chief Justice added to the President of the United States "by the formal services of administering the oath of office."

There was, however, one anomaly that Cummins felt compelled to address, and that was Cheney's canonical status as a valid recipient of orders. Was not Cheney a deposed priest, degraded from the ministry of the church he had pledged to serve and had instead defied? How could one who was no longer a clergyman in good standing in the Episcopal world be made into a bishop? But Cummins replied that it was by no means clear that Cheney's deposition was a legal fact, given the civil injunction on the proceedings that Melvin Fuller had obtained in 1869, plus the defect in the composition of the ecclesiastical trial in which Cheney had been found guilty. And even if Cheney had been canonically guilty, Cummins continued (turning the ideas of the Anglo-Catholics back on them), *"deposition . . . does not destroy or impair the ministerial character,"* because that was received "from the Lord himself." Deposition only *"suspends* the exercise of his functions," for as Cummins was quick to point out, even the most ultra Anglo-Catholics "provide by law for the restoration of the deposed clergyman on certain conditions, but never require a re-ordination." Hence, Cummins concluded, "the ministerial character or *status* remains unimpaired by the act of deposition." And especially in Cheney's case, far from lacking anything essential to the episcopate, Cheney had manifested only the most sterling of qualifications:

> In this city, for the past ten years, most momentous years in its history, you have fulfilled a ministry whose record is before the world and needs no recommendation from me. . . . You have had trials such as fall to the lot of but few men; trials that have come upon you from your loyalty to Christ and fidelity to your conscientious convictions of what is essential to the gospel and to the truth that alone can save the soul. . . . You have been chosen by an almost unanimous vote of both the clergy and laity among your brethren, to the office of a Bishop in this Church. Your fellow presbyters have come from distant places to unite in the solemn act which ratifies your election by the Council. . . . If your heart fails as you approach this burden, look to Him who has never left you nor forsaken you in the past, and say, "The Lord is my Helper. . . ."

And with that, Mason Gallagher and Marshall Smith, acting as Cheney's presenters, brought Cheney before Cummins, who, "arrayed in his primate's robes . . . on the steps of the altar," laid his episcopal hands on Cheney and uttered his own words of consecration, "Take thou authority to execute the office and work of a bishop in the church of God. . . ."[20]

The next morning, the reaction of the Episcopal press, and the newspapers sympathetic to the Episcopal Church, was predictable and savage. The *Chicago Times*, a Democratic paper that had never particularly admired Cheney, now attacked him as a schemer after the purple, "equivocal and suspicious" with "the reverence of a communist, the order of a mutineer, and the principle of a politician."[21] The old Ohio diocesan paper, *Standard of the Cross*, which had reeled from Cummins's letter of 1869 refusing to condemn Cheney, now claimed: "If Christ Church, Chicago, and its Rector had resisted the temptation of the new door that Bishop Cummins has opened, how finely would Dr. Cheney have gathered the interest and sympathy of the whole Church to his cause." But now, Cheney "voluntarily abandons all his strongholds and the brave assertions and efforts of these last two years are surrendered in a day." The tartest comment of all was the full-page cartoon run in a New York newspaper, picturing Cheney kneeling before a leering Bishop Cummins, while lining up below him appeared Henry Ward Beecher, the liberal Congregationalist, and Octavius Frothingham, the Unitarian theologian. "If Cheney, why not Beecher and Frothingham?" the cartoon asked; while the caption at the bottom added, "Apostolic Succession Conferred by a Disbeliever in it." An accompanying box sharpened the cartoon's point:

> It will be remembered that one of the chief reasons moving Bishop Cummins to leave the Episcopal Church and to found a private church of his own was his avowed disbelief in the doctrine of apostolic succession. . . . Naturally enough the spectacle amuses those irreverent radicals, Messrs. Beecher and Frothingham; and as they believe in apostolic succession quite as much as the two bishops hitherto have professed to, it would be a jovial compliment to them were Dr. Cummins to consecrate them both bishops *in partibus infidelium.*[22]

Once again, Cummins did not lack for vindicators, and sometimes from unexpected quarters. One Anglo-Catholic priest from Alabama, John Fulton, published a lengthy study of the canonical standing of Cheney's consecration, and after a review of the Nicene and other patristic canons, he surprisingly concluded, "But what are we to do about it? Well, at present, *Nothing.*"

> . . . If he [Cheney] and Bishop Cummins should insist upon the point that his Episcopal *rank* must be conceded, I see no objection to that. Let him by all means have the name of Bishop, and be styled Right Reverend. . . . I believe that Dr.

Cheney might be very properly permitted to confirm in any Diocese, provided he were so authorized by the Bishop of that Diocese; and so, in effect or even name, he might be a Suffragan Bishop; ordination being, of course, reserved to his Diocesan.[23]

But all the same, Cummins's consecration of Cheney did raise some serious questions. Entirely apart from the business of Cheney's canonical status or Bishop Smith's attempt to revoke Cummins's episcopal authority, there was still the highly irregular fact that Cummins had proceeded to consecrate Cheney single-handedly, rather than in the traditional company of two or more other bishops. Although single consecrations were neither unprecedented nor invalid, there was nevertheless something slightly untoward and overeager in the impression it created.

The haste of Cummins's journey to Chicago to consecrate Cheney raised yet another question. As the New York cartoon had indicated, it was not a little odd that an ecclesiastical organization like the Reformed Episcopal Church should claim on the one hand its disbelief in any inherent grace in bishops, and then rush at top speed to have its one canonical bishop make another "valid" bishop before his canonical deadline expired. Whatever Cummins may have thought about the nature of a "true, simple Episcopacy," it is striking that his suggestion at the Association Hall meeting that a new bishop be elected was greeted (according to the newspaper reports, but not in the published text of the council journal) by cheers "to see the apostolic succession maintained" and seconded by fears "that the succession might be lost through the death of the presiding bishop."[24] And whatever Cummins might have said in his sermon about bishops being merely a historical development out of pre-Christian synagogue elderships, the fact remained that he as a bishop had conducted the consecration, and in virtually the old liturgical form. However much the Reformed Episcopalians would deprecate Anglo-Catholic obsessions with episcopal orders, they themselves had taken as their first major step an action that seemed to place the question of episcopal orders right back at center stage. Cummins and Cheney might not believe in apostolic succession; the point of the consecration cartoon was that they certainly seemed to behave as though they did.

Cheney, for his part, saw no irony in this at all. For him, the procedure simply affirmed the thoroughgoing Episcopalianism of the new movement. In a series of lectures delivered in 1888, Cheney asked: "Why does [the Reformed Episcopal Church] continue to consecrate bishops by bishops and thus perpetuate a succession to which it attaches no importance?" He answered the question this way:

> Reformed Episcopalians *do* attach importance to their historic Episcopate. We do not hold that it is necessary to the existence of a valid ministry and a true church. But we believe that it links us with the glorious Reformers of the English Church. Their polity is ours. . . . But that is not all. . . . The work of this Church must always be largely in the line of opening a refuge for Episcopalians. It must be a home for men who love a liturgy and Episcopal government, though loving the Gospel better. And to such it is able to say, "Whatever you had in your mother Church, of historic value, you have here also. If your old Church claimed to give you an Episcopate historic beyond all question, so do we."[25]

But to Benjamin Leacock, any sign of fussiness over proper consecrations or preservation of a "historic episcopate" sat dangerously at cross-purposes with the very reason the Reformed Episcopal Church had been called into existence. "The danger to the Reformed Episcopal Church . . . is the link of the so-called 'Apostolic Succession,'" complained Leacock. "We are now satisfied with boasting that we have this Apostolic Succession for whatever it is worth," something Leacock denounced as a contradiction of "the more precious truth" of the gospel "that ought to draw and bind us firmly and lovingly to the Protestant bodies around us." Leacock warned that "the religion of the natural heart revels in the idea of a tactual succession from the Apostles," and he prophesied that "the time may come when we will esteem it as something more than it is worth." And when that time came, Leacock declared ominously, "what we have done in the Protestant Episcopal Church, others may have to do in the Reformed Episcopal Church."[26]

In Cheney's mind, the Reformed Episcopal Church could not disassociate itself too greatly from its identity with the Episcopal Church without losing its character as a *reform* movement and becoming just another Protestant sect. But for Leacock, a Reformed Episcopal Church that harped too much on its Episcopalianism might as well never have taken the trouble to secede from the Episcopalians. Thus, almost from the first, the Reformed Episcopalians discovered that their movement was more complex than they themselves had anticipated and that it was going to be plagued by a fundamental ambivalence about its very identity. And they would discover, too, that in Cheney and Leacock they had only heard the beginning of a fateful struggle between two skilled and determined partisans.

Laying No New Foundation

For the moment, there was no time for either Cummins or Cheney to contemplate the technicalities or consequences of their actions. Cummins had already received an application from St. George's Chapel, Chicago, for admission into the new church as early as November 25 (it was received on December 18 as Emmanuel Reformed Episcopal Church), and a candidate for ordination had presented himself to Cummins even before his departure for Chicago.[27] Now, an urgent call came from Peoria, Illinois, 160 miles south of Chicago, for Cummins to come and organize a new congregation there. Because this appeal had been issued by Alexander H. Tyng, brother of Stephen Tyng Jr., Cummins lost no time in dragging his retinue of clergymen, including Cheney, down to Peoria. Arriving by train on the evening of December 16, Cummins held an organizing meeting in the borrowed facilities of the Second Presbyterian Church of Peoria. "Ritualism cannot be put down by the bishops either in this country or in England," Cummins defiantly announced to the overflow crowd. "A reform must come outside of the church, and I chose to go out and assist in the reform, and I would go out a thousand times rather than again officiate in a ritualistic church." He then went on to sum up what the Reformed Episcopal Church would stand for:

> The Reformed Episcopal Church is going back to the old system. It proposes to use the prayer book of 1785 instead of that of 1789. It does not accept or preach the doctrine of apostolic succession. It will treat all clergymen of other denominations as equal with us. If they join us we shall not ask that they be ordained. We shall commune with evangelical Christians of every denomination. We shall omit from the baptismal rite the word "regenerate." We shall omit everything tending to sacerdotalism. We shall pray for all ministers and all people, not for Episcopalians only. We shall take as our standard the Bishop White prayer book. We shall restore, not destroy.[28]

Cheney and Aycrigg followed Cummins with "a fervent appeal," and by the end of the meeting enough members had been recruited and funds pledged to organize a new congregation and hire a minister.

The Peoria and Chicago congregations were only the beginning. Cummins seems to have given little thought to the possibility that his protest would find willing hearers outside the United States, but sometime in December he received an appeal from a group of Evangelical Anglican people in Moncton, New Brunswick, to extend the Reformed Episcopal jurisdiction to them. Cummins leapt at the opportunity to bring Evangelical refugees from the Anglican Church of Canada under his wing, and on January 11, 1874, he sent William Feltwell to organize a new congregation in Moncton. The Moncton Evangelicals had the bad fortune to have as their bishop one of the strongest Anglo-Catholics in the Maritime Provinces, and their old parish had been the scene of repeated and ugly confrontations between clergy appointed by the bishop to represent his opinions, and clergy elected by the congregation to represent theirs. "The congregation dwindled almost altogether away," wrote an American observer. "Only the movement of Bishop Cummins could deliver them."[29] It took them only one day to be thus delivered. After hearing Feltwell preach on January 11, the old congregation organized itself as St. Paul's Reformed Episcopal Church, with Feltwell as rector, and bade farewell to their bishop.[30] Without in the slightest measure expecting it, Cummins had acquired an international episcopate.

In fact, Cummins scarcely needed to do more than beckon to get responses. In most cases, existing Episcopal congregations either tried to switch allegiances as parishes or formed new parishes on their own and petitioned Cummins for recognition. In the East Falls neighborhood of Philadelphia, the newly organized Episcopal parish of Trinity Church was about to dedicate its new building on April 8, 1874. Trinity Church had originated in a mission set up by six laymen in 1871 and had found a sponsor in the pharmaceutical magnate Thomas H. Powers. Both Powers and the first two clergymen employed by the infant congregation, John Fugette and Walter Windeyer, were strongly Evangelical in sympathy. Powers, in particular, had severed his ties with another Philadelphia church, St. James the Less (and broke with many of his family who remained members at St. James's) in protest against its prevailing Tractarianism. With the news of Cummins's secession, Powers saw no reason not to walk out of the Episcopal Church altogether, and because he owned the Trinity Church building and employed a large number of the congregation in his factory, Trinity Church and the Rev. Mr. Windeyer walked out with him. On the very day when Trinity Church would otherwise have become a full parish in the Diocese of Pennsylvania, it suddenly became Grace Chapel / First Reformed Episcopal Church, Philadelphia, and Powers and Windeyer and all the others associated with them became the first Philadelphia Reformed Episcopalians.[31]

Other congregations began to sprout spontaneously, each of them, like so many squalling orphans, demanding Cummins's personal attention. In Cummins's old diocese of Kentucky, a committee of forty was formed on January 16, 1874, to organize a Reformed Episcopal parish in Louisville. "It would not be a proper estimate," wrote one delighted sympathizer, "were we to state that if a Reformed Episcopal Church was immediately organized in this city, over six hundred members would be enrolled, acknowledging their adherence to the doctrines of the Reformed Episcopal Church."[32] But before a new church could be formed, an already existing parish, Emmanuel Church, took the lead and bolted from the Diocese of Kentucky on July 16, 1874.[33] "The congregation, under its new organization, retains their former house of worship, with their former vestry and wardens," reported *The Episcopalian*, "and we presume will shortly be admitted into communion with the Reformed Church."[34] On July 21, Cummins accepted Emmanuel Church into the Reformed Episcopal Church, and in October he conducted a visitation of the church and arranged for the installation of a new rector, John K. Dunn.[35]

Two other Emmanuel Churches also claimed Cummins's oversight. On September 8, 1874, wielding a silver trowel specially inscribed for the occasion, Cummins laid the foundation stone for Emmanuel Church, Ottawa, where Mason Gallagher would be the temporary rector for a congregation of like-minded Orangemen.[36] In December 1874, Cummins and Gallagher were back in New Jersey to preside at the organizing meeting for Emmanuel Church in Newark, where "over fifteen hundred people" were present to hear Cummins rehearse once again the reason and motives for the Reformed Episcopal Church.[37]

But of all the places that required Cummins's immediate presence, none was more critical than New York City. Cummins began to fulfill his pledge to the first General Council to organize a parish there on the first Sunday of 1874. With Benjamin Leacock and William Feltwell assisting him in the use of the 1785 prayer book, and using hymns printed in a leaflet, Cummins addressed a congregation of nearly 2,000 packed into Steinway Hall.[38] Once more, Cummins rose to speak in terms of restoration and reform, to deny innovation and revolution, to put the Reformed Episcopal Church on as secure a Protestant and Whiggish base as he could:

> We are laying no new foundation. We are building alone upon the old. We have no new Gospel to preach. If there are any people in this land who expect we shall preach science, civilization, or philanthropy, God un-deceive them today; we have nothing but the simple Gospel to preach, now and for ever, Jesus Christ. . . . We are not laying foundations, we are seeking to remove the unsound superstructure men have built upon, and to plant ourselves upon the solid rock. . . . But in resisting and rejecting these human fabrics . . . we are returning to the old, the sure, the tried, the elect, the precious cornerstone. We make no new departure; it is the old departure, begun 1,800 years ago by the Sea of Galilee, restored and purified by the reformers of thc sixteenth century, and sought to be established on this new world by the patriots of the American Revolution. We are part of the historic Church of Christ. Our faith, our ministry, our worship, belong to the old way, the good way of our fathers. The very prayer-book we use today, the first time since the lapse of 84 years, was the revision effected by men, some of whom were signers of the Declaration of Independence. . . . On this foundation, then, do we take our stand—Christ Jesus, His Gospel in its purity, His church in its ancient simplicity, His worship holy and uncorrupted by superstitious ceremony and rite. . . . We build in hope, hope of a better day, a day of the re-union of Christians, of a church of the future, that shall not be sectarian, but a confederation of all Protestant churches.[39]

Leacock found Cummins's sermon "a grand exposition of the simple Gospel." But he seems to have missed in the process the ambiguities that lurked in this sermon as much as in the Chicago consecration sermon. Although Cummins stressed repeatedly that the Reformed Episcopal Church was not a new foundation, he just as repeatedly employed metaphors—"It is the same Gospel that Paul preached at Rome and Peter preached at Jerusalem"—which implied that he wanted to start over from the earliest points of the New Testament, and not just "the sixteenth century" or "the patriots of the American Revolution." That, in turn, raised a question about Cummins's intentions: Did he mean to slough off just the excesses of the Anglo-Catholics, or, in conventional sectarian fashion, was he also holding himself free to jettison anything else that fell under the rubric of mere "tradition" (including Anglican tradition)? There was also another question buried in this sermon about Cummins's oft-repeated pledge of ecumenicity: Just what shape did Cummins imagine the relationship between the Reformed Episcopal Church and "all Protestant churches" would assume? It is fairly clear that Cummins, like Muhlenberg, rather naively believed that all evangelical Christendom really hungered for unity, and especially unity under a suitable Anglican banner. Relieve Episcopalianism of its Tractarian offenses, Cummins reasoned, and American evangelicals of whatever denomination would flock to become Anglicans. Hence, what Cummins really expected the Reformed Episcopal Church to provide was the starting point for *organic* union, in which the evangelical denominations would happily blend themselves into the Reformed Episcopal movement. But, running parallel to this idea in almost all of his utterances was the reluctant recognition that the touchy denominational pride of Presbyterians, Methodists, and Congregationalists was no easy creature to tame and would have to be placated by inoffensive protestations of friendliness and respect. And it was at those moments that Cummins began to speak of *federal* union rather than *organic* union. Instead of being the catalyst that would bring together all evangelical Christians, the Reformed Episcopal Church would simply be a friendly member of a "confederation of all Protestant Churches." Like so many nineteenth-century ecumenists, Cummins was caught between the ideal of organic union and having to settle for federal union among churches as the best one could hope for in the highly competitive and sectarian atmosphere of evangelical Christianity. Some, like Philip Schaff (who had shared the platform of the Evangelical Alliance with Cummins), pleaded that denominationalism was not necessarily inconsistent with a "true catholicity of spirit."[40] But in the case of the Reformed Episcopalians, the tragedy of settling for federal union as a second-best was that it allowed other American evangelical denominations to welcome the creation of the Reformed Episcopal Church without feeling the slightest incentive to do anything else. In his eagerness to show that he was not challenging the validity of other evangelical churches, Cummins was unwittingly inviting them to treat the Reformed Episcopal Church as merely another sect rather than the harbinger of "evangelical catholicity."

Finally, on February 15, after a month and a half of morning services in Steinway Hall, and evening services in Lyric Hall, Cummins called for the formal organization of the congregation as the First Reformed Episcopal Church of New York City.[41] A committee

chaired by Benjamin Aycrigg superintended the creation of a constitution and a set of bylaws, and on Monday, March 9, First Church
was duly incorporated, with Cummins named as rector.[42] By now,
however, the strain of six months of unabating stress and activity
had begun to tell on Cummins, and after little more than one week
as rector of the new church he suffered a complete physical collapse.[43]
"At first his physicians hoped that a short rest from constant labor
would restore him," wrote Alexandrine Cummins.[44] But Cummins
was more seriously ill than his doctors suspected, and on March 18
he resigned as rector of First Church and withdrew to the quiet of
Summit, New Jersey, the summer home of Stephen Tyng Jr. Not
until September would Cummins be strong enough to resume leadership of the Reformed Episcopalians.

Meanwhile, Cummins's resignation precipitated a major crisis
within First Church. "The fact was," recalled Benjamin Leacock,
"he had drawn about him . . . that wandering tribe that are on the
lookout for sensation."[45] When Cummins went, so did the bulk of
his hearers, and Leacock soon found himself preaching to an evening
congregation of thirty in the emptiness of Lyric Hall. But at just the
moment when it appeared that First Church was about to founder,
the Rev. William Tufnell Sabine, who had been among Cummins's
counselors at the conference at the Dakes' six months before, and
who was the immensely popular Evangelical rector of New York
City's Church of the Atonement, announced in April that he would
withdraw from the Protestant Episcopal Church to join Cummins.
First Church at once offered him the vacant rectorship, and he at
once agreed on April 30, preaching for the first time as the new
rector on May 3. Sabine was First Church's rescue, for he brought
with him a considerable store of talents and prestige. He was "evangelical, a strong controversialist, a brilliant preacher; withal, a
Christian gentleman and a devoted pastor."[46] Equally important for
the moment, Sabine also brought with him 200 members from the
congregation of the Church of the Atonement. Within another
week, the now-revived First Church moved out of Steinway Hall
for good and into a building at Forty-Seventh Street and Madison
Avenue owned by none other than Stephen Tyng Jr.'s Church of
the Holy Trinity (Tyng himself assumed responsibility for the
lease). Eventually, in May 1876, the vestry of First Church was able
to purchase three lots on Madison Avenue between Fifty-Fifth and
Fifty-Sixth Streets for what was, even then, the remarkably inex-
pensive sum of $42,450. The downpayment was made by one of the
vestry, and the church was able to erect the building which would
be its home for the next half-century.[47]

Cummins's illness now put the full burden of episcopal leadership

onto Bishop Cheney, who, like Cummins, already had his hands
full. On January 4, 1874, Cheney revisited the new congregation in
Peoria and saw to its incorporation as Christ Church. "We can already count over fifty communicants," wrote one member jubilantly. "We look forward to Lent and Easter as a Gospel feast, under
the pure teaching of the Reformed Episcopal Church, and feel sorrow for those all over the land who must still starve on Heresy and
Schism, Apostolical Succession, Baptismal Regeneration, Church
Architecture and History, and other Churchly subjects."[48] Perhaps
such rejoicing was a little too jubilant, for Cheney quickly found it
necessary to issue a pastoral letter, chiding his new charges for too
much neglect of "churchly subjects," such as Lent itself. But he
could not afford to bestow too much time on any Peoria enthusiasts.
Calls from St. Louis, Missouri; Lawrence, Kansas; and Chillicothe,
Illinois, pulled Cheney around the Midwest to organize congregations. In addition to all this, he still had to be pastor of Christ
Church, and on the same day as his visitation to Peoria he somehow
managed to conduct his first confirmations in Chicago (forty-six
people confirmed). On February 25, he had the satisfaction of seeing
Christ Church officially organized as a Reformed Episcopal parish.[49]

In spite of the difficulties posed by Cummins's absence and the
burdens of Cheney's responsibilities, by the time the Second General
Council was due to convene in New York City in May 1874 there
was nothing to hand around but congratulations and good cheer. In
addition to Cummins and Cheney, and the other five founding clergymen (Smith, Feltwell, Bourne, Leacock, and Gallagher), ten new
clergymen had added themselves to the clergy roll, all but one of
them transferring credentials from the Protestant Episcopal Church,
and all in less than six months. But no less surprising were the ten
parishes already up and operating, two each in New York City and
Chicago, two in Canada, one in Philadelphia, and the rest scattered
through the West and Midwest, as far as Denver. Where had they to
go but forward? "Beloved brethren of the clergy and laity of the
Reformed Episcopal Church," exclaimed Cheney in his sermon to
the Council, "let us today lift our hearts in thanksgiving for what
God hath already wrought."[50]

One Great Family

By the time one more year had passed, the "brethren of the clergy
and laity" had quadrupled, as many Evangelical Episcopalians, who
had been sitting on the ecclesiastical fence to see whether the Re-

formed Episcopalians would survive their first six months, now came down from their perches and threw themselves behind Cummins and Cheney. In November 1874, William Rufus Nicholson, secretary of the American Church Missionary Society, resigned as rector of the influential parish of Trinity Church, Newark, and came over into the Reformed Episcopal Church. Born on January 8, 1822, in Green County, Mississippi, Nicholson was the son of a devout Methodist judge, and because Nicholson was once described as having preached his first sermon at age fourteen, it appears that he had early inclinations toward the Methodist ministry.[51] After graduating from LaGrange College in LaGrange, Alabama (a Methodist Episcopal institution), that was precisely what he did, being ordained as a deacon in the Methodist Episcopal Church in 1842. Then, abruptly, his ministry took a sharp turn, for on February 14, 1847, Nicholson submitted to reordination as a deacon in the Protestant Episcopal Church at the hands of Bishop Leonidas Polk, the pioneering missionary bishop of the South. This was quickly followed by ordination to the priesthood of the Protestant Episcopal Church the following April in Christ Church, New Orleans.

It is impossible to say just what Nicholson thought his reordination meant or symbolized, but one thing is certain: it did nothing to discourage his emergence as an Evangelical of the most fiery stamp. His talents as a preacher carried him from his first parochial charge at Grace Church, New Orleans, north to St. John's Church in Cincinnati, Ohio, in June 1849. It was while serving there in 1857 that Nicholson was awarded an honorary doctor of divinity degree by Kenyon College, the institution founded and built by the other pioneering missionary bishop of the day, Philander Chase. In 1859, Nicholson was called to succeed one of the most prominent of the Evangelicals, Alexander Vinton, at St. Paul's Church in Boston. There he stayed until 1872, when he transferred to the charge of Trinity Church in Newark.

Although both Nicholson and Cummins seem to have known each other as early as the 1860s through their mutual interest in the American Church Missionary Society, and though both men shared a common background in Methodism, Nicholson and Cummins represent some interesting contrasts. Whereas Cummins looked for his agenda back to the Muhlenberg Memorial of the 1850s and the prayer book debates of the late 1860s, Nicholson is much more of a transitional figure in terms of what American evangelicalism, as a whole, was soon to become. By the turn of the century, the incapacity of Protestant evangelicalism to shape and give respectability to American culture was slowly shrinking and hardening the old

evangelicalism into the culturally impotent carapace of fundamentalism and becoming more ingrown, defensive, and distracted by the
development of strange new forms of millennial and prophetic theology. This is especially evident in Nicholson's early and vigorous
espousal of dispensationalism, a dramatic brand of eschatology filled
with vivid portrayals of the imminent return of Christ to the earth,
the conversion of the Jews, and the end of the world—or, looked at
another way, of a resignation by evangelicals of any attempt at defining culture and replacing it with an anxious longing to escape
from it. Nicholson was an important figure in the highly popular
and publicized "prophecy conferences" of the 1880s and 1890s, and
it was probably Nicholson's personal influence that helped bring
many other "dispensational" devotees, such as James M. Gray and
Arno Gabelein, into the Reformed Episcopal Church.[52]

But in 1874, it was Nicholson's talents as a leader and preacher,
not his dispensationalism, that caused Cummins to welcome him
into the ranks of the Reformed Episcopal Church. Charles Edward
Cheney, who had little use for Nicholson's "very pronounced beliefs on certain theological and eschatological points," nevertheless
acknowledged Nicholson's forcefulness and strength in the pulpit:

> I would say that the very first idea with which Bishop
> Nicholson impressed me was one of unusual *power*. Possibly
> his grand physical frame, towering stature, and almost ma-
> jestic presence, contributed to this result. But when one came
> to hear him in public address, there was a massive force in his
> marshalling of arguments, and a sledge-hammer weight in
> his reasoning, which made the listener, whether he agreed or
> disagreed with his conclusions, feel that whatever else
> Nicholson was, he was an intellectual athlete, a spiritually
> strong man.[53]

That same forcefulness was also evident in the letter of resignation
he wrote to the wardens and vestry of Trinity Church on November 18, 1874. "The Church principles now so universally believed
and taught . . . are, in my judgement, not only Scripturally untrue,
but also (I mean no offense) deeply dishonoring to the Lord and
Master, and especially so to the Holy Spirit," Nicholson wrote.
"The General Convention has made tenfold more intense the anti-
Protestant errors of the now-prevailing churchmanship, and never
till there is a revised Prayer-book can such errors be counter-acted."[54]
With that, he parted company with the Episcopal Church and placed
himself under Cummins's jurisdiction, and sat down to wait on his
future.

He did not wait for long. A new Reformed Episcopal congregation had organized in Philadelphia in May 1874 as the Second Reformed Episcopal Church, and it quickly offered the rectorship to Nicholson. He just as quickly accepted, and preached for them for the first time on December 6, 1874.[55] Beginning with 130 communicants on his first Sunday, Nicholson went on to build Second Church into a major Reformed Episcopal institution with 550 communicants, a Sunday School of 575 members, and an imposing stone edifice at Twenty-First and Chestnut Streets. Not even a disastrous fire in 1889, which destroyed the church building, daunted Nicholson. The church was promptly rebuilt and renamed St. Paul's Church in 1890. But Nicholson had too much energy, and carried with him too much influence, for Cummins to limit him solely to one parish. In May 1875 the Third General Council elected Nicholson to fill the missionary bishopric Cummins had once wanted for Muhlenberg. Nicholson's consecration on February 24, 1876, was a significant event, and not only for the 600 people who crowded the unfinished chapel of Second Church. In an effort to give dramatic public testimony to his message of ecumenical brotherhood, Cummins had invited as a co-consecrator, with himself and Cheney, Bishop Matthew Simpson, the first and principal figure of the Methodist Episcopal Church. "The most noticeable feature in the whole ceremony was that clergymen of other denominations had been invited to take part in the ceremony and to assist in the administration of Holy Communion," marveled the *Ottawa Times*, which took the trouble to cover the event. Cummins was even more exultant. "This day," he said, "is a day worth living to see. No such scene has been witnessed for centuries in the Episcopal Church."[56] Indeed it had not, although Cummins might have had some cause to temper his jubilation had he foreseen exactly what Nicholson's consecration was going to mean for the church.

Three thousand miles away, Cummins found another supporter of like standing and abilities in the person of the Very Reverend the Dean of Victoria, British Columbia, Edward Cridge. Born in Bratton Fleming, Devonshire, in 1817, Cridge was a Cambridge man, ordained in 1848 and sent out in 1854 as the missionary pioneer of Anglicanism on the Canadian Pacific Coast. He started as chaplain to the Hudson's Bay Company post in Victoria and minister of the District Church; in 1860, when a new diocese for British Columbia was organized, the District Church became Christ Church and was converted into the diocesan cathedral, with Cridge as rector and dean. At the same time, however, Cridge began to run afoul of the new bishop of British Columbia, George Hills, an ardent Tractarian. On December 5, 1872, Bishop Hills put up his new archdeacon, William Sheldon Reese, to preach the sermon at the reopening of the cathedral (after a rebuilding program), and Reese proceeded, to Cridge's horror, to extol Hills's new rituals along with the new architecture. Cridge arose before the benediction could be given and bluntly informed the cathedral congregation that "it was the first time since the church had been built and he its minister, that such doctrine had been advocated, and, with God's help, he would see that it was the last, as long as he was its minister."[57]

It took a great deal to provoke a man like Cridge. He was, like Nicholson, a big, burly man, but gracious and self-effacing to a fault and addicted to playing the cello. (As an undergraduate, Cridge had been one of the founders of the Cambridge University Musical Society.) But Bishop Hills received Cridge's declaration as a personal rebuke and accordingly demanded that Cridge apologize to Reese and to himself. Cridge refused, and on September 22, 1874, Hills proceeded to suspend Cridge from the ministry and put him on ecclesiastical trial for "brawling in church." The ecclesiastical court shortly found Cridge guilty. But the cathedral's congregation supported Cridge rather than their unpopular and high-handed bishop, and they refused to admit Hills to the church building to conduct services. Hills upped the ante still further by taking Cridge and the congregation to the provincial Supreme Court over control of the property of Christ Church, and at that point, Cridge offered to pacify Hills with a qualified apology (Cridge would make the apology, but without acknowledging Hills's right to demand it). But Hills knew he held the legal high ground in British Columbia. He rejected Cridge's offer, and on October 24 the Supreme Court issued an injunction barring Cridge from Christ Church. Now there was no other choice, and on October 27 three-quarters of the congregation voted to organize a new church with Cridge as rector.[58] "We are not seceding from the Anglican Church," Cridge insisted in an address to the rump congregation that had followed him, "because the Anglican Bishop [has] virtually seceded from the Anglican Church, and tried to draw the congregation with him; up to last Sunday week we all were more nearly connected with the Anglican Church (with all respect) than the Bishop himself."[59]

Up to that point, Cridge had had no contact with the Reformed Episcopalians. But on the morning of November 1, 1874, just before Cridge was to open a meeting for his new parish, newspapers from Ottawa came across his desk with notices of the opening of Emmanuel Church, Ottawa, and its connections with Cummins. Cridge at once seized on these reports, and as soon as he had successfully organized his new congregation in Victoria as the Church of Our Lord, Cridge applied for admission into the Reformed Episcopal Church.[60] Cummins was only too happy to accept. The Church of Our Lord not only gave the Reformed Episcopalians an important outpost on the Pacific Coast and in Canada, but also put Cridge's own prestige at Cummins's disposal.

While Nicholson and Cridge were anchoring the Reformed Episcopal Church on either side of a continent, a third and equally interesting recruit appeared out of the Midwest. Samuel Fallows was, like Cridge, English-born (in 1835), but he emigrated to Deansville, Wisconsin, with his family in 1848. His parents were Wesleyan Methodists, and after taking his degrees at the infant University of Wisconsin in 1857–59, Fallows became a Wesleyan Methodist minister and served several congregations across Wisconsin. When the Civil War broke out, Fallows marched off as chaplain to the 32nd Wisconsin Infantry. Quickly tiring of so passive and unadventuresome a role, Fallows resigned his chaplaincy and returned home to raise his own regiment, the 40th Wisconsin, which he commanded as lieutenant-colonel. By the end of the war, he had risen to colonel of the 49th Wisconsin and the brevet rank of brigadier-general. The war made him something of a hero in Wisconsin, and in 1870 he was rewarded with the political plum of State Superintendent of Public Instruction, and in 1874, he was named president of Illinois Wesleyan University.

Fallows's interest in education marked him as a maverick among the Wesleyan Methodists, who had been organized as something of a protest against the creation of formal theological colleges for Methodist clergy. But that only served to put him in sympathy with other mavericks, principal among which was Charles Edward Cheney. Through his wife, Lucy Huntingdon, Fallows was related to one Episcopal bishop and several other Episcopal clergy, and in the early 1870s he had seriously considered finding freer air among the Episcopalians. But the Cheney case, and Bishop Whitehouse's highhanded rule of the Diocese of Illinois, discouraged him from finding an Episcopal answer to Methodist troubles. Those fears vanished, however, with the organization of the Reformed Episcopal Church and Cheney's election to its episcopate. Once he had wound up his affairs with Illinois Wesleyan in June 1875, Fallows presented himself to Cheney. As a gesture of evangelical solidarity, Fallows was taken into the Reformed Episcopal ministry without a word uttered about reordination.

A good many other words might have been said about Fallows,

not all of them complimentary. A man of tremendous energy, it
became easy to set him down as a man of equally tremendous ambition, willing to use his position within the Reformed Episcopal
Church largely as a springboard into prominence in other affairs. He
was relentlessly interested in social and educational reform, serving
by turns as director of the American Medical Missionary Society
(1887), director of the Illinois Anti-Saloon League (1904), president
of the Cook County Temperance Union (1882), vice-president of
the Chicago Red Cross (1883), president of the Board of Managers
of the Illinois State Reformatory (1891–1912), and vice-president of
the National Temperance Society (1890). In 1895, he even organized
a "Home Salon" in Chicago, which promised to slack the working-
man's thirst for liquor by selling a low-alcohol potion known as
"Bishop's Beer." He parlayed his Civil War service into the Chap-
laincy-in-Chief of the politically powerful Grand Army of the Republic, and found himself in the company of presidents and senators
(he served on President Taft's fact-finding Commission in the Phil-
ippines in 1913) and even the Archbishop of Canterbury. And he
dreamed of founding a "University of the West"—not another
Wesleyan cow college but a midwestern Harvard that would open
up the American heartland to science, literature, and religion as
never before. This incessant rush from one program to another
made Fallows nationally famous. It also made him suspicious in the
eyes of eastern Reformed Episcopalians, who (either from envy or
irritation) wondered how dedicated Fallows really was to the church
that had given him a platform from which to speak.

A far more damning word than "ambitious" to describe Fallows
was "liberal." If William Rufus Nicholson would come to represent
the forces tugging the Reformed Episcopal Church in a fundamentalist direction, then Fallows would come to stand for movement to
the opposite pole. In 1875, the thinking that would gradually become known as "liberalism" or "modernism" was still under the
horizon of American religion, but only just. The radical impact of
German higher criticism, together with the damaging consequences
of Darwin's evolutionism, staggered the self-confidence of traditional Christians in their own beliefs. Many, trying to hold onto
some pieces of their religion and still maintain their place in the
Victorian scheme of things, attempted either to alter or amend
Christian doctrine, or to deflect its attention from spiritual to more
this-worldly concerns. In so doing they crossed not only the authority of the Bible but also the evangelical Protestant confidence in natural-law rationality and common-sense theology. For those who

were unwilling to abandon either, "liberalism" was simple intellectual treason.

The first major confrontation of theological liberalism and conservatism occurred only two years after Fallows's admission to the Reformed Episcopal Church in the famous (and futile) trial of Chicago Presbyterian David Swing on charges of heretical departures from the Westminster Confession of Faith. Fallows had been privately, if not publicly, sympathetic to Swing during his trial and thereafter, and he made no secret of his own inclination toward a moderate but definite liberalism. Early in his career, Fallows (according to his daughter and biographer, Alice) "learned the great truth which he was to spend the rest of his life unfolding—that creeds and formulas are not religion, but the definitions of religion; that virtue and sin are relative terms, changing as men change; that good may live in the heart of evil and that all men under their differences are brothers."[61] Professions of that sort were a far cry from the preaching of Cummins or Cheney, and it is worth asking what a man like Fallows thought he saw in the Reformed Episcopal Church. The answer to that lies in the fact that in the 1870s the Reformed Episcopal blow against the constrictions of Anglo-Catholic ritualism was itself viewed as a "liberal" movement, at least in the sense of rebelling against formalism in favor of tolerance and openness. It was not easy for Cummins's contemporaries to see that Cummins's notion of tolerance and openness did not extend to unorthodox or unevangelical theology. It sufficed for many rising liberals to hear what they wanted to hear in Cummins's call for church unity and ecclesiastical freedom, and like Fallows, they were pleased to see the Reformed Episcopalians as a progressive group of innovators who sought to slough off "thought-confining creeds, the antique liturgy, and the medieval sacerdotalism of their High Church adversaries."[62]

And so Fallows, the friend of Shailer Mathews as much as of Dwight L. Moody, threw off the tightening bands of Wesleyan Methodism for what he saw as the broader garments of the Reformed Episcopalians. Little did he dream that his compulsive dogoodism and midwestern liberalism would actually help to further blur the already unsteady identity of the infant church. At first the Reformed Episcopalians saw in Fallows only a preacher and administrator of exhilarating eloquence and unbelievable physical stamina. Oddly enough, like William Rufus Nicholson, his first pastoral task in the Reformed Episcopal Church would be to build up yet another St. Paul's Church, this time in Chicago (within ten years, St. Paul's, Chicago, had 360 communicants on its rolls—third-largest in the

Reformed Episcopal Church—and the largest parish budget in the entire movement). And again, like Nicholson, he was singled out for consecration to the episcopate in 1876.

Fallows, Cridge, and Nicholson represent only the most dazzling new recruits to the Reformed Episcopal movement. Following hard behind them were still others, of lesser fame at the time but not lesser abilities. John Howard-Smith, born in 1820 and yet another graduate of Virginia Theological Seminary, had already spent a quarter-century of his life as the rector of the Church of the Intercession in Washington Heights, New York, and St. John's Church in Knoxville, Tennessee, when he finally gave up all hope for the Evangelical cause in the Episcopal Church and on April 23, 1875, joined ranks with Cummins. Contemplative, soft-spoken, with a forbidding set of mutton-chop whiskers thicker even than Cheney's, Howard-Smith was, theologically speaking, almost everything Fallows was not. More like Nicholson, with whom he would work very closely in the 1880s and 1890s, Howard-Smith stubbornly defended the exclusive authority and divine inspiration of the Bible in determining Christian belief.

> *All* Scripture is God-inspired. Strong in that mighty word, we trample under foot all such sayings as "the Bible *contains* the word of God," leaving man to decide by *his* human inspiration, what is, and what is not God's Divine inspiration. Our watchword, as it has been through the ages past in the church of God, is this: The Bible is the word of God so simply, so sheerly God's word, that even when it records the errors and sophisms of men, or the lies of the devil, the *record*, in all its parts, is the Lord's record to serve distinctly the Lord's purpose.[63]

On the other hand, Howard-Smith pulled up considerably shy of Nicholson's full-blown fundamentalism. He gloried in his Episcopalianism and, like Cheney, never considered that in coming into the Reformed Episcopal Church he had ever left Anglicanism. To the contrary, he lauded the Reformed Episcopal Church as "the now real church of the English Reformation." He passionately believed that a church without roots in the overall history of Christianity was a pointless and perhaps pernicious endeavor. In *The Historic Basis of the Reformed Episcopal Church* (1883), Howard-Smith would vigorously criticize the superficiality of American Protestants who were only too willing to cut themselves off from the testimony of the doctrine and practice of ancient Christianity:

> The Churches of the post-Reformation era have largely elim-
> inated this element of history. . . . They have sought an or-
> ganization that shall not only be harmonious with the written
> Scripture, but shall be so exclusively Scriptural as to ignore
> the subsequent history of the Church as in any sense a factor
> in the development of Christian thought or the flow of
> Christian life.[64]

Others beside Howard-Smith crowded into the Reformed Episcopal Church in the 1870s. James A. Latane, who had greeted the
news of Cummins's withdrawal with such dumbfounded relief in
West Virginia, withdrew from the Episcopal Church in the summer
of 1874 and promptly began organizing Reformed Episcopal missions in Virginia. Latane would soon be elected a bishop, virtually
by acclamation, at the third General Council in 1875, only to decline
the election: four years later, he would be elected again and would
relent and begin a twenty-two-year career in the Reformed Episcopal episcopate in Baltimore, Philadelphia, and Canada. Edward D.
Neill was received without reordination from the Presbyterians in
1874 after having served as private secretary to both Presidents
Abraham Lincoln and Andrew Johnson, then as U.S. Consul to
Dublin, and finally as rector of Macalester College in Minneapolis.
He too set about organizing a new Reformed Episcopal church in
Minneapolis. William Morton Postlethwaite, an old associate of
John Howard-Smith, left the Episcopal Church to join Cheney in
Chicago in 1875, but he spent the largest part of his life in the Reformed Episcopal Church at West Point, where he became the chaplain to the United States Military Academy in 1882. James M. Gray,
a Bostonian and protégé of William Rufus Nicholson, was ordained
in the Reformed Episcopal Church in 1877, but he (like Postlethwaite) achieved his greatest success outside parish ministry, as the
first president of the celebrated Moody Bible Institute in Chicago.
Charles William Quick, who had been ordained by Bishop Meade
of Virginia in 1848 and who was received into the Reformed Episcopal Church by Bishop Nicholson in 1877, never actually served in a
Reformed Episcopal parish. But he brought to the church the prize
of the Evangelical church newspaper, *The Episcopal Recorder*, which
Quick both owned and edited and which now became the principal
news organ of the Reformed Episcopal Church.

By the time the third General Council met in Cheney's own
Christ Church in Chicago on May 12, 1875, the clergy roll of the
Reformed Episcopal Church had swelled to forty-two presbyters
and deacons, more than twice the number enrolled in 1874 and six

times as many as had joined Cummins in New York on the day of the Association Hall meeting—and all this had occurred in little more then eighteen months. What was more, all but seven of the presbyters were old Episcopal men, with long histories of service in the Episcopal Church. "With what agony of soul each of us has been led, conscience-bound, to leave the roof which has been the abode of a life-time, to sever associations cemented by long years of friendship, He only knows who searcheth the heart," said Cummins, as he preached the council's opening sermon.[65] But there was nevertheless every bright hope that the rapid momentum of the new church would snowball year by year until it would rival the old church.

> Already by the good hand of our God upon us you have builded wisely and well. You have completed a work which has been left unfinished for three centuries. . . . You present to the world such a Church as under God would have united the Reformers of England, under Edward VI, and the Reformers of the Continent in one great family; . . . a Church holding to such an Episcopacy as Calvin and Knox would not have rejected . . . such as Evangelical men in the Church of our Fathers have ever claimed to be most in harmony with the Word of God.[66]

Jim Crow and John Bull Among the Reformed Episcopalians

The year 1875 also brought to the side of the Reformed Episcopal Church two of the most startling accessions it would ever receive, one from England and one from the American South. The end of the American Civil War in 1865, and the passage of the Thirteenth Amendment to the Constitution, brought an end to the system of slavery that had kept American blacks in bondage since colonial times. But freedom from slavery did not necessarily translate at once into freedom for opportunity and advancement. Under slavery, Southern whites claimed to own both the work and the bodies of their slaves, but at the same time they were also expected (either legally or morally) to provide some minimum of food and shelter and some form of basic education in Christianity. In South Carolina, where the old prerevolutionary influence of Anglicanism was still strong, this meant providing either separate chapels-of-ease for slave congregations (although always with white presbyters officiating) or separate "slave galleries" in already-existing white churches. But with the end of slavery, and the military occupation of the South by federal soldiers, Southern whites threw off all sense of responsibility for their former chattels and used various forms of official discrimination (in the form of "Jim Crow" laws) to drive the "freedmen" as far from their sight as possible.

Most Southern whites were equally prepared to apply the spirit of "Jim Crow" to their churches as well as to their laws. In 1868, the prominent Virginia Presbyterian theologian, Robert Lewis Dabney, argued violently against any move to ordain freed blacks, "because that race is not trustworthy for such position. . . . If you trust any portion of power over your church to black hands, you will rue it."[67] Even in the midst of the Civil War, the Georgia legislature had actually tried to place a civil ban on black preaching of any sort. The measure was rescinded only after pressure from Georgia Baptists and Methodists was applied, but even then their concern was motivated as much by outrage over state interference in church affairs as by a concern for Georgia blacks.[68] Not even the Episcopalians were exempt from the spirit of "Jim Crow." In 1875, St. Mark's Church in Charleston, South Carolina, whose membership was entirely composed of former slaves, applied for admission to the Diocese of South Carolina, only to be refused on the ground that black Episcopalians could never be considered the equals of white Episcopalians. The diocesan convention explained: "The Church is bound to recognize, in all its relations to the world, and its offices to mankind, that distinction between the races of men which God has been pleased to ordain, and to conform its polity and ecclesiastical organisms to his divine ordinance." The best that the diocesan bishop, William Bell White Howe (who had bravely opposed the exclusion), could offer African-Americans was the vague promise that a separate missionary jurisdiction could be set up for them.[69]

The offer of a "Jim Crow" jurisdiction had little appeal to black Episcopalians in South Carolina. It was also a blow to the handful of white Episcopalian clergy who had put their energies into training the most gifted of the former slaves for ministry in the Diocese of South Carolina. Chief among these men was Peter Fayssoux Stevens, a "cradle" Episcopalian and onetime commandant of the South Carolina State Military Academy in Charleston, and the commander of Stevens' Battery during the bombardment of Fort Sumter, at the opening of the Civil War in 1861. Stevens left military service in October 1861, when he was ordained by then Bishop Thomas Frederick Davis, and from then until 1875 he served five different South Carolina parishes "with a self-denial, devotion and zeal which are beyond all praise of man" (according to Bishop Davis) "sometimes keeping his appointments on foot."[70] At the same time, and rather unexpectedly for a former Confederate officer, Stevens devoted a good deal of his attention to the spiritual well-being of South Carolina blacks, rebuilding and repairing old chapels and establishing new ones. After the war, he banded together with two other priests, Benjamin Johnson of Trinity Church, Abbeville, and A. Toomer Porter of Holy Communion Church, Charleston, to prepare a new generation of free blacks for the priesthood.

But Stevens's pupils came to no better end in the diocese than the congregation at St. Mark's. While rector of Trinity Church, Pinopolis, Stevens established two "colored" chapels, Nazareth and Emmanuel, and astounded Bishop Howe there in 1879 when he presented the bishop with a confirmation class of ninety-nine people, ninety-five of whom were "persons of color."[71] In 1868, while still serving at Pinopolis, Stevens began preparing two former slaves, Frank C. Ferguson and Lawrence Dawson, for the ministry, even paying for Ferguson's education at St. Augustine's College in Raleigh out of his own pocket. But despite the encouragement of the bishop and a favorable examination by two examining chaplains, the diocesan Standing Committee refused to consider the notion of ordaining blacks, and it was not very discreetly hinted that if blacks wanted some kind of ordained ministry they ought to seek it with someone else.[72]

"This, of course, put us in an awkward position," Ferguson explained later, with some degree of understatement. Both Ferguson and Dawson had been raised, first under slavery and now as free men, to love the Book of Common Prayer and the Episcopal Church as their spiritual father and mother, only to be disowned on the specious ground of race the moment they offered to serve them. "You were either to do without the Episcopal Church, and go and join the various organizations among the colored people, whether it suited our spiritual appetite or not," or submit quietly to the triumph of color over catholicity.[73] And as Stevens realized, this posed a challenge to more than just Ferguson and Dawson. "Without ministers of their own, only a very few congregations could be served by the two or three white ministers who were trying to preach to the colored people," Stevens recalled, and that raised the very good question of whether there was any future for blacks anywhere in the Diocese of South Carolina.[74]

But Ferguson was not content to sit idly by. He wrote: "I told my friends we need not be in despair, that there's a Reformation going on in the PEC, and that God may work out events yet in our favour." That, at least, was how Ferguson understood the news of Cummins and the Reformed Episcopal Church. But even though Ferguson knew hardly more than that, he also knew that this "Reformation" might offer the only hope black Episcopalians would have to move forward to full opportunity without sacrificing their identity as Episcopalians. On November 18, 1874, Ferguson called together representatives from four black Episcopal missions in Charleston, Pinopolis, and Oakley, South Carolina, and put to them the inevitable question of their future:

> Brethren, our object here tonight is a most peculiar one. We are here to consider our situation in the Episcopal Church of which we claim to be members. Has the Protestant Episcopal Church given the Negro a Church or not? I answer, "No." Four colored men have been turned away from the doors of her ministry. Where this will end, we do not know. Have we an organization as a church? I contend that we need one for ourselves and our children.[75]

Ferguson first asked for a motion to withdraw from the Episcopal Church, to which the delegates responded, with a noisy assent, "We will withdraw from it, if the Church still refuses to organize us." But then where shall we go? asked Ferguson. One delegate—and this was surely no coincidence—was on his feet at once: "I move that we go to the Reformed Episcopal Church." And so the motion was carried, "without one dissenting voice," and Ferguson was authorized to establish contact with Cummins.[76]

Establishing that contact proved harder than it might have seemed. Ferguson had only the dimmest idea of where Cummins might be found, and he had to borrow a copy of the Church Almanac from a nearby Episcopal rector in order to locate Cummins's address.[77] Even then, the only address in the almanac was Cummins's old episcopal residence in Kentucky, and so the letter Ferguson addressed there took eight months before it finally came into Cummins's hands in New York City. But late was better than never. Cummins, ever since his early days in Norfolk, had "always felt a deep interest in this neglected race" (according to Alexandrine Cummins, who conveniently overlooked her husband's 1861 sermon on colonization), and he hastened to reply.[78] Moreover, he had an ideal messenger at hand. Benjamin Johnson, Peter Stevens's old associate, had come over to the Reformed Episcopal Church early in

1875 and had been appointed (at Cummins's behest) as an itinerant "Evangelist for the South," with his headquarters in Baltimore. Cummins now sent Johnson back to his old diocese, and on June 6 and June 13, 1875, Johnson held two mass meetings with Ferguson and his loyalists and was welcomed with a triumphant confirmation of their decision to join the Reformed Episcopalians. Then, in an equally strategic move, Johnson called on P. F. Stevens, who had moved to Anderson, South Carolina, in 1873, and persuaded Stevens to join him in the Reformed Episcopal Church and return to Pinopolis to give oversight to his "old field of labor."[79]

All told, Johnson brought five African-American churches—Redeemer, Emmanuel, Nazareth, Bethlehem, and St. James's—and 500 communicants into the Reformed Episcopal Church at one stroke, along with starting a new mission, Holy Trinity, in the heart of Charleston.[80] In November 1875, Cummins himself visited Charleston and Pinopolis, preaching beside Stevens and Johnson to overflow congregations in twelve places. "With exquisite taste, and tender propriety, Bishop Cummins everywhere preached the *Gospel!*" one of Cummins's defenders wrote. "Those who went for curious controversy, heard only the grand argument of the *Cross!*"[81] He also took the long-awaited step of ordaining Frank Ferguson a deacon on December 5, accompanied by Lawrence Dawson on December 19 and another Charleston black man, Edward A. Forrest, on December 17.[82]

"As anticipated," Johnson remarked afterward, Cummins's decision to welcome Ferguson, Dawson, and the African-American congregations into the Reformed Episcopal Church on an equal footing with the northern and midwestern white congregations "has prejudiced no little our work among the whites."[83] Indeed it had. Bishop Howe, frantic at the loss of the black congregations, bitterly denounced the principles of the Reformed Episcopalians from the nearest pulpit to Pinopolis he could find. P. F. Stevens immediately found himself a social outcast in Charleston, not only for committing ecclesiastical treason but also for associating himself with a northern "carpetbagger" movement.[84] But Cummins had scored an important moral point by rising above the "color line" and making the Reformed Episcopal Church's declarations about openness and liberty more than theological vocabulary. Of course, Cummins had not imagined that either he or the Reformed Episcopal Church would become pioneers of racial justice, and in the 1870s he faced as much reluctance from Northern whites in his own General Council as from South Carolina whites in their diocesan convention. But Cummins could not square his own dreams of ecumenicity with racial exclusivism. He had seen enough of exclusivism from other quarters to know better. "It is enough for us to know that we have accepted the Divine policy," Benjamin Johnson declared. "In its true Catholicity our Church is 'no respecter of persons'; Barbarians, Scythians, bond and free, have their rights of Church and of soul. The overruling of human prejudices is God's work."[85]

An invitation of a very different kind and from a very different quarter came to Cummins little more than two weeks after the organization of the Reformed Episcopal Church, when he received from a total stranger in England—one F. S. Merryweather—an abrupt notice that the Reformed Episcopal Church was neither alone nor even the first in its protest against ritualism:

> By the last mail I have forwarded documents descriptive of the principles and work of the Free Church of England. This Church was established some years ago to counteract the growth of Ritualism in the Church of England. . . . The ground you desire to take is exactly the ground we occupy, and it seemed to me that this circumstance, in the hands of an All-Wise Providence, may be the means of effecting a powerful Protestant Union for the maintenance of Evangelical Church Principles in both Countries. . . .
>
> Faithfully yours in Christian fellowship,
> F. S. Merryweather[86]

The Free Church of England was the result of some of the same issues and personalities that had produced the Gorham Judgment, in that the Free Church of England and the Gorham Judgment had Bishop Henry Philpotts of Exeter as their protagonist and Tractarianism as their issue. In 1832, the eleventh Duke of Somerset opened a private chapel for his servants in Bridgetown, in what was then the Diocese of Exeter. As minister for his chapel, the duke hired a Church of England clergyman, James Shore. Private chapels were a fairly common way for wealthy noblemen to get the kind of ministry they liked without interference from the diocesan bishop. But if a bishop could not intervene in the affairs of a nobleman's private chapel, he could certainly make life miserable for the clergyman hired for the chapel, because the clergyman could only minister within the diocese by the bishop's license. That, unhappily, is what happened to James Shore, who was as thoroughgoing an Evangelical as Bishop Philpotts was a High Churchman. In 1842, rankling over Shore's ill-concealed objections to the influx of Tractarianism in the Diocese of Exeter, Philpotts refused to renew Shore's license to preach and politely suggested that he find other employment. The Duke of Somerset, unwilling to have *his* clergyman pushed around by a mere bishop, reorganized his chapel in Bridgetown on a non-Anglican basis and invited Shore to continue as the minister. Shore accepted, continuing to use the Book of Common Prayer and his Church of England surplice and scarf, but now in a "free" Church of England parish. Unamused, Philpotts arraigned Shore for officiating "as a dissenter," and in a series of Trollopean legal maneuverings Shore found himself in jail for three weeks.

Shore received no shortage of supporters and sympathizers, principal among which was the Rev. Thomas Elisha Thoresby, a minister in the Countess of Huntingdon's Connexion, a small Methodist-like denomination that had also emerged a century earlier from disputes over episcopal control of private chapels. It was Thoresby's ambition to hitch the Countess of Huntingdon's moribund string of proprietary chapels to the sensationalism of Shore's case and revive and reorganize the Connexion as a new, more identifiably Anglican and anti-Tractarian body. It actually took Thoresby fourteen years to draw up the necessary constitution and other legal documents, but in August 1863 he finally succeeded in gaining legal recognition for the new body, to be known as the Free Church of England, based upon a Deed-Poll registered in Chancery on August 31, 1863.

For all of Thoresby's intentions, the new Free Church of England never attracted any significant number of disgruntled Anglicans. The Free Church had no episcopate, and without bishops it could hardly expect to appeal to many Anglicans as a refuge. In 1868, in an effort to supply by ingenuity what was lacking in orders, the president of the Free Church Council, Benjamin Price, was permitted to take the title "bishop."[87] But such legal fictions did little to make the Free Church more appealing to other Anglicans, and it would inevitably take them further from Anglicanism the more they were applied.

It was at this juncture that the news of Cummins's secession from the Episcopal Church hit the English newspapers. At once, not only F. S. Merryweather (the secretary of the Free Church Council), but also Thoresby and Price, dashed off letters of congratulation to Cummins. And not only congratulations—in his letter, Merryweather had dangled ever so gingerly before Cummins the hint that the Free Church of England and the Reformed Episcopal Church should both find themselves working together for "Protestant Union," and both Thoresby and Price broadly suggested that "we are willing to take counsel together and to co-operate on the ground of perfect equality."[88] As all three Free Churchers surely saw at once, union with the Reformed Episcopal Church would be a fresh tonic to the labors of the Free Church of England and grant them new standing as a part of a larger, pan-Anglican movement. Moreover, the Reformed Episcopal Church possessed in Cummins a fully valid bishop who might well be persuaded to grant to the Free Church the kind of episcopal succession it deplored in its published principles but yearned for with all its heart. Thus, on March 10, 1874, Price and the Free Church Council proposed to the Reformed Episcopal General Council's Executive Committee "a complete and actual union between the two churches."[89]

Cummins, for his part, had been delighted with the overtures of the Free Church since he saw a similar advantage for the Reformed Episcopalians in claiming a connection with a parallel protest already under way in the ancestral homeland of Anglicanism. "If the Free Ch. of England could become organizationally one with us, it would be a very desirable thing," Cummins wrote to Colonel Aycrigg in June 1875. To that end, he sent Aycrigg to England as his personal envoy to the Free Church's Annual Convocation.[90] But other voices within the Reformed Episcopal Church were more suspicious of the Free Church's motives. Marshall Smith warned Aycrigg, "The FCE is not just what is required to meet the want of English Evangelicals. . . . It has too much Congregationalism and Methodism in it, and is quite a heterogenous body."[91] Other objections were even stronger. Aycrigg was informed by one English correspondent that "the trustees of the six churches wh. constitute the entire property of the FCE were decidedly Dissenters & for the most part opposed to Episcopacy even of the mildest type."[92] Hence, when Price's and Thoresby's suggestions for union were brought to the Second General Council in 1874, the Reformed Episcopalians would agree only to enter into a "Federative Union" with the Free Churchers, which did little more than establish the same mutual recognition of each others' ministries that the General Council extended to most other legitimate denominations. More than that, the Council agreed, was impossible because "a careful examination of the 'Deed- Poll' and 'By-Laws' of the Free Church of England have shown us . . . that a close organic union would not be practicable, without very material changes."[93]

Undaunted, Price and Thoresby offered to make any "material changes" the General Council deemed necessary. In April 1875, the Free Church Council rewrote its constitution and canons to conform to the Reformed Episcopal canons, and in February 1876 the Free Church made an even more dramatic concession by offering to adopt the new Reformed Episcopal ordinal—if the General Council would also agree to provide a bishop to preside at a future Free Church consecration.[94] Impressed by such evident tokens of sincerity, the Fourth General Council, meeting in July 1876, voted to receive the Free Church's amended canons and to send the newly elected Bishop Edward Cridge to participate in a "consecration" of Benjamin Price in August.[95] It does not seem to have occurred to the General Council (at least not on its public record) that, by the logic of Cummins's consecration sermon for Cheney, Price's "election" as "bishop" in 1868 was as valid as it needed to be and that a subsequent "consecration" by Cridge would suggest clearly that episcopacy actually was something conferred by the touch of other bishops, rather than by the will of the church. Nevertheless, to England Cridge went, almost as fast as Cridge himself could be consecrated, and on the evening of August 15, 1876, Cridge consecrated Price at Christ Church, Teddington, outside London.[96] Five days later, Cridge and Price together consecrated yet another bishop for the Free Church, John Sugden.

As if to confirm the worst croakings of the nay-sayers, at that moment the Free Church's interest in union with the Reformed Episcopal Church promptly vanished. Alfred Richardson, one of Aycrigg's many English acquaintances, wrote Aycrigg six months after Price's consecration to say that the moment the Free Church captured its piece of the episcopate, British national pride at once reasserted itself. "The argumentation [in the Free Church Council] . . . circled very much round a strong remark of the Treasurer that 'we were not going to have an *American Ch brought over here*'—that we had got *all we wanted.*" Now, said Richardson, "the upshot of it all is that . . . the Free Ch *does not want unity & will not have it.*"[97] Within three more years, the General Council would find the Free Church so uncooperative that a separate branch of the Reformed Episcopal Church would have to be founded in Britain to represent the General Council's principles. By 1881, the "Federative Union" would be abrogated, and not until the 1920s, after much battering, jealousy, and struggle, would the Reformed Episcopal Church and the Free Church of England finally arrive at a meeting of ecclesiastical minds. And even then, that meeting would fall significantly short of the "organic union" Cummins had hoped for half-a-century earlier.[98]

In 1876, however, the unpleasant climax of this part of the Reformed Episcopal Church's founding and organization was still unknown and unsuspected. That spring, the new church had experienced nothing but growth and satisfaction and expected only more of the same. After less than three years, it had fifty congregations all over Canada and the United States and had recruited as Cummins's lieutenants an impressive array of leaders: Cheney and Fallows in Chicago, Cridge in Victoria, and Nicholson in Philadelphia. To a man like Nicholson, sitting at his desk that June and preparing the sermon for the opening of the Fourth General Council in Ottawa, the conflicts and crises of the past in the Episcopal Church must have seemed far gone and away, and the future fair with new enthusiasm and security.

Then, with nine words, the future crashed to the floor, and Nicholson would find the Reformed Episcopal Church ushered to the brink of collapse and disintegration. The telegram, hurried into his study, read: "Bishop Cummins is dying: come by the first train."[99]

VI

THE HAND LEAVES THE HELM

Tell Them to Go Forward

No one would have guessed from looking at George David Cummins's photographs in the early 1870s that he had ever been anything but the robust and vigorous figure they saw there. The heart disease that had dogged his college days had made no reappearance since the discipline of his early outdoor circuit-riding adventures, and a nineteenth-century physician would have been tempted to conclude that the athletic recreation of itinerant preaching had worked its own cure for Cummins. But the mental turmoil Cummins had endured over the ritual controversies in Kentucky and in the General Convention—added to the savage confrontations with Tozer and Potter in the national newspapers, the ordeal of his resignation, the organization of the Reformed Episcopal Church, and the responsibilities for leading and building not only a new church but a new parish in the heart of New York City—had cost him dearly in health and strength. The first cracks had begun to show in February 1874, when Cummins's physicians advised him to take a vacation somewhere outside New York. He went to Philadelphia, where he spent his time promoting the organization of the Reformed Episcopal Church there. By March, Cummins's exhaustion was critical, and on March 18 he officially resigned his new rectorship of First Church and retired to Summit, New Jersey, the summer home Stephen Tyng Jr. had put at his disposal.

Cummins remained out of action until September 1874, when he finally resumed active episcopal work again by conducting a visitation in Canada. "For well-nigh four months I was a very great invalid and sufferer, utterly unable to engage in a single service," Cummins wrote in 1875, but "on the 1st of September, I ventured forth upon work again, trusting in God to give me strength to perform it. From that time until the present I have continued my work, and have not lost a single Sunday, though I am yet far from being in my once vigorous health."[1] All through the winter of 1874–75, he was back at his accustomed routine, visiting new parishes from Kentucky to New Jersey. In April 1875, Cummins was finally able to move his personal possessions out of the old diocesan residence in Louisville and rent a small stone cottage in the Baltimore suburb of Lutherville. The house in Lutherville had the twin advantages of moving Cummins closer to the epicenter of Reformed Episcopal growth in the East (Lutherville was a convenient stop on the Northern Central Railroad, giving Cummins easy access to rail transportation, north and south as he needed it) while also giving him a quiet country home to retreat to and recuperate his energies. He presided (and preached the council sermon) at the Third General Council in Christ Church, Chicago, in May 1875 and was soon back on the road to New York, to New Jersey, to Washington, and most dramatically, to South Carolina to make his visit and welcome to the black congregations in late 1875.

But the incessant grind of travel and the strain of carrying the new church largely on his own shoulders could not be made up for even by the country air of Lutherville. In June 1876, after making an emergency call in Baltimore, Cummins caught a mild cold, and then on June 21 suffered the first in what seem to have been a series of heart attacks. He lingered for four days, conscious but in "such suf-

fering . . . as to require the unremitting services of those around
him." By Monday morning, June 26, his physician finally gave up
hope, and in another hour and a quarter Cummins was dead.[2]

The suddenness of Cummins's death shook the Reformed Episcopal Church to its still-short roots. "Words are utterly feeble to express the keenness of our sorrow," stammered Cheney's new church
newspaper, The Appeal. "The stroke is a heavy one for the Reformed Episcopal Church to bear."[3] Cheney, who conducted the
funeral service on June 28 in the new Church of the Redeemer in
Baltimore, stoically eulogized Cummins there as a soldier who "has
died like a warrior, sword in hand and with battle harness."[4] But a
week later, preaching a memorial tribute to Cummins at Christ
Church, Cheney's grief overflowed the formal boundaries of Evangelical stoicism and became a heart-wrenching testimony to the
memory of a friend who had stood by him in his darkest hour:

> So in loneliness stand I today, while the busy world, like the
> Jordan, hurries past me. But yesterday, he who was to me
> more than a brother, stood at my side. We clasped hands in
> Christian love. We talked of the coming kingdom. We held
> sweet fellowship in prayer. To-day I stretch out my hands in
> vain. What though, in the ineffable glory of that dying hour,
> I catch the flashing of chariot wheels, and see the vision of
> "an innumerable company of angels," my heart still cries,
> "My father, my father, the chariot of Israel and the horsemen
> thereof."[5]

William Rufus Nicholson, addressing a still-dazed General Council
in Ottawa three weeks later, acknowledged, "Great indeed is our
loss. No other man, be he how transcendent as he may, can ever
stand to the Reformed Episcopal Church in the same relations, *for he
was our Luther.*"[6]

But Cummins's death had a sharper significance for the Reformed
Episcopal Church than the outpouring of sympathy and mourning
could measure. Cummins's dying charge to the Reformed Episcopalians (and we have Nicholson to thank for recording this saying
from the family members who gathered around Cummins's death-
bed) had been, "Tell them to go forward, and do a grand work."[7]
But who would steer the ship, now that Cummins was gone, was a
very good question. So long as Cummins had lived, his preemi-
nence in the church had been unchallenged, even though he was
temperamentally reluctant to assert it as such. With Cummins gone
and no clear heir apparent among the surviving bishops, the General

Council would descend into a protracted internecine struggle between those who believed that the purposes of Evangelical reform had been achieved simply by the organization of the Reformed Episcopal Church (and who, like Cheney, sought to maintain as much as possible of their old Episcopal identity intact) and those who saw the organizing of the Reformed Episcopal Church as merely the *beginning* of reform (and who would now seek to question, not just baptismal or eucharistic practices but *every* Episcopal distinctive). And so, for the next twenty-odd years, the course of the Reformed Episcopal Church would be brutally jerked back and forth by competing interests and personalities, and the church would find itself launched into strange and unknown seas, never imagined (it is safe to say) by George David Cummins.

Descent into Confusion

In truth, those competing interests were already feverishly engaged in their struggle even before Cummins's death, and they made their first appearance as combatants as early as the Second General Council, in New York City, in May 1874. No issue had given more common grievance to the Episcopal Evangelicals than the prayer book, and it was no surprise that the Reformed Episcopalians would closely identify their movement with prayer book revision. It was evident that Cummins, at least at first, looked on the rediscovery of the 1785 Book of Common Prayer as the all-purpose solution to that need, without any need for further liturgical tinkering or invention. Between October 1873, when Marshall Smith first provided an astonished Cummins with a copy of the 1785 prayer book, and December 1873, however, it had gradually begun to dawn on Cummins that the 1785 prayer book suffered from some serious practical defects, not the least of which was the absence of any forms for ordination or consecration, for installations or institutions of clergy, or for consecrations of church buildings. Moreover, Cummins had also begun to entertain equally serious doubts about the theology of the prayer book, since he gingerly mentioned his own personal regret at the omission of the Nicene Creed and the "descent into hell" from the Apostles' Creed during his address to the Association Hall meeting. Obviously, the 1785 prayer book would not do without amendment, and from December 1873 until May 1874 Cummins and the Executive Committee of the church labored to bring the 1785 prayer book back into the pale of liturgical legitimacy.

But when discussion of these amendments was brought to the floor of the Second General Council, an acrimonious debate over the amendments broke out, taking Cummins (who had dragged himself out of his convalescence to chair the Council) entirely off guard. Had Cummins stuck by the 1785 prayer book in its entirety and demanded its adoption as such by the Council, few would probably have felt themselves strong enough to challenge Cummins or to challenge a book with such close historical associations with the founding of the Episcopal Church. But once Cummins himself had sanctioned amendment of the prayer book, all inhibitions dissolved and anyone's ideas for revision would be as worthy of a hearing as anyone else's.

And that was what now greeted Cummins. Now that all bets were off, a clamor of suggestions for further, and sometimes bizarre, alterations now arose from the floor of the Council. Cummins, true to his expressed reservations, had reinserted the "descent into hell" into the Apostles' Creed in his amended forms, but Joseph Dawson Wilson, an Episcopal clergyman from Pittsburgh who had only just joined the Reformed Episcopalians, and Randolph Bourne (one of the seven "founders") now rose to call for its excision. Although Marshall Smith desperately tried to stall Wilson's motion by calling for a vote by orders (i.e., clergy and laity in the Council voting separately), the motion was carried. The "descent" now disappeared again from the creed, and all Cummins had to show for his disapproval was the permission, stuck into a prefatory rubric, for ministers to use it in their congregations if they liked.[8] What Cummins had intended as reform and amendment was now about to be carried into revolution.

Nor did it stop with the Creed. Bourne and Charles H. Tucker (another recent convert from the ranks of the Episcopal clergy) next called for the elimination of "catholic" from the Apostles' Creed as well, while Jeremiah Taylor and Benjamin Leacock offered separate motions to strip "catholic" out of the communion prayers.[9] Thomas Moore, a Philadelphia layman, stood up to demand abandonment of the term "collect" to designate prayer; repeated calls were heard for softening all of the communion injunctions to self-examination and confessions of unworthy reception; and according to Thomas Powers of Philadelphia, even the word "sacrament" ought to be replaced by "ordinance." Powers successfully moved the Council to consider adding, in addition to the baptismal office for infants, an order for the "dedication of infants" that would drop not just declarations of regeneration but also the use of water itself.[10]

The sum of all these demands would have so altered the shape of any new liturgy that use of the word "Episcopal" to describe it would have failed on the lips. And it was at that moment that the ambiguity hidden within Cummins's consecration sermon the previous December in Chicago now came to light. Was the Reformed Episcopal Church to remain a self-consciously Episcopal enterprise, looking on itself primarily as an Evangelical refuge from Anglo-Catholic triumphalism? Or was it to be instead a completely new evangelical Protestant denomination, using episcopal government and liturgy as congenial and convenient, but holding itself free to redefine or scrap either as its evangelicalism inclined it? That was the real question posed by the motions of Wilson, Bourne, and the others, and no one saw it more clearly for what it meant than Colonel Benjamin Aycrigg.

Listening to the rising crescendo of liturgical oddities in the Council, Aycrigg was aghast. No church that butchered the traditional prayer book forms with such ham-handed delight would ever be able to demand recognition as "Episcopal" in any historically meaningful sense of the word, and Aycrigg was fearful that adoption of any of these novelties would shift the Reformed Episcopal Church from its proper place as a movement of Episcopal reform and turn it into the private plaything of a few determined radicals. "All that we ask," Aycrigg pleaded in response, "is to let us have a Church that corresponds with the views of the Old Evangelicals in the P.E.C."[11] That, at least, was what Aycrigg thought the Reformed Episcopal Church had been formed to represent, and he was by no means alone in his plea. With him stood Charles Edward Cheney, who would insist to his dying day that Reformed Episcopalians "hold no doctrine which was not held by the English Reformers, and by the founders of the Episcopal Church in America."[12] Writing to Aycrigg in 1878, Cheney affirmed: "I do not desire to see a solitary change made in our present Book" and prayed for "an end to further tinkering with our Liturgy."[13]

Behind Cheney, there also stood clergymen like Marshall Smith, Edward Neill, and (on strictly prayer book issues) William Sabine of First Church. There was an even larger body of laypeople who made their own sentiments clear in the editorials of the *Episcopal Recorder* and a handful of private, anonymous pamphlets, such as "The Episcopate: Views of a Layman." An 1881 *Recorder* editorial reminded would-be revisers and rewriters:

> As its name imports, the R.E. Church is *Episcopal* in its government. And if a mistake has been made in its name, it is in calling it the *Reformed* Episcopal—whereas, in point of fact, it

is *the Old* Protestant Episcopal Church! We hold it to be a matter capable of the clearest demonstration that the [Protestant Episcopal] Church has drifted away—far away—from its moorings at the time of the Reformation; and is throwing to-day the influence of its name and teachings *against* the doctrines of the *Reformers. They would find their representatives in the R.E. Church to-day.*[14]

And the unknown author of "The Episcopate: Views of a Layman" insisted in a similar vein: "We call ourselves the Reformed Episcopal Church but in fact we are Reformed Protestant Episcopalians; in other words our church was intended to be, and is, the Protestant Episcopal Church cleansed from its errors. Our policy should be to change nothing that is not required by unsound doctrine, unwise policy, or evident bad taste, to be changed."[15]

But Cheney and Aycrigg lacked the one essential thing they needed to resist the assault on the Book of Common Prayer, and that was a decisive intervention in this debate on the part of Cummins. This was not for want of sympathy on Cummins's part. Alexandrine Cummins, writing to Aycrigg in 1880, remarked that when her husband

left home, position, influence, and friends, to found the R.E.C., he had no wish that it should be a Methodist or Presbyterian Church. He dearly loved the Church for which he had spent the best years of his life, and when he could no longer minister at her "*altars*" or see her simple liturgy changed into a poor imitation of the gorgeous ritual of Rome, his own wish and intention was to bring together those who were true Protestant Episcopalians, that they might form a pure Church, free from Romish germs—*but this was all.* Had he wished to unite with his Presbyterian, or Methodist, or Reformed brethren, he could have easily done so; and great suffering and sacrifice on his part would have been saved. But when asked, in Nov., 1873, whether he meant to unite with either of these sister Churches, he answered, "*No*; I wish a pure *Episcopal* Church, that it may be a refuge for those who, like myself, prefer a liturgical service." The writer was present when Bishop Cummins revised the communion office with one of his dear brethren, when a suggestion was made for further changes. The Bishop replied, "No, we only want to take out all that can be interpreted as teaching false doctrine—the rest should remain as it is. The fewer changes we make the better; ours is an *Episcopal* Church, and we do not wish to do away with our offices and liturgy."[16]

Cummins originally had little sympathy for the prayer book revision party and had only slowly and reluctantly admitted the need for revision in order to restrain the excesses of the Ritualists. He had no desire now to indulge a similar dose of Evangelical excesses. In 1876 he assured Aycrigg, "I am thoroughly opposed to the adoption of any radical change in our system, and should discountenance the agitation of the subject."[17]

But Cummins hesitated to use his episcopal authority in the 1874 debate for a few basic reasons. One of them was his health at the time. Although he presided at the opening sessions of the 1874 Council, the Council journal shows him frequently out of the chair and otherwise absent from the floor. The prayer book debate touched off "skirmishing hot and heavy along the entire line" (according to the *New York Herald* report), and because this was exactly the sort of atmosphere Cummins needed least to breathe, he simply moved himself off the scene of the debate, to the disappointment of Aycrigg and Cheney and the emboldening of the radicals.[18]

But even if his health had been the best, it is difficult to imagine Cummins staging a forceful intervention into the debate. Cummins, under any circumstances, loathed confrontation and combat. Even his decision to secede from the Episcopal Church was stretched out over four years, to a point where observers then and now have wondered whether Cummins simply waited too long to resign and therefore lost any genuine chance to affect outcomes within the church. Instinctively (and sometimes unwisely), Cummins looked to accommodate rather than alienate. It was Benjamin Leacock's despair to watch Cummins make one charitable but disastrous mistake after another in dealing with people. The bishop who "was too honest himself to suppose men anything otherwise than they seemed" failed utterly to see that "some of the men who joined us, and whom after a few days' contact he described as 'Splendid fellows', 'Valuable accessions', 'Men of the first ability', have proven utter failures, and others have given us much trouble." Even in the best cases, Cummins "hated to run counter to the wishes of anyone, especially if they were his friends," and that would make it especially hard for him to face down the Wilsons, the Bournes, and the Powers on critical prayer book matters.[19]

One other consideration also acted to stay Cummins's hand, and that was his long-cherished desire to promote evangelical Protestant ecumenicity in the Reformed Episcopal Church. In his second sermon to the Lyric Hall congregation in New York City, Cummins predicted that the Reformed Episcopal Church would finally bring to pass a happy marriage of episcopal order and evangelical fellowship. We have "taken our place, not outside of the historic Church, or a Church Episcopally constituted," Cummins said. "We separate from one small body of Christians in the hope of a larger & better Union, to include even them."[20] Clear and compelling as this desire has seemed to Evangelicals from Muhlenberg to Cummins, no one had ever been called on to give such ecumenicity practical shape. Now that the Reformed Episcopalians were out of the Episcopal Church, that desire suddenly became a necessity, but now that the old Episcopal restraints were gone, there was no guideline, no time for experimentation, to determine how far the Reformed Episcopalians could go with their experiment before it ceased to be recognizably Episcopal.

So, for example, the first set of canons enacted by the Association Hall meeting openly repudiated exclusive episcopal ordination as the basis of the church and permitted ministers with nonepiscopal ordinations to be fully welcomed. But did that mean that any and all could be taken into the Reformed Episcopal Church without any condition? No one was sure, and in his urge to stress ecumenical fraternity, Cummins allowed a number of unpredictable clergymen from the ecclesiastical twilight of the Episcopal Church (and elsewhere) into the ranks of the Reformed Episcopalians. Fallows, the Wesleyan liberal, was one example, but far more startling were William Cooper, an "annihilationist" who scandalized the more conservative Evangelicals by frankly proclaiming his disbelief in "the eternal punishment of the wicked," and Joseph H. McElray, who sought ordination from Cummins in 1875, only to leave the Reformed Episcopal Church in 1884 "to join the Universalists."[21]

And then, in addition to these curiosities, there were the simple incompetents, who were unable to make a decent livelihood for themselves in their own denominations and were fleeing to the Reformed Episcopalians as a convenient port in a storm. "Our experience with Mr. [Johnston] McCormac should lead the Standg. Committee to earnestly and attentively consider the importance of adopting strict rules for the reception of Ministers into our church," complained the senior warden of Christ Church, Ottawa, to Colonel Aycrigg in December 1874. "I am [he continued] firmly convinced that he should never have been received as a Minister of the Reformed Epis. Ch."[22] The trouble was that no practical method as yet existed to screen out the incompetent or the oddballs without seeming to contradict Cummins's expressed determination to repudiate Episcopal exclusiveness, and it would take years to weed them out. Until then, the well-intentioned desire of the Reformed Episcopal Church to promote ecumenicity would leave it vulnerable to becoming (in Aycrigg's acidulous phrase) an "ecclesiastical Texas" where people went "to get out of the reach of settled law."[23]

The same inability to discriminate between ecumenicity and folly goes a long way toward explaining Cummins's failure to respond to the outlandish liturgical changes sanctioned by the 1874 General Council. Wanting with all his heart to make the Reformed Episcopal Church as perfect a model of openness as the old church had been of shut-mindedness, Cummins feared to draw any lines that might put him in the same place as Bishop Potter. Therefore, much as Cummins himself had little sympathy with the changes coming out of the debate, he begged Aycrigg "to take a more cheerful view of the outlook" and wait until the furor had died down and the Church had a chance to reflect on its actions. Then, he was sure that cooler, more conservative heads would prevail and restore the old forms, and without needlessly provoking the hotter and unwiser heads which were making their demands. "In every work of reform of which I have read, there were rash and wild agitators, and we cannot expect to escape them," Cummins reasoned. One need only wait until the storm had blown over, and the ship would right itself.[24]

But time was not on Cummins's side. His sudden death in 1876 removed the one possible obstacle that the radicals might have had to respect. Although agitation for revision died away substantially in the 1875 General Council, the Fourth Council of 1876, which met shortly after Cummins's death, behaved as though Cummins's funeral was a signal for a liturgical open season. William Rufus Nicholson now assumed, for all practical purposes, the leadership of the radicals and pressed for the gutting of Morning Prayer, from the "Declaration of Forgiveness of Sins" at the beginning (too much clerical authority implied by that) to the petition "and take not the Holy Spirit from us" (it contradicted the peculiarities of Nicholson's dispensationalism, which taught that the Holy Spirit could not be "taken" from Christians "in this age").[25] Nicholson, along with William Feltwell, had also pushed for the "Dedication of Infants" service, and he was joined by William Cooper (who for his own reasons wanted the elimination of "damnation" from the Litany and was delighted that all mention of hell was now gone from the Apostles' Creed) and by Randolph Bourne (who now urged that "one baptism for the remission of sins" be struck from the Nicene Creed).[26] Two years later, at the Sixth General Council in Newark,

New Jersey, the most sustained assault on the prayer book yet was launched. At its head, again, was Nicholson, who proposed dumping the traditional Prayer Book Catechism of King Edward VI in favor of one composed by himself. Following close behind Nicholson was Charles Tucker (and his renewed motion to strike all mention of "body" and "blood" from the communion office), Joseph Malone, rector of Emmanuel Church, Philadelphia (who was still pressing to eliminate "catholic" from the Apostles' Creed), William Cooper (who wanted to jettison use of the term "sacrament" and who was still urging the council to drop "damnation" from the Litany), and even one layman who was seriously proposing to alter the Apostles' Creed yet again by replacing the fleshy-sounding belief in the "resurrection of the body" with the more idealized "resurrection of the dead."[27]

However seriously Nicholson regarded these efforts, his erstwhile brethren of the Episcopal Church press treated them as a gift, demonstrating the instability and folly of the Reformed Episcopalians. "This past week has witnessed the meeting of the Council of the R.E.C.," remarked *Church and State* in May 1874. "It has been a sad spectacle of what is likely to become of men who drift away from their historical moorings. . . . They are just beginning to get a glimpse of the dreary waste of fanaticism and folly which stretches before them. They will find that there are plenty who will wish to reform their Church just as they have attempted to reform upon the Church they have left."[28] In 1874, during the Second General Council, the *New York Herald* impatiently remarked that "the Reformed Episcopal Church does not yet fully comprehend its mission, if it has any. It ought not to concern itself too much about 'old clothes' if it means to make its mark in the world. The active modern world cares less about old-fashioned names than about work. We advise Bishop Cummins to be done with all this rubbish and get to work."[29] The *New York Tribune* similarly remarked about the 1874 council that "the scrupulous attention to minor points which the Council gave in its revision of the prayer-book must have appeared almost trivial to such on-lookers."[30] William Augustus Muhlenberg grew so fearful of being personally associated with the new Reformed Episcopal notion of prayer book revision that he took the trouble to repudiate the new church in the columns of the *Tribune*.[31]

All this sank Colonel Aycrigg deeper and deeper into despair. In a chilly letter to Joseph Dawson Wilson in 1882, Aycrigg declared that the new revisions had, in his mind, flown directly in the face of the Declaration of Principles. "Because one of the terms of the old Creed, as it has stood since the seventh century, has been erased from the text," Aycrigg wrote angrily, "the remainder, as it stands in our Prayer Book, is erroneously called 'the Apostles' Creed.'" As such, it "is not the legitimate Creed of the R.E.C., since the Declaration expressly makes it 'The Creed commonly called the Apostles' Creed,' one of the 'fixed and unalterable' standards of the R.E.C."[32] Aycrigg seriously considered abandoning the Reformed Episcopal Church to its own devices, only to be dissuaded by Charles Edward Cheney. But even Cheney was shaken by the relentless agenda of Nicholson and the others. "I have actually known a lay member of the Old Church to be agreeably surprised to find that we held the doctrine of the Trinity, and others who supposed that we worshipped without the aid of liturgy," Cheney sardonically remarked in 1888.[33]

It would be easy to dismiss the liturgical enthusiasms of Nicholson, Cooper, Tucker, and Bourne as merely a bad case of nerves brought on by protracted conflict with the equally peculiar liturgical enthusiasms of the Anglo-Catholics. On those terms, the radical assault on the prayer book in 1874 and 1876 can be interpreted as the simple desire, however irrational, to claw as far in the other direction from Episcopal ritualism as one could get. But taking that view of these liturgical controversies, while generous, also underestimates the extent to which all these strange demands have a single and perfectly coherent thread running through them. That common element lay in the steady drift of the old evangelicalism into the new fundamentalism.

The Evangelicals and the fundamentalists were in many respects the same movement, only in different phases of development. Nevertheless, there were significant points of departure, all of which show up in the demands for prayer book change made in the Reformed Episcopal Church. For instance, although fundamentalism remained as deeply concerned as the old Evangelicals with directing people to personal and individual responsibility for sin and salvation, fundamentalists consistently preferred to shorten the time spent on mourning for sin lest it interfere with making a "decision" for Christ and having "joy in the Spirit."[34] That was certainly reflected in the successful bid to prune out such self-accusatory sentences in the communion prayers as "the burden of them is intolerable" or "so is the danger great, if we receive the same unworthily" (both of which *did* appear in the 1785 prayer book).[35] Benjamin Leacock, who emerged as one of the other principal promoters of radical agendas in the Reformed Episcopal Church, even attacked the continuance of Lent in the prayer book calendar on the grounds that "to fast and pray with renewed diligence at a certain period of the year, because it is a time-honored custom, is no part of that Gospel system which is joy and peace in believing."[36]

Other fundamentalist yearnings also underlay the radical attack on the Creed and the vocabulary of the Communion order. Fundamentalism has rarely been a movement friendly to history, because it has often described the history of the church as a record of apostasy and decline from the New Testament. Even the idea of the church itself held little attraction for the radicals; the dispensationalism so beloved of Nicholson and Leacock taught that the Christian church was merely a "parenthesis" in God's overall plan to restore a theocratic kingdom in Palestine.[37] Any appeal to the "catholic" sense of the church, or its unity down through the ages, was wasted on the radicals.

The radicals thus struggled to rid the Reformed Episcopal Church of any idea of its connection with, much less its reliance on, the Christian past. Confident in dispensationalism's assurances that the end of the Christian age was near at hand, the radicals were suspicious of glorification of anything material in worship, such as the use of crosses or pictures, or even the use of wine for Communion. Thomas Powers, Nicholson's fellow Philadelphian (and it is striking in that regard how much of this radical drive had its headquarters in the Philadelphia parishes) frankly confessed to Marshall Smith in 1878: "About some points I feel most anxious, namely, that if we must have the word *sacrament* introduced, we ought to have that of 'ordinance'. . . . Then again, any allusion to a material cross ought to be carefully avoided."[38]

Similarly, in 1877, the radicals induced the Fifth General Council to pass a resolution giving its blessing on "the progress of the temperance revival throughout the country." At that, the unhappy Colonel Aycrigg exploded. Seeing in the "temperance" resolution nothing but the hidden hand of a radicalism utterly foreign to his own experience as an Episcopalian, Aycrigg objected to "this metaphysical Christianity." It was little else than

> agreeing with those who reject the communion entirely; and with those who at communion use the bread, but refuse the wine; and with those who use water, as do the Mormons; and with those who use unfermented grape juice under the fictitious title of "unfermented wine"—in opposition to the express command of Christ when He instituted the communion; and to the personal habits of Himself and followers.[39]

For "metaphysical," Aycrigg might as easily have said, "fundamentalist."

But it was not in prayer book revision, or even in their reduction-
ist approach to doctrine and practice, that the radicals left their most
enduring mark in the Reformed Episcopal Church. That mark was
made in 1875 at the Third General Council, when Nicholson and
Leacock introduced a thorough and in some respects disastrous rewriting of the Thirty-Nine Articles of Religion. This rewriting reduced the number of Articles to thirty-five, but even more important it reduced their doctrinal content to the plainest minimum.
Nothing more clearly illustrates Nicholson and Leacock's determination to set the Reformed Episcopal Church off in directions
other than the ones envisioned by Cummins than the very idea of
subjecting the Articles of Religion to the scrutiny of revision. Although the prayer book had been revised not a few times since the
days of the Reformation, no serious effort had ever been made to
rewrite the Articles since the end of the sixteenth century. Moreover, the Articles had long been viewed as the last bastion of Evangelical authority in the Church of England and for that reason were
firmly imbedded in the Declaration of Principles. But even so, the
Articles were evidently not enough to satisfy Nicholson and Leacock or the other partisans of radicalism, and so even the Articles of
Religion went onto the same procrustean bed from which the prayer
book had just arisen.

That the Thirty-Nine Articles ever came up for revision at all can
be laid entirely at the doorstep of Benjamin Leacock. In 1874, as one
of the seven founding clergymen of the Reformed Episcopal
Church, Leacock was made chairman of the General Council's
Committee on Doctrine and Worship, a committee created under
the canons to oversee "all alterations of, or additions to, the prayer
book offices or Articles of Religion of this Church."[40] The committee seems to have been intended primarily as a committee of reference, but Leacock, from the beginning, was determined to take a
more active role in shaping the doctrinal life of the new church and
to use the committee as his vehicle.

The justification for placing the Articles of Religion under scrutiny had come harmlessly enough in a motion by Marshall Smith on
the last day of the 1874 General Council, and it is not difficult to see
why—the General Council had only just approved the use of the
Apostles' Creed *sans* the "descent into hell," and it would therefore
be necessary to do something with Article III of the Articles of Religion ("Of the Going Down of Christ into Hell"). On top of that,
the embarrassing word "priest" turned up in Articles XXXI,
XXXII, and XXXVI, and some action was needed to authorize re-

placing it with the Reformed Episcopalians' term of choice, "presbyter." But the motion to refer the matter to Leacock's committee placed all further discretion on the subject in Leacock's hands, and without any stipulated restraints on what he might come up with. And so, in the spring of 1875, having already taken counsel with Nicholson, Leacock placed before an unprepared and confused committee a new set of "Articles of Religion" to replace the old Thirty-Nine.

In later years, Leacock complained of the revision as an unwanted task he was compelled to undertake without very much help from the other committee members.[41] But all the contemporary evidence points in the other direction. In a letter to Benjamin Aycrigg in 1882, Joseph Dawson Wilson, one committee member, complained in equal terms that Leacock had actually kept all the proposed work of revision in his own hands until the final meeting of the committee before its report to the 1875 General Council, and then introduced not just a revision of four articles, but an overhaul of them all. Moreover, Leacock introduced into the committee's debate no less than William Rufus Nicholson, who was not a member of the committee but who proceeded to enter into discussion of the Articles as though he were. The reason was unpleasantly obvious: "Bp. Nicholson was, I understand, the author of them and he was brought into the Com[mittee] to discuss them," Wilson wrote. "When Dr. Leacock asked as a personal favor to bring Bp. Nicholson in, I could not be so discourteous as to object."[42]

Knowing the mind of Leacock and Nicholson makes it easier to understand the radical principles represented by the new Articles of Religion they were proposing. Not only were the Articles renumbered from Thirty-Nine to Thirty-Five, but their content was drastically altered. Article III of the old Articles (the offending article on the "descent into hell") was, of course, omitted entirely. Article IV, "Of the Resurrection of Christ," was also rewritten to include a paragraph on "His Second Coming" that effectively wrote dispensational premillennialism into the article. Nicholson's old Methodist Arminianism reasserted itself in the revision of Article X ("Of Free Will"), where "the grace of God by Christ preventing [going ahead of] us" was watered down to "the grace of God by Christ inclining us." But that Arminianism was even more apparent in Nicholson's entire elimination of Article XVII ("Of Predestination and Election") and its replacement with a weak-willed sort of laissez-faire:

> While the Scriptures distinctly set forth the election, predestination, and calling of the people of God, . . . they no less

positively affirm man's free agency and responsibility, and that salvation is freely offered to all through Christ. This Church, accordingly, simply affirms these doctrines as the Word of God sets them forth, and submits them to the individual judgement of its members.[43]

Common to almost all these changes were Leacock's and Nicholson's abiding and thorough suspicions of the institutional church. They consistently tilted the thrust of the Articles away from the faith of the corporate and visible church to the private experience of the individual Christian in repentance, in conversion, and in fellowship with the Holy Spirit. Although the new Articles retained most of the old declaration of Article II that "The Church hath power to decree Rites or Ceremonies and authority in Controversies of Faith," that affirmation was effectively voided by the wording of the new Article XXIII, "Of the Authority of General Councils," which made private moral choice the determining factor in Christian thought and life:

No law or authority can override individual responsibility and therefore the right of private judgement: For the individual Christian as Christ distinctly affirms, is to be judged by the Word.[44]

When Leacock and Nicholson turned to the sacraments, the same tone of private sentimentality prevailed. The sacraments were reduced from being "certain sure witnesses, and effectual signs of grace" (Article XXV) to being "only a symbol or sign divinely appointed." The "Supper of the Lord" now became merely "a memorial of our Redemption by Christ's death," and the original declaration in the old Article XXVIII, that "the Body of Christ is given, taken, and eaten, in the Supper, only after an heavenly and spiritual manner," was replaced with what amounted to a flat denial of the need for the sacrament at all, provided personal prayer and Bible study were practiced:

We feed on Christ only through his Word, and only by faith and prayer; and we feed on him, whether at our private devotions, or in our meditations, or on any occasion of public worship, or in the memorial symbolism of the Supper.[45]

Even the new article on "Faith" (for which there was no corresponding article in the old Thirty-Nine) was couched not in the objective vocabulary of the Reformation but in the purely experiential terms of evangelical Victorian piety[46]:

> The faith which brings justification is simply the reliance or dependence on Christ which accepts him as the sacrifice for our sins. . . . We may thus rely on Christ, either tremblingly or confidingly; but in either case it is saving faith. If, though tremblingly, we rely on him in his obedience for us unto death, instantly we come into union with him, and are justified. If, however, we confidingly rely on him, then have we the comfort of our justification. Simply by faith in Christ are we justified and saved.

All this pointed the Reformed Episcopal Church away from its roots in the English Reformation and threatened to define it as simply another Americanized evangelical sect. But for just that reason, it required all of Nicholson's "moral weight" combined with Leacock to push the new Articles through the Committee on Doctrine and Worship. And when the new Articles were introduced into the business of the Third General Council, they were met with a clamor of disapproval. Colonel Aycrigg, as with prayer book revision, hotly opposed the new Articles on the grounds that the Declaration of Principles had already established the Thirty-Nine Articles as the Reformed Episcopal statement of the "Doctrines of Grace." "I wished to let these two [Nicholson and Leacock] especially understand that no one would be allowed to depart from this higher law [i.e., the Declaration of Principles] without serious opposition," Aycrigg wrote to a foreign correspondent. "But neither of them appeared to think that we were under this 'higher law.' "[47]

Aycrigg was especially incensed at Leacock's "efforts . . . to produce numerous illegitimate changes in the 'Doctrine, Discipline and Worship' of the R.E.C." and accused Leacock of manipulating the Committee on Doctrine and Worship "in the hope that he could raise a party among the new comers, sufficient to break the compact."[48] Leacock, as Aycrigg wrote to Joseph Dawson Wilson, "was the only founder on your Committee and he has been the most persistent iconoclast in the R.E.C."[49] But Nicholson and Leacock fought back with equal energy. Nicholson (as William T. Sabine remembered with wholehearted admiration almost four decades later)

> stepped to the head of the centre aisle of Christ Church, Chicago, to advocate the final adoption of our Thirty-Five Arti-

cles of Religion and standing there, pleaded for the great truths of the Gospel with a fervor of utterance, a majesty of statement, and a passion of conviction, united with a rush of feeling and tenderness which seemed at once to unite the graces and power of the very highest eloquence.[50]

Joseph Dawson Wilson was less impressed. "It was a case of gush," he wrote later to Aycrigg.[51]

The deadlock might have been resolved—maybe even entirely averted—had Cummins (in what would be his last General Council) stepped in with some decisive gesture. He had already put himself on record as opposing alterations in the Articles of Religion, and Aycrigg beseeched him to oppose Nicholson's new articles openly. But as with the revisions of the prayer book, Cummins feared the effect public argument would have on the image of the new church, feared alienating powerful men like Nicholson, and feared (perhaps more than anything else) simply being disregarded no matter what he said. And so the solution to the deadlock came not from Cummins but from Cheney.

Cheney had no particular desire to see Nicholson's new-model articles supplant the Thirty-Nine Articles, but he was willing for the sake of unity (and perhaps at Cummins's behest) to propose an ingenious compromise. Cheney noted that the Declaration of Principles stated only that the Reformed Episcopal Church embraced the "doctrines of grace as set forth in the Thirty-Nine Articles of Religion." Accordingly, he proposed that the new Articles be received as "containing substantially the great truths known as the 'Doctrines of Grace'" (i.e., not as a replacement of the Thirty-Nine but as a commentary of sorts on them) and that they be received *as a resolution* of the Council (i.e., as an expression of the Third General Council's mind on the "Doctrines of Grace" and not as a permanent Statement of Faith).[52] The Council was relieved to act on a compromise that said so little so artfully. Cheney's resolution (which he successfully insisted be included as a preamble to all printings of the new Articles) was gratefully adopted, and the Thirty-Five Articles were allowed to replace the Thirty-Nine in the new Reformed Episcopal prayer book.

The result, however, was that the Council effectively left unclear exactly what the Reformed Episcopal Church professed to believe. The doctrines of the Thirty-Nine Articles were not those of the Thirty-Five. Cheney's compromise resolution notwithstanding, the two documents are fundamentally incompatible, and Reformed Episcopalians have continued to oscillate between the doctrinal mind-set of the two to this day. And it could not really have cheered Benjamin Aycrigg to read Joseph Dawson Wilson's clumsy attempt to look on the sunny side: "I see no use of making a moan about it. . . . Articles of religion cut but little figure in the practical theology of a church anyhow."[53]

Remodeling a Church Government

It was almost inevitable that disagreements as deep as these should soon take on a political color and begin to harden around a few prominent individuals. After Cummins's death, Cheney spoke the loudest for Episcopal traditionalism within the Reformed Episcopal Church, and the nine parishes that now clustered around him in Chicago were generally understood to be of one mind with him. In the East, William Rufus Nicholson emerged as the principal voice of the radicals, and the New York–Philadelphia axis, comprising almost twenty parishes, moved almost exclusively under his influence. Eventually, Chicago came to see itself as the guardian of the true Episcopal flame and to see New York and Philadelphia as self-destructive Evangelical zealots; while in New York and Philadelphia, the Reformed Episcopalians saw themselves as the vanguard of an evangelical revolution, and saw the Chicagoans as a suspicious band of Tories who needed watching.

Unpleasant as these suspicions were for the atmosphere of the new church, none of them would have welled up into outright conflict had it not been for the two unexpected and unwelcome developments. The first of these involved numbers. Although no reliable statistics in the Reformed Episcopal Church were in the General Council journals until the 1880s, it was fairly plain from 1875 on that the eastern parishes were outstripping the western ones in growth, and consequently in representation in the General Council. That imbalance fed trouble into a second unlooked-for problem— the political structure of the General Council. As initially organized in 1873, the General Council was organized like a single national diocese, with Cummins as diocesan bishop and Cheney as a sort of missionary assistant. In 1875, episcopal authority was redistributed somewhat by the General Council's creation of seven "missionary jurisdictions"—St. John (the Canadian Maritime provinces), Ottawa (Central Canada), Pacific (the United States and Canadian west coast), South (everything below the Mason-Dixon line and west to the Mississippi), and Northwest and West (the midwestern states and the western territories)—and bishops were eventually conse-crated for all of them.[54] But this changed the picture only slightly. From being a single national diocese, the Reformed Episcopal Church now began to resemble a Methodist "jurisdiction," with cir-cuit-riding missionary bishops. That impression was reenforced by the provision in the Constitution and Canons of 1874, which ruled that all episcopal appointments were made, and could be unmade, by the General Council: "The Bishops of this Church shall be cho-sen or received agreeably to such rules as shall be fixed by the Gen-eral Council; and their jurisdiction, powers, and duties, shall be such as the General Council may hereafter define."[55]

As Cheney watched the disagreements between eastern and mid-western Reformed Episcopalians widen and fester, that provision took on ominous overtones. As it was, the quasi-Methodism of the canons rankled Cheney's episcopal sensitivities. Even worse, how-ever, by the terms of the canons it could easily be imagined that the Philadelphians, under Nicholson's direction, would one day be able to muster enough votes in General Council to cancel Cheney's episcopal authority in Chicago and substitute one of their own per-suasion as bishop. In September 1875, Cheney decided to move first. Calling together representatives from all the Illinois parishes at St. Paul's Church in Chicago, Cheney took advantage of a provision in the canons that permitted the organization of "synods" (a word that was probably intended to describe only small-scale, local organ-izations, the equivalent of a rural deanery) and declared the creation of the Synod of Chicago. Cheney was promptly elected bishop of the synod by the assembled delegates, and significantly without so much as a by-your-leave to the General Council.[56] This new stand-ing as Bishop of Chicago put Cheney's episcopal authority on an entirely different footing from that of a mere missionary appoint-ment, and presumably secure from meddling by hostile radicals in the General Council.

This unilateral action, however, had to receive at least the formal approval of the next General Council in order to square itself with the canons, and when Cheney deposited his little fait accompli on the doorstep of the General Council in July 1876, the Council's first reaction was to balk. Cheney immediately upped the ante: recogni-tion of the Synod of Chicago *plus* repeal of the canon granting right of all episcopal appointment to the General Council.[57] Uncertain just how far to push Cheney, the Council nervously delegated discussion of the matter to a Committee of Five (none of whom were from Chicago), with instructions to report to the next meeting of the General Council in 1877.

Over the course of the following year, the argument over synodical jurisdiction had plenty of time to heat up. The Council's General
Committee (as the old Executive Committee had been renamed)
was strongly inclined not to recognize Cheney's synod. Herbert
Turner, one of the lay members of the committee, implied that the
synodical plan was intended for "a dissatisfied clergyman gathering
a few parishes around him and making himself bishop," leaving his
hearers with little doubt as to whom he considered a "dissatisfied
clergyman."[58] Mason Gallagher likewise attacked the synodical system as that "which accords neither with the Spirit of the New Testament, nor with American Institutions."[59] But Cheney had his partisans too. One of his presbyters published a short, sharp tract that
accused the opponents of Cheney's synodical plan of subverting the
fundamental principles of Episcopal government:

> This Church recognizes Episcopacy as an ancient and desir-
> able form of Church government. It does not invent a pol-
> ity—it recognizes one. However excellent may be the mod-
> ern form of church government, it prefers the ancient form.
> However modern its name or its separate legal existence, it
> claims to be ancient, both in retaining primitive apostolic
> doctrine and in retaining a primitive polity. . . . The proposal
> to abolish the local Episcopate is a proposal violently, by leg-
> islative enactment, to reverse the process which God, by his
> kindly Providence, has enacted. It is a proposal to introduce a
> method which certainly is not ancient, which does not be-
> long to Episcopal government, which is adverse to the origi-
> nal theory of our constitution, and which is full of danger.
> . . . [It] proposes to give to a majority of the General Coun-
> cil, however small, ill-informed, or prejudiced that majority
> may be, power to force a bishop upon an unwilling people.[60]

When the Fifth General Council convened in Nicholson's Second
Reformed Episcopal Church in Philadelphia in May 1877, the debate
on the issue was "warm and exciting," and according to Mason Gallagher "a rupture appeared almost inevitable."[61] "It had been the
theme of somewhat heated controversy in our Church papers," recalled an anxious Cheney, "and a new constitution and canons had
been proposed which wholly deprived any local body from electing
a bishop."[62] But surprisingly the report of the Committee of Five
cautiously approved the Synod of Chicago's organization and recommended that the General Council amend the canons to suit the
new situation. "And the Council" (as the Council Journal noted) "—

as an expression of gratitude to the Great Head of the Church, for the presence, the influence, and the aid of the Holy Spirit, in harmonizing widely differing opinions—rose and sang the 'Gloria in excelsis.'"[63]

It was at this point the turn of Cheney's critics to wonder, now that Cheney had secured a measure of independence for himself, whether they ought to do likewise for the sake of *their* independence. On October 30, 1877, delegates from the ten Reformed Episcopal parishes in New York City and northern New Jersey met under the leadership of Bishop Nicholson at the Church of the Incarnation in Brooklyn to discuss the organization of their own synod.[64] A few of the delegates argued to the bitter end against the synodical plan. Leacock, demurring from Nicholson's willingness to surrender the point, fought synodical organization to the last ditch, appealing to the expense of maintaining a synodical bishop and then to the simple uselessness of synods. "The General Council is to us a general council and a synod," Leacock pleaded. "We can do nothing outside the General Council. The only benefits, then, that we would gain by a synod would be spiritual ones."[65] But Leacock was argued down, and eventually voted down, and in January 1878 the Synod of New York duly adopted a constitution and set of bylaws.

The New York synod promptly became an example of just what Cheney had most feared from the Eastern Reformed Episcopalians. Unable to decide on a bishop (Nicholson would have been their choice, but Nicholson's church was in Philadelphia, and the Philadelphia parishes were now contemplating their own organization), the synod elected as their "chairman" a layman, Stewart L. Woodford, of the Church of the Incarnation. The synod then proceeded to pass a series of resolutions, stridently denouncing "the participation of communicants of this Church in what are commonly called worldly amusements." But when the synod moved to censure the General Council itself for not having dealt more severely with those who failed to teach "the eternal punishment of those who die in their sins," Woodford, the lay chairman, announced that he "did not believe in eternal punishment, in the Jonathan Edwards sense of the term" and resigned. After a good deal of anguished fumbling, and a call for prayer by the host rector, James M. Gray, the synod backed down and claimed that its censure applied only to "ministers and teachers in the Bible class and Sunday-school." Woodford then "withdrew his resignation" and "again took the chair."[66]

In October 1879, Nicholson agreed to election as "president" of the synod, but not "bishop," and so the matter of choosing a synodical bishop dragged on through two more synodical meetings in

April and November 1880.[67] At last, on April 6, 1881, the laggardly Philadelphia parishes united with the New York synod to form a united Synod of New York and Philadelphia at Christ Church, Rahway, New Jersey, and Nicholson was unanimously elected synodical bishop.[68] The Canadian Reformed Episcopalians followed suit at approximately the same time, organizing the First Synod of the Dominion of Canada on May 26, 1880, in Montreal and electing Edward Wilson (rector of St. Bartholomew's, Montreal) as their first bishop.[69]

All in all, the movement toward synodical (or, to use the proper term, "diocesan") bishops had been a long draft of gall and wormwood for the easterners. But nothing so decisively put an end to the "missionary bishop" episcopate, or so thoroughly justified Cheney's suspicions of exclusive General Council control of the bishops, than the scandalous affair of Thomas Huband Gregg, the General Council's "missionary bishop" for Great Britain. Although the Reformed Episcopal Church and the Free Church of England had agreed to the "Federative Union" in 1877, discontent with the agreement and with the Free Church soon began to surface within the Reformed Episcopal General Committee. "If I had known as much as I do now of the character of the 'Deed Poll' of the F.C.E. my vote would not have been given . . . to enter into a Federative or any other description of union with the F.C.E.," wrote Henry Alexander, a General Committee member from Ottawa, to Benjamin Aycrigg in October 1877. "I consider it unfortunate that we ever had anything to do with them."[70] Aycrigg himself, who had played a leading role in the formation of the Federative Union, was now one of the most disenchanted with the F.C.E., and he and Marshall Smith now began to formulate plans for planting a separate Reformed Episcopal Church in England, independent of the Free Church, almost as an act of atonement for their original misjudgment.

The Free Church evidently discovered these intentions early on. In February 1877, F. S. Merryweather, the Free Church Council secretary, warned Henry Alexander: "It would not be a wise thing for the Reformed Episcopal Church to seem to encourage division . . . by the establishment of a Branch of their church in this country separate from the Free Church of England."[71] The following June, the Free Church's Convocation anxiously passed a resolution deploring "the appearance of division and rivalry between two Episcopal bodies so thoroughly one in the great work of evangelization."[72] But by this time, Aycrigg and Smith already had reason to wonder whether the Free Church was really an *episcopal* body after all, and whether the Reformed Episcopal Church had forfeited a chance to make a legitimate appeal to Church of England Evangelicals by designating the Free Church as its mouthpiece in England. That view was encouraged, whether Merryweather realized it or not, by a disgruntled faction within the Free Church led by Philip Norton and Alfred Richardson, both of whom shared Aycrigg's perception that the Free Church represented only a sham Anglicanism and urged the Reformed Episcopalians to establish a thoroughgoing episcopal alternative for them in England. "I carefully prepared a paper," Norton wrote to Aycrigg in February 1877, "with the principal reasons for wishing to have a Branch of your Church here; dwelling chiefly upon the unsatisfactory nature of the Poll-Deed which is the legal constitution of the F.C.E."[73]

Aycrigg might well have wondered why Norton and Richardson did not simply move ahead on their own, organize such a "branch" of the Reformed Episcopal Church in England, and then petition the General Council for recognition. The problem with that solution, as Norton and Richardson admitted, was that neither of them had originally been ordained in the Church of England. Lacking that essential credential, neither of them could realistically assume leadership for an "authentic" episcopal movement. But later in 1877, the Church of England obligingly provided Aycrigg with the ideal candidate. In one of the long string of bitter court actions that grew out of Evangelical and Anglo-Catholic strife in the Church of England, the Judicial Committee of the Privy Council (the same body that had found in favor of Gorham twenty years earlier) agreed to hear charges against the Rev. C. J. Ridsdale, Anglo-Catholic vicar of St. Peter's, Folkestone, for various ritual offenses. Surprisingly, the committee acquitted Ridsdale and declared his ritual innovations permissible within the ambit of Church of England canon law. The decision sent a shiver of outrage through Church of England Evangelicals, and among those thus outraged was Thomas Huband Gregg, vicar of St. John's, East Harbourne.

Gregg was a short, hot-tempered Anglo-Irishman with the fierce look of a spoiled child perpetually on his face. Born in 1840 in Ballymahon, Ireland, he graduated from Trinity College, Dublin, and was ordained deacon, and then priest, in the Church of England in 1863 and 1864. He served his curacy at St. Paul's, Wolverhampton, and in December 1869 was appointed vicar of East Harbourne. Unable to stand still with only one profession, Gregg had also picked up a medical education at Queen's College, Birmingham, and became a Fellow of the Midland Medical Society, with a view to opening a general medical and preaching mission to the poor.[74] But Anglo-Catholic ritualism and the Ridsdale case pushed him over the brink of patience. "In the Church of England as by law established, . . . *the Church herself* by her highest earthly tribunal has *officially sanctioned* the adoption, by her 'priests,' of the eastward or *sacrificial* position at her 'altars,'" Gregg complained, and in May 1877 he resigned his living in protest.[75]

Gregg did not, however, turn automatically to the Free Church of England as an alternative. He had been corresponding with Alfred Richardson and Benjamin Aycrigg as early as December 1876 and had fallen in completely with their scheme for a Reformed Episcopal organization in England independent of the Free Church. "A branch of the REC in organic union with that in America, appears to me to be what is wanted in this country," Gregg announced to Aycrigg on December 16, 1876.[76] And, writing to Richardson on February 16, 1877, Gregg declared:

> None (as you know) can more thoroughly sympathize, than I do, with the *work* of the F.C.E.: but when one examines your Poll-Deed wh. is the *legal* constitution, then scarcely anything could be more unlike . . . the Constitution and Canons of the R.E.C. According to the Poll-Deed the F.C.E. consists really of Bishops & churchwardens as its "orders" and appears to me to be an attempted amalgamation of Presbyterianism, Congregationalism, and such an Episcopacy as makes all Presbyters Bishops . . . & ignores entirely the very idea of consecration. . . . I fear . . . that the F.C.E. is but showing . . . that it is not one & does not desire to be one with the (I use the words advisedly) *most magnificent work of the present century—the Reformed Episcopal Church.*[77]

This was sheer music to the ears of Alfred Richardson and Benjamin Aycrigg, and both seized on Gregg and the "missionary bishop" scheme as the solution to their dilemma in England. "Gregg is a man of good family—high scholarship—administrative ability—a public power," Richardson wrote breathlessly to Aycrigg on January 29, 1877. "He is your man for a Missionary Bishop & I predict that within twelve months he will have founded twelve good churches."[78]

Aycrigg and Marshall Smith leapt to the opportunity to designate Gregg a missionary bishop for England. In early May 1877, two weeks before the meeting of the Fifth General Council, Aycrigg and Smith presented to the General Committee their case for organizing a separate Reformed Episcopal jurisdiction in England under the direct authority of the General Council and with Thomas Gregg as its missionary bishop. The General Committee was wary of the proposal, and Charles Edward Cheney was especially hostile to the designation of a missionary bishop for what amounted to an end run around the Free Church.[79] But the prevailing disillusionment with the Free Church, combined with Aycrigg's extravagant predictions that Gregg was precisely the man who would draw disaffected Church of England Evangelicals into the Reformed Episcopal orbit, won the day. Gregg was officially received as a presbyter into the Reformed Episcopal Church by the General Committee on May 9, 1877. Less than a week later, on Benjamin Leacock's nomination, Gregg's reception was confirmed by the General Council and Gregg was elected a missionary bishop "for the Kingdom of Great Britain and Ireland."[80] In mid-June, with £70 lent to him by Benjamin Aycrigg, Gregg sailed for America and was duly consecrated in First Church, New York, by the then-Presiding Bishop, Samuel Fallows (with Bishops Nicholson and Cheney assisting) on June 20, 1877.

Gregg returned to England on July 4, 1877, and promptly set about erecting a provisional synodical council and recruiting clergy and laity—most of them, as it turned out, from the Free Church. A newly organized Free Church congregation in Southend-on-Sea installed Gregg as their rector and became the first official Reformed Episcopal parish in England. Within a year, Gregg had brought over six Free Church clergymen, including Philip X. Eldridge, Alfred Richardson, Gordon Llewellyn, Hubert Bower, Francis Aske, and Philip Norton, and even one Free Church bishop, John Sugden. But over the course of the same year, Gregg began to display a streak of ambitious self-aggrandizement that brought him into increasing collision with his own followers and with the General Council in America. He began experimenting with his own revision of the prayer book and the lectionary, resubstituted the Thirty-Nine Articles of Religion as the doctrinal standard of the Church, created canonical requirements for the use of vestments, and sought to concentrate all power for licensing and receiving clergy in his own hands as (what he now called himself) the "Primate of England." In November 1877, Aycrigg and Marshall Smith were sufficiently alarmed at Gregg's innovations to write a letter of mild protest.[81] But Gregg's response to any American criticism was an abrupt and almost hysterical accusation that the Americans were trying to manipulate what rightfully was a British concern. "We have something to bear," Gregg complained, "in being so constantly reminded that we must go to Yankeeland, to be told what we must do."[82]

Gregg's letters infuriated Aycrigg, and all the more since it began to dawn on Aycrigg that he had been used by Gregg in the same way he had been used by the Free Church. "The R.E.C. does not profess to be an *American Church* in any sense of the word," Aycrigg replied. "The R.E.C. is 'Yankee' [only] in so far as that the first Anglican Bishop to lead us in the reform that has been so ardently desired in England and America was found in this country, and that the majority of the R.E.C. and the Standing Committee are in this country."[83] Consequently, when Gregg appealed to the next General Council in 1878 for permission to draft a constitution and canons for the English Reformed Episcopalians, the Council agreed only with the vital condition that three commissioners appointed by the Council would review any new canons before they would actually take effect.[84]

It was now Gregg's turn to become furious. "There must not be any *British* dictation to the United States, neither must there be any *United States* dictation to British subjects," declared Gregg's church magazine. Instead, "there must be the fullest and most complete ecclesiastical Home Rule, consistently with the integrity of the R.E. empire."[85] When one of the American commissioners, Herbert Turner, met with Gregg's newly created "General Synod" in mid-September 1878, Gregg refused to negotiate any point of question and eventually walked out on him.[86] One month later, Gregg wrote to the General Council to request a letter dimissory from the General Council on the grounds that he was no longer able to consider himself merely a missionary bishop of the General Council but was now the bishop of an independent national province of the Reformed Episcopal Church.

This threw Gregg's newly formed parishes into an uproar, since most of their members had left the Free Church to join the Reformed Episcopal Church and not Thomas Huband Gregg. A number of the clergy, including Norton and Richardson, resisted Gregg's grab for power, only to be notified individually in late October and November that Gregg no longer considered himself as operating under the American canons and that all English Reformed Episcopal clergy would have to obtain new licenses directly from him in order to continue their ministries. To finish his unilateral declaration of independence from America, Gregg proceeded to consecrate Nicholas Rounsdell Toke, a former Church of England clergyman, as a bishop without even bothering to notify the Reformed Episcopal General Committee.[87]

In Britain and in America, the second thoughts and recriminations began to fly thick and fast. "I fear we have misjudged Bishop Gregg," Joseph Dawson Wilson wrote to Aycrigg, suddenly discovering "I don't like him personally."[88] "Gregg has turned out to be a thorough Judas," wrote Philip Norton. "It is our duty to cut him down."[89] By the time the General Committee met in January 1879 to consider Gregg's demand for a letter dimissory, opinion concerning him had turned poisonous:

> In asking letters of dismissal under the circumstances, it is clear that there is no authorized body to which he could be dismissed. . . . This action must, therefore, be regarded as a secession from the R.E.C., for the furtherance of his own ambitious principles. . . . His assumption of certain prerogatives and titles, and his demand of an oath of allegiance at the consecration of bishops, are features in his system of Church work, contrary to the genius of Protestantism, and to the spirit of the R.E.C. So far then from bring able to bid him God Speed, the Presiding Bishop feels bound to protest against his unprotestant and arrogant assumptions.[90]

On February 8, 1879, Presiding Bishop Fallows wrote Gregg a lengthy letter, reviewing the English situation, questioning Gregg's authority, and refusing his request for a letter dimissory.[91] Eventually, in May 1880, William Rufus Nicholson, acting as Fallows's successor as Presiding Bishop, simply removed Gregg's name from the clergy roll of the Reformed Episcopal Church.[92] Meanwhile, the General Council appointed the former Free Church bishop, John Sugden, as bishop of the General Synod of the English Reformed Episcopal Church to challenge Gregg's authority, and in June 1879 the Council elected Alfred Richardson to be consecrated as Sugden's assistant.[93]

But Bishop Gregg declined to disappear as neatly as that. Claiming that he alone represented the legitimate authority of the Reformed Episcopal Church in England, Gregg proceeded to organize the "Reformed Church of England." Since he held the British copyright for the Reformed Episcopal Prayer Book in his own name, he was able to keep Sugden and Richardson from using it in General Synod churches, thus reducing them to using the Church of England Book of Common Prayer with all the necessary Reformed Episcopal emendations penciled into the margins. Gregg also lured a number of General Synod laypeople into his fold. "No right-minded member of the Church of England, aware of the circumstances of the case, *could ever think of joining any body under the auspices of* Messrs. *Sugden, Richardson, and Norton,*" wrote one of Aycrigg's English correspondents. "I write to ask you . . . whether . . . you have contented yourselves with only one side [of Gregg's case]."[94]

Gregg also successfully appealed to the anti-"Yankee" prejudices of a number of Canadian Reformed Episcopalians. Brandram B. Ussher, one of Cheney's ordinands and the new rector of St. Bartholomew's Reformed Episcopal Church in Montreal, threw in his lot with Gregg in the summer of 1879. In the process, Ussher declared that the General Council had tampered so much with the prayer book, the Articles of Religion, and the whole notion of episcopal order that Gregg's movement was the only hope for hanging onto a recognizable Anglican identity:

> The views expressed by leading gentlemen in the Eastern States who mould the legislation & doctrine of our church are such as to convince me, that I am even less likely in the future than in the past to recognize in the R.E.C. . . . the Church in which I was baptized and brought up, with which I had only one fault to find, viz. the Romanism in her Prayer Book. If the United States authorities will not keep faith with me, in harmony with the views expressed to me by Bishop Cummins, . . . then with God's help I shall keep faith with myself, and identify myself with that branch of an R.E.C. . . . that affords some guarantee of usefulness to one who desires to live and die a Protestant Episcopalian.[95]

There was little the General Council could have done to prevent such secessions. The Easterners' devotion to the missionary bishop scheme had induced them to consecrate a virtual stranger, and it had now backfired in their faces. "Bp. Gregg was a simon pure Missionary Bishop, elected by us, appointed to his field by us," admitted Joseph Dawson Wilson in a letter to Benjamin Aycrigg in 1879, "but it has turned out badly. Let us face the fact like honest men and confess ourselves mistaken."[96] That lesson, at least, was well learned. The General Council elected no more missionary bishops for another fifty years.

The Vestments Controversy

Wrenching as the struggles over episcopal jurisdiction, the prayer book, and the Articles turned out to be, nothing so divided and tormented the Reformed Episcopal Church after George David Cummins's death as the comparatively minor question of vestments. The Reformation in England had cut the dress of the clergy

down to "such ornaments . . . as was in the Church of England by
authority of the Parliament in the second year of the reign of King
Edward the Sixth," which was generally understood before the Ritualists came onto the scene to mean that the parish clergy of England were to vest in the long black cassock, the white surplice (to
go over the cassock), and the four-pointed Canterbury cap. For
bishops, it meant the rochet (a billowy white episcopal surplice) and
chimere (a long black or scarlet vest). But the regulations that prescribed this dress proved difficult to enforce, chiefly because no one
was entirely sure what had been worn "in the second year of King
Edward the Sixth." The Puritans of the seventeenth century refused
to wear the surplice, or even the university gown, on the grounds
that any distinctive dress for the clergy would only point the way
back to popery. The Latitudinarians of the eighteenth century finished what the Puritans began, and by the 1760s the surplice had
disappeared from all but the most rustic of parishes. The fashionable
clergy of the age of Johnson and Hogarth instead preferred only the
plain black cassock and, instead of the surplice, a black don's gown,
open at the front. Powdered wigs and tricorn hats replaced the
pointed caps, and bishops donned aprons, breeches, gaiters, and
shovel hats for all but their formal portraits.[97]

Since American Episcopalianism was planted during this very period of black-gown minimalism, the standard Protestant Episcopal
dress reflected the same pattern of cassock-and-gown. The earliest
surviving portrait of George David Cummins, drawn during his
days as rector of Trinity Church, Washington, shows him dressed in
cassock and an open-front don's gown with a pair of white preaching bands at the throat.[98] It was therefore easy for many of Cummins's contemporaries to assume that this status quo enjoyed a
quasi-official position as the proper dress of American Episcopalians. James A. Latane recalled: "When I first remember, the surplice was almost unknown in the Diocese of Virginia. . . . In few of
the Dioceses was it universally worn, and in none, I think, was it
used in the pulpit."[99] Even in Samuel Seabury's Connecticut, the
surplice "was worn to read the service and then the minister
changed it for a black gown to preach his sermon—frequently passing down the whole length of the Church to get to the robing or
Vestry-room in the [church] porch."[100]

All this changed with the appearance of the Ritualists (the Tractarian phase of Anglo-Catholicism was comparatively indifferent to
the question of vestments). In their effort to restore the public image
of the Anglican parson as the successor to the Apostles, they revived
any and all vestments that they thought would appear to give testi-

mony to their continuity with Catholic order. "Come with me to
the City of Baltimore," exclaimed one outraged Evangelical. "We
will enter the Protestant Episcopal Church of St. Mary the Virgin—
significant name surely—situated on Orchard Street."

> The Rev. Dr. Batterson, of Philadelphia, preaches the ser-
> mon, arrayed in a crimson cassock and white surplice, with a
> doctor's purple band which is fastened with a brooch of dia-
> monds. After the reading of the lesson the altar is "censed"
> by Rev. Mr. Perry, who wears a handsome white cope, upon
> the back of which is embroidered a beautiful sunburst. After
> the offertory, clergy and choristers march down the middle
> aisle and make the circuit of the church in the following or-
> der: Incense bearer, crucifer, with two acolytes in red sur-
> plices and zuchettas; nine little girls dressed in white and
> wearing long white veils, choristers with banners, acolytes,
> clergy. . . . The Rev. Dr. Houghton, of the Church of the
> Transfiguration, has his white locks crowned with a black
> biretta, and his body enveloped in a robe of gold silk, heavy
> with gold embroidery, two acolytes *bearing the train of the
> robe.* . . . No comment is necessary upon such a performance
> as this in a Protestant (!) Church, but . . . it may be interest-
> ing to particularly note the color of some of the vestments in
> this instance, comparing it with the common evangelical in-
> terpretation of Revelation xvii, where the same color figures
> conspicuously.[101]

The movement toward greater and grander vestments began with
the surplice, as the most basic step beyond the simple black cassock.
In so doing, they meant only to use the restoration of the surplice
(which was, after all, the dress of the Reformation rather than the
Middle Ages they so adored) as a stepping-stone toward reintroduc-
tion of other, more "Catholic," vestments like the alb, chasuble,
amice, maniple, and eucharistic stole. But the surplice had been so
long out of common use that it was lumped in with all the others as
a Ritualistic tool, so the surplice became the object of heated assault
by Evangelicals, such as the Earl of Shaftesbury, who announced to
a public meeting in 1850, "I would rather worship with Lydia on the
banks of the river than with a hundred surpliced priests in the gorgeous temple of St. Barnabas."[102]

In time, as the battleground between Ritualists and Evangelicals
shifted to the openly eucharistic vestments, the surplice and scarf
reassumed their traditional status as the dress of Evangelical Angli-

cans. The "innovation" of the surplice was almost lost sight of in the uproar over baptism and liturgy. But the irritation was there in some Evangelical minds all the same. "In its origin, its history, and its association, it is to my mind clearly and distinctively a *sacrificial vestment*," Latane declared, and on those terms it could be only a matter of time before some Reformed Episcopalians began to call for the abolition of the episcopal rochet and chimere, as well as the surplice.[103]

That call actually came within a day of the founding of the Reformed Episcopal Church, and from no one less than George David Cummins. On December 3, 1873, when Cummins met for the first time with the newly designated Executive Committee, one of the first suggestions he made was to lay aside his rochet and chimere and revert to the use of cassock and gown. Benjamin Leacock remembered:

> The subject of using vestments, other than the black gown, was brought up by the Bishop. He had previously spoken to me on the subject of the episcopal robes, and had expressed his decided disapprobation of their use. He now asked the opinion of the Committee. One after another gave his opinion, and the judgement was unanimous against the use of the robes. The Bishop expressed himself as greatly satisfied with the result. He gave it as his opinion, that the use of these robes had a most unspiritualizing influence upon their wearers—that their effect was to separate and make them conspicuous, and thus to engender self-importance, pride, and arrogancy.[104]

It is worth noting, however, that Cummins's decision was based on the inexpediency of the rochet and chimere, rather than on theological principle. He did not imply, as Leacock wished he had, that the episcopal vestments were "sacerdotal" in nature or symbolism. Cummins's personal indifference to the question was demonstrated a week later, as Cummins was about to depart for Chicago to consecrate Charles Edward Cheney.

Cheney had always worn the cassock, surplice, and scarf, even on the day Bishop Whitehouse had walked out of the Christ Church vestry room for the last time. Cheney had continued to wear them all through his long years of exile, as a way of demonstrating that he, and not Bishop Whitehouse, was still upholding the principles of the Episcopal Church as he had always known them. To have cast them aside would, in Cheney's mind, have been tantamount to con-

ceding the truth of Whitehouse's attack on him, conceding that he
was no Episcopalian, that he had abandoned the church, and that
Cheney's congregation had been led astray into some form of quasi-
Methodism. When Cheney learned of Cummins's intention to dis-
pose of his robes (Cummins had, in fact, already given the bulky
rochet and chimere, which in Victorian fashion were sewn together, to
his wife to take apart) and do the consecration in cassock and gown, he
anxiously cabled Cummins: "Bring your robes with you." Cummins
cabled back, "They are taken to pieces." Cheney replied just as
quickly, "Bring them as they are," for as Cheney explained later,

> By doffing the distinctive habit of a bishop, [Cummins]
> would proclaim that he had not merely "transferred his work
> and office to another sphere," but had inaugurated a church
> that in outward things was widely different from the usages
> of the Evangelical Episcopalians whom he had claimed that
> he and we represented. So deep and strong was the sentiment
> that it threatened a schism in my own parish.[105]

Cummins had proposed to abandon the rochet and chimere to
avoid having a bishop of the Reformed Episcopal Church look too
mighty. On the other hand, he had never intended, by that action,
to make Reformed Episcopal bishops seem like anything less than
bishops, and he was alarmed that the absence of the robes might
somehow sabotage Cheney's consecration. "Bishop Cummins informed us that Mr. Cheney was very desirous that he should wear
his robes," Leacock remembered. "His reasons were that [Cheney's]
congregation were used to them—that they would expect him—
that not seeing them would occasion a shock that might produce a
revulsion of feeling and cause some to regret the change they had
made in their church relations."[106] Cummins could ill afford to make
Christ Church stumble on the very threshold of the Reformed Episcopal Church, and because the question for him was only one of
expedience, the unsewn robes were thrown into a trunk and put on
the train to Chicago, where Alexandrine Cummins hurriedly pieced
them together in time for her husband to perform Cheney's consecration in full dress.[107] Cummins thereafter lent his rochet and
chimere to Cheney for use at confirmation (until Christ Church was
able to present Cheney with his own rochet and chimere) and continued to use them himself afterward on episcopal visitations in
Canada.[108] After his death, Cummins "was clad in them when laid
away in the cemetery near Baltimore where he rests now awaiting
the resurrection."[109]

There were others, however, who would have been only too happy to have buried rochets, chimeres, and surplices once and for all with Cummins. Once again, the question would involve the same personalities and, at the root of the question, the same basic issue of Reformed Episcopal identity and purpose. Benjamin Leacock never made any secret of his dislike for the surplice or of his conviction that the surplice was a badge of the episcopal identity he hoped would be suppressed in order to allow the Reformed Episcopalians to become one with the background of American Protestantism. The surplice, explained Leacock,

> draws a line of very decided and offensive demarcation between ourselves and the Protestant bodies about us. Offer the ministers of the different bodies what else we will, and there is at once sympathy and affiliation. Show them our *Articles* and they approve of them; hand them our *Declaration of Principles*, and they will thank God for the vindication of His truth: give them the Prayer Book, and they will use it with satisfaction; ask them to put on the black gown, and they do without hesitation; but offer them the episcopal robes, and the same must be said of the surplice, and they will fling them from them with scorn and would to God our Church had done so at the first.[110]

But this kind of argument, when stripped of its rhetoric, was really asking Reformed Episcopalians to fling aside more than just surplices. Essentially, it urged Reformed Episcopalians to assassinate their own ecclesiastical identity, and if it was put as nakedly as Leacock did, it would frighten off more Episcopalians than it would attract. For that reason, Leacock—aided by William Rufus Nicholson and James A. Latane—sought to persuade Reformed Episcopalians to ban the surplice from the Reformed Episcopal Church, not because it was too Episcopalian but because it was too popish, and they had in their favor the argument that the cassock and gown, rather than the surplice, had long been the customary dress for many Evangelical Episcopalians. Leacock, writing the *Episcopal Recorder* in 1894, tarred the surplice with a Ritualist brush by claiming that the surplice was merely a stalking horse for popish dogma:

> [The Ritualists'] errors had begun to exert their pernicious influence on the Church. Consciously or unconsciously, the evil leaven was working. The result was ritualism. Very sim-

ple, very innocent at first. Flowers, glorias, postures, chant-
ing, wafer-bread, surplices, that was all. But doctrine was
back of it. It always has been so. We hide our eyes to the fact
but history is against us.[111]

But this connection was by no means as settled in the minds of
Reformed Episcopalians as Leacock wanted to believe. Benjamin
Aycrigg, who as a layman had no particular interest in surplice-
wearing, peremptorily dismissed the guilt-by-association rhetoric of
Leacock and Nicholson. "As I understand the matter," Aycrigg
wrote in 1876 in reply to Charles W. Quick, "the Surplice is not 'a
linen rag of popery,' nor 'a Babylonish garment.' . . . It does not
'indicate the claim and discharge of sacerdotal functions,' except of
late years by the Tractarians who, in like manner, have put a ritualistic construction on Baptism and the Lord's Supper. On the contrary, the Surplice is used exclusively by *Protestants.*"[112] In addition to
Cheney's argument for the rochet, chimere, surplice, and scarf as
the visible proofs of the Reformed Episcopal Church's continuity
with the larger Anglican world, other voices argued that the issue of
whether one should wear certain vestments or not was simply irrele-
vant so long as Evangelical doctrine was being preached. It was this
argument that lay behind the most eloquent appeal on behalf of the
wearers of the surplice, which came from Peter F. Stevens, in his
address to the Twelfth General Council in 1889. Stevens, like
Aycrigg, had no personal interest in the surplice or bishop's robes,
but he defended the users of them on the grounds of Luther's old
argument, the freedom of the Christian:

> What matter whether a garment be white or black, if only
> Christ is preached, what matter whether a few words more
> or less, in or out of the Prayer Book be used, if God is wor-
> shipped in spirit and in truth, what matter where a man was
> born if the truth as it is in Jesus be his guide and aim—where
> Christ is truly preached, and His truth truly rules, there is the
> Church, and there are our brethren. In the positive prescrip-
> tions of our Canons we have uniformity enough to make and
> mark us one and the same Church; let us preserve unim-
> paired the liberty granted by those same Canons.[113]

But arguments from liberty fell on deaf ears when addressed to men
like Nicholson, Leacock, and Latane. "The details of ceremonial,
which otherwise might appear trivial, really derive magnitude from
being acts done in the prosecution of an important purpose," the

unknown author of *Questions and Answers About the Protestant Episcopal Church* darkly warned.[114] As Latane reminded his readers, "Those vestments, like other elements of a false ritualism, have a self-propagating quality which may be safely trusted, if only a fair field be given them, to bring the entire Church into subjection to them."[115] Thus, for the first quarter-century of the life of the Reformed Episcopal Church, the successive General Councils were increasingly pockmarked by acrimonious debates (which were hurriedly expunged from the public record) and personal infighting (much of which went on in the anonymity of cloakrooms and church vestibules).

Cheney naturally became the lightning rod to which most of the antivestment electricity was attracted. In 1874, he was forcibly prevailed on not to wear his rochet and chimere while preaching the opening sermon at the Second General Council.[116] In 1875, he successfully faced down an attempt to include "vestment" among a list of "direct or symbolic teachings . . . of a sacerdotal character" to be banned by the Reformed Episcopal canons. In July 1876, he narrowly escaped a resolution of censure from the Fourth General Council for performing confirmations and other episcopal acts in his episcopal robes. Cheney had tried to placate his detractors by voluntarily putting the robes by at Nicholson's consecration the previous February, and by giving free rein to his presbyters in Chicago to wear what they wished.[117] But nothing Cheney did or pled satisfied the enemies of the vestments. Meanwhile, the constant badgering of the arguments widened the split between eastern and midwestern Reformed Episcopalians, helped poison relations with the Canadian parishes (not to mention adding fuel to the appeal of Bishop Gregg's schism), and at length finally exploded into a ferocious public battle in 1897 on the floor of the Fifteenth General Council.

The prelude to the 1897 confrontation occurred during the winter of 1894–95 in a shower of brilliant polemical fireworks staged by Latane and Cheney on the pages of the *Episcopal Recorder*. Latane opened his attack on the surplice in the October 25, 1894 issue, declaring: "There is no Church in Christendom . . . in which the surplice, or white linen vestments, of any kind, are used in the services of the Church, *except in Churches where the idea of priest and sacrifice prevail.*" As proof of this association, Latane insisted that, since the surplice "was almost unknown" in his experience in Virginia until it was introduced by the Anglo-Catholics, its introduction could have no other purpose but for it to act as the handmaiden of popery. "Its use in this country steadily advanced with the doctrine of a priesthood in the ministry, a sacrifice in the Lord's Supper, and altars in the churches."[118] Furthermore, he added, "there is no authority in the Word of God for the use of special vestments of any kind in the worship and service of the Church of Christ"—how could their use have anything other than sinister purposes? Far better, Latane claimed, "that the East could give up its monkish cassock, and the West its sacrificial surplice" and meet on "the common ground of the black gown" only.[119]

Cheney, stung by Latane's thinly veiled accusation that the use of the surplice was a Trojan horse for Ritualism, volleyed back a reply, which appeared on November 15. In it, Cheney hotly asserted that "the surplice *alone* was never considered a badge of the priestly office. . . . The minister who makes himself a sacrificing priest is never satisfied with that garment as a sign of his sacerdotal claim." Cheney also appealed to the identity of the Reformed Episcopal Church as an Episcopal movement. Bishop Cummins "had pledged himself to make this Church the representative of the 'old and true Protestant Episcopalians.' . . ."[120] Any attempt by Latane to strip away the surplice was also an attempt to strip the Reformed Episcopal Church of its true identity, and thus of any continued rationale for its existence. "I beg you, my dear brethren of the clergy and laity, to remember that the only ground for our existence as a church lies in the fact that there was a pressing need, not for another Presbyterian Church—not for another Baptist Church—not for another Methodist Church—but for another Protestant Episcopal Church," Cheney told his synodical council in Chicago in 1884. "The moment we cease to emphasize those peculiarities which make us Episcopalians, that moment we acknowledge that we have no right whatever to exist."[121] Now, Cheney argued, the introduction of Latane's black-gown-only proposal would actually be fully as much an "innovation," in terms of the history of the Episcopal Church, as the vestments introduced for their part by the Ritualists. What made one innovation purer than another?

It was now Latane's turn to be stung. Finding that Cheney had neatly turned the tables of "innovation" on him, Latane rounded on Cheney's argument that the surplice was "the badge of *an* Episcopal ministry." But, Latane inquired, "of *what sort of an Episcopacy is* it the badge?" And answering, Latane happily conceded that he had none of Cheney's interest in maintaining any ties to the Episcopal past, since "the surplice is the badge of *exactly that form of Episcopacy* which the Reformed Episcopal Church has renounced and forsaken."[122] Nor did Latane propose to let Cheney hide behind a plea for "liberty." "Does he not know," Latane wrote angrily, "that the cry of 'Christian liberty' in such a connection is utterly misleading, and that it is just the cry with which every Romanizing priest in the old Protestant Episcopal Church seeks to defend his introduction into that Church of some Romish service or ceremony or symbol or vestment?"[123] And in an attempt to turn the tables of gender on Cheney (as the Evangelicals had long tried to turn them on the Anglo-Catholics), Latane brazenly inquired what could be the purpose of Cheney's request "allowing him to wear in his mother's house old Mrs. Roma's petticoats" unless it was to put "old Mrs. Roma . . . in charge of the whole establishment."[124]

It was in an atmosphere thick with such flammable remarks that the Fifteenth General Council met in First Church, New York, in June 1897. It had been assumed from the beginning that this Council would witness the final showdown on the vestments question, and the assumption was not disappointed. In the very first afternoon session on June 9, a resolution on vestments was introduced by the Presiding Bishop, Thomas W. Campbell, bishop of the Canadian synod since 1891. Although Campbell himself disliked the wearing of the surplice, his resolution called for tolerance of the gown, surplice, and scarf for presbyters, and the rochet for bishops. Latane, however, at once proposed a conflicting resolution, calling for the outright abolition of all but the black gown except—and this was to be a sop thrown to Cheney—in parishes where the old vestments were still being worn. The debate over the resolutions worked its way through committees and over dinner tables for two days, until the Council, voting by orders, defeated Campbell's tolerance resolution. Then (with a difference of only six votes among the clergy) the Council upheld Latane's abolition resolution.[125]

Up until this point, Cheney had deliberately taken no part in the debate. But he now rose and asked for the floor to read a general letter to the Presiding Bishop. What he read aloud was a thundering indictment not only of the abolition resolution but also indirectly of everything the Reformed Episcopal Church had become in the twenty-one years since the death of George David Cummins. "The final vote," Cheney declared, "I believe to be a fatal blow at all Christian liberty in the Reformed Episcopal Church." But worse, "it is a deliberate violation of the solemn pledge given by Bishop Cummins to his co-adjutors in the founding of the Church." Thus, Cheney announced, "we . . . distinctly depart from the customs of 'the old and true Protestant Episcopalians'" and "say that the 'old paths' . . . to which Bishop Cummins declared that we returned, are paths leading directly to Rome." On those grounds, Cheney could not "with good conscience hold any office in the gift of a Council which I am convinced has 'laid the axe at the root' of all Christian liberty in this Church." And as Latane looked on stonily, Cheney submitted his resignation from all Council committees "and from any other place which I may hold by the authority of the General Council."[126]

The wonder was that Cheney simply did not leave the Reformed Episcopal Church altogether. But Cheney had put too much into the church to leave it now, and it was a very good question as to where, at age sixty-one, he could now expect to go. Instead, he stayed on at Christ Church, running the Synod of Chicago as his own episcopal fiefdom with Samuel Fallows's assistance, and defiantly wearing his rochet and chimere up until his death in 1916. Others felt no such restraints. Presiding Bishop Campbell left the Reformed Episcopal Church in disgust before the end of the year, as did two of Cheney's own presbyters, Frederick Walton and William Fairley. But worse than the loss of individuals, the 1897 "black-gown" resolution symbolized the closure of the original spirit of the Reformed Episcopal Church. It heralded, instead, the quiet descent of the Reformed Episcopalians into an ecclesiastical conundrum where they would always be too obviously Episcopalian to satisfy most non-Episcopalians, and too stridently anti-Episcopalian in thought, word, and dress ever to be able to persuade significant numbers of Episcopalians to join them.

The "black-gown" resolution was, in that sense, only the culmination of a series of contradictions that had shown up in the fabric of the Reformed Episcopal Church right from the beginning, and some of the men who had founded the Reformed Episcopal Church had seen this coming for more than a decade. William Feltwell, one of the original seven clergymen who stood with Cummins on that snowy day in December 1873, went with Bishop Gregg. Marshall Smith, who had taken down in pencil Cummins's dictation of the "Call to Organize," also resigned in April 1882 and returned to the Reformed Church in America. "I have my doubts whether our movement now amounts to much, either in England or in this Country," Smith wrote sadly to Aycrigg. "The *radicals* have destroyed its symmetry and the *whims* of the theologians have broken the helm."[127]

VII

RECOVERY AND DISILLUSION

They All Ended in Failure

Both the Anglo-Catholics and the Reformed Episcopalians existed in a strangely symbiotic relationship, in that both were dramatically antimodern movements and both thought there was
good reason for being so dramatic about it. In their eyes, the loss
of religious authority in Anglo-American Victorian culture, and
the impact of complex national and international market empires,
spelled a serious loss in moral meaning and individual autonomy.
The urban, industrial self appeared fragmented and illusory, a
Jamesean flow of consciousness without weight or significance,
an exercise in irrationality tossed up and about on the storms of

the unconscious.[1] The Reformed Episcopalians struck back at the tide of modernism by wishing themselves back to the coherent self of the Scottish philosophy, the Evangelical model of rationalism in which the self could be known immediately as a whole. The Anglo-Catholics offered an ecstatic medieval piety that washed away doubt in a bath of Romantic history. Both Reformed Episcopalians and Anglo-Catholics were thus traditionalists, and shared what might be called a traditional outlook. And both were part of the overall struggle of Christian orthodoxy to negotiate "new vehicles of consent" that would somehow affirm some kind of continuity with the past while giving a fresh sense of order and stability to class and social relations.[2]

Still, this symbiosis should not be mistaken for an identity of intent. The Reformed Episcopalians, like other Anglo-American evangelicals, sought to bend the weapons of reason to their own defense; Anglo-Catholicism sought to escape secularism by eluding, rather than affirming, the trammels of reason. As it turned out, neither in the long run could successfully fend away the shrinking walls of the house occupied by religion in the Victorian world. One telltale but subtle measure of the real intellectual distance between both parties occurs in the peculiar vocabulary of English and American Anglo-Catholicism. Like so many other nineteenth-century imperialisms, Anglo-Catholicism invented a new language, full of arcana to Protestant ears, larded with "the Blessed Sacrament," "Father" as a term of clerical address, sanctuary lamps, ciboriums, crucifers, and so forth. The aggressive and provocative implications of Anglo-Catholic language are usually treated simply as one more instance of their urge to break lances with a Protestant culture, and as such they leave little doubt about Anglo-Catholicism's inherent imperialism. What is more likely to be missed is how this clutter of terminology actually functioned as a short-circuit around rationality. The thicket of Anglo-Catholic religious language is, after all, strangely matched to the dearth of serious Anglo-Catholic theological speculation—unless, of course, Anglo-Catholic language is recognized for what it was, an active and conscious repudiation of the theological rationalism so beloved of the Evangelicals, in favor of a dialect based on religious sentiment. Nothing galled the Reformed Episcopalians so much, on a personal level, as the use of the term "Father" as a personal salutation, because the usage reeked not only of Romanism but also of a blatantly unrepublican claim to patriarchy. Just on terms like that, as an exercise in antimodernist symbols, Anglo-Catholicism affords more pure delight than any other movement in American history. At least, more than any place else in nineteenth-century American thinking, Anglo-Catholicism is composed and defined as a relationship of signs. And it was in Anglo-Catholicism, in the Episcopal Church in Milford, Pennsylvania, that the father of semiotics, Charles Sanders Peirce, found his last comforts at the end of a petulant and stormy life.[3]

As compelling as its signs might appear as a justification of religion, the unpleasant fact was that Romantic intuitions of medieval glory were doomed to yield less and less in the way of satisfaction as the capitalist and technological tightening of language in the nineteenth century "raised the question whether intuition qualified as knowledge at all."[4] The Anglo-Catholics embody the most extreme propensity of Victorian religion toward statements of belief that were "tenuously established, floridly expressed, elaborately vague."[5] Thus, whatever their overtly antimodern pose might appear to be, the fact was that their antimodernism actually was Janus-faced, in that it provided a bridge over which reluctant conservatives could cross into a mass-industrial society without having to immerse themselves in the fiery brook of secularism that rolled beneath it. T. J. Jackson Lears remarks:

> In America as in Europe, antimodernism had a dual significance: it promoted accommodation to new modes of cultural hegemony while it preserved an eloquent edge of protest. . . . In the United States, antimodernism revitalized familiar bourgeois values and paved the way for new ones: it eased the transition from classical to corporate liberalism, and from a Protestant to a therapeutic world view. . . . In the United States, the social impact of antimodernism was wide-ranging and complex. Antimodern impulses helped WASP elites to become a unified and self-conscious ruling class. Gothic architecture and medieval heraldry provided collective symbols—often with Anglophile overtones—for an emerging national bourgeoisie.[6]

Anglo-Catholicism thus accomplished little in terms of a theological agenda in the American Episcopal Church—but it did become immensely popular as a religious refuge for the financiers and aspiring bourgeoisie who were modernity's most relentless apostles. And it could accomplish their self-defeating *volte-face* because it offered an international capitalist elite just the right juxtaposition of resistance and acceptance of bourgeois culture it needed to prosper in an uncertain and complex world system, a juxtaposition nowhere more obviously celebrated than in the passion for Gothic architecture indulged by Episcopalianism's greatest stockmarket and railroad tycoons.

By contrast, the Reformed Episcopalians, with their fervent dedication to Protestant union and republican simplicity, seem to have had before an American audience every advantage the Anglo-Catholics did not have. Furthermore, with their early interest in fundamentalism and premillennialism, hardly any group would have been in a better position than the Reformed Episcopalians, after the turn of the century, to present themselves as a highly attractive, broadly based conservative Protestant denomination. Instead, however, these putative advantages served only to work against the Reformed Episcopalians. The fundamentalism represented by William Rufus Nicholson played into serious conflict inside the church with the liberalism represented by Samuel Fallows. Outside the Reformed Episcopal Church, fundamentalism turned into a homogenizing theological attitude that cut across denominations, rendering separatisms like the Reformed Episcopalians moot and individual denominational traditions meaningless. And as for the enthusiasms of such Reformed Episcopal premillennialists as Nicholson and his disciple, James M. Gray, they were more easily captured by organizations like the great premillennial conferences, which operated more like voluntary societies than a liturgically based denomination whose most obvious signs were prayer books and bishops.[7]

But the Reformed Episcopalians' most basic difficulty lay precisely in the antiquated version of antimodernism that stood at the core of their self-identity. Unlike the Anglo-Catholics, the Reformed Episcopalians remained rooted in the Whig rhetoric of rational theology and common sense—theirs was an antimodernism of the most consistent but also most outdated cloth. The twentieth century would reveal that there was no viable method for coalescing industrial capitalist society with Whiggish religion, and that fact alone rendered the Reformed Episcopal enterprise (as well as the fundamentalist enterprise) a marginal one from the first.[8] Thus, instead of creating the kind of dialogues Cummins envisioned as the beginning of a pan-Protestant movement, the Reformed Episcopalians, misunderstanding each other and misunderstood by others, created monologues with each other. The one major exception to this was Cummins's extraordinary outreach to the South Carolina blacks, but the opportunity to explore the dramatic potential of that outreach fizzled after Cummins's death. Consequently, the Reformed Episcopalians noticed none of the great transformations of American culture that occurred between 1870 and 1930. They became, rather, a culture of their own, and that in turn highlights the fatal significance of what was, in almost everyone else's eyes, a tempest in the ecclesiastical teapot—the vestments controversy.

The vestments controversy, along with the disastrous affair of Bishop Gregg and the internal wrangling over power and jurisdiction between the New York–Philadelphia Synod and the Synod of Chicago, would never have happened if the Reformed Episcopalians had not already defeated Cummins's plea that they look outward to the Protestant world as a whole, rather then inward on their own obsessions. And because these controversies signaled such closure, they dealt the public reputation of the Reformed Episcopal Church a blow from which it never fully recovered. It was difficult for outsiders, either from the Episcopal Church or elsewhere, to believe Cummins's promise that the Reformed Episcopal Church would be the wave of the ecumenical future when its members were so bitterly divided over their own identity and purpose. "You know how I feel about the new rubrics on candles, altar, etc.," wrote one embittered Reformed Episcopal layman to his bishop in 1930, who continued:

> In my opinion these things are harmless. They mean nothing to me, but if they would bring people into the churches, I would fill the churches with them. . . . We split our Church in half once on the surplice question which was not worth five minutes consideration. We have never recovered from that catastrophe.[9]

Reformed Episcopal membership statistics supported this complaint only too well; communicant membership in the church stalled and then faltered after 1897. In 1878, when the first records of communicant membership were gathered by the General Council, the Reformed Episcopal Church had 5,808 communicants (and that after only five years of growth), with approximately twice that many listed as "attendants on worship" and another 9,000 on the rolls of Reformed Episcopal Sunday Schools. By 1889, the figure had almost doubled to 9,283 communicants, and in 1894 communicant membership stood at 10,665 and "attendants" were estimated at nearly 40,000.[10] But the events of 1897 chilled all further hope of growth. Communicant membership stalled at the 10,000 mark until 1912; it then blipped upward to just over 11,000 from 1915 to 1921, and then settled into a long, slow slide.

The vestments controversy was not the only reason for this decline. One silent but major factor was age. By 1900, the first generation of Reformed Episcopal leadership, who had been recruited from the ranks of the old Episcopal Evangelicals, had begun to die off. Benjamin Leacock died in his native Barbados in 1896, followed by William Rufus Nicholson in Philadelphia in 1901. James Allen Latane briefly succeeded Nicholson as bishop of the New York and Philadelphia Synod, only to die suddenly in February 1902. John Howard-Smith followed them in death in 1903. The last lay member of the original Council in Association Hall, Charles Kellogg, died in 1914, leaving Charles Edward Cheney as the sole survivor of the Reformed Episcopal founders until his own death two years later. After that, the only leader left to the Reformed Episcopalians with any kind of national stature was the elderly Samuel Fallows. "Who, in our church, has made a success?" wailed William Russell Collins in 1928. "A few in the first generation, like Sabine, Nicholson, Cheney and Fallows, had a few years of success, . . . [but] they all ended in failure, and they were our best educated, most scholarly, most influential and commanding men." Collins did not lavish any approval on the noisy and aggressive band of fundamentalist boosters whom he saw coming up through the thinned Reformed Episcopal ranks. "Succeeding them, our most relatively successful men have been our crudest, of small education, crude manners, and the vocabulary of the peasantry, . . . and among these not a single scholarly man nor a well-trained Episcopalian."[11]

Collins's fear that the Reformed Episcopal Church was coming to represent merely a sort of déclassé Episcopalianism was shared by others in the church. The *Episcopal Recorder* admitted as early as 1881 that "it is evident that social position is an important factor in the problem of the growth of the R.E. Church." However much rank-and-file Episcopalians might grumble at the Anglo-Catholic ascendancy in their church, "they have not the moral courage to subject themselves to the social ostracism which they fear attaches to any who leave its ancient fold and enter the R.E. Church."[12] That fear of "social ostracism" was based on the increasingly obvious fact that, apart from a handful of large urban parishes, like First Church in New York City, St. Paul's in Philadelphia, and Christ Church in Chicago, the Reformed Episcopal Church was turning into a largely lower-middle-class denomination. Even in the great urban parishes, lower-middle-class social identity freely and sometimes defiantly asserted itself. In 1902, William T. Sabine (who had succeeded Nicholson and Latane as bishop of the New York and Philadelphia Synod) found himself powerless to keep a splinter group of "working people" from walking out of St. Paul's in Philadelphia to form their own congregation, the Church of the Mediator. "It is composed of a middle class of working people who are not fairly recognized in St. Paul's," Bishop Sabine wrote in his visitation book, but (he added approvingly) they "are zealous and faithful."[13]

Not only was the Reformed Episcopal Church becoming lower-middle-class in ethos, its official statements began to seethe with the kind of social moralism that lower-middle-class resentment of Episcopalian high society used as a form for protest against the economic misery of the Gilded Age. Beginning in 1878, the General Council had adopted standing resolutions condemning "all theatrical exhibitions, dances, and gaming" and other "forms and assemblies of pleasure in which the children of this world find their chosen joy." In 1881, yet another resolution added Reformed Episcopal disapproval of "the great and crying evil of intemperance," and in 1887 and 1897 still more resolutions followed, condemning "the enormous traffic in intoxicating liquors." The condemnation of upper-class pleasures was, after all, a relatively safe way of threatening upper-class power (which was, in the late nineteenth-century in England and America, almost always most visible in its pleasures). Subtle class-signals about the social identity of the Reformed Episcopalians cropped up in other contexts too. In 1907, Henry McCrea, rector of Trinity Church, Philadelphia, was singled out for praise at a New York and Philadelphia synodical council for having "abolished fairs, shows, entertainments, and everything of a spectacular character" as fund-raising tools for the parish—including, one presumes, that most typical Episcopal church function, the church bazaar.[14] On those terms, to leave the Episcopal Church for the Reformed Episcopalians was to commit a breach of etiquette as much as to make a theological statement. There was no doubt that "the social question retards our growth," admitted W.A.L. Jett, rector of St. Luke's Church, Murray Hill (New Jersey). "In many cases to unite with [the Reformed Episcopal Church] means social ostracism."[15]

Meanwhile, the fundamentalist radicals and the church traditionalists continued to savage each other on council floors and in print. The elderly Cheney doggedly persisted, almost to his last breath, in declaring that "Bishop Cummins' earnest efforts were directed toward making this Church as clearly and undoubtedly *Episcopal* as the Church from which it sprang."[16] In New York City, at the twentieth anniversary celebrations of the Association Hall meeting in 1893, D. O. Kellogg took up the same theme: "The Reformed Episcopal Church . . . is only reformed incidentally, for in gist and core it is a restoration, and should have been called the Restored Episcopal Church if its true relation to the organization from which it was cloven is to be indicated in its name."[17] Thirty years later, at the half-century mark, William Russell Collins and Willard Brewing (soon to become bishop of the First Synod of Canada) were still trying to wave the old Episcopal flag. "The Reformed Episcopal Church in 1873 . . . never ceased to exist as a part of the Episcopal Church," Collins claimed, but only "assumed a new name under an independent Episcopate."[18] And with rather more optimism than evidence, Brewing announced that "when one comes into a Reformed Episcopal Church, it is not difficult to detect to what branch of the Church we belong. The atmosphere is unmistakably Anglican."[19]

But Brewing and Collins both knew that they were only whistling to keep their courage up after 1897. Fundamentalism, and its dispensationalist offspring, had acquired a substantial influence within the Reformed Episcopal Church, due in large part to William Rufus Nicholson. That influence was strengthened in the eastern parishes by James M. Gray, Nicholson's disciple and later first president of the Moody Bible Institute, and by Daniel Miner Stearns, a former Congregationalist who was rector of Grace Church, Scranton, and the Church of the Atonement in Philadelphia from 1886 until his death in 1920. For Stearns, the "prophetic scheme" espoused by dispensationalism, which was predicated on the return of a Jewish state to Palestine and the subsequent conversion of the Jews to Christianity, was almost requisite to salvation. "To fulfill the word of God, the restoration of Israel becomes an absolute necessity," Stearns wrote in 1882. "To shake our faith in this would be to shake the assurance of our own personal salvation inasmuch as the ground of both is the infallible testimony of the Word of God."[20] Far from promoting an "unmistakably" Anglican atmosphere, Stearns, Gray, and others of the same mind were intent on promoting the diametric opposite.

That they succeeded was not always due to their skills in persuasion. Herman Hoffman, a Moravian clergyman who brought his entire Philadelphia congregation over into the Reformed Episcopal Church in 1881, spent most of his career as a Reformed Episcopalian (which included election as a stand-in bishop for Canada in 1903) on a personal rampage against the surplice. Arrogant, not a little pompous, and plagued throughout his life by an assortment of physical ills, Hoffman was not particularly threatening to the traditionalists on his own terms. What did make him a force to be reckoned with was the very considerable fortune that came into his hands through the death of his first wife, Elizabeth Looney Hoffman. When Hoffman himself died in 1913, his will created a church extension fund that lent out generous sums of money at minuscule interest rates for any new Reformed Episcopal church building—provided "there shall never be used in its edifice of worship any vestments . . . in accordance with the Standing Resolution bearing on vestments of the Reformed Episcopal Church, passed by the General Council of the said Reformed Episcopal Church that convened in the City of New York in May 1897."[21] By dangling the prospect of unlimited free money in front of struggling parishes and vestries, Hoffman hoped to out-bid, rather than out-debate, the hapless partisans of cassock and surplice.

To complicate matters further, alongside the fundamentalists and the traditionalists, there still remained odd lots of unrepentant liberals who were equally convinced that they represented the "true spirit" of the Reformed Episcopal Church. Bishop Cheney had grown more and more suspicious of the orthodoxy of his fellow bishop and Chicagoan, Samuel Fallows, whom he regarded as "loose-jointed, sensational, unreliable."[22] Surprisingly, when Fallows at last succeeded Cheney in Chicago in 1916, he turned out to be more tame than Cheney had feared, and Fallows's lengthy term as Presiding Bishop (from 1902 to 1922) was unruffled by any public flourish of liberal opinions. It was not Fallows who stirred up liberalizing troubles, but Willard Brewing, the handsome, dapper Canadian bishop. Well might he love the Reformed Episcopal Church's "Anglicanism"—he did not seem to love much else about the church. As Cheney discovered to his horror in 1914, Brewing "held the crudest views of Christian truth of any man I ever met. . . . I am quite sure that he took the position once that if Jesus had died a natural death it would have sufficed; he rather abhorred the thought of salvation by the blood."[23] Finally, in 1929, Brewing had enough of being reminded by his fellow bishops "that there is not much in common between Brewing and our founders in doctrine or polity or form of worship," and he left the Reformed Episcopal Church to become moderator of the newly formed United Church of Canada.[24] He was not greatly missed.

Brewing and Fallows got their reputations for liberalism chiefly because they could not resist displaying it. Others, such as Joseph Dawson Wilson, kept up a reputation for Evangelical orthodoxy while privately entertaining their own individual liberalisms and keeping them under wraps. Wilson candidly admitted to William Russell Collins in 1916 that he was virtually a Universalist, since he believed "God was not going to keep a vast number of blaspheming wretches in existence for ever, but would ultimately have a universe free from sin." But Wilson was a smoother man than Brewing. "All our bishops understand my position," Wilson claimed—so long as he was discreet. Nor was he alone, he confided to Collins: "[William Morton] Postlethwaite . . . held the same view," and "Mason Gallagher was much impressed" with it.[25] How many others held similar cards up their sleeves can only be guessed.

These deep and persistent divisions of mind within the leadership of the General Council of the Reformed Episcopal Church not only discouraged growth but actually encouraged the individual congregations of the Reformed Episcopal Church to start looking out for their own interests before those of the Reformed Episcopal Church as a whole. The first sets of canons of the Reformed Episcopal Church had granted to the parishes of the church considerable latitude in governing their own affairs, and after 1897 many parishes converted that latitude into virtual independence. The bishops reigned, but they did not, and in many cases could not, rule. And lacking any single leader among the Reformed Episcopal bishops with sufficient stature to bend the alienated factions of the church into unity, the parishes drifted apart, setting their own private courses and building their individual parish empires. In 1918, D. M. Stearns congratulated the vestry of the Church of the Atonement on the pages of the *Episcopal Recorder* for having pledged $26,000 to foreign missions in that year, making a total of $209,000 over the twenty-five years he had been their rector. What Stearns neglected to mention was that almost all of it had gone to support non–Reformed Episcopal agencies selected by Stearns. In his visitation book for 1902, Bishop Sabine fumed helplessly that, under Stearns's leadership, "the church is now more undenominational than Reformed Episcopal in character. . . . The R.E. liturgy is only partly used." Nor was Church of the Atonement the only parish to go its own way. Stearns's former parish, Grace Church, Scranton, had given more than $1,200 in 1901 to "benevolent purposes, but of this amount only $234.00 are reported as going to Reformed Episcopal causes." Even the tiny Church of the Sure Foundation in West Chester, Pennsylvania, gave only $3 out of its benevolence budget of $679 in 1901 to "home denominational causes."[26]

The congregations shortchanged their own Reformed Episcopal rectors as well as Reformed Episcopal causes. Although no records on clergy salaries were kept in the early council journals, Bishop Sabine kept in his visitation book an informal record that gives the earliest reliable data on what Reformed Episcopal clergy were being paid at the turn of the century. According to Sabine, the top salary in the New York and Philadelphia Synod belonged to the ever-irritating D. M. Stearns, who earned a very comfortable $2,500 a year (when the average minister's salary nationally was $737). Hard behind him came William DuBose Stevens of Emmanuel Church, Newark (New Jersey), whose salary stood at $1,800, and William

Freemantle of St. Luke's, Philadelphia, who was paid $1,200. After that, however, the salary figures trailed off dramatically. The Church of the Reconciliation in Philadelphia paid Francis H. Reynolds only $300, Joseph Kitchen at Bishop Cummins Memorial Church in Baltimore earned only $250, and George Worrell at Grace Church, Collingdale (Pennsylvania), would probably have starved on the $150 paid him by the parish had his wife not been a niece of Herman Hoffman "and is understood to receive a living income from him." Twenty-five years later, in 1929, the best estimate of clergy salaries in the Reformed Episcopal Church put the average salary at $2,200, with the lowest coming in at $1,800; but even that lagged seriously behind other professions in 1929. "The congregations of the church," concluded George W. Huntingdon at a New York and Philadelphia synodical council in 1907, "do not give their pastors a living support."[27] And even those who did, did so grudgingly by contrast with the wealth of the Protestant Episcopal Church. Bishop Sabine never confided to his visitation book what he was paid by First Church, New York, but William Russell Collins, who grew up under Sabine's ministry, knew all too well, and he told Thomas J. Richards in 1924,

> No greater sacrifices have been made in our church, than those made by our far underpaid ministry, which has virtually supported the church and sustained its life in sacrificial service. . . . I think of Bishop Sabine, who would have been valued at $10,000.00 a year, easily in another church, serving ours in the pastorate for $4,000.00 and giving $1,000.00 a year with millionaires sitting in the pews giving less, and serving in the Episcopate for no salary.[28]

Each of these problems—the divisions of purpose, the disappearance of leadership, the lack of cooperation and support—fed further and further on each other. As the Reformed Episcopal Church quarreled over its identity, puzzled Episcopalians pulled shy of joining it. Those who actually joined were often "working people" like those of the Church of the Mediator, who were incapable of sustaining the costs hidden in the structure and expectations of an Episcopal church. The individuals and parishes who did have the means to support the work of the Reformed Episcopal Church hesitated to invest their money in a movement that might collapse after only a few more years. And as the levels of support remained low, the Church was unable to recruit clergy and leaders of sufficient talent and status to deal with the fitful problem of identity. And so the Reformed Episcopalians faltered, and a deadly sense of ennui succeeded the strife of controversy. The "grand work" looked like it had gone as far as it was likely to go. "I fancy that, outside of Philadelphia and Chicago, very little is known of the Reformed Episcopal Church," Joseph Dawson Wilson complained in 1914, forty years after George David Cummins had been front-page news. "It has given rise to a questioning of the rightfulness of our existence at all."[29]

Miss Benson's Seminary

The remarkable thing is that the Reformed Episcopal Church did not, despite itself, go out of existence. "It might well be asked, is there a single Church in Christendom today which, for a like period of existence, has committed more blunders, or sustained more harassing misfortunes, than have we?" exclaimed William H. Cooper in 1882. "And yet, thank God! we live."[30] In 1911, after more blunders and misfortunes, Charles Edward Cheney was still prompted to make the same judgment. "Its first five years of life were contemporaneous with the most appalling and long-continued financial depression that the United States has ever known," Cheney recalled, "but nevertheless this young Church has lived through it all. . . . Calamities which seemed beyond all human power either to avert or overcome, have been strangely made the vehicle of blessing."[31] Cheney did not specify precisely what calamities or vehicles of blessing he had in mind, but undoubtedly the principal reason the Reformed Episcopal Church was still around in 1911 to be thus marveled at by Cheney was the one outstanding success story of its first quarter-century of existence, not to mention the single most remarkable institution the Reformed Episcopal Church ever produced—its theological seminary in Philadelphia.

The founders of the Reformed Episcopal Church had seen from the start that they could not depend solely on defectors from the Episcopal Church to supply the ranks of their clergy. So, as early as 1875, Marshall B. Smith had called on the General Council to create a recommended course of study for candidates for the Reformed Episcopal ministry. A reading list approved by the General Council in 1877 gives away a good deal of what the early Reformed Episcopalians saw as the core of their theology: Bishop Butler's celebrated *Analogy of Religion* and McIlvaine's *Evidences* in apologetics; the stark Presbyterian Calvinists, Charles and A. A. Hodge, on theology, along with Bishop Pearson on the Apostles' Creed and Bishop Burnet's commentary on the Thirty-Nine Articles; Bishop J. B. Lightfoot's famous essay on the ministry in the early church, along with Hooker's *Lawes* and Lord Peter King (whose book on church government had unconvinced John Wesley of the need for apostolic succession); Philip Schaff and George Park Fisher on church history; and back to the Calvinists, Noah Porter and James McCosh, on "mental and moral philosophy." It was a strictly low-church list, containing an odd amalgam of Scottish common-sense philosophy and Calvinist theology (Hodge, McCosh, Porter) and a stiff dose of latitudinarian churchmanship (King, Pearson, and Burnet). Oddly, almost no Church of England Evangelicals made it onto the list, and only one American Evangelical (McIlvaine).

At almost the same moment the curriculum was finalized, the General Council was given the chance to put a roof over the curriculum's head. On March 21, 1877, one of Samuel Fallows's wealthy and intimate friends, Edward Martin of Red Hook, New York, offered the General Council a gift of 160 acres of land outside Chicago that had been bought in 1836 at a Chicago Canal Trustees sale. Martin expected that the land would be developed to provide an income to fund a theological seminary in Chicago to be known unblushingly as the "Martin College of Theology." This, in turn, would become the nucleus for a "University of the West," which the Reformed Episcopal Church would organize and operate as a nursery for ecumenical Protestantism in the Midwest. This unlooked-for bounty dazzled the Reformed Episcopalians, and the 1879 General Council actually got as far as nominating a faculty for the new institution: John Howard-Smith as dean and instructor in biblical, exegetical, and pastoral theology; James A. Latane as instructor in systematic theology and New Testament exegesis; Mason Gallagher as instructor in history and polity; Joseph Dawson Wilson as instructor in apologetics; William Newton as instructor in mental and moral philosophy; and Marshall Smith as instructor in Hebrew.

But Martin's proposal turned out to have several important strings attached. Martin had stipulated that the land was to be given to the Reformed Episcopal Church strictly to provide an income for the seminary; none of it could be sold, nor could the rental income itself be used to erect buildings. In fact, Martin required that the General Council must raise the $10,000 necessary to put up a building for the seminary, or the entire gift would revert back to him. Furthermore, for as long as it took the church to build the seminary and get it into operation (and he set a maximum of twelve years),

Martin required the General Council to pay the taxes on the property, and if the General Council should at any time default in paying the taxes (almost $8,600 a year), the gift of the land and anything the Reformed Episcopalians had built on it would revert to Martin.

As stiff as these conditions might seem, Martin had a reason for them. By preventing the use of the income from the land to cover operating expenses, he was closing off any temptation there might be to accept his gift and then, years later, sell it all off to meet other denominational expenses. And by demanding that the Reformed Episcopal Church assume responsibility for the taxes (and threatening to resume control of the land if the church failed to pay them), Martin was providing an incentive for the church to get on with building and operating the seminary as fast as possible. "Mr. Edward Martin . . . has conditionally presented our Church with land in the suburbs of Chicago containing over 1700 city lots worth now over $250,000 . . . as a free gift for the Reformed Episcopal Theological Seminary," Mason Gallagher explained in the *Episcopal Recorder*. "He naturally asks our 8000 communicants to contribute a small sum . . . to indicate that we appreciate the benefaction, and to show that as a Church . . . we are in some degree worthy of so magnificent a gift. . . . *Surely the hand of God is in this thing!*"[32]

However, one person's incentive is another's burden. William Rufus Nicholson opposed the project from the first, and Herbert B. Turner, the first secretary of the General Council objected that managing a project as large as that proposed by Martin was simply beyond the means of the General Council:

> Is it not time that this child's play should stop? It is very evident that Mr. Martin entirely misapprehends the position of our Church, and the resources of its members. He asks for nothing more than is reasonable . . . but our Church is in no such position. It lacks three elements necessary to such a college, money, professors, and students, and the sooner we stand aside and let some Christian body strong enough to do the work claim the benefit of this most liberal agent, the better it will be for the general cause.[33]

But there may have been deeper motives behind Nicholson's and Turner's strange prudence. A "University of the West" had long been a private project of Samuel Fallows, and locating a Reformed Episcopal theological seminary at the center of Fallows's plans—and Cheney's jurisdiction in Chicago—would have put the theological education of the Reformed Episcopal Church squarely in the lap of the Chicagoans. It did not help, either, that the four trustees whom Martin had appointed to oversee the property—Samuel Beers, Gordon Hubbard, William Aldrich, and Fallows himself—were all Chicagoans. If the Chicago Synod could capture the new seminary within its own bounds, it could at one stroke redress the imbalance of power between itself and the East and control the climate of opinion that would shape the future clergy of the Reformed Episcopal Church. Cheney's plea on behalf of the Martin College scheme— that "there is an *esprit de corps*, a love for the Church itself, which cannot be expected of those who are not educated in its own ways, and whose early associations have not been with its organic life"— was read by the New York and Philadelphia Synod as a threat to inculcate the ways of Chicago into the heads of Reformed Episcopal seminarians.[34]

Probably as much for that reason as any other, the easterners successfully throttled the plan. In the face of the anguished disbelief of Fallows and Cheney, the Tenth General Council in 1885 finally decided that the payment of taxes and other encumbrances on the land were more than the Reformed Episcopal Church could bear, and it voted to return the land to Martin's ownership. That, however, left the church back where it had been in 1877, with no seminary at all. The interest stirred up by the Martin College proposal had at least underscored that something had to be done about theological education to get it on a permanent footing, and on October 24, 1884, even before the Martin College of Theology had breathed its last, Bishop Nicholson met with Cheney's nemesis, James Latane, to discuss the establishment of a school within the bounds of the New York and Philadelphia Synod. In September 1885, Nicholson and Latane authorized John Howard-Smith and William Wallace Lovejoy to begin taking on the instruction of candidates for the ministry, although the only facilities for doing so were the rooms of Howard-Smith's tiny Church of the Atonement in Brooklyn. Meanwhile, Cheney organized theological instruction for five students, using the parlors of Christ Church for schoolrooms and the clergy of the Synod of Chicago for instructors. Cheney gave his little endeavor the grandiloquent title "The Divinity School of the Synod of Chicago," but in neither his case nor in Howard-Smith's case was there any dependable funding or resources. At that point, theological education seemed doomed to remain, at best, a part-time and a localized, synodical affair.

But then, on March 16, 1886, Nicholson was approached by Miss Harriet Benson, one of his parishioners at St. Paul's, Philadelphia, who made him an astounding offer. The daughter of a well-heeled

Philadelphia family (and commanding personal wealth in excess of $5 million), Benson proposed the creation of a trust of $200,000, under whose terms the General Council was to build and administer not only a denominational theological seminary but also a massive new church in West Philadelphia, and a $50,000 endowment to operate it. This offer, unlike Martin's, was virtually free of strings, except for the provision that Nicholson be appointed dean of the seminary. The General Council, however, was not disposed to kick at a goad that minor, and Benson's trust was unanimously received by the General Council on May 16, 1887. So confident was Nicholson the Council would act that way that he had authorized the cornerstone-laying of the chapel of the new church on September 19, 1886, and a second cornerstone-laying for the adjoining seminary building on October 21, 1886. On February 20, 1887, Nicholson was ready to consecrate the chapel of what was to be known as Christ Memorial Church (the cornerstone for the rest of the church, a massive 500-seat Gothic cathedral designed by Isaac Pursell of Philadelphia, would not be laid until May 28, 1887). And on September 30, 1887, it was Nicholson who presided at the "devotional meeting" that opened the doors of the seminary to its first class of students.

The first eleven students who entered the new seminary that day were uncommonly united in purpose and identity. William Russell Collins, Joseph J. Lewis, William DuBose Stevens, Henry F. Milligan, George S. Vail, Robert Westly Peach, and Rowland W. Mott were all Reformed Episcopalians, or shortly became such. William Stevens was in fact the son of South Carolina's bishop, Peter F. Stevens, and Rowland Mott was the organist of St. Paul's, Philadelphia. Only H. Grattan Guinness Vincent, among the regular students, had no connection with the Reformed Episcopal Church, and he later went to the Protestant Episcopal Church. There were also three special students in Hebrew: Francis H. Reynolds (then thirty-seven years old, Reynolds had been ordained by Cummins in 1876 after spending only a year at the Virginia Theological Seminary in Alexandria), Alexander Sloan (also ordained by Cummins in 1875 and in 1887 rector of Grace Chapel, Philadelphia), and Hendrik Van Ommeran (who had just been ordained in February 1886 by Nicholson and who was serving as minister-in-charge of the short-lived St. John's Church, Philadelphia). The first catalog of the seminary promised that "they who seek the privileges afforded by the Seminary will find the doctrines taught within its walls to be only those of a Protestant Evangelical Faith, as drawn from the infallible word of Divine Revelation." But the course of study was little other than the 1877 prescribed list of reading, with Nicholson as professor of Bible interpretation and homiletics, Howard-Smith teaching systematic theology, William Wallace Lovejoy teaching biblical literature, and Mason Gallagher, Herman Hoffman, and William Newton filling in other gaps in history and polity. Not the best faculty that could have been assembled, it was still successful in at least one respect: it clearly excluded any influence from the Chicago Synod or from the western and Canadian liberals. By the time James M. Gray was persuaded to join the faculty in 1893 as a lecturer in a new English Bible series, theological education in the Reformed Episcopal Church had been brought securely under the viewpoint of the New York and Philadelphia Synod—which was to say, a mild mixture of the old Evangelical theology with a touch of dispensationalism, a thoroughgoing biblical conservatism, and a decided taste for the lowest common denominator in churchmanship. As a result, the geographical center of the Reformed Episcopal shifted away from New York City, where it had been founded, to Philadelphia, and from 1887 on the fortunes of the Reformed Episcopal Church become bound to personalities and events in Philadelphia and in Pennsylvania.

The first students seem to have learned a few other things beyond what the seminary curriculum promised. They successfully provoked the seminary house-parents into resignation by eating the seminary refectory out of business; they tried to duck out of attending Reformed Episcopal services (Faculty minute, 1890: "they are not prohibited from attendance at other places of worship, but the habit of attendance at other churches is deprecated"); and they indulged a number of "frivolities unbecoming a Theological Student" (Faculty minute, 1890: "There shall be no smoking of tobacco in the Seminary building"). Higher learning and high-jinks seemed to go hand-in-hand, and the faculty found it as difficult to impose the one as to suppress the other.

All "frivolities" aside, the new students did manage to learn, and at the end of their three-year course, to graduate. A few faded from view almost at once. Hendrik van Ommeran resigned from the Reformed Episcopal Church in January 1888 to join the Congregationalists and was heard from no more; Rowland W. Mott developed tuberculosis and died within two years of graduation, at age thirty-one. But the others became the vital second wind of the Reformed Episcopal Church, in terms of both leadership and spirituality. Robert Westly Peach rose to become a bishop in 1924 and Presiding Bishop in 1930. He was the prime mover in the revision of the Reformed Episcopal prayer book between 1912 and 1930 (the chief effect of which was to move it closer, rather than further, from the revision of Protestant Episcopal Book of Common Prayer accomplished in 1928), and also taught church history and apologetics at the seminary until his death in 1936. The ill-paid Frank Reynolds, the last survivor among George David Cummins's ordinands, went on to serve a succession of parishes in the New York and Philadelphia Synod until his death in 1943. William DuBose Stevens was ordained by his father the bishop and served Reformed Episcopal parishes in Canada, New Jersey, Philadelphia, and New York City until World War I. Then, even though he was long past the age when anyone expected heroics, he volunteered to go to France as a Red Cross chaplain. There he died, not from bullets but from heart failure, on September 29, 1918.

The faculty of the seminary similarly grew in wisdom and stature. After Nicholson's death in 1901, he was followed as dean by John Howard-Smith, and when Howard-Smith died in his sleep in April 1903, Joseph Dawson Wilson became "Chairman of the Faculty" (Bishop Sabine, as one of the bishops who "knew" Wilson's "position," drew the line at awarding Wilson the title "dean") but only after privately promising never to air his opinions in the seminary on universalism. He never did. (William Wallace Lovejoy, on the other hand, did and was kicked off the faculty and out of the church in 1890.) At the same time, the faculty added W. Max Muller as professor of ancient languages and Old and New Testament exegesis. Muller was unquestionably the finest scholar ever to teach in the seminary. Born in 1862 of devout Lutheran parents in Bavaria, Muller had not only a Ph.D. from Leipzig but also a part-time post teaching Egyptology at the nearby University of Pennsylvania. Muller was joined by another Penn graduate, Josiah H. Penniman, who taught liturgics from 1894 to 1904, when he was elected provost at the university. Joshua McDowell Leavitt, a former president of Lehigh University, also joined the faculty in 1889 to teach church history and polity. And when the hapless Muller drowned in a swimming accident in 1919, his place was quickly filled by George Handy Wailes, who had already gone through stints as professor of Hebrew at Temple University and head of the Greek Department at Ursinus College and who would continue to teach at the seminary until 1959, when he was ninety-three years old. The same year Wailes joined the faculty, the seminary nearly acquired the services of one of the most prominent Church of England Evangelicals of the day, W. H. Griffith-Thomas, only to be cheated by Griffith-Thomas's death in 1924.[35]

By the 1920s, the seminary had the full potential to emerge, thanks to Harriet Benson's unlooked-for beneficence, as one of the preeminent conservative theological institutions in the nation. As it was, Philadelphia had emerged after the Civil War as the effective capital of American evangelicalism, and the location of the seminary and other critical Reformed Episcopal agencies in Philadelphia promised to position the new enterprise at the tactical center of evangelical Protestantism in the United States. "The establishment of our Seminary has exerted a most healthful influence upon the entire Reformed Episcopal Church," Herman Hoffman jubilantly announced to the Twelfth General Council in 1889.

> It has [continued Hoffman] given a permanence to our move-
> ment and has imparted stimulus and enthusiasm to every de-
> partment of our denominational work. It has become a bond
> to unite all the scattered and isolated parishes of our commu-
> nion. . . . No human sagacity can forecast what a mighty
> fortress and centre our Seminary will be in the great future
> for the defense of Protestant Evangelical truth. As Witten-
> berg was identified with every movement of the German
> Reformation, as Halle was the home of pietism, and as Ox-
> ford was the prime mover in and feeder of Ritualism, may
> we not aspire to make our Seminary a representative and cit-
> adel of a sound and evangelical theology?[36]

The Long Shadow of Robert Livingston Rudolph

None among the seminary's graduates came closer to embodying that potential or did more to pull the Reformed Episcopal Church's capsized affairs upright again than its premier graduate of the Class of 1894, Robert Livingston Rudolph. Born in New York City on December 29, 1865, the son of a German immigrant, Robert Rudolph was raised under the eye of William Sabine at First Church, New York. Up until the year he entered New York University, young Rudolph's school expenses were actually paid out of Sabine's pocket. Rudolph graduated from New York University in 1892, then went on to the Reformed Episcopal Seminary from 1892 to 1894, and from there on still further to Princeton Theological Seminary for a year under the celebrated Calvinist heavyweight Benjamin Breckinridge Warfield. Rudolph returned to New York University one last time to earn a master's degree in 1896, although, restless for more study, he later wangled a sabbatical to read theology in Germany under Theodore Zahn at Erlangen. For the most part, however, after 1896, Rudolph settled down to the duties of the ministry in the Reformed Episcopal Church. He was ordained deacon (in April 1895) and then presbyter (1896) by Bishop Nicholson, and he served as Sabine's assistant at First Church from 1895 to 1903. After the death of John Howard-Smith at the seminary in Philadelphia, Rudolph was invited to take up the responsibilities of teaching systematic theology, a position he held until his death (and that required him to abandon his New York City residence to live most of the year in Philadelphia). Finally, in 1909, after Herman Hoffman's retirement from episcopal duties had left the entire weight of the New York and Philadelphia Synod on Sabine's seventy-one-year-old shoulders, Rudolph was elected bishop coadjutor for Sabine. At Sabine's death in 1913, Rudolph automatically succeeded him at the head of the New York and Philadelphia Synod. In 1924, after the death of Samuel Fallows, the General Council unanimously elected him Presiding Bishop. Although forty-four years old at the time of his consecration, Rudolph was the first Reformed Episcopal bishop never to have been in charge of a parish.

In the end, that omission did not mean much, for along with Peter F. Stevens, the pioneer missionary bishop of the Carolina freedpeople, Rudolph was one of the greatest bishops of the Reformed Episcopal Church, and the only one after Cummins with the kind of political energy and intellectual stature that could have restored the Reformed Episcopal Church to its original course. Stevens even seems to have been Rudolph's model as a bishop. After the aging Stevens's health failed in 1909, Rudolph was detailed to make a visitation to the Carolina churches, ordaining clergy and confirming 147 new members. Rudolph's last visit to Stevens, in late December 1909, left a deep impression on the newly minted bishop.

> Though in his eightieth year [Rudolph recalled] and suffering infirmities of body and mind which completely incapacitated him for work, the one burden of that last conference, his passionate prayer, was that he might be permitted to go out again and labor for the salvation of his colored brethren.[37]

For the next twenty years, Rudolph did little more than spend himself just as freely as "this man of the martyr spirit."[38]

In one respect, Rudolph had little choice but to do so, if the Reformed Episcopal Church were to survive. Lacking the numbers and resources to afford an administrative substructure of deans, canons, or archdeacons (although Cheney briefly appointed one of his clergy

as an archdeacon for his Ohio parishes), the church threw all of its
organizational burdens onto its bishops, and after Sabine's death in
1913 Rudolph had to attend to all things major and minor himself.
This meant that he was compelled to suffer the fools among his
clergy with as much gladness as he could summon. They beseeched
him incessantly to solve the pastoral problems they had caused for
themselves. One of them, an immature and hysterical deacon in his
first parish, half-appealed and half-demanded that Rudolph "appoint
a court that shall try William Broomall and Mrs. Hilary Fox for
lusting after each other and using the Church Bldg. for such im-
moral purposes . . . and instruct Fred Kopke, our S.S. Supt. [that it]
. . . is not his right to select a Burlesque show for the Christmas
entertainment of the S.S. as he & his wife did last Xmas in open
defiance to my expressed opposition and conviction."[39] Sometimes
Rudolph had no alternative but to pick up the pieces of a shattered
parish and glue them back together by sheer force of his own personality. In 1917, when the Church of the Cornerstone in Newburgh, New York, was ready to sink for the last time, Rudolph
took himself up to Newburgh, and

> after five weeks of earnest work among them on Fridays,
> Saturdays and Sundays, in preaching, visitation and by corre-
> spondence, we met on Friday evening, [November] 30th,
> fifty in number, and decided to continue the testimony. We
> found that by united, prayerful effort we had secured pledges
> almost sufficient to meet the requirements for the year. Mr.
> [Thomas W.] Gladstone was called to the rectorship of the
> church, and received on his arrival a most hearty welcome.[40]

Sometimes the lay leadership of the parishes drew his fire. Independently wealthy through his marriage to Anna Knight (1869–1964),
Rudolph refused to accept a salary as bishop, but he ceaselessly hec-
tored the parishes for not paying their own rectors decently. "Brethren! some of the conditions which prevail ought not to be allowed
to continue for another month," he threatened the 1919 New York
and Philadelphia synodical council. "Love and sacrifice would enable
you to honor yourselves and God. If you fail, the Divine judgment
will be manifested in the loss of leadership and in your despairing
helplessness."[41]
　　The one satisfying aspect of having to deal single-handedly with
so many crises was that whatever successes Rudolph won in rebuilding the church were incontestably his alone. In 1925, he took the
opportunity to remind the New York and Philadelphia Synod that

during the previous sixteen years he had held 370 confirmations, and received 4,035 men and women into communicant membership in the Reformed Episcopal Church—a figure equal to almost the entire communicant membership of the synod at the time of his consecration. In eight visits to the Carolina churches, he had confirmed 606, and he confirmed 11 more at the Church of Our Lord in British Columbia during a visitation there in 1912.[42] And twice, in 1914 and 1915, Rudolph set a record for the size of his confirmations. On one Sunday in 1915, after a Billy Sunday revival had roared through Philadelphia, Rudolph confirmed 390 people at St. Paul's in the morning (along with welcoming 136 transfers of membership) and another 87 at Emmanuel Church, Philadelphia, in the evening (with 5 more transfers), making "a total accession for one day of 618."[43] Like Caesar before the Nervii, Rudolph had to go everywhere and do everything, but also like Caesar, everywhere he went he conquered. After only four years in the episcopate, the *Episcopal Recorder* editorialized, "Bishop Rudolph has done his work well."

> He has never declined to answer a call to the most distant parish in the jurisdiction. Often, when suffering physical pain and when less devoted men might have found an excuse, he has fulfilled his engagements, and at great financial sacrifices to himself he has served the Synod. But not only has he served the New York and Philadelphia Synod, but also the whole Church in ways that it is given few men to do. Every year he visits the Special Missionary Jurisdiction of the South, and covers the many and far distant parishes of our colored friends in the South. . . . He has crossed the continent that he might do the work made necessary by the death of Bishop Edward Cridge, D.D. . . . In labors more abundant, Bishop Rudolph has served our whole Church, and is worthy of the highest honor that either the Synod . . . or the General Council can confer upon him.[44]

One of his last students in the seminary described Rudolph more simply and succinctly: "an excellent theologian . . . and a prince among men."[45]

The fuel for Rudolph's relentless energies was his passionate attachment to the principles and worship of the Reformed Episcopal Church. Rudolph was among the first generation of Reformed Episcopalians who had grown up knowing no other church but the Re-

formed Episcopal Church, and his close personal ties to Bishop
Sabine and Bishop Stevens made the consideration of other ecclesiastical alternatives a moral impossibility. "My love for our dear
church would compel me to repudiate my own son if I felt that his
influence was detrimental to the life of the Church," he wrote to
Fred Mackenzie, rector of Grace Church, Scranton, in 1928.[46] That
close personal identification of his own life with the life of the
church also left him with no room for sympathy for the fashionable
theological liberalism of the 1920s. In 1924, he firmly announced:

> Since this Synod was organized, no man has ever crept into
> the ministry with a doubt in his mind as to the Deity of
> Christ, the utter helplessness of man, the full efficacy of the
> shed blood when the sinner believes, or the irrevocable loss
> of those who finally neglect this Gospel of grace. We are free
> from modernism, thank God, and such men as we can find in
> any one of our pulpits.[47]

Theologically speaking, Rudolph's days at Princeton Seminary had
imparted a deep and thorough tinge of old-school Calvinism to his
thinking. Hodge's *Outlines* remained the flagship theology text in
his seminary classroom, and as one member of the Class of 1929
recalled, "The influence of the theology of those days was apparently Calvinistic."[48] Years later, Rudolph's son, Robert Knight
Rudolph, who succeeded his father as theology instructor in the
seminary, had little more to do than "maintain the old Princeton
position to which he [Robert Livingston Rudolph] was devoted."[49]
    Yet for all his Presbyterian theologizing, Rudolph never lost some
sense of being an Evangelical Episcopalian. "Let us not drift into a
selfish individualism, a parochialism," he warned his parishes in
1914, or "we will lose character as an Episcopal Church. When we
lose that, there will be no longer need of our existence."[50] In 1927,
he vigorously reiterated the same point: "What dost thou think of
this sect? Do you know that it is not a sect? Do you know that it is a
Church with a Gospel for a special need?" What the parishes of the
Reformed Episcopal Church needed was not just a generic evangelicalism, "not merely men who know the Gospel but men who can
speak to the times out of our historic background."[51] He had little
personal patience with those who sat lightly by their Episcopalianism.
He wrote off an elderly clergyman, Edward Benson Barker, in 1924
as "not a loyal Reformed Episcopalian," and his distaste for D. M.
Stearns knew no limit—"not in any sense an Episcopalian," he tartly

informed the senior warden of the Church of the Epiphany, Cleveland, in 1923.[52] Rudolph also consistently forced Reformed Episcopalians to define themselves against the standard of the Episcopal Church, and he took every occasion he could to remind them of the rock from whence they had been hewn:

> Are we justified in maintaining a separate existence as a Church, as Bishop Cummins and his associates were justified in establishing a separation? The answer is readily at hand to the most casual observer. When, under the corporate name, Protestant Episcopal, seven hundred bishops and priests assemble in council in Philadelphia, within this very month, proclaiming themselves Anglo-Catholics, profess all the sacerdotal dogmas of Rome, celebrating high pontifical Mass . . . when, under the boasted unity and generous catholicity of this so-called Protestant Church, we find variously preached modernism, conservatism, traditionalism, socialism, and Romanism, and these all mutually denunciatory, constituting a wondrous catholic schism, we ask again, is our separation justified? And we answer, Yes, a thousand times over.[53]

Ironically, it was precisely the depth of his passion for the Reformed Episcopal Church that prevented Rudolph from emerging as the second Cummins, for he was never able to sympathize with those who did not love the Reformed Episcopal Church in precisely the terms he conceived of it. As a child of First Church and a product of the seminary at the height of William Rufus Nicholson's influence as dean, Rudolph took the New York and Philadelphia Synod's mentality as the norm for the entire Reformed Episcopal Church without so much as a glance sideward. In the midst of the General Council debate over vestments in 1897, Rudolph emerged as "one of the strongest advocates of the Geneva gown." He told the *New York Herald*: "We regard the surplice as the badge of the priestly office which we reject. . . . The young men [have] determined that it should not be left as a legacy for us, but should be settled once for all." And he dismissed Cheney's resignation from office after the 1897 Council with unbelievable callousness: "Bishop Cheney has always pursued the same tactics when he was beaten of refusing to play any more, and we hope he will get over this as he has got over other defeats."[54] Thirty years later, he had still refused to yield an inch in sympathy to Cheney or his heirs in Chicago. When in 1928 Rudolph attempted to use his position as Presiding Bishop to bully

St. Andrew's Church in Chicago into giving up the use of the surplice, the rector, Richard L. Sonne, informed him straightly that
there was more than one way to be a Reformed Episcopalian:

> Because I had been reared as a child in the R.E. Church, and
> because I think it is the jewel of denominations and sincerely
> love it for all that it stands [for], I am endeavoring to build
> up the church of St. Andrew's as an evangelical, not a ritual-
> ist. . . . We have an entirely different problem to meet in
> Chicago than in Philadelphia, Bishop—and have differently
> trained people. You can never realize the heartache we Chi-
> cago boys suffered when we saw how our beautiful service
> was mutilated by some of the eastern brethren who think and
> act more like Methodists than Episcopalians. Much as I re-
> spect your opinions, Bishop, and as highly as I regard you, I
> am sure that your request to tear out the surplice from St.
> Andrew's would result only in unfriendliness and harm; and
> engender animosity that is always very undesirable and
> weakening.[55]

Rudolph's personal animosity toward the Chicago traditionalists
found a particular target rather closer to Philadelphia in the person
of Dr. William Tracy, the redoubtable rector, from 1888 to 1926, of
the seminary's parish in Philadelphia, Christ Memorial Church. A
Welshman by birth and a former assistant to Cheney in Chicago,
Tracy had turned Christ Memorial and its 460-member congregation into an outpost of Chicago sentiments on every issue. (This
includes the surplice issue; Tracy had spoken on the floor of the
1897 General Council on Cheney's behalf and ever after persisted in
wearing his cassock rather than a Geneva gown in church.) The relationship between Rudolph in the seminary, and Tracy in Christ Memorial Church next door, gradually became poisonous. As late as
1929, when Tracy was in retirement, he was still "a dangerous man"
to Rudolph, and Rudolph's friend, William Russell Collins, warned
Rudolph: "He cannot become any more your enemy than he has
always been. . . . He can still talk. And there are those who visit
him and afford him opportunity to talk and who believe."[56]

One of those who had believed Tracy, and who came thoroughly
under his influence, was the benefactress of the seminary, Harriet
Benson. Tracy's quarrels with the leadership of the New York and
Philadelphia Synod effectively subverted Benson's obvious intention
that the immense Gothic pile of Christ Memorial Church should
function as the cathedral of the Reformed Episcopal Church, with a

resident bishop in the chancel and the seminary faculty in the carved oak stalls as a cathedral dean-and-chapter. But in these quarrels, Benson took Tracy's side rather than Nicholson's or Latane's, and blamed the bishops rather than Tracy. Although she remained throughout her life a member of St. Paul's Church, Philadelphia, she withdrew all her endowments from St. Paul's and put them into Christ Memorial Church. When the climactic vote on the surplice was taken in 1897, her close confidante and spokesman, Charles Morton, rose to announce to the Council that Miss Benson was retaliating against the antisurplice party (including Rudolph) by withdrawing a $300,000 bequest she had made in 1889 for a Special Church Extension Trust.[57] When she died in 1902, Benson left Christ Memorial trust funds amounting to nearly $500,000 and left Tracy a $10,000 pension.

The vestments issue was only one among many blinders Rudolph wore. In his New York University days, he had won an early reputation for ardent Prohibitionism, and classmates poked gentle (but discerning) fun at him when they suggested that "he ran for President on the Prohibition ticket, but wasn't elected," although they did allow that he would likely become "President of the Prohibitionists' Widows' and Orphans' Home."[58] Rudolph was not amused. As bishop he was responsible, more than anyone else, for what had become a crusade for both liberals and fundamentalists in the 1920s: the replacement of the wine and the chalice in the communion service with unfermented grape juice and individual thimble-sized glass communion cups. To a horrified Benjamin Aycrigg in the 1880s, this had represented an outrageous departure from Episcopal tradition, and Rudolph heard the same expressions of outrage forty years afterward when he publicly sanctioned the change. "All must admit that the small individual cups are a recent innovation, differing from the universal custom of Protestant churches since the Reformation," protested J. J. Robinson, a Canadian Reformed Episcopalian serving Grace Church, Havre-de-Grace (Maryland) in 1922.

> Satan [Robinson went on] is ever striving to make God's people want to do just the opposite of whatever the will of God may be. . . . Our Lord having said, "All of you drink of this cup," the adversary tries to terrify God's people with imaginary dangers. . . . The change to individual cups has been made because of a lack of faith in God's protecting care, and we need to remember that "WHATSOEVER IS NOT FAITH IS SIN." . . . There is danger that the New Testament Feast may repeat this sad history, ceasing to be the Lord's Table, and

becoming merely the individual functions of various discordant sects.[59]

But Rudolph was unpersuaded, and by the end of his episcopate the silver chalices and patens of the old Reformed Episcopal parishes in the New York and Philadelphia Synod had been replaced by grape juice and the glass thimble-cups.

Blinkered to all argument as Rudolph might be in what he considered matters of principle, he was willing to suspend some principles for the sake of people who were close to him. William DuBose Stevens was judged by one member of First Church, New York, as a pastoral and professional flop—"He was a dismal failure in Newark and the church he is in now in Phila., Pa., is going to pieces"— but he was a close friend of Rudolph's, and when the rectorship of First Church fell vacant after Bishop Sabine's retirement in 1908, Rudolph used all the votes of his family and relatives to swing Stevens's election as rector. "So you see," complained Miss E. G. Porter to Bishop Fallows, "the Johnstons [Rudolph's in-laws] and the Rudolphs are bound to give us Stevens of Phila. Mrs. Johnston [Rudolph's sister] said her daughter may well cry her eyes out if she don't have the Stevens children to play with and to attend her theatre parties."[60]

A more serious example of Rudolph's favoritism erupted in 1915 over yet another of Rudolph's friends, William A. Freemantle, rector of St. Luke's Church, Philadelphia, and editor of the *Episcopal Recorder*. An Englishman by birth, Freemantle had brought the entire congregation of St. Luke's into the Reformed Episcopal Church from the Episcopal Church in 1891. He had not been able to get his wife to see matters the same way, however, and in 1903 she left him and returned to England. This de facto separation would normally have been sufficient embarrassment to terminate Freemantle's, or any other clergyman's, career in 1915. But with Rudolph's friendship and the sympathy of his congregation, Freemantle had been permitted to labor on. Then, in January 1915, Freemantle quietly divorced his wife and, in July, without a word of announcement, left a church picnic and went off and married Anna Hoffman, the second wife and widow of Bishop Herman Hoffman. Freemantle's separation had been bad enough in 1903. The sudden divorce and remarriage, and to Hoffman's widow, sent the New York and Philadelphia Synod into moral shock. Freemantle's vestry demanded and got his resignation from St. Luke's, and in October William Tracy led a charge to have Freemantle ousted from the synodical Standing Committee.[61] But Rudolph unaccountably stuck by Freemantle. The Church of the Redemption, and then the prestigious Church of Our Redeemer in Philadelphia, were found for Freemantle, and Tracy's bid to unseat Freemantle from the Standing Committee was squelched.[62] Rudolph's rigorism turned out to be surprisingly selective.

Only a bishop of tremendous personal force could have pulled Freemantle out of such a fire; only a man of deep personal loyalties would have tried. On both counts, Robert Livingston Rudolph left an indelible stamp on the Reformed Episcopal Church. He took up the episcopate at just the point in time when it seemed that the Reformed Episcopal Church was going gradually to founder, but when he died, without warning, of heart failure on September 30, 1930, at his beloved summer retreat in Dorset, Vermont, a still-vigorous sixty-four years old, he had successfully righted the ship, pushed its numbers as high as they had ever been, and given the church a stability it would enjoy without serious threat for the next half-century. However, there was a price to be paid for Rudolph's brand of stability. His style of personal government and his rigid self-definitions of what constituted Reformed Episcopalianism made it difficult (then and now) to be sure that he was not manufacturing mere stasis rather than real stability. Although he successfully imbued the Reformed Episcopal Church with his own principles and prejudices, he did it such a way as to guarantee that the Reformed Episcopal Church would survive for the next half-century looking little different from the way he had left it in 1930—in fact, looking more like the church of Robert Livingston Rudolph than that of George David Cummins. Still, it must be said that without Robert Livingston Rudolph, the church of George David Cummins would probably not have survived at all.

Our Bitter, Mendacious, and Unscrupulous Enemy, Dr. Gregg

The ascendancy of Philadelphia and the theological seminary in the 1890s, and of Robert Livingston Rudolph in the early 1900s, were only the most obvious indications of how the Reformed Episcopal Church was able to restore a measure of order to its divided and unruly house. There was other good news too. The happiest and probably least looked-for development of this sort was the surprisingly mild end of the fantastic schism of Bishop Gregg in 1894.

Thomas Huband Gregg's repudiation of the General Council in

1879 split the Reformed Episcopal Church's General Synod for England into two competing jurisdictions, the first being Gregg's own self-styled "Reformed Church of England," the other being the battered rump of the General Synod under Bishops Alfred Richardson and John Sugden. Both of these, moreover, remained at odds with the Free Church of England. In Canada, Gregg not only attracted B. B. Ussher and St. Bartholomew's, Montreal, to his cause, but also consecrated Ussher as a bishop in 1882, to sow the seeds of the "Reformed Church of England" in Ontario. For a while, Gregg enjoyed a modest amount of success. He single-handedly built up Trinity Church, Southend-on-Sea, pumped out a monthly magazine called *The Reformed Church Record*, fought off local challenges to his title to the Trinity Church property mounted by Richardson and Sugden, made numerous visits to Canada and the United States, and in 1886 opened a "Christian Medical Mission" for the indigent where "all services were given gratuitously."[63] He broke rhetorical lances with a number of Church of England bishops in the letters columns of local newspapers, gave lectures, made visitations, and in 1889 announced that the time had come to organize the British Empire into "Reformed Church" dioceses. He announced with a flourish to his handful of churches: "England and Wales have been divided into Dioceses which have received official recognition from Her Majesty the Queen (the Head of the Established Church) by assigning to our Senior Bishop [i.e., Gregg himself] an official seat at Her Majesty's Jubilee Service, in Westminster Abbey on June 21st, 1887." Whether the Queen intended that Bishop Gregg should draw so great a conclusion from so slender a premise is doubtful. But Gregg persisted in signing himself as the "Bishop of Verulam," and he dispensed to his "dioceses" a string of archaic Anglo-Saxon names straight out of a Walter Scott romance: Selsey, Dunoc, Caer Memphric, Caer Leiron, St. German, Caerleon, Pengiven, Wyke, Hexham, Menevia, Margam, Alaunum, and Clausentum.[64]

Richardson and Sugden, by contrast, sulked in their tents. "Bp. Sugden is old & *does nothing*," Richardson complained to Charles Kellogg, secretary of the General Council. "The whole burden of work, with all the abuse, suffering & responsibility rests upon me. I have no Stipend & am a *martyr*."[65] But Richardson was by no means above reproach. In 1889, he and Sugden consecrated Thomas Greenland, a former Church of England clergyman, as an assistant bishop for the work of the sluggish Reformed Episcopal General Synod. But the words of consecration had hardly been uttered over Greenland before Greenland and Richardson collided. "I was anxious to help forward a movement which I believed would . . . afford a pure, simple, and spiritual worship for aggrieved members of the national Church," Greenland wrote afterward. He soon found that Richardson's synod, "instead of being bound together by one common bond of union and mutual sympathy would more and more drift, as it was drifting, into Congregationalism." But the measures Greenland proposed for counteracting this drift, such as a Sustentation Fund and a plan "to have all the Churches joined by Trust Deed with the R.E.C.," met with stony refusals from Richardson.[66] At length, when Richardson unilaterally dismissed one of the General Synod clergy without bothering to consult the Standing Committee of the Synod, Greenland challenged him, and in May 1889 Greenland withdrew from the General Synod to organize the "Free Protestant Church of England Mission." There were now *three* competitors in England for the title "Reformed Episcopal."

Across the ocean, Charles Edward Cheney was serving his second stint as Presiding Bishop of the Reformed Episcopal Church (1887–89), and he cast a distinctly cold eye on Richardson's ecclesiastical antics. Forgetting his initial skepticism about Gregg and all such "missionary bishop" schemes, Cheney increasingly came around to the conclusion that Gregg was (rather like himself) a martyr for traditional Anglicanism who had been wantonly sacrificed by the radicals in the General Council for the same reasons that he was suffering in Chicago—vestments, the prayer book, the Thirty-Nine Articles. "I am more and more convinced that the majority of our General Committee made one of the most fearful blunders ever committed when they turned the cold shoulder to Bishop Gregg, and subsequently put Bishop Richardson in the position which he now occupies," Cheney wrote to Charles Kellogg in 1889. "All that I learn from England convinces me more and more that Richardson is an exceedingly dangerous man; that he is not a Reformed Episcopalian at heart, but a scheming fellow ready to take up anything which will advance his personal interest."[67]

Cheney, in fact, had remained in personal, although surreptitious, contact with Gregg in England and with Ussher in Canada ever since 1879. When he became Presiding Bishop in 1887, Cheney set the wheels in motion toward a reconciliation, first with Ussher in 1888 and then with Gregg in 1889. Two rather feeble attempts to talk Ussher back into the Reformed Episcopal Church had been made by Bishop Fallows and by Bishop Edward Wilson in the early 1880s. But neither had offered Ussher any particularly good reason for rejoining the General Council, and Ussher's consecration as bishop by Gregg in 1882 appeared to have put Ussher completely beyond the pale. But in 1888, Cheney dispatched the persuasive and omnicompetent Peter F. Stevens to Montreal to negotiate with

Ussher, and after a series of meetings between delegates of Ussher's breakaway congregations and the rest of the Canadian Reformed Episcopal churches in May and June 1888, an agreement was finally reached. The Canadians would hold a re-union synod in September 1888; Ussher would relinquish his claims to episcopal jurisdiction in Canada and allow the reunited synod to elect a new bishop; but Ussher would be recognized as a validly consecrated bishop by the rest of the Reformed Episcopal Church and invited to minister in another Reformed Episcopal jurisdiction (which, to no one's surprise, turned out to be the Chicago synod).[68]

Stevens's settlement touched off an uproar among the radicals in the General Council, who not only looked on Ussher as a turncoat but also refused to recognize Gregg's consecration of Ussher as valid. It is odd that their argument against Ussher was not that recognition of the validity of his consecration would undermine the value of the episcopate, but instead that it would make it appear *too* valuable. Ussher's consecration had not, of course, been confirmed by the General Council (or much of any council, for that matter), and its validity rested almost entirely on Thomas Huband Gregg's authority as a bishop to convey orders to whomever he laid his hands on. That was entirely too expansive a notion of episcopal order for the radicals to stomach. Predictably, James A. Latane bitterly denounced any move to welcome Ussher back into the General Council. "He is not a *Missionary Bishop* of this Church, because he has never been elected such by a vote of the General Council," Latane protested, "and he is not the *Bishop of a Synod*, because he has never been elected such by the vote of any Synod of this Church, and even if he had, that election would not constitute him a Bishop of this Church, until such election had been confirmed by the General Council."[69] Mason Gallagher was even more blunt in his opposition to Ussher. In a paper circulated before the meeting of the 1889 General Council in Boston, Gallagher argued: "To allow . . . that the laying on of hands by a Bishop in England, could confer the Episcopate on this Brother, who, as we have seen, was destitute of a regular and valid election, is to directly affirm the doctrine of Apostolic Succession."[70]

But Cheney was not about to surrender the case tamely, especially because he saw that his own episcopal authority as much as Ussher's was under attack. "There can be no question, in my judgment, that under our canons, Bishop Ussher is just as much a bishop as Bishop Nicholson, Bishop Fallows, or myself, only that he is a bishop without jurisdiction," Cheney explained to Charles Kellogg in February 1889. "The canons of our Church seem to me perfectly clear and conclusive upon this point."[71] In the end, the General Council chose to see matters Cheney's (and Peter F. Stevens's) way. Ussher retained his episcopal title, but he never was given any further episcopal responsibilities either, and after serving as rector of Christ Church, Kansas City (Missouri), and Christ Church, Peoria, Ussher retired from active pastoral work in 1897. However, he stayed on the rolls of the Synod of Chicago as *Bishop* Ussher until his death in California in 1925.

Cheney might have been able to pull off the same arrangements for Thomas Huband Gregg as well, if only Gregg had allowed him. In January 1889, Cheney opened up his own inquiries into the state of affairs in the General Synod in England under Richardson and Sugden. He did little to conceal his intention of disowning the General Synod and bringing Gregg's "Reformed Church of England" back into communion with the General Council. In ominous terms, Cheney announced to Sugden that the time had come to "settle" English affairs: "The ceaseless controversy which seems to be carried on in Great Britain between the two organizations into which the Reformed Episcopal Church has been divided since 1879 leads me to feel that the time is very near when our General Council must decide upon some definite course of action in regard to them."[72] Richardson and Sugden had no difficulty reading between Cheney's lines, and they at once began bombarding their American friends with a mixture of alarm and threat. "Am I right in my apprehension that Bishop Gregg is coquetting with some of our American brethren?" Sugden asked William Sabine in February 1889. "Personally, I have no quarrel with Bishop Gregg," Sugden hastened to say, but, he added, "I think that he has wronged us, and that he has been and is autocratic."[73] Richardson, who knew something of what autocracy was, reacted more vehemently. "Many letters to persons in this country, from Bishop Cheney, have been handed to me," Richardson erupted to Charles Kellogg on March 13, 1889,

> & from them all I learn, beyond controversy, that for ten years past your "presiding bishop" has been in "constant & friendly" correspondence with our bitter, mendacious & unscrupulous enemy, Dr. Gregg. It is not pleasant for us to know this. Not one honest man among us would dream of having anything to do with Dr. Gregg & we feel it bitterly indeed that the "presiding bishop" of our Church should increase the difficulties of our very difficult work, by helping our worst enemy to hinder & spoil it. Under the circumstances, some of us are very seriously inclined to pause & consider![74]

Not content with dispatching frantic letters only, Richardson and Sugden sent one of their own men, Philip X. Eldridge, as an observer to the General Council session in Boston that May expressly to ensure that no rehabilitation of Gregg would occur. *"He is a match for Gregg,"* Richardson wrote to Charles Kellogg the day after Eldridge sailed for America. "He will smite Gregg hip and thigh."[75]

Richardson might have saved himself the trouble. No matter whether Gregg was as "mendacious & unscrupulous" as Richardson painted him, it was certainly true that Gregg's behavior in 1879 had been erratic and unreliable. He had not grown any less so over the years, as his fantasies about enjoying the Queen's favor reveal. When Gregg learned of Cheney's behind-the-scenes labors to put matters between the General Council and the "Reformed Church of England" to rights, Gregg immediately burst out in a public display of self-righteous triumph. He unwisely proceeded to publish Cheney's letters to him in *The Reformed Church Record* and in an "Open Letter" demanded that Cheney grant him a public forum at the General Council in Boston to justify himself.[76] Gregg's bombastic ultimatum covered Cheney with embarrassment. In a letter written to Gregg on March 29, 1889 (and published two weeks later in the *Episcopal Recorder*), Cheney stiffly corrected Gregg's assumption that all was now forgiven. "My individual opinion is one thing, my loyalty as a member of the General Council to the decision of that body is another," Cheney informed Gregg. "None of us will consent to allow such a firebrand to be cast into the approaching meeting of our supreme Church legislature as would be involved in your personally presenting your appeal."[77]

And that was that. To the assembled General Council that May, Cheney candidly admitted: "I have never been able to see the question [of Bishop Gregg] with precisely the same eyes as the majority of my brethren." But, Cheney continued, "I have honestly endeavored to divest myself of all prepossession and prejudice, and however painful it might be, was obliged to decide that the conclusion arrived at by the General Council was final, admitting of no appeal, and that therefore Bishop Gregg could not be entitled to a seat in this body."[78] The English General Synod's ambassador, Philip X. Eldridge, understood clearly what this meant and tactfully refrained from expressing more than "a few words of fraternal acknowledgement and greeting." After that, all mention of Thomas Huband Gregg in the councils of the Reformed Episcopal Church came to an end.[79]

Cheney should have seen earlier what others around him had seen all too clearly, that Gregg had moved over the years from being merely erratic to being downright unstable. But Cheney was, in this case, too preoccupied by his controversies with Nicholson and Latane to realize that Gregg was far from being an unsullied witness to traditional Anglicanism. In the end, the fact that it was Gregg, and not Nicholson or Latane, who forced Cheney to withdraw his overtures was providential, for Gregg only went from bad to worse. In July 1891, Gregg finally went to pieces mentally. Charged by one of his churchwardens with seducing the warden's wife, Gregg responded by suing the warden for libel and unilaterally dismissing his vestry and wardens at Trinity Church.[80] On July 16, 1891, he preached his last sermon at Trinity Church, a babbling, incoherent stream of words in which he claimed that the Queen had "cuddled me in her arms" in Westminster Abbey.[81] Two weeks later, Gregg was in an insane asylum in Ticehurst, Sussex, where he died, "much quieter," on March 31, 1896.[82]

The removal of Gregg from the scene also removed the principal reason for the division between Gregg's "Reformed Church of England" and the General Synod parishes. When Alfred Richardson withdrew himself from the General Synod over a personal dispute, the way was clear for a reunion. In May 1894, on the motion of no one less than Gregg's own son, Francis T. Gregg, the "Reformed Church of England" rejoined the General Synod, with Philip X. Eldridge as the Presiding Bishop of both groups. There was, once more, a single Reformed Episcopal Church in England. That, in turn, raised again the question of the General Synod's relationship to the Free Church of England, which had been almost forgotten by Reformed Episcopalians in England during the turmoil over Richardson and Gregg. In 1916, the General Synod made the first overture to the Free Church on the subject of union, and after a decade of haggling, negotiation, and joint convocations, the Free Church and the Reformed Episcopal General Synod voted to merge on June 15, 1927.[83] The new union retained the title "Free Church of England," with "otherwise known as the Reformed Episcopal Church" as its subtitle. Fifty-four years had passed since George David Cummins's first correspondence with the Free Church, and only now was his original plan to carry his new work into the Church of England finally coming to fruition.

The Special Jurisdictions

It is ironic that it was easier for the Reformed Episcopalians to transplant themselves to India and other points foreign than to the mother country of Anglicanism. Foreign missionary work had been one of the fondest objects of Evangelical Anglican energies in the nineteenth century, and American Protestantism lavished huge sums of money and the lives of some of its most exemplary youth in foreign mission work. Missionary work, in fact, became something of a barometer of the sincerity of a denomination's evangelical principles. For Reformed Episcopalians, who felt more keenly than others the need to demonstrate their evangelical *bona fides* despite the implications of their episcopal name, the urge to push forward foreign missions volunteers was immediate. In 1877, lacking a missions agency of its own, the Fifth General Council voted to endorse the work of the Womens' Union Missionary Society (chiefly because of the leadership of a Reformed Episcopal laywoman, Harriet Brittan, in the WUMS), and in 1881, the Eighth General Council organized a Reformed Episcopal Board of Missions.[84]

Unfortunately, the new Board of Missions had no independent source of funding. Emma Eberle, of St. Paul's, Philadelphia, volunteered for missionary service in India in 1886 but had to seek the sponsorship of the WUMS, and when G. Milton Gardner presented himself in 1889 for missionary work in China, the Board of Missions had no alternative but to recommend him to a Congregational mission agency for employment. The first full-fledged Reformed Episcopal mission had to wait until late in 1889 and the widowhood of Elizabeth Mercy Bacon. Charles A. Bacon had been one of the charter members of Christ Church, Peoria, and when he died suddenly in 1887, his widow Elizabeth "was led to deep heart-searching and prayer to learn what God would have her do to fulfill his purpose and to mitigate her anguish." She chose the Evangelical *beau geste* and sailed for Calcutta at the end of 1889. Unlike her forlorn predecessors in Reformed Episcopal missions, Elizabeth Bacon possessed her own means and could afford to finance her undertaking as a purely Reformed Episcopal work. She bought seventy-nine acres in the central Indian town of Lalitpur (including a building once used as a Hindu temple) and converted the properties on her land into a school for girls.[85] In 1897, when a famine swept through central India, Bacon was unexpectedly left with 135 orphans under her wing, and her school perforce turned into an orphanage. This influx of orphans not only changed the nature of her work but also nearly swamped her ability to manage the property, and in desperation she appealed to the General Council to send her an assistant.

Unfortunately, there was not much the General Council could do, and the Board of Missions was on the brink of recommending that she transfer her orphan work to another denomination's missionary agency. However, on October 11, 1898, as the Board of Missions met to debate how to surrender the Lalitpur mission to bigger hands, the board secretary was presented with a letter from one of the seminary students, David T. Van Horn, who offered to leave at once for India. "When the letter was read, a strange emotion filled every member of the Board present," and William Rufus Nicholson melodramatically rose to declare: "This is of the Holy Ghost. I came to vote for the disbanding of the work. I had letters to read on the transference of it to other hands. God certainly means that we shall not do what we purposed doing."[86] Funds were quickly pledged to support not only Van Horn (who left for India five months later) but also two other assistants, Elizabeth Graydon of Toronto and Martha Bartley of Philadelphia, who joined Bacon and Van Horn in 1899.

Even with Van Horn's nearly miraculous sense of timing, the story of the Lalitpur mission was not an easy one. Bacon herself, her own personal funds exhausted, died in 1900 in a cholera epidemic that killed more than one hundred of the orphanage's children.[87] Van Horn fell victim to smallpox in April 1914, and his memorial service at St. Paul's, Philadelphia, "caused much searching of heart, and led to the conclusion that we at home had no very worthy share in this self-sacrificing work."[88] Yet, the Lalitpur mission survived both Bacon and Van Horn and went on to prosper under Van Horn's ebullient and energetic successor, Howard Guiler Hastings. Where Bacon and Van Horn shrouded their work in a drapery of moral self-sacrifice, Hastings (who had been recruited from the ranks of the Presbyterian Church) bounced into mission work with the glee of the happy warrior. In a letter to Bishop Rudolph in 1915, Hastings gave some idea of what he was making of the mission with a combination of the talents of a camp superintendent and the tactics of a salesman:

> Wednesday of this week I visited a town of 25 miles south on another road, fortunately a good road, and went on my motorcycle, with another man, one of the mission workers sitting on the parcel carrier behind my seat. We went to visit the landlord of the village to arrange for the placing of a mission worker as teacher and preacher in his village. . . . I find my cornet a big help in these country villages, and use it quite a bit. I am at present teaching one of my workers here at Lalitpur to play a tenor horn which I brot out from America with me. He has some music in his system (tho he sometimes has difficulty in getting it out) for he has a little hand

harmonium on which he can play native tunes and some simple hymns, so I think he will make out all right on the horn. I might add that these villagers are not close musical critics, and I suppose that my cornet playing would sound the same as that of Bohumir Kryl or Herbert Clarke.[89]

Rudolph had an easier time dealing with Hastings than with the other major Reformed Episcopal mission work in India, the Harriet Benson Memorial Hospital in Lucknow. Spurred by the example of Elizabeth Bacon, but too elderly herself to emulate it, Harriet Benson decided to add a missionary hospital to her long list of Reformed Episcopal benefactions, and after her death in 1902 her will provided for the purchase of land and the erection of a hospital in Lucknow. Charles R. Cook, a Canadian graduate of the seminary's Class of 1893, had served briefly in parishes in Des Moines and Montreal and went out to Lalitpur to assist Van Horn as a medical missionary in 1900. In 1903, he accepted charge of the new hospital being built in Lucknow, where he served under conditions even more hair-raising than those in the orphanage in Lalitpur. In 1912, 1913, and 1914, Cook reported treating a total of 43,496 medical cases, with a little bit of preaching thrown in on the side:

As usual during the year we have had all classes among the patients attending the hospital and forming the congregations for preaching services. . . . And all these thousands have had the gospel impressed upon their attention in accord with the Lord's command: "Preach the Gospel to every creature." In the wards, where we only take the serious cases that can remain, there are added opportunities for personal work. That we have had some success to cheer us is proved by the fact that during the period under review there were 76 baptisms. . . . This past year we have been particularly grateful for the realization of our long-deferred hopes regarding a mission home. . . . As the land about here is rather low, the floor level of each house is controlled by the level of the roadway. This necessitates a high plinth which I welcome on account of the numerous snakes that are about. . . . As we killed more than 80 of them during the building of the house I am afraid we won't be free of them in the seasons when they make their appearance.[90]

Cook worked on in Lucknow with only one furlough (in 1909–10) until his retirement in 1929. He then astounded Bishop Rudolph by selling the entire hospital property, pocketing the proceeds, and returning to America to live out his remaining years in comfort. Shocked by what he considered the basest form of theft from the General Council, Rudolph had Cook arrested the moment he stepped off the boat in New York.[91] But as it turned out, the canny Miss Benson, unwilling to trust the General Council after the surplice debacle, had authorized Cook to take title to the hospital in his own name. Moreover, his salary had been paid out of the Benson estate through the vestry of Christ Memorial Church, not by the General Council. William Tracy (Rudolph's bête noir) had also freely encouraged Cook to ignore Rudolph's protests and take what was legally if not entirely rightfully his.[92] Rudolph's suit against Cook collapsed ignominiously (although some of the Lucknow funds that had come from the General Council were later recovered), and at least one major Reformed Episcopal mission simply disappeared, leaving a substantial amount of egg on the episcopal face.

Bishop Rudolph, and the Reformed Episcopal Church as a whole, was more successful in maintaining the church's pioneering work among the African-Americans of South Carolina. When Peter F. Stevens retired from his episcopal work in Charleston in 1909, he had built up the "Special Missionary Jurisdiction of the South" into 39 churches and 2,734 communicants, with more than 1,100 children in 80 Sunday Schools.[93] The General Council deputized as Stevens's successor a youthful Canadian who had only just graduated from the Philadelphia seminary that May—Arthur Lorne Pengelly. The selection of Pengelly, who had no prior pastoral or administrative experience and who was not even a United States citizen in 1909, was never fully explained and actually admits of only one explanation: no one in the General Council was willing to put a black South Carolinian in charge and thus put a black man on an equal footing with the white leadership of the North, and no one else in the North could be persuaded to take responsibility for the blacks.

Despite the relatively enlightened position on racial equality adopted in the 1870s by Bishop Cummins and the first generation of Reformed Episcopalians (the seminary admitted its first African-American student in 1903, a generation ahead of many other northern institutions), the black Reformed Episcopalians in Charleston were the poorest jurisdiction in the church and were treated by their northern and midwestern brethren with a distinct air of white condescension. From the beginning, no one, either black or white, seems to have been interested in seeing the South Carolina churches expand to become a fully multiracial synod. Both the freedpeople in the new Reformed Episcopal parishes, and the northern whites who had helped them, were content to see the South Carolina churches remain an all-black affair, almost as though white converts were either not entirely welcome or as though northern whites paled at the thought of sponsoring an "amalgamationist" church.

So, rather than seeing the Southern Reformed Episcopalians as full partners in the Reformed Episcopal movement, white Reformed Episcopalians in Chicago and Philadelphia interpreted the South Carolina churches and missions as a carefully controlled experiment in racial paternalism. The wife of one Chicago clergyman explained the backwardness of the "Special Jurisdiction" in terms of racial inferiority, not in terms of the institutionalized racism of white Southerners, "because they are of that race which is only beginning to show the effects of its late birthright to freedom and education."[94] Charles Edward Cheney congratulated himself on "my love for the Negro Race . . . and because of the advanced position taken by our church at its very beginning," but he still referred patronizingly to the black Reformed Episcopalians as "our dusky brethren."[95] In 1919, Robert Livingston Rudolph was approached by a black West Indian Anglican priest, George Alexander McGuire, who had offered to organize a series of missions for blacks and West Indians in New York under the aegis of the Reformed Episcopal Church. Rudolph briefly received McGuire and his Church of the Good Shepherd into the New York and Philadelphia Synod. But McGuire was dreaming dreams of black independence and self-determination that were a generation ahead of their time, and he soon found Rudolph indifferent to his black nationalist aspirations. In January 1921, McGuire withdrew from the Reformed Episcopal Church to organize what became the African Orthodox Church, and the New York and Philadelphia Synod remained a thoroughly white enterprise.[96] Even Peter F. Stevens, for all his undoubted devotion to the welfare of the Carolina African-Americans, never once seems to have challenged the civil status quo of "Jim Crow" legislation, and even suggested in 1894 that it would be a good idea if some of his "Afric-Americans" could be repatriated to Africa to "culminate in a colony of Reformed Episcopalians emigrating to Liberia."[97] White Reformed Episcopalians were quick to take pride in their racial progressiveness, but few wanted to do more than enjoy it from afar, or take it so seriously as to grant the "Special Jurisdiction" its own self-elected black bishop. In the absence of an experienced white bishop willing to work with the blacks as Stevens had, there was no alternative to sending the untried Pengelly.

At first, Pengelly was such an unknown quantity that the General Council would only agree to give him the title of "superintendent." Episcopal duties, such as ordination and confirmation, were volunteered by Robert Livingston Rudolph. The older black clergy of the "Special Jurisdiction" were not always disposed to cooperate with the twenty-nine-year-old Canadian. As Pengelly reported to Rudolph after one of the "Special Jurisdiction" convocations:

> Our Convocation has come and gone. . . . Everything went along pretty fair till the Standing Committee met to go over my list of appointments. I had made some drastic changes as I had promised earlier in the year to do, [Rev. D. J.] Mack and [Rev. Stephen] Bash, Trinity and Israel [Churches], being most affected. These two and R. D. Simmons being on the committee made it a little embarrassing and things would have gone smoothly but for Simmons making an objection to Bash, which he had no business doing in such a meeting, because he was injecting personal dislike and we were dealing with a general situation, that had to be looked at in a broader light. The appointments were read and all went smoothly till I got a letter from Bash. I considered it insulting and insinuating and wrote him to that effect and demanded an apology. I have put up with his intimidating kind of nonsense as long as I could. It would be ruinous to my position to put up with any more.[98]

Pengelly eventually outgrew his awkwardness and inexperience, and in 1914 Rudolph successfully proposed him for election and consecration as a missionary bishop. He gave promise of becoming yet another Stevens—he constantly promoted the needs of the "Special Jurisdiction" to northern donors, arranged for reliable salaries to be paid to African-American pastors, built membership to more than 3,000, and secured land titles and building repairs. But that promise was cut short by a fatally neglected appendicitis in 1922.

To replace him, the General Council could think of nothing better than to repeat the experiment with Pengelly. Another Canadian, Joseph E. Kearney, a graduate of the Ontario Bible College and fresh out of seminary in May 1923, was sent south as superintendent almost at once. Kearney was eventually elected and consecrated missionary bishop for the South in 1930, and he served the second-longest episcopate in the Reformed Episcopal Church—twenty-eight years—until his retirement in 1958. But Kearney's longevity was no cure for the same steady erosion in numbers that afflicted the rest of the Reformed Episcopal Church. Southern membership, which at Kearney's consecration stood at 3,335, slowly ebbed out, until by 1970 communicant membership in the "Special Jurisdiction" remained almost solidly black and stood at only 2,177. Even then, no one suggested that it was time that black Reformed Episcopalians be given their own synodical organization on a par with Chicago or Philadelphia. To the contrary, in 1960, yet another white superintendent from the North, William Henry Stuart Jerdan, was sent to Charleston to govern the black churches. In Jerdan, however, the black Reformed Episcopalians finally found their second Stevens. A relentless promoter and organizer, Jerdan identified himself deeply with the black Reformed Episcopalians' patient wait for ecclesiastical autonomy. After his consecration as a missionary bishop in 1962, it was Jerdan who campaigned to have the "Special Jurisdiction" raised to the synodical level in 1973, with its own constitution and canons, sponsored the election of a black assistant bishop, Sanco K. Rembert, in 1966, and stepped down as synodical bishop in 1987 to allow Rembert to become the first black bishop at the head of the South Carolina parishes. It had taken the better part of a century for it to happen, and until then black membership in the Reformed Episcopal Church had remained at a virtual standstill.

In one sense, that judgment could easily have been rendered over the entire Reformed Episcopal Church by the end of Robert Livingston Rudolph's life in 1930. The establishment of the seminary, the long afternoon of Rudolph's episcopate, the healing of the Gregg schism, and the missions work in India and the South—all were welcome signs that the Reformed Episcopal Church really had the strength to put its own house in order, and they underwrote the survival of the Reformed Episcopal Church after the traumas of the 1890s. But at the same time, these developments managed to provide little more than mere survival. The membership of the church never grew materially after the embarrassment of the 1897 General Council, and the seminary, after Rudolph's death, gradually turned inward on itself and, instead of producing fresh growth, only trained its students to build the walls of the Reformed Episcopal ghetto still higher. Although the Reformed Episcopalians had survived, they were unable, as Cummins had wanted and expected, to "go forward and do a grand work."

EPILOGUE

Few Episcopalians and few American evangelicals today are seriously troubled with much knowledge of the Reformed Episcopal Church. But the circumstances and personalities that went into the founding in 1873—including the secession of a full-fledged Episcopal bishop who was assumed to have a significant future before him—were easily the most sensational that had ever overcome the Episcopal Church. Throughout the last quarter of the nineteenth century, Cummins and his new-modeled church threatened to destabilize the Episcopal Church, fragment its membership, and reorganize the Anglican presence in America on rigorously Evangelical lines. They were headline news for months (and in an age when headlines meant something), and for the next twenty-five years were an ongoing source of study, comment, and carpet-chewing rage, from the House of Bishops to the pages of the *Mercersburg Review*. Nothing, until the affair of Bishop Pike in the 1960s and the controversies over liturgy and the ordination of women in the 1970s, so nearly rocked the Episcopal Church to its foundations.

The subsequent disappearance of the Reformed Episcopalians from active Episcopal interest was due partly to the self-destructive ironies of the Reformed Episcopalians themselves, and partly to the instinctive Anglican desire to efface all records of past unpleasantness. But beyond even those considerations, the forgetting of the Reformed Episcopalians involved a larger strategy in the life of the Episcopal Church than merely the wish to marginalize one unhappy group of dissidents.

Anglo-Catholicism won a much more complete victory in American Episcopalianism than in the Church of England, and that accomplishment allowed it to write a good deal of later Episcopal history pretty much as the history of its own successes. To do so required erasing the objectionable blot of the Reformed Episcopalians, for starters, but once begun it also became necessary to mute the substantial voice Evangelicals had once uttered in the Episcopal Church in the early nineteenth century, and which rose to a climax in the organization of the Reformed Episcopal Church. A survey of the standard Episcopal Church histories of the last hundred years—Tiffany, Manross, Addison, and Perry—reveals either a dismissal of the Evangelicals as an unavoidable fluke of nineteenth-century life, or merely a harmless phase in the life of the Episcopal Church that yielded gracefully and without murmur to a synthetic hegemony. Only Chorley's *Men and Movements in the American Episcopal Church* (1950) and Raymond Albright's *History of the Protestant Episcopal Church* (1964), which leans heavily on Chorley, give the Evangelicals their due and acknowledge that the Catholic hegemony was won only after intense and bitter conflict.

Recovering the lost history of the "Old Evangelicals" of the Episcopal Church forces us to see the founding of the Reformed Episcopal Church as one of the most dramatic examples of the steady disintegration of Anglican identity in the nineteenth century, not merely as a sectarian event. And even beyond the unaccustomed excitement of seeing Episcopalians at each other's throats, the case of the Reformed Episcopalians is directly related to the larger question of Anglican identity in the larger Christian world. On one side, the organizers of the Reformed Episcopal movement were of course related to other Anglicans, such as Bishop Ryle, who believed that Anglicanism was becoming entirely too much of a "mingle-mangle" by tolerating those who clearly burst the bounds of sixteenth-century Protestant doctrine. But the Reformed Episcopalians were also related to those, like Stephen Neill, who were willing to play loosely with Anglican identity in terms of liturgy and ministry in order to promote a primitive version of ecumenicity.

One of the chief grievances of the Reformed Episcopalians at the time of the formation of the Reformed Episcopal Church was precisely that the Anglicanism of their day was becoming entirely too restrictive by breaking off contact and communion with other non-Anglican churches. By the same token, what they, as Evangelicals, objected to in Anglican comprehensiveness was that in their day Anglicanism seemed bent on accommodating the wrong people, and on drawing artificial doctrinal distinctions that excluded the correct ones. The Reformed Episcopalians, in effect, simultaneously declared that they had an identity when they were really all the while groping for a different one.

This failure of identity was far from being simply an unhappy accident. It was, on the contrary, the result of two conscious and deliberate sacrifices that, at the time, seemed to be the proper conclusions for Evangelicals to grasp but that in fact were deadly symptoms of the pathology of group identity. The most obvious of these decisions was the early decision by the Reformed Episcopalians to drop all claim of an "apostolic succession" in the episcopate of Cummins and his successors, in favor of justifying their new-model episcopacy on grounds that were more pragmatic but at the same time more acceptable to non-Episcopalian evangelicals whom they confidently expected would gather admiringly around their banner. The odd blind spot of this decision was the otherwise obvious fact that no other American Protestant evangelicals had ever really wanted a church order built on anything less than divine fiat, and that an episcopal structure that had been carefully vetted to avoid confrontation was not going to pull into it those undecided Evangelical brethren who still dallied on the old church's shore. To the degree that the Reformed Episcopalians calmly depreciated the episcopate, undecided Evangelicals who still hesitated to leave the Episcopal Church feared to take them seriously. In the meantime, the Reformed Episcopalians themselves, with nothing but their own anti-Anglo-Catholic rhetoric ringing in their ears, lost any sense of why they retained an episcopate at all. Gradually, any sense of continuity with their own Episcopal past or their Evangelical kin still within the old church slipped away.

The second, and unwittingly fatal, decision made by the Reformed Episcopalians was to dramatically decentralize authority within their new church, so as to better avoid the heavy-handed dictatorships they felt had been laid on by them by High Church bishops in their old dioceses. What they did not anticipate was that such decentralization only ensured that the new church would disintegrate into loose-floating islands that the further removed in time from their break with the Episcopal Church, the more removed they would become from each other, as each island developed its own ways of meeting its own needs. In the Reformed Episcopal experience, this disintegration fell out along geographical lines, with diocesan synods in Chicago, Charleston, Montreal, and the New York–Philadelphia corridor increasingly representing differing, and then warring, ways of constructing a reformed Anglicanism. None of these four houses triumphed completely over the others, and so the life of the Reformed Episcopal Church became permanently tainted with suspicion and disaffection over points that to the uninstructed eye could only have seemed morbidly picayune. The loss of continuity occasioned by the first decision might not have been so painful had not this second decision made it almost inevitable that whatever new identity might arise out of the ruins of separation from the Episcopal Church would be diffused and dissipated among its competing and often mutually mistrustful synods.

This identity was to be not only fatally diffused but also badly dislocated. Especially within the New York–Philadelphia Synod, Reformed Episcopalians accepted the evangelical rather than the episcopal aspect of their inheritance as the key element of a Reformed Episcopalian, and that led them to adopt more and more "standard" Victorian evangelical poses and appearances, and fewer and fewer Episcopal ones. But these poses and appearances—such as premillennialism, dispensationalism, and revivalism—which eventually came to displace the old republican Whiggism of the founders and sway the mind of the New York–Philadelphia Synod, could not be mixed easily with the structured sacramental piety of the Book of Common Prayer (which, with a few editorial revisions, remained the liturgical usage of the Reformed Episcopalians). Nor would the American fundamentalism of the 1920s and 1930s (which grew up out of the old Victorian evangelicalism) ever completely trust the Reformed Episcopalians, no matter what their explanations, so long as they kept prayer books in their hands and bishops in their offices.

Thus began a Sisyphus-like struggle by Reformed Episcopalians to appease evangelical expectations by any means short of abandoning the Book of Common Prayer or their bishops. What they eventually learned, however, was that no appeasement would ever suc-

ceed in the American fundamentalist environment *except* the abandonment of prayer book and bishops. This inevitably produced a
sense of futility and exhaustion that runs as a countertheme through
every Reformed Episcopal Council journal from the 1880s on. And
when this appeasement came into confrontation with traditionalist-
minded Reformed Episcopalians in Chicago and Canada, who
thought of themselves as Episcopalians first and Evangelicals second, the resulting conflicts served only to further destabilize the
shaky security of the new movement and deflect its attention onto
trivialities that seemed safer to argue about.

It is easy, in retrospect, to diagnose mistakes. And it is so easy in
this case that it is difficult not to describe such errors simply as cata-
strophic failures of common sense. But before any leap to easy judgment is made, it is worth remembering that Anglicanism itself at
this time was increasingly plagued by the same diffusion and dislocation of identity and has struggled for almost as long as its Reformed Episcopal offspring with the dilemmas of a ruptured sense
of the past and a crumbling arrangement of order. The mistakes the
Reformed Episcopalians made were made by all too many others,
and for not entirely dissimilar reasons. Without wishing to overload
the word "irony," it may be that the ultimate irony of the Reformed
Episcopalians is that, in their effort of 1873 to escape from the contradictions of Anglicanism, they only transposed them to an Evangelical key.[1]

Much of this unorganized and unplanned-for groping took place
because by 1930 two of the most critical components of the Reformed Episcopal identity—the expectation that the Reformed Episcopal Church would become a magnet for Evangelical Anglicanism
in America, and the parallel expectation that the Reformed Episcopal Church would also become an agent for Protestant ecumenism—gradually disappeared from the agendas of the Reformed
Episcopal Church. Instead, the Reformed Episcopal generation that
came to maturity after 1930 (the first that had no significant personal
contact with Cummins or his associates) identified itself with the
host of fundamentalist sects and Reformed splinter groups that
sprang into being in the 1930s as a response to the ascendancy of
liberal theology in the "mainline" American churches.

The most serious of these disappearances was the gradual attenua-
tion of the Reformed Episcopal Church's sense of itself as an Anglican movement. During the first decade of Reformed Episcopal existence, the still-smoldering resentments of the Evangelical-Tractarian
debates and the personal connections many Reformed Episcopalians
had with the Episcopal Church kept alive a sense of engagement

with Episcopal concerns. "The most powerful among the instruments arrayed upon the side of Christ to-day is, in my opinion, the Anglican Communion," Joseph Dawson Wilson told the Seventh General Council in 1879, adding to that admiring declaration his conviction that "God has brought the Reformed Episcopal Church into being for the purpose of revivifying the Anglican Communion."[2]

By the time Wilson died in 1924, it was harder and harder to hear voices like that. Instead, the Reformed Episcopalians quickly turned their controversial energies on each other and proceeded to fight among themselves over vestments, liturgy, and the nature of the episcopate. For Latane, Nicholson, Leacock, Cheney, and all their followers, the old enemy of Anglo-Catholicism faded out of sight and was replaced by a new enemy, which in this case was each other. The Reformed Episcopalians thus spun themselves into a dense cocoon of recriminations and suspicions, arguing over issues that had meaning only for themselves and only glancing occasionally over their shoulders at the larger Episcopal Church they had left.

Ironically, the creation of this cocoon must be blamed in part on the success of the theological seminary in Philadelphia. As long as the Reformed Episcopal Church relied on defectors from the Episcopal Church to replenish its supply of clergy and laity, it maintained simply through their presence a living interest in overall Episcopal affairs. But after the 1880s, when the seminary took over as the chief source of Reformed Episcopal leadership, the church's contacts with the wider Anglican world began to dry up. A leadership formed exclusively within the Reformed Episcopal Church and within the Philadelphia orbit would inevitably be shaped only by the interests and problems existing inside the New York and Philadelphia Synod, and to the extent that the seminary was able to meet the needs for clergy training, it taught the new generation of Reformed Episcopal clergy to think of themselves only as inhabitants of the cocoon, and not as Episcopalians. By institutionalizing education, the Reformed Episcopalians actually narrowed rather than broadened their horizons.

But another part of the blame must go to the Episcopal Church itself. For one thing, after the 1890s there were fewer and fewer Evangelical Episcopalians left in the Episcopal Church with whom the Reformed Episcopalians could establish any ties. One Sunday in the summer of 1880, Marshall Smith paid a visit to Stephen Tyng Sr.'s old parish of St. George's, New York, and what he saw there shocked him:

On Sunday afternoon I went to St. George's (Dr. Tyng's old Church). There were present in this immense and costly edifice only *33* persons, including Minister, Choir & Sexton! The young Deacon who officiated knelt with his back to the people at the center of the Chancel rail when he came in. He only read prayers, and there was no Sermon. Must it be said of St. George's "Ichabod"?[3]

Although Cummins was often criticized by the Evangelical leadership in the Episcopal Church for having bolted too precipitously, the truth was that he had waited entirely too long. By 1873, the Anglo-Catholic grip on church education and appointments had forced a substantial number of Evangelicals out of the Episcopal Church, and what Cummins took out with him were actually only a handful of the remnant who were left. Those who stayed within the Episcopal Church were either too old to leave (such as William Sparrow, who died in January 1874, or Henry Lee of Iowa, who died the following September, or John Johns of Virginia, who died in 1876) or too mistrustful of Cummins's leadership (like Heman Dyer, who prayed for the Reformed Episcopalians until his death in 1900, but who never joined them in prayer).[4] Either way, Evangelical Episcopalianism perished on the vine, either disappearing in its old vineyards entirely, or declining into the peculiar latter-day latitudinarianism known as "Low Churchmanship." Benjamin Leacock recalled:

> The Evangelical party had been a great power in the Church. When circumstances called it into existence, it had almost the entire field to itself. It was composed of some of the most distinguished of the Bishops and Clergy of the Church of that day. As a party it had established its Evangelical Knowledge Society, its Missionary Association for the West, and its Society for the Education of Young Men for the Ministry. It controlled not only powerful churches but whole Dioceses, electing bishops, and naming Rectors. In those days it was worthwhile being a prominent man and leader in such an organization, and yet . . . ritualism and sacerdotalism made steady advances and won away from the Evangelicals church after church, and Diocese after Diocese.[5]

Even Charles Edward Cheney helplessly admitted in 1888: "To day the old evangelical party is like the race of moundbuilders of our Western plains. It is hopelessly extinct."[6] Once the old Evangelicals were gone, there were no new ones to replace them, and no one in the Episcopal Church with whom the Reformed Episcopalians could develop any meaningful fellow-feeling.

But a much more serious reason for the slow death of the Episcopal ethos in the Reformed Episcopal Church was the sheer hostility of the Episcopalians. Once Cummins left the Episcopal Church in November 1873, there was no shortage of ecclesiastical invective directed at the Reformed Episcopalians by their former brethren. It is significant that Cummins's fellow bishops made no attempt at reconciliation; to the contrary, the bishops of the Episcopal Church scrambled to disown Cummins and his associates as rapidly as they could. The High Church bishop of Minnesota, Henry Benjamin Whipple, who had once tried to save Charles Edward Cheney from the wrath of his bishop, saw "no way to reconcile [Cummins's] act with the honor and fidelity of a Christian man to his plighted faith."[7] William Bacon Stevens, the bishop of Pennsylvania, and one who was far from being sympathetic to the Anglo-Catholics, told his diocesan convention in 1874 that "this unfaithfulness to [Cummins's] threefold vows of ordination, this needless rending of the Church of Christ, he has crowned by an act unparalleled in the annals of Christ's Church—the consecrating by his single self of a lawfully-deposed clergyman to the work and office of a bishop."[8] Joseph Kerfoot of Pittsburgh publicly characterized Joseph Dawson Wilson's resignation from Calvary Church, Pittsburgh, to join with Cummins as "the distressed act of a man frightened by a nightmare" and guilty of "great lack of memory, of history, of theology, of logic and of love."[9] Morgan Dix, who had been the cause of no little part of Cummins's agitation, dismissed the Reformed Episcopalians as scarcely worthy of Episcopal notice:

> It is not too much to say, that hundreds rise up early and late take rest, haunted by the fear that we are all going over to Rome, or that we shall be devoured alive by the "Reformed Episcopal Church." [But] . . . there are not a few of us . . . who regard the Cummins schism as one of the feeblest, most inconsequent, and most ridiculous of all ecclesiastical movements.[10]

In 1888, the bishops of the Episcopal Church advised the Lambeth Conference of that year that Cummins's consecration of Cheney was defective on the grounds of intention, thus invalidating all subsequent Reformed Episcopal orders, and when the General Convention of the Episcopal Church was prevailed on to review the question again in 1910, the only conclusion it came to was that it would be "inadvisable" to pursue the matter further.[11] In 1905, when Bishop William Montgomery Brown of Arkansas delivered a series of lectures, recommending the Episcopal Church (as Cummins had done) as "the church for Americans," he took the opportunity to swipe at "Dr." Cummins:

> Dr. Cummins held his Bishopric solely for use in the Catholic Church and not outside or against it. There was no pre-existing organic unity between him and his followers making them in any sense a Church or a constituent part thereof sharing with her inherent self-perpetuating power. They were simply an aggregation of persons who organized themselves into a body which hitherto had no corporate existence of any kind. . . . By joining the Reformed Episcopalians a person no more becomes a member of the Anglo-Catholic Communion than if he were to join the Methodist or Presbyterian body.[12]

That summed up the attitude the Episcopal Church and its leadership chose to take toward the Reformed Episcopalians for another thirty years.

In the teeth of such contempt, it is not entirely surprising to find Reformed Episcopalians turning their backs on the old church as "old Mother Damnable." Not until 1937 did the Episcopal House of Bishops authorize a Commission on Approaches to Unity to open up negotiations toward reunion with the Reformed Episcopal Church. By then, much of the animus that lay behind the contempt of Dix and Brown had faded, largely because the issues that had burned so brightly in the 1870s had ceased to be issues for the Episcopal Church. Thus, the leading edge of the negotiations (which lasted from 1937 until 1941) was taken by no one less than Frank Wilson, Bishop of Eau Clair and the most ultra Anglo-Catholic in the Episcopal Church. Wilson was prepared to be surprisingly generous to the Reformed Episcopalians. On February 16, 1938, Wilson met with an eight-person commission of Reformed Episcopalians, headed by then-Presiding Bishop Frank V. C. Cloak, and offered to create a uniate relationship between the two bodies. "Their bishops would be invited to sit in our House of Bishops and ours in theirs," Wilson reported in *The Living Church*. "Clergy could move freely back and forth accepting calls to parishes in either direction and communicants would be received without discrimination." As for the question of validity, Wilson was remarkably untroubled by any defects in Cummins's "intention" or in Cheney's 1873 consecration. "There appears to be little reason for questioning their orders."[13]

By this time, however, such offers of reconciliation from the Episcopal Church no longer had much meaning for the Reformed Episcopalians. Robert Knight Rudolph, who had inherited his father's position as professor of systematic theology at the Reformed Episcopal Seminary, rejected Wilson's proposition out of hand: "I could never agree to the required statement that our two Churches were [a] True Church of Jesus Christ according to the Scriptures—I had found much that was scripturally untrue brought to the surface as we learned the convictions of each other, . . . that I therefore [was] compelled to vote *no*."[14]

In the place of Evangelical Episcopalianism, much of the Reformed Episcopal Church embraced the fundamentalist identity promoted by Nicholson and Leacock in the 1880s and 1890s, and it began to see its real kinship lying with Presbyterian separatists like J. Gresham Machen, and fundamentalist Bible schools like Moody Bible Institute, which had two Reformed Episcopalians for presidents (James M. Gray and Bishop William Culbertson) for more than half of its institutional life. William Montgomery Brown's stinging assessment that "the Reformed Episcopalians are nothing more or less than Prayer Book Methodists" had come narrowly close to the truth.[15] And so the proposals for negotiation with the Episcopalians died on the table. Not for another fifty years would serious dialogue begin again between the Episcopal Church and the Reformed Episcopalians.

The loss of its Episcopal identity was only the first casualty among the expectations of the Reformed Episcopal Church's founders. The other great expectation—that the Reformed Episcopal Church would prove to be a catalyst for American Protestant church unity—did not long survive the question of Episcopal identity. Indeed, the wonder is that this expectation enjoyed as long a life as it did, since in many respects it was doomed by forces beyond any Reformed Episcopalian's control. Cummins's well-intentioned but nearsighted belief that only the Anglo-Catholics were keeping evangelical Protestants from stampeding into the Episcopal fold was staggered at the very beginning by the realization, once the Reformed Episcopal Church was organized and functioning, that the rest of evangelical Protestantism could not have cared less.

Even among the Protestants who sympathized with Cummins, there was a fatal reluctance to talk about unity in any other terms than mere friendly cooperation. Much as enlightened church leaders would wag their heads in mournful deprecation of division and disunity, denominational identities and boundaries proved far tougher than they liked to admit or than Cummins had imagined. Few of those leaders were willing to challenge their own lay followers' persistent love for the safety of ecclesiastical ghettoism, so they settled for talk about "fraternal union" rather than the much more risky prospect of organic union. The result was that, at one General Council after another, delegates from other denominations greeted the Reformed Episcopalians, uttered a few evangelical pleasantries, and then departed without any further display of interest in joining Cummins's crusade for unity.

In fact, the failure of church unity to advance beyond the platforms of the Evangelical Alliance was not simply a Reformed Episcopal problem. Philip Schaff, who had shared the Evangelical Alliance's platform with Cummins in that fatal convention in New York in 1873, went to the last Alliance Convention twenty years later still promoting federation rather than organic unity: "Federal or confederate union is a voluntary association of different churches in their official capacity, each retaining its freedom and independence in the management of its internal affairs but recognizing one another as sisters with equal rights and cooperating in general enterprises such as the spread of the gospel at home and abroad, the defense of the faith against infidelity, the elevation of the poor and neglected classes of society, works of philanthropy and charity and moral reform."[16]

It was, in fact, the example of the Alliance, rather than Muhlenberg's and Cummins's hope for the organic re-union of Protestants, that set the ecumenical example. The persistence of disunion and Protestant parochialism defied the best efforts of an entire generation, even though the four decades between 1890 and 1930 saw the greatest push toward American Protestant church unity that had ever been seen. In 1894, the Open and Institutional Church League was organized by New York Presbyterian Charles L. Thompson to provide a common network to coordinate the educational and social work of various big-city churches. In Maine, William D. Hyde of Bowdoin College sponsored the creation of the Interdenominational Commission of Maine, and in 1899 the Connecticut Bible Society became the basis of a statewide interchurch movement. From the cities and states, the ecumenical urge spread outward. In 1900, a national "Ecumenical Missionary Conference" convened in New York City with delegates from a variety of denominational mission boards, and an attendance roughly estimated at 150,000. One year later, a "National Federation of Churches and Christian Workers" was organized under the direction of Elias B. Sanford, a Connecticut Congregationalist who confidently predicted that "Protestantism in its historic development has passed beyond its divisive age and is now to fulfill and prove its power, as a divinely guided movement, in gathering its forces into closer unity of spirit in thought and action."

Even the Episcopalians, embarrassed by the Reformed Episcopal separation and unwilling to appear to be talking from two sides of their mouths about "catholicity," made their own gesture toward ecumenical unity at the General Convention in Chicago in 1886. The idealism that Muhlenberg had embodied in the Episcopal Church, and for which Cummins had suffered in 1873, found a new and persuasive voice in William Reed Huntington. A distant relative to Samuel Fallows (of all people), Huntington published a dramatic and open-handed proposal for organic church union in 1870 in his book *The Church Idea: An Essay Toward Unity*. Like Muhlenberg, Huntington frankly urged on his readers the necessity for organic rather than mere federal union among the churches, and like Muhlenberg again, he believed that the Protestant Episcopal Church could provide the platform for that unity if the Episcopal Church would be willing to set forth a brief statement of Christian "essentials" on which all other Christian bodies could agree.

Huntingdon's own proposal for those "essentials" bore some rather unusual resemblances to Cummins's Declaration of Principles. Like the Declaration, Huntington reduced the "essentials" down to four succinct articles: the Scriptures as the word of God, the Nicene Creed as a sufficient statement of Christian belief, the use of two sacraments (Baptism and the Lord's Supper), and the "historic episcopate" (Huntington deliberately shied away from invoking any terminology suggesting apostolic succession) as the preferred form of church government. Rather like Cummins, Huntington hoped that by simplifying the Episcopal Church's statement of what it considered essential the mists of confusion over orders, validity, and sacramental theology would blow away on their own and leave Churchmen and Nonconformists, but even more, Episcopalians and Roman Catholics, able to embrace each other without reservation.

And indeed, there was little that even the most hardened Anglo-Catholics in the Episcopal Church could really say *against* Huntington's plan. Therefore, in a bid to wipe out the uneasiness caused by Cummins's secession and to surpass in generosity the calls of other American Protestants for church union, the Episcopal General Convention of 1886 decided to go them all one better and adopt Huntington's "quadrilateral" as its offer of organic union. It framed Huntington's proposal in these words:

. . . as essential to the restoration of unity among the divided branches of Christendom, we account the following, to wit:

1. The Holy Scriptures of the Old and New Testaments as the revealed Word of God.

2. The Nicene Creed as the sufficient statement of the Christian Faith.

3. The two Sacraments—Baptism and the Supper of the Lord—ministered with unfailing use of Christ's Words of Institution, and of the elements ordained by Him.

4. The Historic Episcopate, locally adapted in the methods of its administration to the varying needs of the nations and peoples called of God into the Unity of His Church.[17]

And not stopping there, the Lambeth Conference of 1888, meeting at the behest of the Archbishop of Canterbury, adopted the General Convention's proposals as a general statement of the entire Anglican Communion's desire for unity.

Whatever Huntington might have meant by "the historic episcopate," it soon became apparent that the only construction the bishops who now sat on the bench intended to allow on that phrase was "the apostolic episcopate," and that meant in practical terms that any ministry seeking unity under the umbrella of the Lambeth Quadrilateral would also have to seek reordination at episcopal hands. This no other Protestant church was ever willing to do in Huntington's lifetime. The Presbyterian Church's General Assembly conducted unity discussions based on the Quadrilateral from 1887 until 1896, but it eventually discovered that the Episcopal Church had no real intention of recognizing "the Presbyterian Church to be a Church of Christ and its ministry a divinely authorized ministry," and the negotiations died on the vine.

That meant the most successful proposals for unity among American churches would come not from Episcopalians but from the Congregationalist Elias Sanford, from a Presbyterian, William H. Roberts, and from William Hayes Ward, another Congregationalist, who together in 1902 projected the most ambitious church union meeting yet: the "Interchurch Conference on Federation."[18] This conference, which finally met in Carnegie Hall, New York City, in 1905, with delegates from twenty-nine different denominations (including the Reformed Episcopal Church) was an important advance on the road to ecumenical unity.

In a significant departure from the program of the Evangelical Alliance, which was really an association of *individuals* from different denominations, the conference invited the participation of official representatives of the different American Protestant denominations.[19] The conference hammered together a Plan of Federation for what was to be called a "Federal Council of the Churches of Christ in America" (FCC) and over the next three years, the plan was referred back to the conference's participating denominations for ratification. Finally, in December 1908, the inaugural sessions of the Federal Council of Churches were convened in Philadelphia, with representatives of thirty-three American denominations gathered together for the first time as a "federal union."

However, so long as the Federal Council of Churches was proposed only as a *federal* union, rather than an organic one, and so long as no one seemed willing to trifle with the identities and loyalties of the participating denominations themselves, the FCC's pursuit of unity was often more apparent than real. Although the Plan of Federation explicitly stated that the participating denominations were gathering themselves together under the headship of the "Divine Lord and Saviour Jesus Christ," the FCC's constitution acknowledged that the council had "no authority to draw up a common creed or form of government or of worship."[20] Charles L. Thompson, by then a veteran of ecumenical networking, rebuked delegates at the Philadelphia convention who called for the demolition of denominationalism. "The best place to learn Christian federation," said Thompson, was not in plans for organic unity but "on the battlefield of Christian service."[21] Presumably, denominational independence was not going to be seriously challenged; the best the Federal Council could promote was "co-operation."

Even then, not much cooperation seemed to be forthcoming. As the *Christian Century* observed in 1932, "it is difficult for any but the initiated to realize how tenuous a connection this body has with its constituent denominations, how little authority is committed to it and how jealously the denominations guard their own prerogatives against any encroachment or usurpation by the Council which is their creature."[22] And this institutional weakness quickly became apparent at every level of the Federal Council, including the unpleasant subject of money for the FCC's operations. The member denominations who congratulated themselves on having achieved "unity" through the creation of the Federal Council proved to be notoriously reluctant to contribute funds to sustain the FCC's meager annual budget of $14,000.[23]

Stinginess was not the only threat to the stability of the Federal Council of Churches. The writers of the FCC constitution knew all too well that they could draw the boundaries of the Federal Council only so far without offending vital denominational constituencies.

The tighter the boundaries, the more denominations would refuse to join the FCC, and the fewer member denominations, the more absurd the FCC would appear. Survival alone, then, dictated that the FCC's membership be kept as theologically open as possible. But the more open the membership was, the more likely it was that the Federal Council would take on an increasingly liberal theological cast—and that would cause conservative member denominations to stalk out of the FCC in protest.

The Federal Council of Churches struggled to maintain a generally evangelical tone in its early years, and even specifically excluded the Unitarians from membership. But precisely because it lacked the authority to address real theological issues, its attention was more and more deflected onto the theologically safer issues of social service and public moralism. Because those were the issues of paramount interest to theological liberals, however, the liberals eventually came to dominate the governance and agenda of the FCC. Predictably, when that happened, the conservative denominations dropped out. In 1912, the Southern Presbyterian Church lodged a formal complaint against the FCC's Social Service Commission for dabbling too much in what Southern Presbyterians considered to be purely political matters. Even though an investigation of the complaint found that the Social Service Commission "has both kept within its constitutional provisions and has given full and effective expression to the unity of evangelical Christianity," the Southern Presbyterians remained dissatisfied. In 1931, still unhappy, they left the FCC entirely. They were joined in their exodus by the Mennonites (disgruntled over the FCC's chest-beating support of World War I) and the Church of God, who walked out in 1933 to protest the FCC's attempt keep them from founding more churches of their own in geographical areas where other member denominations were already well planted.[24]

Nevertheless, even with its struggles over poor support, theological mistrust, and its incapacity to arrange for anything more than "co-operation," the Federal Council still represented the best hope for channeling the energies of Protestant sectarianism toward Protestant unity instead. In the eyes of Reformed Episcopalians, these activities, however limited, seemed to be the very things the Reformed Episcopal Church had been founded to promote. "It is our firm conviction that our Church carries in its doctrine, worship and polity the principles of a reunited Protestantism," William Freemantle editorialized on the pages of the *Episcopal Recorder* in 1918, "and when that goal is reached our Church will have finished its testimony and gladly and thankfully merge into the great body of a united Church."[25]

For that reason, the Reformed Episcopalians, small as they were in numbers, took a major leadership role in the early years of the FCC's formation. On November 27, 1908, shortly before the first inaugural sessions of the FCC were to convene, Bishop Sabine (then Presiding Bishop) appointed William Tracy, William Freemantle, Joseph Dawson Wilson, and Robert Livingston Rudolph as the Reformed Episcopal delegates to the FCC.[26] They all returned to report in glowing terms to the Nineteenth General Council in 1909, which in turn reappointed Rudolph and Tracy as delegates to the FCC.[27] Rudolph, surprisingly, became one of the strongest proponents of the Federal Council, serving alternate terms as a vice-president along with Joseph Dawson Wilson. In 1915, Rudolph welcomed Charles McFarland, General Secretary of the Federal Council, to the platform of the Twenty-First General Council, which formally expressed "our heartiest appreciation of his address" and extended "through him, to the constituent bodies of the Federal Council, our fraternal greetings."[28] In 1918, Rudolph again put the FCC on a Reformed Episcopal platform by inviting Albert G. Lawson, chairman of the FCC's Administrative Council, to address the Twenty-Second General Council in Philadelphia. And once Lawson was done, Rudolph called for "a hearty vote of thanks to the Federal Council of Churches of Christ in America for sending us their representative." Rudolph's motion sailed through the General Council without a single dissenting vote.[29]

The apparent success the Reformed Episcopalians enjoyed in their association with the FCC actually fostered an unaccustomed atmosphere of smugness among Reformed Episcopalians. "Here we may humbly claim to be the *Pioneers* of Christian Union," Bishop Frank Vaughan of the English Synod informed the theological seminary's Class of 1924 at commencement ceremonies.[30] In 1913, when the Anglo-Catholic missionary bishop of Zanzibar, Frank Weston (ironically, the successor in the same diocese of the Bishop Tozer who had precipitated Cummins's crisis of conscience in 1873), wrecked a proposal for Anglicans and other British Protestants to create a missionary federation in East Africa, the *Episcopal Recorder* was led to contrast this with the enviable record the Reformed Episcopalians were establishing on church federation. "Will it end by some Church of England people seeing what Bishop Cummins and his sympathizers saw?" the *Recorder* coyly inquired, and continued:

> The Anglican Church is in an exceedingly anomalous position. It either has to take up the position of our own Church concerning orders and intercommunion, or stiffen its medi-

evalism and become as cast iron as the Roman Church. . . . Whichever course it takes, it will have to show its hand in the matter of reunion, which it professes is so dear to its heart. If it moves towards Protestantism, it will move still further away from Rome. . . . If it moves away from Protestantism, it will not be one whit nearer reunion with Rome, for the Papal hierarchy smiles indulgently when the Anglican Church claims any apostolic authority and order.[31]

Moreover, not content with the federative union espoused by the FCC, the Reformed Episcopalians now began upping the ante of church union with a dramatic call for "the union of the several Evangelical branches of the Church of Christ." In 1912, Robert Westly Peach (who would succeed Robert Livingston Rudolph as Presiding Bishop in 1930) urged the FCC to endorse a plan of his that would see the Reformed Episcopal Church "appoint a Commission on Church Union . . . to confer officially or unofficially with commissions, committees, or individuals of other denominations."[32] Peach argued:

> Our denominational attachments and rivalries have caused us to build, perhaps, over 100,000 superfluous churches, at a cost of far over $500,000,000. Their upkeep and the salaries incident to maintaining services make necessary the raising annually of millions of wasted dollars; make necessary, moreover, gruelling efforts to raise money. Inevitably, there has arisen The Great Protestant Order of Mendicant Pastors and Sisters, unincorporated. . . . In our division, our people are groaning under the burdens caused thereby, and under the reproach of incompetency, not only they, but the unchurched masses ignore our weakened testimony and reject our appeal; our problems are multiplied, our fellowship is marred, our Lord is dishonored. Those are the conditions organic unity is set to cure.[33]

In the heady atmosphere created by the FCC, this was a difficult argument to resist, and the commission that was ultimately appointed and also chaired by Peach laid the groundwork for Peach to call a "Preliminary Conference" in Philadelphia in 1918 that would draw up proposals for "a Constitutional Convention on Organic Union of the Churches."[34]

But were the Reformed Episcopalians really serious? Or was the talk about organic union merely a rhetorical amusement to reassure the Reformed Episcopal Church that it still had a purpose to serve as a church? The fact is that when Peach was actually able to bring his "Preliminary Conference" together in Witherspoon Hall in Philadelphia in February 1920 to write a constitution, the shape of his proposed "organic union" looked little different from just another federation scheme. Peach stated:

> In the interest of the freedom of each and of the co-operation of all, each constituent Church reserves the right to retain its creedal statements, its form of government in the conduct of its own affairs, and its particular mode of worship. In taking this step, we look forward with confident hope to that complete unity toward which we believe the Spirit of God is leading us. Once we shall have co-operated whole-heartedly . . . we are persuaded that our differences will be minimized and our union become more vital and effectual.[35]

In fact, the "union" became neither vital nor effectual. Although representatives from seventeen different denominations participated in drawing up the constitution for the "American Council on Organic Union of Evangelical Churches," Peach could not get anyone to actually endorse the plan as an operative reality.[36]

Part of the reason Peach's organic unity plan fell through so badly was that the closer the possibility of an organic union scheme came, the more Reformed Episcopalians realized that they did not particularly like the idea after all. "Is Church Union desirable?" asked Joseph Dawson Wilson in 1918, and continued:

> That depends on the kind of Church Union we seek. If all denominations should unite in one organization, the results would be striking. Massive church buildings would be reared and ably manned with a sufficient corps of workers. The neglected places would not be neglected, and the poor would have the Gospel preached to them. Questions of procedure and differences of administration could be determined by a congress. The visible results would be impressive. But doubt arises whether this would be according to the Lord's will. . . . Let us be on our guard. We long for a union of Christian forces. It grieves us to see the Church frittering away its energies in the competition of divided sects, and the word "union" has a magic fascination; but union may be purchased at too great a price. The surrender of vital elements of the faith is too much to pay.[37]

The next year, the even more venerable Malcolm T. McCormick (who had been received from the Episcopal Church in 1875 by Cheney) voiced the same complaint, only more pungently. "Let our unity, then, be with *individuals* and not with churches," McCormick urged. And in a single sweeping repudiation of the entire scheme of unions, he added: "When I know Methodists, Presbyterians, Baptists, etc., who are truly born of God, I love to be with them and work with them as *individuals*; but would hesitate to work with them as churches."[38] Not surprisingly, James M. Gray, the fundamentalist president of Moody Bible Institute, raised the same objection: "Let us do all that we can legitimately do to reform the city and the State and to promote international morality and world peace," he conceded, "but when it comes to the formation of a World Church union to promote such things, important as they are, let us be aware that we are found fighting against God, betraying the Lord for thirty pieces of silver and selling our birthright for a mess of pottage."[39]

Gray's concern about "selling our birthright" is a curious one, considering that by the time he wrote those words in 1919 the Reformed Episcopalians were not sure what their birthright was. However much they professed their interest in church union, it was clear that whenever the moment came for actual commitment, even on the most favorable terms,ʲ the Reformed Episcopalians would balk and retreat. No more dramatic example of this ecclesiastical acceptance/avoidance complex exists than the debacle of Robert L. Rudolph's advocacy of the Church of Jesus in Puerto Rico.

In 1911, D. M. Stearns approached Rudolph with an unusual opportunity that his limitless missionary interests had brought him into contact with—a former Roman Catholic priest named Manuel Ferrando. In addition to superintending a mission in New York City for prosletyzing Spanish-speaking Roman Catholics and editing a magazine named *The Converted Catholic* for "the instruction of Protestants regarding Romanism and for the enlightenment and conversion of Roman Catholics to the Evangelical Faith," Ferrando was the unofficial leader of a string of Protestant mission stations in his native Puerto Rico. Ferrando had protested his admiration for the Reformed Episcopal prayer book and polity to Stearns, and Stearns in turn suggested to Rudolph that he visit Ferrando's Puerto Rican missions to consider absorbing them as a Reformed Episcopal missionary jurisdiction. Accordingly, Rudolph visited Puerto Rico with Ferrando and was utterly won over by "the simplicity of the faith and life of the people."[40] Rudolph returned from Puerto Rico determined to take the Church of Jesus under the Reformed Episco-

pal wing and to have Ferrando elected and consecrated a Reformed
Episcopal missionary bishop for the job.

However, confronted with church union on its own doorstep, the
Reformed Episcopalians promptly slammed the door in Ferrando's
(and Rudolph's) face. "I am strongly convinced that it would be an
error to take up the Porto Rican Mission as a Jurisdiction of the Ref.
Epis. Church, and to consecrate Dr. Ferrando as a Missionary
Bishop of our communion," Charles Edward Cheney warned Ru-
dolph. Cheney suggested as an alternative simply consecrating Fer-
rando as a bishop for his own people and leaving it at that.[41]
Rudolph, unfazed, proceeded to receive Ferrando as a Reformed
Episcopal presbyter (ironically, on the strength of his ordination as a
Roman Catholic priest) and introduced him socially throughout the
New York and Philadelphia Synod.[42]

But when Rudolph appealed to the synod to elect Ferrando a missionary bishop in October 1912, the delegates unhesitatingly rejected
the appeal.[43] Rudolph was forced to settle for Cheney's plan: Ferrando was consecrated in November 1912 after a special session of
the General Council, but solely as a bishop for the Church of Jesus
in Puerto Rico. The Church of Jesus itself was left to its own devices, a reaction that understandably puzzled and offended them.
"Allow us to say, dear brethren, that we never intended to add a
new denomination to the already too many existing divisions in the
Church of Christ," Ferrando told the General Council in 1915:

> We have been brought up in our Christian life to love you
> and regard you as our parent Church. We have even been
> proud to call ourselves a branch of the Reformed Episcopal
> Church, . . . but now your act has made a degree of separa-
> tion between us, which we regret. We never intended to be a
> burden upon you, any more than we have been in the past,
> and as we try to live according to the Word of God and in
> conformity with your Declaration of Principles and Liturgy,
> we cannot understand why we should nominally be a sepa-
> rate body.[44]

He could not have known it, but Ferrando was really signing the
death warrant on Cummins's dream of "the union of all Evangelical
Christendom."

The hesitancy of the Reformed Episcopalians to commit themselves to the ecumenical relations that were supposed to be their
raison d'être was matched (and in some measure caused) by the unwillingness of other denominations to make more than token com-

mitments themselves to the Reformed Episcopalians—or in some cases, to take advantage of Reformed Episcopal naiveté. Cheney was incensed in 1912 when a new Reformed Episcopal mission in Detroit located an ideal site for a building, only to have a neighboring Presbyterian mission rush in and buy up an option on the property. Then, Cheney went on, "in a way that seemed to me only comparable to the taking of the one little 'ewe-lamb' in Nathan's parable," the presbytery of Detroit proposed that the members of the Reformed Episcopal mission join in organizing a new Presbyterian church on that very ground. It took another seven years, but finally the Detroit Reformed Episcopalians caved in and voted to "unite with the Presbyterian Church."[45] As Presiding Bishop, Cheney was forced to preside over a similar situation with another Reformed Episcopal mission in South Ozone Park, in New York City. Christ Reformed Episcopal Church had been organized in South Ozone Park in 1902, and by 1916 it was able to begin construction on its own building. But before the construction was "half completed," an Evangelical Lutheran mission, armed with substantial Lutheran funding, was built next door and "attracted to itself more than half the membership of Christ Church and Sunday School." The South Ozone Park mission, like the Detroit mission, ended up by surrendering themselves to the Presbyterian Church, in 1921. One of the hazards of ecumenicity George David Cummins had not recognized in 1873 was that other denominations might look on ecumenical relations with the Reformed Episcopalians simply as an opportunity for their own self-aggrandizement.

Nothing for the Reformed Episcopalians undercut the mythical memory of the Evangelical Alliance more than the indifference and occasional greed of "our fellow Christians of other branches of Christ's Church" in these incidents. But the blame for the death of ecumenicity among the Reformed Episcopalians cannot be transferred entirely to others. Nothing stood in starker contrast to Cummins's immediate response in 1875 to the call of the Charleston freedmen than the repulse of the Church of Jesus in 1912. And so, over the course of its first generation, the Reformed Episcopal Church shifted on its axis, moving away from its Anglican foundations and ecumenical commitment and leaving only the shell of Cummins's words behind as evidence that the church had once occupied a very different position.

None of this was helped by the fact that the Federal Council of Churches, and other church union schemes like the InterChurch World Movement, were increasingly associated in Reformed Episcopal eyes with doctrinal liberalism. By 1930, even Robert Westly

Peach had to acknowledge "the dominance of advanced liberals in some union movements of late," and in 1934 Peach actually accused the FCC of succumbing to the "idiom of liberalism." In 1936, the year of Peach's death, the General Council toyed with a resolution calling for withdrawal from the FCC, and although the resolution was tabled it resurfaced at the next General Councils in 1939 and 1942. Finally, in 1945, with Robert Knight Rudolph leading the way, the Reformed Episcopal Church formally withdrew from the Federal Council of Churches.[46] The great age of ecumenical endeavor in the Reformed Episcopal Church was over, and with it the most important reasons for the existence of the Reformed Episcopal Church.

And yet—the very history of the Reformed Episcopal Church would be impossible to write except for the irony that phrase disguises. The virtual destruction of the most cherished ideals of the founders of the Reformed Episcopal Church by the generation which followed them ought, by all ecclesiastical logic, have ended up by ringing down the curtain on the Reformed Episcopal movement, certainly by the 1960s if not earlier. And if we were to judge solely in terms of numbers, it came close to that. The slide in communicant membership that began after Robert Livingston Rudolph's peak year in 1915 continued unabated thereafter. Even though Bishop Howard David Higgins could announce at his retirement in 1972 that, as bishop of the New York and Philadelphia Synod, he had founded "almost one-third of our present churches" during his episcopate, he glided over the fact that he had also closed just as many and that the totals for communicant membership in the synod were less in 1972 than they had been in 1926, when Higgins began his ministry as an assistant at First Church, New York.

And yet, the Reformed Episcopal Church still lived, still operated its theological seminary (where in the 1970s enrollment was reaching all-time highs), and still supported its synods in Chicago and Charleston and its mission at Lalitpur. It is surprisingly easy to discover that, beneath the riot of change that swept over the Reformed Episcopal Church between 1897 and 1930 and that threatened to sweep away entirely its Episcopal identity, there remained ironic evidences of persistence showing that despite the blunders and failures not everything had really been lost after all. Take the botched agenda for ecumenical unity—the urge for church union disappeared, for all intents and purposes, from the public posture of the Reformed Episcopal Church after the 1920s. *And yet*, the practice of comprehensiveness on the parish level with other evangelical churches continued to be one of the distinguishing motifs of the

Reformed Episcopal experience. Or take the matter of the episcopate. Nothing seemed more self-contradictory in the 1870s than the Reformed Episcopal decision to define the episcopate not as an apostolic order that represented and embodied the *esse* of the church, but in the functional terms reminiscent of William White's original 1782 call for the organization of the Episcopal Church: as a presidency chosen from among the presbyters of the church who is to function as a symbol of unity for the *bene esse* of the church. *And yet*, in 1969 Graham Leonard, Eric Mascall, Colin Buchanan, and J. I. Packer recommended, as the blueprint for the "integration of ministries" into a new United Church of England (in *Growing into Union*), almost the very same plan for recognition of nonepiscopal ministries (and even the larger notion of episcopal authority) that the Reformed Episcopalians have been trying to operate with for over a century. And in their obsessive determination to banish the term "priest" from their prayer book and replace it with the more cumbersome "presbyter," the Reformed Episcopalians unwittingly showed themselves somewhat ahead of the times rather than behind them, as is indicated not only by the post-1920s usage of the Church of South India but also even the Lima document, "Baptism, Eucharist, and Ministry," and, once again, *Growing into Union*.

The Reformed Episcopalians turned out to be neither quite so conservative as might have been expected (as in the pursuance of ad hoc ecumenicity) nor quite so radical as their Episcopal critics painted them. Consider the *practice* of episcopal government (as opposed to the *theory*) among the Reformed Episcopalians. In whatever ways they tried to minimize the prelatical aspects of the episcopate, the Reformed Episcopal ordinal still consecrated Reformed Episcopal bishops almost word-for-word by the pattern of 1662, right down to the "Veni Creator Spiritus." Confirmation remained an episcopal prerogative, and a careful consecration list from Cummins onward was kept in all General Council journals (a labor that would be needless if the Reformed Episcopalians had really meant what they said about bishops being nothing but first-among-equal presbyters). For all the departures from, and depredations on, classical Anglicanism, there remained an inarticulate but altogether genuinely Episcopalian instinct among the Reformed Episcopalians, and even with all the caveats and protestations firmly in place, there still remains a thoroughly recognizable notion of Anglican episcopacy in the Reformed Episcopal Church. Despite the Reformed Episcopal Church's dalliance with separatist fundamentalism in the 1930s and 1940s, it somehow contained within itself an ecclesiastical gyrocompass that kept the church on an eccentric but still Anglican course. Nor can the Reformed Episcopalians be blamed too severely for conducting such a dalliance. Evangelicals in the Church of England, over the same period, lapsed into the same fundamentalistic ghetto, saw their numbers dwindle in the same proportions, and suffered in the same measure from the lack of vigorous leadership.

Today, of course, a good deal of that has changed. The great Anglican Evangelical conferences at Keele in 1967 and at Nottingham in 1977 were evidence not only of a renascence of Evangelical vigor in the Church of England, but also of a renewed Evangelical commitment to Anglicanism and the Church of England. The most recent studies of Anglican Evangelicals reveal that nearly half the ordinands of the Church of England at the time of the 1988 Lambeth Conference identified themselves as Evangelicals, and the newest Archbishop of Canterbury is one himself. Even in the United States, a surprising upsprouting of Evangelical clergy and parishes has appeared in the Episcopal Church since the 1960s, modeled variously on Keele and Nottingham and even on the Catholic charismatic movement.

What is interesting in this regard is to note how some Reformed Episcopalians, without any apparent prompting, have undergone some of the same changes, and followed virtually the same arc of reconciliation with their Anglican identity, as their Evangelical counterparts in the Church of England and the Episcopal Church. For just as the 1970s saw the pendulum of enthusiasm swing in the Evangelical favor in England and in the Episcopal Church, so in the 1980s something of the same resurgence of Anglican interest and life occurred in the Reformed Episcopal Church. Reformed Episcopalians began showing up at meetings of Anglican traditionalists in Fairfield, Connecticut, in 1985 and 1986; in 1988, the General Convention of the Episcopal Church sanctioned the opening of discussions; and in 1989, the Episcopal Synod of America (a joint venture of Episcopalian Evangelicals and traditionalist Anglo-Catholics) welcomed a Reformed Episcopalian onto their platform. Even the rochet and chimere for Reformed Episcopal bishops, and the surplice and scarf for the other clergy, have resurfaced within the New York and Philadelphia Synod.

Of course, this tentative reaffirmation of the Reformed Episcopalians' Anglicanism assumes that one knows what this "Anglicanism" is that is being reaffirmed. Unfortunately, the diffusion and dispersion of identity which has been Anglicanism's greatest weakness renders this reaffirmation problematic, and for the Anglican Evangelicals fully as much as the Reformed Episcopalians. The Reformed Episcopalians may well have come back to Anglicanism only to discover that no one is quite sure what Anglicanism is. That could possibly mean that there is no longer any viable reason for Episcopalians to see the Reformed Episcopalians as being outside of official Anglicanism, but it could just as well mean that the Reformed Episcopalians have lost so much of their original *raison d'être* that *they* no longer see any reason to remain outside official Anglicanism, or it could mean that there really is no Anglicanism left to come back to.

What may lie more stubbornly in the path of this reaffirmation is the problem of the slowly diminishing size of the Reformed Episcopal Church—or perhaps not the size, exactly, but the sociology of sectarianism that small-sized American denominations breed. A comparison of the recovery of an Anglican identity among the English Evangelicals with a rediscovery of Anglicanism by Reformed Episcopalianism may well not be apt, because the Anglican Evangelicals are much more numerically stronger and already exist within the official Anglican establishment.

By contrast, the modern Reformed Episcopalians now number less than half of their greatest total membership in 1921 (no more than 6,000 communicants, according to the figures published in 1990). More serious is the critical shortage of lay or clergy leadership within the Reformed Episcopal Church who have had sufficient direct exposure to Anglicanism to guide this "rediscovery." With the closing of the Reformed Episcopal seminary's historic buildings in Philadelphia in 1993, the pool of that leadership will only get smaller. Within an atmosphere as numerically close and confined as the Reformed Episcopal Church, even a reaffirmation of "Anglicanism" may easily turn into a mere party platform, or a tool for personal politics, rather than a recovery of principle.

One of the more unpleasant truths about American Protestantism and its endless divisions and subdivisions is that ecclesiastical tininess leads to insularity, and insularity is perhaps the one certain object Anglicanism opposes. It may be that after more than one hundred years in self-imposed isolation from Anglicanism there is simply insufficient room in the Reformed Episcopal Church for the reflection and tolerance required for a genuine reaffirmation of so sprawling a creature as "Anglicanism." In the sociology of sectarianism, insularity tempts small churches like the Reformed Episcopal Church to reward antiintellectualism and eccentricity and punish genuine breadth of theological opinion. The result is that "Anglicanism" (or any other "ism") can easily become defined in the shallow terms of controversy (vestments, terms of address, and the like) rather than in serious self-examination and self-criticism. Instead of self-examination, the oversize powers and influence of individuals or individual leaders in small denominations can promote cronyism, conformity, and an influx of religious opportunists who hope to maximize their desires for status through the desperation of a small church to recruit members. In such an atmosphere, movements as small-scale as the Reformed Episcopalians are likely to turn themselves into self-authenticating and self-accrediting agencies that are impervious to criticism and incapable of embracing a larger religious discourse (like Anglicanism or ecumenicity) on any other scale except self-interest.

The past history of the Reformed Episcopal Church does not give quick encouragement that these shoals can be easily avoided in the current "Anglican turn." The Reformed Episcopalians have, from time to time, already grounded heavily onto all these sociological reefs, only to float off again in somewhat worse shape than before. They have uncritically accepted the Thomas Greggs, deliberately turning a blind eye to their real intentions of self-promotion, and clung to them long past the moment when it was clear that the Greggs had been a big mistake. And they have groped wildly for a series of "isms"—Calvinism, dispensationalism, fundamentalism, and, more recently, Christian Reconstructionism—less with a concern for how well these "isms" matched the reasons for their founding than with an urge to hitch the Reformed Episcopal wagon to any vehicle that looked like movement. The recent turn to "Anglicanism" may yet turn out to be just another "ism," imposed from the top as part of a political agenda (like Nicholson's *Articles of Religion*) or advertised as yet another restorative against the church's slow extinction.

And yet, the Reformed Episcopal Church has always stood significantly apart from the dozens of equally small Protestant sects on the American religious horizon, and it would be a rash observer who would offer predictions about a denomination with traditions so rich, with a resilience so remarkable, or with a history so ironic. And anyway, the story of the Reformed Episcopal future is a different story from this one, and will have to be the substance of a different book.

Notes

INTRODUCTION

1. Kit and Frederica Konolige, *The Power of Their Glory: America's Ruling Class, the Episcopalians* (New York: Wyden Books, 1978), pp. 32–33.

2. Robert Bruce Mullin, *Episcopal Vision/American Reality: High Church Theology and Social Thought in Evangelical America* (New Haven, Conn.: Yale University Press, 1986), p. x.

3. Paul Avis, *Anglicanism and the Christian Church: Theological Resources in Historical Perspective* (Edinburgh: T. & T. Clark, 1989), p. 163.

4. W. J. Hankey, "Canon Law," in *The Study of Anglicanism*, ed. Stephen Sykes and John Booty (London: SPCK, 1988), p. 208.

5. Avis, *Anglicanism and the Christian Church*, pp. 167–172.

6. Stephen Neill, *Anglicanism* (1958; New York: Oxford University Press, 4th ed., 1977), p. 387.

7. John Whale, "Comprehensive Church: Anglican Readiness to Receive All Believers," *Church Times*, April 15, 1988, p. 11.

8. David Ousley, "Unity and Authority," *Churchman* 104 (1990): 147–152.

9. Stephen Sykes, *The Integrity of Anglicanism* (London: A. R. Mowbrays, 1978), p. 19. Sykes recently wondered aloud in an editorial leader in the March 23, 1990, *Church Times* whether the theological disarray of the Church of England had become so far advanced that "the removal of the establishment would not precipitate the ending of the Anglican experiment altogether." In the same article, however, Sykes also defended "Christianly reasoned dissent" and allowed that everything, "beginning with the very word 'God' itself, is open to question and has been questioned and discussed by theologians with the Church from the very beginning." But even an upright Anglican liberal like Alec Vidler would vigorously reject the notion that the Church of England ought to behave "as a sort of league of religions." He says: "I have nothing to say for such an unprincipled syncretism" (*Essays in Liberality* [London: SCM Press, 1957], p. 166). For a view on theological comprehensiveness from a more disgruntled angle, see Eric Mascall, "Whither Anglican Theology?" in *When Will Ye Be Wise: The State of the Church of England*, ed. C. A. Anthony Kilmister (London: Blond & Briggs, 1983), pp. 30–49.

10. G. V. Bennett, "The *Crockford's* Preface," in *To the Church of England: Essays and Papers*, ed. Geoffrey Rowell (Worth, W. Sussex: Churchman, 1988), p. 224.

11. Neill, *Anglicanism*, p. 387.

12. Victor Conzemius, "The Concept of Schism," in *Sacramentum Mundi: A Encyclopedia of Theology*, ed. Karl Rahner (New York: Herder & Herder, 1970), vol. 6, pp. 6–8.

13. Kreiger, "Sykes on Liberalism and Liberalism on Sykes," in *The Future of Anglican Theology*, ed. M. Darrol Bryant, Toronto Studies in Theology 17 (New York: Edwin Mellen Press, 1984), p. 99.

14. I am indebted for a number of these insights to Michael O'Brien, whose article "On the Mind of the Old South and Its Accessibility" pointed out the difficulties historians have experienced in the recovery of Southern intellectual history and had peculiar parallels to the difficulties historians have in opening up Episcopal history as well. See *Intellectual History Newsletter* 4 (Spring 1982): 3–12.

15. Martin Marty, *Modern American Religion: The Irony of It All, 1893–1919* (Chicago: University of Chicago Press, 1986), pp. 317–319.

CHAPTER 1

1. Benjamin B. Leacock, *Personal Recollections Connected with the Reformed Episcopal Church*, ed. R. K. Rudolph (Philadelphia: Reformed Episcopal Publication Society, 1964), p. 5.

2. Edwin Scott Gaustad, *Historical Atlas of Religion in America* (New York: Harper & Row, 1962), pp. 43, 52–53, 66–70, 74–81.

3. Sidney Ahlstrom, *A Religious History of the American People* (New Haven, Conn.: Yale University Press, 1972), pp. 415–471; Jon Butler, *Awash in a Sea of Faith: Christianizing the American People* (Cambridge, Mass.: Harvard University Press, 1990), pp. 268–282; Martin Marty, *Pilgrims in Their Own Land: 500 Years of Religion in America* (Boston: Little, Brown, 1984), pp. 169–187.

4. Calvin Colton, *The Genius and Mission of the Protestant Episcopal Church in the United States* (New York: Stanford & Swords, 1853), pp. 301–302.

5. Steven H. Tyng, *Memoir of the Rev. Gregory T. Bedell, D.D.* (New York: Protestant Episcopal Society for the Promotion of Evangelical Knowledge, 1859), p. 324. May was, perhaps not incidentally, something of an illustration of Bethune's message, because May had been converted during a Presbyterian revival at Jefferson College and seriously considered entering the Presbyterian ministry before at last deciding to enter the Evangelical Episcopal seminary at Alexandria, Virginia, in 1825. See Alexander Shiras, *Life and Letters of Rev. James May, D.D.* (Philadelphia: Protestant Episcopal Book Society, n.d.), pp. 12–21.

6. William Holland Wilmer, *The Episcopal Manual, Being Intended as a Summary Explanation of the Doctrine, Discipline, and Worship of the Protestant Episcopal Church* (Baltimore, Md.: E. J. Coale, 1829), p. 187. On Wilmer's Evangelicalism, see David L. Holmes, "William Holland Wilmer: A Newly Discovered Memoir," *Maryland Historical Magazine* 81 (Summer 1986): 160–164.

7. Kit and Frederica Konolige, *The Power of Their Glory: America's Ruling Class, the Episcopalians* (New York: Wyden Books, 1978), p. 33.

8. The first Church of England services in North America were probably read as early as 1578 or 1579 by the exploratory expeditions of Frobisher and Drake. See William Stevens Perry, *The History of the American Episcopal Church, 1587–1883* (Boston: James R. Osgood, 1885), vol. 1, pp. 1–15; Charles C. Tiffany, *A History of the Protestant Episcopal Church in the United States of America* (New York: Christian Literature Co., 1895), pp. 3–4; William W. Manross, *A History of the American Episcopal Church* (New York: Morehouse-Gorham Co., 1950), pp. 2–3; Raymond W. Albright, *A History of the Protestant Episcopal Church* (New York: Macmillan, 1964), pp. 12–13.

9. James Thayer Addison, *The Episcopal Church in the United States, 1789–1931* (New York: Charles Scribner's Sons, 1951), pp. 28–31; "Instruccions, Orders and Constitucions . . . to Sr. Thomas Gates, Knight, Governor of Virginia," in *The Three Charters of the Virginia Company of London*, ed. S. M. Bemiss (Williamsburg, Va.: Virginia 350th Anniversary Celebration Corporation, 1957), p. 57. See also Perry Miller's quixotic but surprisingly informative "Religion and Society in the Early Literature of Virginia," in *Errand into the Wilderness* (Cambridge, Mass.: Harvard University Press, 1956), pp. 99–140.

10. Eben Edwards Beardsley, *The History of the Episcopal Church in Connecticut*, 2 vols. (New York, 1865); Lucy Cushing Jarvis, *Sketches of Church Life in Colonial Connecticut* (New Haven, Conn.: Tuttle, Morehouse & Taylor, 1902).

11. Tiffany, *History of the Protestant Episcopal Church*, pp. 125–131.

12. William Stevens Perry, *The History of the American Episcopal Church* (Boston, 1885), vol. 1, p. 254.

13. Quoted in Joseph Ellis, *The New England Mind in Transition: Samuel Johnson of Connecticut, 1696–1772* (New Haven, Conn.: Yale University Press, 1973), pp. 89–90.

14. Perry, *History of the American Episcopal Church*, vol. 1, p. 299.

15. On Seabury, see Bruce Steiner, *Samuel Seabury, 1729–1796: A Study in the High Church Tradition* (Athens: Ohio State University Press, 1972); Eben Edwards Beardsley, *Life and Correspondence of the Right Reverend Samuel Seabury* (Boston, 1881).

16. Samuel Seabury, *A Discourse Delivered in St. John's Church* (Boston, 1721), p. 12.

17. Samuel Seabury, *A Discourse Delivered Before the Triennial Convention of the Protestant Episcopal Church* (New York, 1792), p. 9. See also John F. Woolverton, *Colonial Anglicanism in North America* (Detroit: Wayne State University Press, 1984), p. 33.

18. Woolverton, *Colonial Anglicanism*, p. 28.

19. William H. Seiler, "The Anglican Parish in Virginia," in *Seventeenth-Century America: Essays in Colonial History*, ed. James Morton Smith (Chapel Hill: University of North Carolina Press, 1959), pp. 119–142. See also William H. Seiler, "The Church of England as the Established Church in Seventeenth-Century Virginia," *Journal of Southern History* 15 (1949): 478–508; James K. Owen, "The Virginia Vestry: A Study in the Decline of a Ruling Class" (Ph.D. diss., Princeton University, 1947); Woolverton, *Colonial Anglicanism*, pp. 76–80.

20. David L. Holmes, "The Episcopal Church and the American Revolution," *Historical Magazine of the Protestant Episcopal Church* (hereafter *HMPEC*) 47 (1978): 261–291; William M. Hogue, "The Religious Conspiracy Theory of the American Revolution: Anglican Motive," *Church History* 45 (September 1976): 277–292.

21. Frederick V. Mills, *Bishops by Ballot: An Eighteenth Century Ecclesiastical Revolution* (New York: Oxford University Press, 1978), p. 158.

22. John F. Woolverton, "Philadelphia's William White: Episcopalian Distinctiveness and Accommodation in the Post-Revolutionary Period," *HMPEC* 43 (1974): 279–296. See also Woolverton, *Colonial Anglicanism*, pp. 214–219; William Stevens Perry, "Ancestry and Early Life," in *The Life and Letters of Bishop William White*, ed. Walter Herbert Stowe (New York: Morehouse Publishing Co., 1937), pp. 3–34; Julius H. Ward, *The Life and Times of Bishop White* (New York: Dodd, Mead & Co., 1892), pp. 11–24.

23. William White, *The Case of the Episcopal Church in the United States Considered* (Philadelphia: David C. Claypoole, 1782), pp. 72–73. See also Clara O. Loveland, *The Critical Years: The Reconstitution of the Anglican Church in the United States of America* (Greenwich, Conn.: Seabury Press, 1956), pp. 34–41.

24. See White, *Case of the Episcopal Church Considered*, p. 74; Walter Herbert Stowe, "The Presbyter," in *Life and Letters of Bishop William White*, ed. W. H. Stowe, pp. 63–76; Tiffany, *History of the Protestant Episcopal Church*, pp. 289–312, 327– 352; Albright, *History of the Protestant Episcopal Church*, pp. 125–133.

25. Quoted in Marion Hatchett, *The Making of the First American Book of Common Prayer* (New York: Seabury Press, 1982), p. 46.

26. "An Act of Association of the Clergy and Congregations of the Protestant Episcopal Church in the State of Pennsylvania" (May 24, 1785), in *Connecticut Churchmanship*, ed. Kenneth Walter Cameron (Hartford, Conn.: Transcendental Books, 1969), pp. 25–27.

27. Tiffany, *History of the Protestant Episcopal Church*, pp. 327–348.

28. Frederick V. Mills, "Mitre Without Sceptre: An Eighteenth-Century Ecclesiastical Revolution," *Church History* 39 (September 1970): 371; Loveland, *Critical Years*, p. 288.

29. White, "On Certain Questions Relative to the Eucharist," in *The Common Sense*

Theology of Bishop White: Selected Essays from the Writings of William White, ed. Sydney A. Temple (New York: King's Crown Press, 1946), pp. 139, 147.

30. William White, *Comparative Views of the Controversy between the Calvinists and Arminians* (Philadelphia: M. Thomas, 1817), vol. 2, p. 514.

31. William White, *Commentaries Suited to Occasions of Ordination* (New York: Stanford & Swords, 1848), pp. 60, 90, 207-208.

32. White, "The Source of Knowledge: An Address" (1823), in *Common Sense Theology of Bishop White*, ed. Temple, pp. 36, 56; White, *Comparative Views*, vol. 2, p. 147. See also Woolverton, "Philadelphia's William White," pp. 288-289.

33. Hatchett, *Making of the First American Book of Common Prayer*, p. 57; E. Clowes Chorley, *The New American Prayer Book: Its History and Contents* (New York: Macmillan, 1929), pp. 46-59.

34. E. Clowes Chorley, "The Election and Consecration [of Samuel Seabury]," in *The Anglican Episcopate in Connecticut*, ed. Kenneth Walter Cameron (Hartford, Conn.: Transcendental Books, 1970), pp. 17-39; Eben Edwards Beardsley, *The History of the Episcopal Church in Connecticut* (New York: Hurd & Houghton, 1865), vol. 1, pp. 347-350.

35. Loveland, *Critical Years*, pp. 57-58.

36. Seabury had actually been authorized to seek out the Scottish Episcopalians if all else failed by the Connecticut convention in 1784. See Tiffany, *History of the Protestant Episcopal Church*, p. 314, and the letter of Daniel Fogg to Samuel Parker, July 14, 1783, in *The Diocese of Connecticut: The Formative Period, 1784-1791*, ed. Joseph Hooper (New Haven: Diocese of Connecticut, 1913), p. 17.

37. Loveland, *Critical Years*, pp. 105-106.

38. See Tiffany, *History of the Protestant Episcopal Church*, pp. 322-324.

39. "The Communion-Office for the Use of the Church of Scotland," in *Anglican Climate in Connecticut*, ed. Kenneth Walter Cameron (Hartford, Conn.: Transcendental Books, 1974), pp. 52-63.

40. See Massey Hamilton Shepherd Jr., *The Oxford American Prayer Book Commentary* (New York: Oxford University Press, 1950), pp. 80-83; J. H. Srawley, "The Holy Communion Service," in *Liturgy and Worship: A Companion to the Prayer Books of the Anglican Communion*, ed. W. K. Lowther Clarke (London: SPCK, 1954), pp. 341-354; *Prayer Book Studies IV: The Eucharistic Liturgy* (New York: Church Pension Fund, 1953), pp. 78-92, 260-262.

41. Loveland, *Critical Years*, pp. 137-144; Hatchett, *Making of the First American Book of Common Prayer*, p. 5; Beardsley, *History of the Episcopal Church in Connecticut*, vol. 1, p. 370.

42. Loveland, *Critical Years*, p. 184.

43. Ibid., pp. 200-213; Tiffany, *History of the Protestant Episcopal Church*, pp. 363-365; Albright, *History of the Protestant Episcopal Church*, pp. 132-133.

44. Albright, *History of the Protestant Episcopal Church*, pp. 134-135; Beardsley, *History of the Episcopal Church in Connecticut*, vol. 1, pp. 393-394.

45. Hatchett, *Making of the First American Book of Common Prayer*, pp. 47-48, 60-62, 103, 130; Beardsley, *History of the Episcopal Church in Connecticut*, vol. 1, p. 403; Chorley, *The New American Prayer Book*, p. 55.

46. Loveland, *Critical Years*, pp. 263-268; Tiffany, *History of the Protestant Episcopal Church*, pp. 370-372; Albright, *History of the Protestant Episcopal Church*, pp. 136-138.

47. Tiffany, *History of the Protestant Episcopal Church*, pp. 379-384; Addison, *Episcopal Church in the United States*, pp. 70-72; Albright, *History of the Protestant Episcopal Church*, p. 140.

48. Loveland, *Critical Years*, pp. 284-286.

49. William Wilberforce, *A Practical View of the Prevailing Religious System of Professed Christians* (London, 1798), p. 83.

50. G. R. Balleine, *A History of the Evangelical Party in the Church of England* (London: Longmans, Green, 1908), pp. 156–158. See also Oliver Warner, *William Wilberforce and His Times* (London: Batsford, 1962).

51. Ian Barclay, *The Call to Seriousness: The Evangelical Impact on the Victorians* (New York: Macmillan, 1976), p. 72; Owen Chadwick, *The Victorian Church: Part One* (New York: Oxford University Press, 1966), pp. 440–445; Edward Carpenter, *Cantuar: The Archbishops in Their Office* (1971; reprint, Oxford: A. R. Mowbray, 1988), pp. 300–311.

52. Simeon, "Christ Crucified; or, Evangelical Religion Described," in *Expository Outlines on the Whole Bible* (1847; reprint, Grand Rapids, Mich.: Baker Book House, 1966), vol. 16, pp. 40–41.

53. Ryle, "Evangelical Religion," in *Knots Untied, being plain statements on disputed points in Religion from the standpoint of an Evangelical Churchman* (1877; reprint, Cambridge: James Clarke, 1977), pp. 3–6.

54. Ryle, "Evangelical Religion," p. 5; Wilberforce, *Practical View*, p. 98.

55. See Hugh Evan Hopkins, *Charles Simeon of Cambridge* (Sevenoaks, Kent: Hodder & Stoughton, 1977), p. 28.

56. Ian Barclay, *Call to Seriousness*, pp. 21–22; Hopkins, *Simeon*, p. 62.

57. Ryle, "Evangelical Religion," p. 8 (emphasis in the original).

58. Barclay, *Call to Seriousness*, pp. 66, 69.

59. E. Clowes Chorley, *Men and Movements in the American Episcopal Church* (New York: Charles Scribner's Sons, 1950), p. 32.

60. Albright, *History of the Protestant Episcopal Church*, pp. 149, 154–160.

61. "Joseph Pilmore, D.D.," in *Annals of the American Pulpit*, ed. William Butler Sprague (New York: Carter & Brothers, 1858), vol. 5, pp. 266–270. See also Chorley, *Men and Movements*, pp. 33–36.

62. Manross, *History of the American Episcopal Church*, p. 232; Albright, *History of the Protestant Episcopal Church*, p. 164.

63. Perry, *History of the American Episcopal Church*, vol. 2, pp. 183–184. See also Sprague, *Annals*, vol. 5, pp. 417–418.

64. Addison, *Episcopal Church in the United States*, p. 92.

65. J.P.K. Henshaw, *Memoir of the Life of the Rt. Rev. Richard Channing Moore, D.D.* (Philadelphia: William Stavely, 1842), pp. 30–31.

66. Addison, *Episcopal Church in the United States*, pp. 110–112; Sprague, *Annals*, vol. 5, pp. 368–369.

67. E. R. Goodwin, "Rt. Rev. Dr. William Meade," in *History of the Theological Seminary in Virginia and Its Historical Background*, ed. W.A.R. Goodwin (New York: Edwin S. Gorham, 1923), vol. 1, p. 97.

68. Randolph H. McKim, "Rt. Rev. Dr. John Johns," in ibid., vol. 2, p. 2.

69. Chorley, *Men and Movements*, pp. 46–47.

70. Addison, *Episcopal Church in the United States*, pp. 102–110; Sprague, *Annals*, vol. 5, pp. 453–462.

71. John Seely Stone, *A Memoir of the Life of James Milnor* (New York: American Tract Society, 1848). See also Sprague, *Annals*, vol. 5, pp. 562–571.

72. Norris Stanley Barratt, *Outline of the History of Old St. Paul's Church, Philadelphia, Pennsylvania* (Lancaster, Pa.: Colonial Society of Pennsylvania, 1917), pp. 137–138.

73. William Bacon Stevens, *The Past and the Present at St. Andrew's: Two Discourses preached in St. Andrew's Church, Philadelphia, on the 12th and 19th of September, 1858* (Philadelphia: C. Sherman & Son, 1858), pp. 13–15.

74. Tyng, *Memoir of the Rev. Gregory T. Bedell*, pp. 125, 214. See also Chorley, *Men and Movements*, p. 52; Sprague, *Annals*, vol. 5, pp. 554–560.

75. D. S. Allister, "Anglican Evangelicalism in the Nineteenth Century," in *The Evan-*

gelical *Succession in the Church of England*, ed. David N. Samuel (Cambridge: James Clarke, 1979), pp. 76–78. See also Robert W. Prichard, "Nineteenth-Century Episcopal Attitudes on Predestination and Election," *HMPEC* 51 (1982): 23–51.

76. Stevens, *The Past and the Present at St. Andrew's*, pp. 72–73.

77. Tiffany, *History of the Protestant Episcopal Church*, p. 467; Carl E. Grammar, "Rev. Dr. William Sparrow" and Robert A. Gibson, "The Theology of Sparrow," in *History of the Theological Seminary in Virginia*, ed. W.A.R. Goodwin, vol. 1, pp. 590, 613.

78. Sparrow, "The Wrath of Man the Praise of God," in *Sermons by the Rev. William Sparrow, D.D.* (New York: Thomas Whittaker, 1877), p. 243.

79. Manton Eastburn, *The Moderation of the Protestant Episcopal Church* (Boston, 1849), p. 7.

80. Ibid.

81. William Sparrow, *The Christian Ministry: An Address delivered at The Annual Commencement of the Theological Seminary of the Protestant Episcopal Church of the Diocese of Virginia, June 24, 1869* (New York: American Church Press, 1869), pp. 17, 26.

82. Charles Pettit McIlvaine, *The Chief Danger of the Church in These Times: A Charge delivered to the Clergy of the Diocese of Ohio at the Twenty-Sixth Annual Convention of the Same, in Rosse Chapel, Gambier, September 8th, 1843* (New York: Harper & Brothers, 1843), pp. 17–19.

83. John Johns, *Address delivered at the Seventy-Eighth Annual Council of the Protestant Episcopal Church in Virginia* (Richmond, Va., 1873), p. 8.

84. Sparrow, "Eating the Flesh of the Son of Man, and Drinking His Blood," in *Sermons*, p. 178.

85. James May, *The Advantages of Church Membership with reference to some errors, historically considered* (Philadelphia, 1847), p. 27.

86. Eastburn, *Moderation of the Protestant Episcopal Church*, pp. 23–24.

87. Henry Washington Lee, *Sanctification: The Primary Charge to the Clergy of the Protestant Episcopal Church in the Diocese of Iowa* (Davenport, Iowa: n.p., 1857), pp. 10, 16–17.

88. May, *Advantages of Church Membership*, pp. 28, 30.

89. Perry, *History of the American Episcopal Church*, vol. 2, p. 193.

90. Albright, *History of the Protestant Episcopal Church*, pp. 189–190.

91. Perry, *History of the American Episcopal Church*, vol. 2, pp. 198, 214, 223.

92. Gaustad, *Historical Atlas of Religion in America*, p. 68; Heman Dyer, *Records of an Active Life*, 2nd ed. (New York: Thomas Whitaker, 1886), p. 216; C. W. Andrews, *The Voice of Experience; or, Thoughts on the Best Method of Conducting Missions in the Protestant Episcopal Church* (New York: Stanford & Swords, 1852), p. 10; Addison, *Episcopal Church in the United States*, p. 132.

93. Goodwin, *History of the Theological Seminary in Virginia*, pp. 171–179.

94. Albright, *History of the Protestant Episcopal Church*, pp. 169, 189.

95. Sparrow to Rev. E. W. Syle, October 6, 1854, in Cornelius Walker, *The Life and Correspondence of William Sparrow, D.D.* (Philadelphia: James Hammond, 1876), p. 224.

96. Robert Bruce Mullin, *Episcopal Vision/American Reality: High Church Theology and Social Thought in Evangelical America* (New Haven: Yale University Press, 1986), offers the the most sophisticated interpretation of Hobart's thinking. Hobart's writings have been variously collected in *The Posthumous Works of the Late Right Reverend John Henry Hobart*, 3 vols. (New York, 1832–33), and *The Correspondence of John Henry Hobart*, ed. Arthur Lowndes, 6 vols. (New York: Protestant Episcopal Commission on Archives, 1911–12). See also John Frederick Schroeder, *Memorial of Bishop Hobart* (New York: T. Swords, 1831); Manross, *History of the American Episcopal Church*, pp. 219–228; Addison, *The Episcopal Church in the United States*, pp. 96–102; Perry, *History of the American Episcopal Church*, vol. 2, pp. 153–166.

97. John Henry Hobart, *The Churchman: The Principles of the Churchman stated and explained* (New York: T. Swords, 1819), p. 5. See Mullin, *Episcopal Vision/American Reality*, p. 30; Walter H. Conser Jr., *Church and Confession: Conservative Theologians in Germany, England, and America* (Macon, Ga.: Mercer University Press, 1984), pp. 297–299.

98. Hobart, *Apology for Apostolic Order and its advocates* (New York: T. & J. Swords, 1807), p. 33; Chorley, *Men and Movements*, p. 142.

99. Mullin, *Episcopal Vision/American Reality*, p. 116.

100. Daniel Walker Howe, *The Political Culture of the American Whigs* (Chicago: University of Chicago Press, 1979), chap. 7; Daniel Walker Howe, "The Evangelical Movement and Political Culture in the North During the Second Party System," *Journal of American History* 77 (March 1991): 1216–1239; Charles G. Sellers, *The Market Revolution: Jacksonian America, 1815–1846* (New York: Oxford University Press, 1991), pp. 157–161; George M. Thomas, *Revivalism and Cultural Change: Christianity, Nation-Building, and the Market in the Nineteenth-Century United States* (Chicago: University of Chicago Press, 1989), pp. 79–99. See the evidence on Evangelical and non-Evangelical voting patterns, especially among Episcopalians, in Ronald P. Formisano, *The Birth of Mass Political Parties, Michigan, 1827–1861* (Princeton: Princeton University Press, 1971), pp. 155–158.

101. On the prevailing styles of Anglican clergy dress and the controversies it generated in the nineteenth century, see Janet Mayo, *A History of Ecclesiastical Dress* (London: Batsford, 1984), pp. 102–107; Allen C. Guelzo, "A Test of Identity: The Vestments Controversy in the Reformed Episcopal Church," *Anglican and Episcopal History* 61 (September 1992): 303–304.

102. Robert V. Remini, *Henry Clay: Statesman for the Union* (New York: W. W. Norton, 1991), pp. 686, 781, 783.

103. Eric Foner, *Free Soil, Free Labor, Free Men: The Ideology of the Republican Party Before the Civil War* (New York: Oxford University Press, 1970), pp. 78–79; Salmon Chase, in *Inside Lincoln's Cabinet: The Civil War Diaries of Salmon P. Chase*, ed. David Donald (New York: Longmans, Green & Co., 1954), pp. 56, 60, 102.

104. I am grateful to Diana Butler for the reference to Anna Pierpont's letters to Charles McIlvaine and for her description of McIlvaine's visit to England (Diana Hochstedt Butler, "Standing Against the Whirlwind: The Evangelical Party in the Nineteenth Century Protestant Episcopal Church" [Ph.D. diss., Duke University, 1991], pp. 45–46, 267–270, 278–280, 302–310).

105. On Evangelical Episcopalians and the Liberia mission, see George David Cummins, *Life of Virginia Hale Hoffman* (Philadelphia: Lindsay & Blakiston, 1859), and J. R. Oldfield, "The Protestant Episcopal Church, Black Nationalists, and Expansion of the West African Mission Field, 1851–1871," *Church History* 57 (March 1988): 31–45.

106. Jefferson Davis to Varina Howell Davis, May 16, 1862, *Jefferson Davis, Constitutionalist: His Letters, Papers, and Speeches*, ed. Dunbar Rowland (Jackson: Mississippi Department of Archives and History, 1923), vol. 5, p. 246.

107. Howe, "The Evangelical Movement and Political Culture in the North," *Journal of American History* 77 (March 1991): 1222–1232; Sellers, *Market Revolution*, pp. 157–161.

108. Colton, *The Genius and Mission of the Protestant Episcopal Church*, pp. 172–173, 178.

109. John A. Clark, *A Walk About Zion* (New York: Robert Carter, 1869), p. 59.

110. Henry Codman Potter, *Reminiscences of Bishops and Archbishops* (New York: G. P. Putnam's Sons, 1906), p. 10.

111. Manross, *History of the American Episcopal Church*, pp. 215–219.

112. Stevens, quoted in *Alfred Lee, First Bishop of Delaware* (Philadelphia: James B. Rodgers, 1888), pp. 191–192.

113. Stevens, *The Past and the Present at St. Andrew's*, p. 75.

114. John Cotton Smith, *The Church's Law of Development; or, Different Schools of Opinion in the Church* (New York: T. Whittaker, 1872), n.p.

115. John A. King, "Rt. Rev. John Henry Hobart, D.D.," in *Annals*, ed. Sprague, vol. 5, p. 452.

116. John Henry Hobart, *The High Churchman Vindicated* (New York: T. & J. Swords, 1826), p. 6.

117. Chorley, *Men and Movements*, p. 170; John Henry Hobart, *A Companion for the Festivals and Fasts of the Protestant Episcopal Church* (New York: Standford & Delisser, 1858), pp. 294–295.

118. John Henry Hopkins, *The Novelties Which Disturb Our Peace: Letters Addressed to the Bishops, Clergy, and Laity of the Protestant Episcopal Church* (Philadelphia: John M. Campbell, 1844), pp. 7, 20, 54–55.

119. See Chorley, *Men and Movements*, p. 88; Albright, *History of the Protestant Episcopal Church*, pp. 187–188.

120. "The Early Use of the Surplice in Connecticut," in *Connecticut Churchmanship: Records and Historical Papers Concerning the Anglican Church in Connecticut in the Eighteenth and Early Nineteenth Centuries*, ed. Kenneth W. Cameron (Hartford, Conn.: Transcendental Books, 1969), p. 7.

CHAPTER 2

1. Owen Chadwick, *The Victorian Church: Part One* (Oxford: Oxford University Press, 1966), pp. 7–60; Alec R. Vidler, *The Church in an Age of Revolution: 1789 to the Present Day* (1961; reprint, New York: Viking Penguin, 1985), pp. 40–49.

2. John Keble, "National Apostasy," in *The Oxford Movement*, ed. Eugene R. Fairweather (New York: Oxford University Press, 1964), pp. 42–43.

3. Ian Ker, *John Henry Newman: A Biography* (Oxford: Clarendon Press, 1988), pp. 80–84; Chadwick, *Victorian Church*, pp. 70–72.

4. Newman, "Tract One: Thoughts on the Ministerial Commission," in *Tracts for the Times* (London: J. G. & F. Rivington, 1838), vol. 1, p. 2. See also *The Oxford Movement*, ed. Fairweather, p. 56; R. W. Church, *The Oxford Movement: Twelve Years, 1833–1845*, ed. Geoffrey Best (Chicago: University of Chicago Press, 1970), pp. 81–84.

5. Dieter Voll, *Catholic Evangelicalism: The Acceptance of Evangelical Traditions by the Oxford Movement During the Second Half of the Nineteenth Century* (London: Faith Press, 1963), pp. 29–31, 75, 92, 127–131; John Henry Newman, *Apologia Pro Vita Sua*, ed. D. J. DeLaura (New York: W. W. Norton, 1968), pp. 47–48; Ker, *Newman*, pp. 114, 160–161; Peter Toon, *Evangelical Theology, 1833–1856: A Response to Tractarianism* (Atlanta: John Knox Press, 1979), pp. 21–26; G. R. Balleine, *A History of the Evangelical Party in the Church of England* (London: Longmans, Green, 1908), pp. 215–216.

6. Pusey, "Scriptural Views of Holy Baptism," in Newman, *Tracts for the Times* (1838), vol. 2, part 2, p. 24; Robert I. Wilberforce, *The Doctrine of the Incarnation of Our Lord Jesus Christ in Its Relation to Mankind and to the Church* (New York: E. & J. B. Young, 1885), pp. 288, 305–311.

7. John Henry Newman, *Lectures on the Prophetical Office of the Church viewed Relatively to Romanism and Popular Protestantism* (London, 1837), pp. 20–22. On Bennett, see W. J. Sparrow Simpson, *The History of the Anglo-Catholic Revival from 1845* (London: George Allen & Unwin, 1924), pp. 59–60, and C.P.S. Clarke, *The Oxford Movement and After* (London: A. R. Mowbray, 1932), p. 147.

8. Chadwick, *The Victorian Church*, p. 213.

9. Olive Cook, Graham Hutton, and Edwin Smith, *English Parish Churches* (New York: Thames & Hudson, 1976), pp. 212–213; Peter G. Cobb, "The Architectural Setting of the Liturgy," in *The Study of Liturgy*, ed. C. Jones, G. Wainwright, and E. Yarnold (New York: Oxford University Press, 1978), pp. 478–480; Mark Chatfield, *Churches the Victorians Forgot* (Ashbourne, Derbys: Moorland Publishing, 1989), p. 9.

10. Janet Mayo, *A History of Ecclesiastical Dress* (London: Batsford, 1984), pp. 102–107.

11. Kenneth D. Mackenzie, "Anglican Adaptations of Some Latin Rites and Ceremonies," in *Liturgy and Worship: A Companion to the Prayer Books of the Anglican Communion*, ed. W. K. Lowther Clarke (London: SPCK, 1954), p. 747; Francis Penhale, *The Anglican Church Today: Catholics In Crisis* (London: A. R. Mowbrays, 1987), pp. 50–58. On the response to Neale's innovations, see Eleanor Towle, *John Mason Neale, D.D.: A Memoir* (London: Longmans, Green, 1906), pp. 262–270.

12. Pearson and Wilson, in *The Judgement of the Bishops Upon Tractarian Theology*, ed. W. Simcox Bricknell (Oxford, 1845), pp. 630, 696. See also Toon, *Evangelical Theology*, pp. 26–45.

13. Richard Hurrell Froude, *Remains of the Late Reverend Richard Hurrell Froude* (London: J. G. & F. Rivington, 1838–1839), vol. 1, pp. 336, 389, 393. See also L. I. Guiney, *Hurrell Froude: Memoranda and Comments* (London: Methuen, 1904), pp. 240–247.

14. See Ker, *Newman*, pp. 216–218; Newman, *Apologia*, pp. 71–80; Church, *Oxford Movement*, pp. 182–201.

15. Chadwick, *Victorian Church*, pp. 250–271; Edward Carpenter, *Cantuar: The Archbishops in Their Office* (1971; reprint, Oxford: A. R. Mowbray, 1988), pp. 302–303; Balleine, *History of the Evangelical Party*, pp. 222–227.

16. J. M. Cameron, "John Henry Newman," in *Nineteenth Century Religious Thought in the West*, ed. Ninian Smart et al. (Cambridge: Cambridge University Press, 1985), vol. 2, pp. 81, 104.

17. T. J. Jackson Lears, *No Place of Grace: Anti-Modernism and the Transformation of American Culture, 1880–1920* (New York: Pantheon, 1981), pp. 161–199.

18. Keble, in Owen Chadwick, ed., *The Mind of the Oxford Movement* (Stanford, Calif.: Stanford University Press, 1960), p. 68.

19. Ann Douglas, *The Feminization of American Culture* (New York: Alfred Knopf, 1977), pp. 298–299. See also W.S.F. Pickering, *Anglo-Catholicism: A Study in Religious Ambiguity* (London: Routledge, 1989).

20. On the growth of the Oxford Movement in the American Episcopal Church, see Robert Bruce Mullin, *Episcopal Vision/American Reality: High Church Theology and Social Thought in Evangelical America* (New Haven: Yale University Press, 1986), pp. 149–159; E. Clowes Chorley, "The Oxford Movement in the General Theological Seminary," *Historical Magazine of the Protestant Episcopal Church* (hereafter *HMPEC*), 5 (1936): 177–201; Kenneth M. Peck, "The Oxford Controversy in America: 1839," *HMPEC* 33 (1964): 49–63; George E. DeMille, *The Catholic Movement in the American Episcopal Church* (Philadelphia: Church Historical Society, 1950); James Thayer Addison, *The Episcopal Church in the United States, 1789–1931* (New York: Charles Scribner's Sons, 1951), pp. 152–163.

21. R. W. Harris, *Christian Worship Not Symbolical: A Sermon Preached in St. George's Church, Astoria, L.I.* (New York: Hallet & Breen, 1868), pp. 12–13.

22. Charles Pettit McIlvaine, *The Chief Danger of the Church in These Times: A Charge Delivered to the Clergy of the Diocese of Ohio* (New York: Harper & Brothers, 1843), p. 8.

23. Charles Pettit McIlvaine, *Oxford Divinity Compared with that of the Romish and Anglican Churches: With a special view to the Illustration of the Doctrine of Justification by Faith* (Philadelphia, 1841), pp. 10, 212.

24. John Henry Hopkins, *A Tract for the Church in Jerusalem . . . considered in a Friendly Remonstrance to the Editors of the Church Journal* (Burlington, Vt., 1854), p. 5.

25. Brownell, in Eben Edwards Beardsley, *The History of the Episcopal Church in Connecticut* (New York: Hurd & Houghton, 1868), 2:365.

26. The standard biographies of Muhlenberg are Anne Ayres, *The Life and Work of William Augustus Muhlenberg, Doctor in Divinity* (New York: Thomas Whittaker, 1889); William Wilberforce Newton, *Dr. Muhlenberg* (Boston: Houghton & Mifflin, 1890); Alvin W. Skardon, *Church Leader in the Cities: William Augustus Muhlenberg* (Philadelphia: University of Pennsylvania Press, 1971). See also E. R. Hardy, "Evangelical Catholicism: W. A. Muhlenberg and the Memorial Movement," *HMPEC* 13 (1944): 155–192.

27. Clinton Locke, in E. Clowes Chorley, *Men and Movements in the American Episcopal Church* (New York: Charles Scribner's Sons, 1950), p. 363.

28. Ayres, *Life and Work of Muhlenberg*, p. 173.

29. Newton, *Dr. Muhlenberg*, pp. 75–79, 104–106.

30. On the Memorial Movement, see Mullin, *Episcopal Vision/American Reality*, pp. 181–188; Newton, *Dr. Muhlenberg*, esp. "The History of the Memorial Movement," pp. 123–176; Addison, *The Episcopal Church in the United States*, pp. 177–188; Perry, *History of the American Episcopal Church, 1587–1883* (Boston: James R. Osgood, 1885), vol. 2, pp. 292–310. On the presentation of the Memorial, see *Journal of the Proceedings of the Bishops, Clergy, and Laity of the Protestant Episcopal Church . . . 1853* (Philadelphia: King & Baird, 1854), pp. 181–183.

31. The text of the Memorial is reprinted in *Evangelical and Catholic Papers: A Collection of Essays, Letters and Tractates from the Writings of Rev. William Augustus Muhlenberg, D.D.*, ed. Anne Ayres (New York: Thomas Whittaker, 1875), pp. 79–84. See also Muhlenberg's *Suggestions for the Formation of an Evangelic and Catholic Union: A Paper Read at the Evangelical Conference in Philadelphia, November 9, 1869* (New York: Thomas Whittaker, 1870), pp. 11–12.

32. William A. Muhlenberg, "An Exposition of the Memorial" (November 1854), in *Evangelical and Catholic Papers*, pp. 140–141.

33. Freeman, in *Memorial Papers: The Memorial with Circular & Questions of the Episcopal Commission* (Philadelphia: E. H. Butler, 1857), pp. 180–181. See also Hardy, "Evangelical Catholicism," p. 188; Addison, *Episcopal Church in the United States*, pp. 184–185.

34. Alonzo Potter and Dr. Harry Croswell, in *Memorial Papers*, pp. 110, 245.

35. "Preliminary Report on the Memorial" and "Report of the Commission on Memorial of Rev. Dr. Muhlenberg and Others," in Perry, *History of the American Episcopal Church*, vol. 2, pp. 298, 300–310.

36. William Sparrow, *The Christian Ministry: An Address delivered at the Annual Commencement of the Theological Seminary of the Protestant Episcopal Church of the Diocese of Virginia, June 24, 1869* (New York: American Church Press Co., 1869), pp. 8–9, 17; Alfred Lee, *The Sermon Delivered at the Opening of the General Convention of the Protestant Episcopal Church, Wednesday, Oct. 7th, 1868* (New York: Protestant Episcopal Society for the Promotion of Evangelical Knowledge, 1868), pp. 21–27; John Johns, *A Valedictory Discourse: By the Rev. J. Johns, D.D., Delivered in Christ Church, Baltimore, October 3, 1842* (Baltimore: N. Hickman, 1842), pp. 16–19; Henry Van Dyke Johns, *The Protestant Episcopal Pastor Teaching the People Committed to His Charge* (Baltimore, Md.: N. Hickman, 1842), pp. 14–18.

37. William Meade, *Companion to the Font and Pulpit* (Washington: J. & G. S. Gideon, 1846), pp. 40–53.

38. Charles Wesley Andrews, *Baptismal Regeneration: A Review of the Controversy, with thoughts on the Duty of the Evangelical Portion of the Episcopal Church at the Present Time, Touching on the Toleration of Ritualism* (Alexandria, Va.: J. & W. J. Entwisle, 1869), pp. 5–

13. See also Charles Wesley Andrews, *Notes on the State of the Church* (Philadelphia: J. B. Lippincott, 1874), pp. 47–50.

39. William Rufus Nicholson, *Reasons Why I Became a Reformed Episcopalian* (Philadelphia: James A. Moore, 1875), p. 5.

40. Franklin Rising, *Are There Romanizing Germs in the Prayer-Book?* (New York, August 1868), p. 6.

41. Ibid., pp. 38–39.

42. Ibid., p. 39.

43. Chorley, *Men and Movements*, pp. 364–365.

44. *Journal of the Proceedings of the Bishops, Clergy, and Laity of the Protestant Episcopal Church . . . 1868* (Hartford, Conn., 1869), pp. 140–143, 151–152. The text of the report is in Perry, *History of the American Episcopal Church*, vol. 2, pp. 349–350. See also Chorley, *Men and Movements*, pp. 376–379.

45. Addison, *The Episcopal Church in the United States*, pp. 208–209.

46. Perry, *History of the American Episcopal Church*, vol. 2, p. 355–361.

47. James DeKoven, in *Debates in the House of Deputies in the General Convention of the Protestant Episcopal Church*, ed. D. F. Murphy (Hartford, Conn., 1871), p. 506. See Charles C. Tiffany, *A History of the Protestant Episcopal Church in the United States of America* (New York: Christian Literature Co., 1895), pp. 531–532, and Perry, *History of the American Episcopal Church*, vol. 2, p. 361.

48. *Eli Trembling for the Ark; or, The Action of the Late General Convention and Its Lessons* (New York: Sutton & Bowne, 1869), pp. 9, 11.

49. Chorley, *Men and Movements*, pp. 408, 410.

50. *Eli Trembling for the Ark*, p. 11.

51. Clarence Walworth, *The Oxford Movement in America; or, Glimpses of Life in an Anglican Seminary* (1895; reprint, New York: Johnson Reprint Co., 1974), p. 157.

52. Annie Darling Price, *A History of the Formation and Growth of the Reformed Episcopal Church, 1873–1902* (Philadelphia: James M. Armstrong, 1902), p. 83.

53. *Digest of the Canons for the Government of the Protestant Episcopal Church in the United States of America* (Boston: William A. Hall, 1865), p. 38.

54. Horatio Potter, *A Pastoral Letter to the Clergy of the Diocese of New-York, from the Bishop* (New York, May 1865), pp. 6–7.

55. Ibid., pp. 11–12.

56. Eli H. Canfield, *Review of "A Pastoral Letter to the Clergy of the Diocese of New York, from the Bishop"* (New York, July 1865), p. 23.

57. John Cotton Smith, *A Plea for Liberty in the Church: A Letter to the Rt. Rev. Horatio Potter, D.D., D.C.L.* (Cambridge: Riverside Press, 1865), pp. 4–5.

58. Stephen H. Tyng, *Letter to Rt. Rev. Horatio Potter, D.D.* (New York: John A. Gray & Green, 1865), p. 22.

59. [American Church Union], *The Tyng Case: A Narrative Together With the Judgement of the Court, and the Admonition by the Bishop of New York* (New York: Pott & Amery, 1868), pp. 5–11; Raymond F. Albright, *A History of the Protestant Episcopal Church* (New York: Macmillan, 1964), p. 251; Chorley, *Men and Movements*, pp. 275–277.

60. Effingham H. Nichols, *A Letter to the Right Rev'd Horatio Potter, D.D., LL.D. . . . relating to the Proceedings against the Rev. Stephen H. Tyng, Jr.* (Washington, D.C.: Gibson Brothers, 1868).

61. Muhlenberg, *Suggestions for the Formation of an Evangelic and Catholic Union*, p. 11.

62. "Admonition," in *The Tyng Case*, pp. 20–32.

63. Stephen H. Tyng Jr., *The Liberty of Preaching: Its Warrant and Relations* (New York: John A. Gray & Green, 1867), pp. 8, 23.

64. Charles Rockland Tyng, *Record of the Life and Work of the Rev. Stephen Higginson Tyng, D.D.* (New York: E. P. Dutton, 1890), p. 471.

65. Benjamin Aycrigg, *Memoirs of the Reformed Episcopal Church and of the Protestant Episcopal Church*, 5th ed. (New York: Edward O. Jenkins, 1880), p. 125.

66. Price, *History of the Reformed Episcopal Church*, p. 36.

67. *Berkshire (Massachusetts) Courier*, September 11, 1871, p. 3.

68. Rodney Howat Longmire, "Charles Edward Cheney, Bishop of the Reformed Episcopal Church" (S.T.M. thesis, Lutheran Theological Seminary, Philadelphia, 1965), pp. 2–6.

69. Charles Edward Cheney, *Personal Reminiscences of the Founding of the Reformed Episcopal Church* (Philadelphia: Reformed Episcopal Publication Society, 1913), p. 9.

70. "The Trial of the Rev. Mr. C. E. Cheney," in Ashmead Miscellanies Book, p. 199, Archives of the Reformed Episcopal Church at the Philadelphia Theological Seminary, Philadelphia.

71. Charles Edward Cheney, "Jonah's Gourd," in *Sermons* (Chicago: Cushing, Thomas & Co., 1880), pp. 56, 58.

72. Cheney, "Doubt as a Religious System," in ibid., p. 180.

73. Cheney, "The Reformed Episcopalian at the Baptismal Font," in *What Do Reformed Episcopalians Believe? Eight Sermons Preached in Christ Church, Chicago* (Philadelphia: Reformed Episcopal Publication Society, 1888), p. 7.

74. Cheney, "The Reformed Episcopalian and His Bishop," in ibid., p. 89.

75. Cheney, *Personal Reminiscences*, p. 7.

76. Ibid., p. 2; and Cheney, "The Spiritualism of Christ," in *A Neglected Power and Other Sermons* (New York: Fleming H. Revell, 1916), p. 142.

77. Cheney, "Fidelity and Conscience," in *A Neglected Power*, p. 169.

78. Cheney, "The Reformed Episcopalian at the Baptismal Font," in *What Do Reformed Episcopalians Believe?* p. 10.

79. "In Memoriam: Right Reverend Charles Edward Cheney, D.D., S.T.D." (Chicago: Vestry of Christ Reformed Episcopal Church, 1916), pp. 9, 14.

80. "The Trial of the Rev. Mr. C. E. Cheney," in Ashmead Miscellanies Book, p. 199.

81. Cheney, *The Reformed Episcopal Church: A Sermon Preached in Christ Church, Chicago* (Chicago: Perry, Morris, & Sultzer, 1874), p. 5.

82. Cheney, "The Reformed Episcopalian at the Baptismal Font," in *What Do Reformed Episcopalians Believe?* pp. 22–23.

83. Cheney, *Personal Reminiscences*, p. 8.

84. "Bishop Cheney's Proposed Memorial to the General Convention," in Clippings Book No. 2, p. 7, Archives of the Reformed Episcopal Church.

85. Cheney, *Personal Reminiscences*, p. 8.

86. Keith J. Hardman, *Charles Grandison Finney, 1792–1875: Revivalist and Reformer* (Syracuse, N.Y.: Syracuse University Press, 1987), p. 377.

87. Clinton Locke, *Personal Reminiscences of the Diocese of Illinois, 1856–1892*, ed. R. B. Dibbert (Chicago: Grace Episcopal Church, 1976), pp. 1–2.

88. Samuel H. Kerfoot, *Bishop Whitehouse and the Diocese of Illinois* (Chicago, 1860), pp. 10–12, 45–46; Locke, "Personal Reminiscences," p. 6. See also Leacock Miscellanies Book, pp. 81–82 (Archives of the Reformed Episcopal Church).

89. Kerfoot, *Bishop Whitehouse*, pp. 6–7.

90. "J.S.B.H. and the Scathing Rebuke," in Leacock Miscellanies Book, p. 82.

91. "Bishop Whitehouse and the Rev. Charles E. Cheney," in Leacock Miscellanies Book, pp. 85ff.

92. On the Cracraft incident and the suspicions it aroused concerning Whitehouse's

Copperhead sympathies, see *An Appeal from Grace Church, Galesburg, to the Diocesan Convention of Illinois* (Galesburg, Ill.: D. Myers, 1865); and Bruce T. Brown, "Grace Church, Galesburg, Ill., 1865–1866: The Supposed Neutrality of the Episcopal Church During the Years of the Civil War," *HMPEC* 46 (June 1977): 187–208.

93. "In Memoriam: Right Reverend Charles Edward Cheney," p. 17

94. Whitehouse, in Aycrigg, *Memoirs*, p. 128.

95. "Ritualism: A Protest Against the 'Great Peril' to the Protestant Episcopal Church," in Ashmead Miscellanies Book, pp. 222–223.

96. Edward Pessen, *Jacksonian America: Society, Personality, and Politics*, rev. ed. (Urbana, Ill.: University of Illinois Press, 1985), pp. 199–200. See also Daniel Walker Howe, *The Political Culture of the American Whigs* (Chicago: University of Chicago Press, 1979), p. 166. On the attraction of High Church Episcopalians to the Democratic party in the 1850s and during the Civil War, see Allan Bogue, *The Earnest Men: Republicans of the Civil War Senate* (Ithaca, N.Y.: Cornell University Press, 1981), p. 60.

97. Cheney, *Personal Reminiscences*, p. 9.

98. "Bishop and Rector—The Case of Rev. Mr. Cheney, of Chicago—Affidavit of the Bishop in Support of the Motion to Dissolve the Injunction," in Ashmead Miscellanies Book, p. 210.

99. Cheney, *Personal Reminiscences*, p. 9.

100. "Bishop and Rector," p. 210.

101. Sparrow to T. U. Dudley, July 29, 1869, in *The Life and Correspondence of Rev. William Sparrow, D.D.* (Philadelphia: James Hammond, 1876), p. 297.

102. Longmire, "Charles Edward Cheney," p. 15.

103. "Illinois: The Trial of Rev. Mr. C. E. Cheney," in Leacock Miscellanies Book, pp. 29–30.

104. "Trial of C. E. Cheney," in Ashmead Miscellanies Book, p. 197.

105. Ibid., p. 30.

106. Clinton Locke, who was unwillingly sucked into the legal proceedings against Cheney in 1871, typified the crowd of spectators as "the Cheney women" (Locke, "Personal Reminiscences," p. 32), even though the newspaper accounts make no reference to gender. This is one of only two occasions in which Locke refers to women in his "Personal Reminiscences," and both have to do with Cheney and Cheney's future fellow-separatist, George David Cummins. Perhaps there is a reason for this. Both Clara Emma Griswold Cheney and Alexandrine Macomb Balch Cummins were extraordinarily assertive women. Clara Cheney was a well-known author of children's books and published a best-selling young people's history of the Civil War. Alexandrine Cummins wrote her husband's biography and played a major but largely invisible role in prompting her husband's secession from the Episcopal Church in 1873. (Locke, in fact, snarls at Alexandrine Cummins as a "queer wife" who, although "handsome and agreeable," had not had "the seven devils . . . cast out of her.") In addition, Cummins's first major publication was a biography of the Evangelical Episcopalian missionary to Liberia, Virginia Hale Hoffman, who had been a parishioner of Cummins's in Baltimore (see George David Cummins, *Life of Virginia Hale Hoffman* [Philadelphia: Lindsay & Blakiston, 1859]). All this might suggest that yet another point of contention between the Evangelicals and the Anglo-Catholics—and perhaps between Whitehouse and Cheney—was a division over gender roles and stereotypes, with the Evangelicals willing to defy "catholic" glorifications of male patriarchy and celibacy by empowering Evangelical women. It is in just this spirit that Richard Rankin's forthcoming *Ambivalent Churchmen and Evangelical Churchwomen: The Religion of the Episcopal Elite in North Carolina, 1800–1860* (University of South Carolina Press) proposes that Anglo-Catholicism represented a patriarchal version of Episcopalianism that male elites used to counter the egalitarian demands of their Evangelical

wives, demands that involved conversion to both Evangelicalism and companionate marriage. This classification, however, is complicated by the willingness of Evangelical controversialists to stigmatize Anglo-Catholic ritualism as "effeminate." See R. W. Harris, *Christian Worship Not Symbolical: A Sermon Preached in St. George's Church, Astoria, L.I.* (New York: Hallet & Breen, 1868), pp. 12–13. What is more, the first chapter of Cummins's biography of Virginia Hale Hoffman, "The Christian Woman," lauds Evangelicalism for having made women "man's equal, companion, friend," but also makes it clear that her proper location is "in a home" as a "mother, sister, and wife" (p. 19).

107. Cheney, *Personal Reminiscences*, p. 10.

108. "Re-opening of the Cheney Case," *Chicago Evening Journal*, May 3, 1871, p. 3.

109. Longmire, "Charles Edward Cheney," pp. 18–19; "Illinois: New Proceedings in the Case of Mr. Cheney," *Protestant Churchman*, April 20, 1871, p. 1.

110. "Cheney: Conclusion of the Trial of the Rev. Charles Edward Cheney," *Chicago Mail*, May 4, 1871, p. 1; "Last of the Cheney Case," *Chicago Evening Journal*, June 2, 1871, p. 4; "Deposed: Promulgation of the Sentence Degrading Rev. C. E. Cheney from the Ministry," *Chicago Evening Post*, June 3, 1871, p. 1.

111. Cheney, "Journal of Services" for September 10, 1871, Archives of the Reformed Episcopal Church, Philadelphia Theological Seminary; "The Cheney Case. The Episcopal Visitation of Christ Church on Yesterday," *Chicago Times*, September 11, 1871, p. 1. See also "Bishop Whitehouse's Visitation to Christ Church," *Chicago Tribune*, September 11, 1871; "The Ceremonial War," *Chicago Evening Post*, September 11, 1871; "The Episcopalian Schism Out West," *New York Herald*, September 11, 1871; "Clerical Honor," *New York Times*, September 12, 1871, p. 3.

112. "The Second Act: The Cheney Rebellion Fast Drawing to Its Close," *Chicago Times*, May 28, 1872, p. 1; "Cheney's Chastening," *Chicago Times*, June 21, 1872, p. 3.

113. The day before, Tyng had received a written warning from Whitehouse not to appear at Christ Church, but Tyng ignored it ("Christ Church," *Chicago Times*, June 5, 1871; "Regeneration: A Sermon by the Rev. Stephen H. Tyng, Jr., of New York," *Chicago Tribune*, June 5, 1871, p. 4). See also Cheney, "Journal of Services" for June 4, 1871.

114. "Episcopacy: The Last of the Cheney Case," *Chicago Evening Journal*, June 3, 1871, p. 1. See also Aycrigg, *Memoirs*, p. 131; Chorley, *Men and Movements*, pp. 407–408.

115. W. H. Cooper's copy of the printed resolution is bound into an untitled volume of pamphlets in the Archives of the Reformed Episcopal Church. See also Albright, *History of the Protestant Episcopal Church*, pp. 278–280; Aycrigg, *Memoirs*, p. 130.

116. Cheney's comment is part of an insertion on pp. 141–143 of a notebook entitled "Scrapbook, Volume 3, 1871–1872" Archives of the Reformed Episcopal Church.

117. The interview of Whipple and Lee with Cheney is described in a May 13, 1871, letter to Henry John Whitehouse, in Henry Benjamin Whipple, *Lights and Shadows of a Long Episcopate* (New York: Macmillan, 1899), pp. 328–338. See also "Bishop Whitehouse and His Brother Bishops," *Chicago Tribune*, August 23, 1871, p. 3; "The Cheney Case: The Late Interference by Two Bishops in the Proceedings Against the Degraded Clergyman," *Chicago Times*, August 27, 1871, p. 1.

CHAPTER 3

1. *The Christian Advocate*, December 11, 1873, p. 399, United Methodist Historical Museum, Baltimore, Md.

2. Alexandrine M. B. Cummins, *Memoir of George David Cummins, D.D., First Bishop of the Reformed Episcopal Church* (Philadelphia: E. Claxton, 1878), pp. 265–267.

3. Cummins, in *Journal of the General Conference of the Methodist Episcopal Church Held in Baltimore, Md., May 1–31, 1876* (New York: Nelson & Philips, 1876), p. 526. See also Leacock Clippings Book, Archives of the Reformed Episcopal Church, Philadelphia Theological Seminary, Philadelphia, p. 161.

4. A. Cummins, *Memoir of George David Cummins*, p. 16.

5. Cummins's original license is in the collections of the United Methodist Historical Museum.

6. *General Minutes of the Annual Conferences of the Methodist Episcopal Church, 1835–1844* (New York, 1844), pp. 330, 438.

7. A. Cummins, *Memoir of George David Cummins*, p. 21.

8. Clarence C. Goen, *Broken Churches, Broken Nation: Denominational Schisms and the Coming of the Civil War* (Macon, Ga.: Mercer University Press, 1985), pp. 81–86.

9. George David Cummins, *The African a Trust from God to the American* (Baltimore: John D. Toy, 1861), pp. 16, 18, 19, 20–21, 22.

10. William Taylor, *Story of My Life* (New York: Hunt & Eaton, 1896), p. 63.

11. A. Cummins, *Memoir of George David Cummins*, p. 37.

12. William Francis Brand, *The Life of William Rollinson Whittingham, Fourth Bishop of Maryland* (New York: E. & J. B. Young, 1883), vol. 1, pp. 312–320.

13. Ian Bradley, *The Call to Seriousness: The Evangelical Impact on the Victorians* (New York: Macmillan, 1976), pp. 57–68.

14. Cummins, "The Fruit of the Spirit," in Cummins's sermon manuscript book, Bishop Cummins Memorial Reformed Episcopal Church, Catonsville, Md.

15. A. Cummins, *Memoir of George David Cummins*, p. 44.

16. Cheney, "The Preacher Bishop," in *Sermons* (Chicago: Cushing, Thomas & Co., 1880), p. 242; Benjamin B. Leacock, *Personal Recollections Connected with the Reformed Episcopal Church*, ed. Robert K. Rudolph (Philadelphia: Reformed Episcopal Publication Society, 1976), p. 71.

17. Cheney, "The Preacher Bishop," in *Sermons*, pp. 237, 238.

18. Thomas U. Dudley, "The Protestant Episcopal Church," in J. S. Johnston, *Memorial History of Louisville from Its First Settlement to the Year 1896* (Chicago, 1896), vol. 2, p. 149.

19. Leacock, *Personal Recollections*, pp. 71–72.

20. A. Cummins, *Memoir of George David Cummins*, p. 79.

21. Robert B. Croes to William R. Whittingham, January 25, 1855, in the Maryland Diocesan Archives, Baltimore.

22. A. Cummins, *Memoir of George David Cummins*, pp. 107–108.

23. Cummins to William R. Whittingham, April 1, 1857, in Maryland Diocesan Archives.

24. A. Cummins, *Memoir of George David Cummins*, p. 101.

25. *Christian Advocate*, December 11, 1873, p. 399, United Methodist Historical Society.

26. A. Cummins, *Memoir of George David Cummins*, p. 230.

27. Noah Schenck, *The Preaching of Jesus: A Sermon Preached at the Consecration of Trinity Church, Chicago, Ill., on Sunday, April 24, 1864* (Chicago: Tribune Book & Job Office Print, 1864), p. 33.

28. Charles Edward Cheney, *Personal Reminiscences of the Founding of the Reformed Episcopal Church* (Philadelphia: Reformed Episcopal Publication Society, 1913), p. 6.

29. Cheney, "The Preacher Bishop," in *Sermons*, pp. 239, 240.

30. Cummins, "Returning to the Fold," sermon manuscript book.

31. Cummins, "Healing the Lunatic Child," in *Sermons By Bishop Cummins* (Philadelphia: Reformed Episcopal Publication Society, 1884), p. 85.

32. Cummins, "The Stilling of the Tempest," November 10, 1861, St. Peter's Church, Baltimore, Md., sermon manuscript book.

33. Cummins, "Abraham's Prayer for Ishmael," sermon manuscript book.

34. Cummins, "The Kingdom Come," sermon manuscript book.

35. Cummins, *The Claims of the Prayer Book Upon Protestant Christendom: A Sermon Preached at the Anniversary of the Bishop White Prayer Book Society* (Philadelphia: King & Baird, 1861), p. 43.

36. Cummins, "Have ye received the Holy Ghost?" June 8, 1862, St. Peter's Church, sermon manuscript book.

37. Cummins, "Hazael a warning to young men," sermon manuscript book.

38. Cummins, "Christ's Doctrine its own Evidence," in *Sermons By Bishop Cummins*, p. 38.

39. Cummins, "The Temptation of Jesus," sermon manuscript book.

40. *Journal of the Proceedings of the Bishops, Clergy, and Laity of the Protestant Episcopal Church . . . 1865* (Boston: William A. Hall, 1865), p. 38.

41. A. Cummins, *Memoir of George David Cummins*, pp. 140–141.

42. Cummins, *Claims of the Prayer Book Upon Protestant Christendom*, p. 41.

43. Leacock, *Personal Recollections*, p. 18.

44. A. Cummins, *Memoir of George David Cummins*, p. 334.

45. Cummins, *Claims of the Prayer Book Upon Protestant Christendom*, pp. 31, 33.

46. George David Cummins, *The Prayer Book a Basis of Unity* (Louisville, Ky.: Louisville Courier Steam & Job Print, 1867), pp. 4–5, 8, 10, 11.

47. George David Cummins, *The Christian, in time of National Peril, Trembling for the Ark of God: A Sermon Delivered on Thanksgiving Day in St. Peter's Church, Baltimore, November 29, 1860* (Baltimore: John D. Toy, 1860), p. 18.

48. Cummins to Mason Gallagher, March 11, 1869, in A. Cummins, *Memoir of George David Cummins*, p. 347.

49. Cummins, "Witnessing to Evangelical Truth, A Perpetual Duty," *The Episcopalian*, July 13, 1870, p. 1.

50. Cummins, "Worship in Spirit and in Truth," in *Sermons By Bishop Cummins*, p. 60.

51. Cummins to G. T. Bedell, May 14, 1869, in A. Cummins, *Memoir of George David Cummins*, p. 347.

52. Cummins, "The Memorial Feast," in *Sermons By Bishop Cummins*, p. 55.

53. Cummins, "The Bread of Life," sermon manuscript book.

54. Cummins, "The Christian's Great Calling," sermon manuscript book.

55. Cummins, "What is that to thee? Follow thou me!" November 10, 1861 (St. Peter's Church, Baltimore), and May 8, 1864 (Trinity Church, Chicago), sermon manuscript book.

56. Cummins, "The True Unity of Christ's People—Many Folds but One Flock," in *Sermons By Bishop Cummins*, pp. 9–10.

57. Cummins, "Christ's spiritual presence better than his bodily presence," sermon manuscript book.

58. Cummins, "The Simplicity that is in Christ," sermon manuscript book.

59. Cummins, "Character determining the soul's destiny," sermon manuscript book, "Worship in Spirit and in Truth," in *Sermons By Bishop Cummins*, p. 60.

60. Cummins, *The Christian, in time of National Peril*, pp. 14–15.

61. Cummins, "Worship in Spirit and in Truth," in *Sermons By Bishop Cummins*, p. 60.

62. Cummins, "Our lamps are gone out," January 26, 1862 (St. Peter's Church, Baltimore), and July 23, 1865 (Trinity Church, Chicago), sermon manuscript book.

63. Cummins, "The Memorial Feast," in *Sermons By Bishop Cummins*, p. 53.

64. A. Cummins, *Memoir of George David Cummins*, p. 373.

65. Henry Codman Potter, *Reminiscences of Bishops and Archbishops* (New York: G. P. Putnam, 1906), p. 10.

66. B. B. Smith, "Sermon," in *Forty-Fourth Annual Convention of the Protestant Episcopal Church, Diocese of Kentucky* (Louisville, Ky., 1872), pp. 34–35; "Sermon," in *Forty-Fifth Annual Convention of the Protestant Episcopal Church in the Diocese of Kentucky* (Louisville, Ky., 1873), p. 33.

67. The Smith trial is ably summarized from the original trial documents in Frances Keller Swinford and Rebecca Smith Lee, *The Great Elm Tree: Heritage of the Episcopal Diocese of Lexington* (Lexington, Ky.: Faith House Press, 1969), pp. 108–145.

68. Leacock, *Personal Recollections*, p. 28; A. Cummins, *Memoir of George David Cummins*, p. 250.

69. A. Cummins, *Memoir of George David Cummins*, p. 245.

70. Swinford and Lee, *The Great Elm Tree*, p. 290.

71. *Christian Advocate*, December 11, 1873, p. 399, in United Methodist Historical Museum.

72. A. Cummins, *Memoir of George David Cummins*, p. 280.

73. Ibid.

74. Swinford and Lee, *The Great Elm Tree*, p. 293.

75. George David Cummins, *Following the Light: A Statement of the Author's Experiences Resulting in a Change of Views Respecting the Prayer-Book of the Protestant Episcopal Church, and of the Reasons for Changing the Direction of Ministerial Labors in the Gospel of Christ* (Philadelphia: James A. Moore, 1876), p. 8. See also Ross A. Foster, "The Origin and Development of the Reformed Episcopal Church in America, 1873–1973" (Ph.D. diss., Clarksville School of Theology, 1978), p. 127.

76. "Opening of a New Ritualistic Church in Louisville," *Protestant Churchman*, February 17, 1871, pp. 119–120. See also Swinford and Lee, *The Great Elm Tree*, p. 294.

77. Cummins, *Following the Light*, p. 8. See also Foster, "Origin and Development of the Reformed Episcopal Church," p. 127. See also Warren C. Platt, "The Reformed Episcopal Church: The Origins and Early Development of Its Ideological Expression," *HMPEC* 51 (1983): 246–247.

78. Leacock, *Personal Recollections*, p. 28.

79. Cummins, *Following the Light*, p. 8. See also Foster, "Origin and Development of the Reformed Episcopal Church," p. 127.

80. Cummins, "The Memorial Feast," in *Sermons By Bishop Cummins*, p. 56.

81. Leacock, *Personal Recollections*, p. 48.

82. A. Cummins, *Memoir of George David Cummins*, p. 288.

83. Charles Wesley Andrews, *Notes on the State of the Church* (Philadelphia: J. B. Lippincott, 1874), p. 15.

84. A. Cummins, *Memoir of George David Cummins*, p. 300.

85. George David Cummins, *The Protestantism of the Episcopal Church* (New York: Protestant Episcopal Society for the Promotion of Evangelical Knowledge, 1868), pp. 1, 3, 4.

86. A. Cummins, *Memoir of George David Cummins*, pp. 294, 300.

87. Cummins, *Following the Light*, p. 8. See also Foster, "Origin and Development of the Reformed Episcopal Church," p. 125; Platt, "The Reformed Episcopal Church," pp. 246–247.

88. Cummins, *Following the Light*, p. 9.

89. A. Cummins, *Memoir of George David Cummins*, p. 332.

90. Cummins, in *The Standard of the Cross*, June 26, 1869, p. 1.

91. A. Cummins, *Memoir of George David Cummins*, p. 339.

92. Cheney to Cummins, in ibid., pp. 349–350.

93. Cheney to Cummins, July 3, 1869, in ibid., pp. 351–352.

94. Cheney, *Personal Reminiscences*, pp. 6–7.

95. Swinford and Lee, *The Great Elm Tree*, pp. 304–307.

96. Cheney, "The Preacher Bishop," in *Sermons*, p. 240.

97. See Cummins's address to the Evangelical Education Society in 1871, in *Fifth Annual Report of the Board of Managers of the Evangelical Educational Society of the Protestant Episcopal Church . . . October 12, 1871* (Philadelphia: McCalla & Stavely, 1871), pp. 24–30.

98. Heman Dyer, *Records of An Active Life* (New York: Thomas Whittaker, 1886), pp. 216–219. See also Raymond W. Albright, *A History of the Protestant Episcopal Church* (New York: Macmillan, 1964), p. 218.

99. Delancey, October 2, 1862, in "Convention Debates, 1859–1862," newspaper clippings book, Archives of the Reformed Episcopal Church.

100. Henry C. Lay to Bishop William Whittingham, December 1, 1869, Maryland Diocesan Archives.

101. James Craik to John Cowan and Dr. George Cowan, January 4, 1869, in Swinford and Lee, *The Great Elm Tree*, pp. 300–301.

102. The Rev. Ethan Allen to Bishop William Whittingham, December 31, 1869, Maryland Diocesan Archives.

103. "The Missionary Society," *Philadelphia North American*, October 24, 1873, p. 1.

104. A. Cummins, *Memoir of George David Cummins*, p. 303.

105. Swinford and Lee, *The Great Elm Tree*, pp. 308–309.

106. *Forty-Fourth Annual Convention of the Protestant Episcopal Church, Diocese of Kentucky, 1872*, pp. 27–28. See also Swinford and Lee, *The Great Elm Tree*, p. 310; A. Cummins, *Memoir of George David Cummins*, pp. 404, 406.

107. Cummins, "Witnessing to Evangelical Truth a Perpetual Duty," *The Episcopalian*, July 13, 1870, p. 1.

108. Cummins, in *Fifth Annual Report of the Evangelical Education Society*, p. 26.

109. *Forty-Fifth Annual Convention of the Protestant Episcopal Church in the Diocese of Kentucky* (Louisville, Ky., 1873), p. 41.

110. Cummins, *Old and New St. Paul's Church, Louisville: A Sermon Preached at the Re-Opening, September 4, 1873* (Louisville, Ky.: Maxwell & Co., 1873), p. 16.

111. Ibid., pp. 5, 10.

112. Swinford and Lee, *The Great Elm Tree*, pp. 311–312.

113. Cummins to Cheney, January 28, 1871, in Foster, "Origin and Development of the Reformed Episcopal Church," p. 77.

114. Cummins, "Following the Light," in ibid., p. 127.

115. Cummins to Cheney, January 29, 1872, in Annie Darling Price, *A History of the Formation and Growth of the Reformed Episcopal Church, 1873–1902* (Philadelphia: James M. Armstrong, 1902), p. 47.

116. Hall Harrison to Bishop William Whittingham, May 22, 1871, Maryland Diocesan Archives.

117. A. Cummins, *Memoir of George David Cummins*, pp. 395, 398–399; E. Clowes Chorley, *Men and Movements in the American Episcopal Church* (New York: Charles Scribner's Sons, 1950), p. 408.

118. M. A. Crowther, *Church Embattled: Religious Controversy in Mid-Victorian England* (Newton Abbot, Devon: David & Charles, 1970), p. 107.

119. Arnold to Mr. Justice Coleridge, November 18, 1835, and Arnold to Thomas S. Pasley, December 14, 1836, in Arthur Penrhyn Stanley, *The Life and Correspondence of Thomas Arnold, D.D.* (Boston: Ticknor & Fields, 1860), vol. 2, pp. 24–25, 68.

120. Arnold to W. W. Hull, April 27, 1836, in ibid., p. 39.

121. Arnold, "Principles of Church Reform," in *The Miscellaneous Works of Thomas Arnold, D.D.* (New York: D. Appleton, 1845), pp. 98, 101.

122. Ibid., p. 88. See also Stephen Neill, *Anglicanism*, 4th ed. (New York: Oxford University Press, 1977), p. 246.

123. Arnold, "Principles of Church Reform," in *Miscellaneous Works*, p. 107.

124. Crowther, *Church Embattled*, pp. 68–69; Owen Chadwick, *The Victorian Church: Part One* (New York: Oxford University Press, 1966), pp. 189–190.

125. Walter H. Conser Jr., *Church and Confession: Conservative Theologians in Germany, England, and America, 1815–1866* (Macon, Ga.: Mercer University Press, 1984), pp. 202–207.

126. Arnold to A. P. Stanley, May 24, 1836, in *Life and Correspondence of Arnold*, vol. 2, p. 47.

127. Arnold, "The Oxford Malignants and Dr. Hampden," in *Miscellaneous Works*, p. 141.

128. Arnold to Thomas S. Pasley, December 14, 1836, in Stanley, *Life and Correspondence of Arnold*, vol. 2, pp. 47, 69.

129. Arnold to Mr. Justice Coleridge, November 18, 1835, in ibid., p. 23. See also Avis, *Anglicanism and the Christian Church: Theological Resources in Historical Perspective* (Edinburgh: T. & T. Clark, 1989), p. 245.

130. Arnold, "Principles of Church Reform," in *Miscellaneous Works*, p. 92.

131. Rowland E. Prothero, *The Life and Correspondence of Arthur Penrhyn Stanley* (New York: Charles Scribner's Sons, 1893), vol. 2, pp. 295–296.

132. Neill, *Anglicanism*, p. 247. See also A. B. Webster, "Church Order and Reunion in the Nineteenth Century," in *The Historic Episcopate in the Fullness of the Church*, ed. Kenneth M. Carey (London: Dacre Press, 1954), pp. 84–85.

133. Arnold to the Rev. J. Hearn, April 12, 1836, in Stanley, *Life and Correspondence of Arnold*, vol. 2, p. 38.

134. James Davis, *Historical Sketch of the Origin and Operations of the Evangelical Alliance* (London: W. J. Johnson, 1874), p. 4.

135. Muhlenberg, "An Exposition of the Memorial," in *Evangelical Catholic Papers: A Collection of Essays, Letters, and Tractates from the Writings of Rev. William Augustus Muhlenberg, D.D.*, ed. Anne Ayres (New York: T. Whittaker, 1875), p. 147.

136. "The Evangelical Alliance," *Philadelphia North American*, October 7, 1873, p. 2.

137. "Evangelical Alliance," *Philadelphia Inquirer*, October 6, 1873, p. 1.

138. Paul A. Carter, *The Spiritual Crisis of the Gilded Age* (Dekalb: Northern Illinois University Press, 1971), p. 181.

139. Davis, *Historical Sketch*, p. 12.

140. Ibid., p. 20.

141. "The Evangelical Alliance," *Philadelphia North American*, October 7, 1873, p. 2.

142. Davis, *Historical Sketch*, p. 22.

143. Cummins, "Roman and Reformed Doctrines of Justification Contrasted," in *History, Essays, Orations, and other Documents of the Sixth General Conference of the Evangelical Alliance Held in New York, October 2–12, 1873* (New York: Harper & Brothers, 1874), p. 472.

144. Ibid., p. 467.

145. Ibid., p. 474.

146. A. Cummins, "A Memorable Communion Service," in Leacock, *Personal Recollections*, app. 13.

147. John D. Hall, "A Memorable Communion—George D. Cummins, D.D.," and A. Cummins, "A Memorable Communion Service," in Leacock, *Personal Recollections*, app. 15, 13.

CHAPTER 4

1. "To the Rt. Rev. Dr. Potter, Bishop of New York," *New York Tribune*, October 6, 1873, Clippings Book No. 4, Archives of the Reformed Episcopal Church, Philadelphia Theological Seminary, Philadelphia, pp. 23–24.

2. George Herbert Wilson, *The History of the Universities' Mission to Central Africa* (London: UMCA, 1936), pp. 19, 30; Stephen Neill, *Anglicanism* (New York: Oxford University Press, 1977), p. 343.

3. George Strong, *The Diary of George Templeton Strong*, ed. Allan Nevins and Milton Halsey Thomas (New York: Macmillan, 1952), vol. 4, p. 505.

4. Phillips Brooks, quoted in Alexander V. G. Allen, *Life and Letters of Phillips Brooks* (New York: E. P. Dutton, 1900), vol. 2, p. 80.

5. Benjamin Aycrigg, *Memoirs of the Reformed Episcopal Church*, 5th ed. (New York: Edward O. Jenkins, 1880), pp. 57, 100–101.

6. Cummins's reply to Tozer is reprinted in Alexandrine Cummins, *Memoir of George David Cummins, D.D.* (Philadelphia: E. Claxton, 1878), pp. 412–414. See also Annie Darling Price, *A History of the Formation and Growth of the Reformed Episcopal Church, 1873–1902* (Philadelphia: James M. Armstrong, 1902), pp. 92–93.

7. Cummins, in Price, *History of the Reformed Episcopal Church*, pp. 92–93.

8. A. Cummins, *Memoir of George David Cummins*, p. 416; and "A Memorable Communion Service," in Benjamin B. Leacock, *Personal Recollections Connected with the Reformed Episcopal Church*, ed. Robert K. Rudolph (Philadelphia: Reformed Episcopal Publication Society, 1976), Appendix, p. 13.

9. Tschiffely in *Louisville Courier Journal*, November 15, 1873, quoted in Frances Keller Swinford and Rebecca Smith Lee, *The Great Elm Tree: Heritage of the Episcopal Diocese of Lexington* (Lexington, Ky.: Faith House Press, 1969), p. 314.

10. John H. Drumm, *The Cummins Controversy* (Bristol, Pa., 1874), p. 5.

11. Aycrigg, *Memoirs*, pp. 37, 40, 54, 159, 160. See also "Who Is Responsible for It?" *Southern Churchman*, December 1873, Leacock Miscellanies Book, p. 116, Archives of the Reformed Episcopal Church.

12. Potter, "Bishop Tozer and the Dean of Canterbury," Clippings Book No. 2, pp. 9–10, Archives of the Reformed Episcopal Church.

13. A. Cummins, "A Memorable Communion Service," in Leacock, *Personal Recollections*, Appendix, p. 13.

14. A. Cummins, *Memoir of George David Cummins*, p. 417.

15. Cummins, "Anniversary Exercises," *Philadelphia Inquirer*, October 24, 1873, p. 2.

16. Leacock, *Personal Recollections*, pp. 22–23.

17. A. Cummins, *Memoir of George David Cummins*, p. 428.

18. Leacock, *Personal Recollections*, p. 34. See also Alexandrine Cummins's letter of April 23, 1891, to Leacock, reprinted in the appendix to Leacock's *Personal Recollections*, p. 6.

19. Ibid.

20. A. Cummins, *Memoir of George David Cummins*, p. 445.

21. Cummins's letter is variously reprinted in ibid., pp. 418–420; Price, *History of the Reformed Episcopal Church*, pp. 100–102; *Philadelphia Inquirer*, November 17, 1873, p. 8; and in Clippings Book No. 2, pp. 15–16. A formal printed copy of the letter, which may have been the way Cummins actually sent the letter to Smith, is pasted into the Leacock Miscellanies Book, p. 101.

22. Smith to Cummins, November 13, 1873, in Swinford and Lee, *The Great Elm Tree*, p. 315. See also Aycrigg, *Memoirs*, p. 108.

23. "Louisville Dispatch," *New York Times*, November 15, 1873, p. 7; *Philadelphia Inquirer*, November 15, 1873, p. 1.

24. *New York Times*, November 15, 1873, p. 6.

25. "Louisville Dispatch," *New York Times*, November 15, 1873, p. 7; *Philadelphia Inquirer*, November 15, 1873, p. 1.

26. The text of Smith's official letter of notice, written on November 23, is in Price, *History of the Reformed Episcopal Church*, pp. 105–106.

27. On Cummins's plans, see Gallagher's brief memoir of Marshall Smith in "Rev. Marshall Smith, D.D.," *Episcopal Recorder*, September 23, 1882, p. 1. See also Leacock, *Personal Recollections*, p. 43.

28. Aycrigg gives a short autobiographical sketch of himself and his reasons for leaving St. John's in his *Memoirs*, pp. 99, 111, 122, 148, 174–175. A copy of Aycrigg's letter of resignation from the vestry of St. John's on October 30, 1873, is in the Aycrigg Papers, Archives of the Reformed Episcopal Church.

29. Aycrigg, *Memoirs*, pp. 112–113. See also Price, *History of the Reformed Episcopal Church*, pp. 102–103, 284; Leacock, *Personal Recollections*, p. 38.

30. Gallagher, "Rev. Marshall B. Smith, D.D.," *Episcopal Recorder*, September 23, 1882, p. 1.

31. Aycrigg, *Memoirs*, p. 102.

32. Marshall Smith's handwritten original of the "Call to Organize" is in the Aycrigg Papers, as is a printer's proof of the "Call" with Cummins's penciled corrections. The text of the "Call" is in Price, *History of the Reformed Episcopal Church*, p. 126, and in Aycrigg, *Memoirs*, p. 113. Another copy of the printed "Call" is pasted into the Leacock Miscellanies Book, p. 102.

33. Aycrigg, *Memoirs*, p. 108.

34. Cheney, "Journal of Services," entry for November 27, 1873.

35. Aycrigg, *Memoirs*, p. 33.

36. Rodney H. Longmire, "Charles Edward Cheney, Bishop of the Reformed Episcopal Church" (S.T.M. thesis, Lutheran Theological Seminary, Philadelphia, 1965), p. 23.

37. Leacock, *Personal Recollections*, p. 52.

38. Latane, "The Reformed Episcopal Church: A Reason of the Hope That Is Within Us Respecting It," in *Minutes of the Proceedings of the Fifteenth Council of the New York and Philadelphia Synod of the Reformed Episcopal Church* (Philadelphia: Reformed Episcopal Publication Society, 1895), pp. 55–56. See also Price, *History of the Reformed Episcopal Church*, p. 283.

39. Aycrigg, *Memoirs*, p. 37.

40. Quoted from the *Church Journal* in *Christian Advocate*, November 27, 1873, p. 381.

41. Witte, "Exsurge Domine, adjuva nos" (1873), in Leacock Miscellanies Book, p. 103.

42. Both *The Nation*'s comments and Shipman's sermon were clipped by B. B. Leacock from *Church and State* and pasted into the Leacock Miscellanies Book, p. 112.

43. *New York Times*, December 1, 1873, p. 2.

44. Swinford and Lee, *The Great Elm Tree*, pp. 316–317.

45. "The New Episcopal Church," in Leacock Miscellanies Book, p. 109.

46. "Rev. Dr. Tyng on the Secession," in Clippings Book No. 2, p. 40, and Leacock Miscellanies Book, p. 105. See also Aycrigg, *Memoirs*, p. 37.

47. *Louisville Courier Journal*, November 21, 1873, p. 4, in Swinford and Lee, *The Great Elm Tree*, p. 315.

48. "Letter from the Bishop of Iowa to Bishop Cummins," Clippings Book No. 2, pp. 20–21.

49. A. Cummins, *Memoir of George David Cummins*, p. 431.

50. Cornelius Walker, *The Life and Correspondence of Rev. William Sparrow, D.D.* (Philadelphia: James Hammond, 1876), p. 352.

51. Aycrigg, *Memoirs*, p. 114.

52. Leacock, *Personal Recollections*, p. 71.

53. Ibid., p. 69.

54. Over the next six months, a substantial amount of anxious correspondence flowed back and forth from Smith to his fellow bishops, debating the merits of how to proceed with Cummins. This correspondence is preserved in the "Collection of George David Cummins," Church Historical Society, Austin, Texas. Another large collection of correspondence, stretching from November 1873 to June 1874 and including Smith's correspondence with Bishop William R. Whittingham of Maryland, is in the Maryland Diocesan Archives, Baltimore. Evidently, the High Church bishops had little confidence that Smith would proceed aggressively against Cummins, and several of them appealed to Whittingham to exert pressure on Smith for a public trial (see John Williams of Connecticut to Whittingham, June 2, 1874).

55. Craik to B. B. Smith, December 11, 1873, in the Maryland Diocesan Archives.

56. Aycrigg, *Memoirs*, p. 40.

57. Brooks, in Allen, *Life and Letters of Phillips Brooks*, vol. 2, pp. 80–81. See also Raymond W. Albright, *Focus on Infinity: A Life of Phillips Brooks* (New York: Macmillan, 1961), p. 159.

58. *New York Times*, November 30, 1873, p. 5.

59. *New York Times*, November 22, 1873, p. 6.

60. *New York Times*, December 1, 1873, p. 2; "Unbecoming Haste," *The Episcopalian*, n.d., in Clippings Book No. 2, p. 36.

61. "The Case of Bishop Cummins," *Philadelphia Inquirer*, December 1, 1873, p. 3.

62. Aycrigg, *Memoirs*, p. 118.

63. Ibid.

64. "The Case of Bishop Cummins," *New York Times*, November 30, 1873, p. 4.

65. *New York Times*, December 2, 1873, p. 4.

66. Craik, in Swinford and Lee, *The Great Elm Tree*, p. 319.

67. Muhlenberg, "An Exposition of the Memorial" (November 1854), in *Evangelical and Catholic Papers: A Collection of Essays, Letters and Tractates from the Writings of Rev. William Augustus Muhlenberg, D.D.*, ed. Anne Ayres (New York: Thomas Whittaker, 1875), pp. 79–84. See also Alvin W. Skardon, *Church Leader in the Cities: William Augustus Muhlenberg* (Philadelphia: University of Pennsylvania Press, 1971), pp. 210, 223.

68. Leacock, *Personal Recollections*, p. 49.

69. *New York Times*, December 2, 1873, p. 5.

70. Leacock, *Personal Recollections*, p. 49.

71. A. Cummins, *Memoir of George David Cummins*, p. 439.

72. Leacock, *Personal Recollections*, p. 49.

73. Ibid.

74. *Journal of the First General Council of the Reformed Episcopal Church, . . . December 2d, 1873* (New York: Edward O. Jenkins, 1874), p. 7; "The Cummins Movement," *Philadelphia Inquirer*, December 3, 1873, p. 1.

75. Leacock, *Personal Recollections*, p. 50.

76. Cummins, "Address," in *Journal of the First General Council*, p. 9. The full text of Cummins's address is also reported in a *New York Tribune* clipping in the Leacock Miscellanies Book, pp. 103–104.

77. Cummins, "Address," in *Journal of the First General Council*, p. 18.

78. Ibid., p. 19.

79. Ibid., p. 20; A. Cummins, *Memoir of George David Cummins*, p. 436.

80. Cummins, "Address," in *Journal of the First General Council*, pp. 21–22.

81. "The Cummins Movement," *Philadelphia Inquirer,* December 3, 1873, p. 1. See also *Journal of the First General Council,* p. 22.

82. Leacock, *Personal Recollections,* p. 49.

83. *Journal of the First General Council,* p. 24; "New Religious Movement," *New York Times,* December 3, 1873, p. 8; "The Episcopal Schism," *New York Tribune,* December 3, 1873, in Leacock Miscellanies Book, p. 105.

84. "New Religious Movement," *New York Times,* December 3, 1873, p. 8; "The Episcopal Schism," Leacock Miscellanies Book, p. 105.

85. Leacock, *Personal Recollections,* p. 51.

86. Ibid., pp. 51–52.

87. "New Religious Movement," *New York Times,* December 3, 1873, p. 8; Longmire, "Charles Edwards Cheney," p. 26.

88. "New Religious Movement," *New York Times,* December 3, 1873, p. 8.

89. Leacock, *Personal Recollections,* p. 51.

CHAPTER 5

1. On the links between religious rationalism and the rationalizations of the market, see Christopher Hill, *The Century of Revolution, 1603–1714* (New York: W. W. Norton, 1961), pp. 75–86, and James Turner, *Without God, Without Creed: The Origins of Unbelief in America* (Baltimore: Johns Hopkins University Press, 1985), pp. 133–137.

2. Charles Hodge, *Systematic Theology* (1871–73; reprint, Grand Rapids, Mich.: William B. Eerdmans, 1979), vol. 1, p. 10.

3. The best studies of the assimilation of "Baconianism" and natural-law apologetics into evangelical thought are Herman Hovenkamp, *Science and Religion in America, 1800–1860* (Philadelphia: University of Pennsylvania Press, 1978), pp. 3–49, and Theodore Dwight Bozeman, *Protestants in an Age of Science: The Baconian Ideal and Antebellum Religious Thought* (Chapel Hill, N.C.: University of North Carolina Press, 1977), pp. 3–86. Also highly illuminating are Mark A. Noll, *Princeton and the Republic, 1768–1822: The Search for a Christian Enlightenment* (Princeton: Princeton University Press, 1989); Lefferts A. Loetscher, *Between the Enlightenment and Pietism: Archibald Alexander and the Founding of Princeton Theological Seminary* (Westport, Conn.: Greenwood Press, 1983); and chapter 5 of Bruce Kuklick's *Churchmen and Philosophers: From Jonathan Edwards to John Dewey* (New Haven: Yale University Press, 1985).

4. George M. Marsden, *Fundamentalism and American Culture: The Shaping of Twentieth-Century Evangelicalism, 1870–1925* (New York: Oxford University Press, 1980), p. 20.

5. For a parallel development within an even more rationalized religious culture, see Daniel Walker Howe's discussion of the conflict between old-line and liberal Unitarians in the 1850s, in *The Unitarian Conscience: Harvard Moral Philosophy, 1805–1861* (Cambridge, Mass.: Harvard University Press, 1970), pp. 172–173, 208–209. On the impact of capitalism on American religion, see Ann Douglas, *The Feminization of American Culture* (New York: Avon Books, 1978), p. 111.

6. William G. McLoughlin, *The Meaning of Henry Ward Beecher: An Essay on the Shifting Values of Mid-Victorian America, 1840–1870* (New York: Alfred Knopf, 1970), p. 176.

7. Mason Gallagher, *An Open Letter to Bishop James S. Johnston, D.D., of the Protestant Episcopal Diocese of Western Texas, concerning his address on Cahenslyism* (Philadelphia: James M. Armstrong, 1893), pp. 3–4, 6, 7, 14.

8. "Ritualism and Rome, an Interview with Bishop Potter on the Reform Movement in the Church," *New York Herald,* December 6, 1873, p. 1.

9. "Il Fait Accompli," *The Episcopalian*, December 17, 1873, in Clippings Book No. 2, p. 47, Archives of the Reformed Episcopal Church, Philadelphia Theological Seminary, Philadelphia.

10. "The New Episcopal Church," *The Church Union* (n.d.), in Leacock Miscellanies Book, p. 109, Archives of the Reformed Episcopal Church.

11. Charles Edward Cheney, *The Reformed Episcopal Church: A Sermon Preached in Christ Church, Chicago* (Chicago: Perry, Morris & Sultzer, 1874), pp. 4, 15, 20.

12. "The Protestant Episcopal Church and the New Reform Movement," in Leacock Miscellanies Book, p. 116. See also Alexandrine Cummins, *Memoir of George David Cummins, D.D., First Bishop of the Reformed Episcopal Church* (Philadelphia: E. Claxton, 1878), pp. 443–444.

13. Benjamin Aycrigg, *Memoirs of the Reformed Episcopal Church* (New York: Edward O. Jenkins, 1880), p. 120.

14. Ibid., p. 39.

15. Ibid., p. 120; Annie Darling Price, *A History of the Formation and Growth of the Reformed Episcopal Church, 1873–1902* (Philadelphia: James M. Armstrong, 1902), p. 152.

16. "Consecration of Bishop Cheney in Christ Church, Chicago," in Leacock Miscellanies Book, p. 111.

17. Ibid., p. 110. See also Rodney H. Longmire, "Charles Edward Cheney, Bishop of the Reformed Episcopal Church" (S.T.M. thesis, Lutheran Theological Seminary, Philadelphia, 1965), p. 34.

18. "Appendix D," in *Journal of the Proceedings of the Second General Council of the Reformed Episcopal Church, held in the First Reformed Episcopal Church, New York City, Commencing Wednesday, May 13, and ending Tuesday, May 19, 1874* (Philadelphia: James A. Moore, 1874), p. 21.

19. The first published text of Cummins's sermon is found in a special supplement to *The Episcopalian*, December 17, 1873, and was later published in pamphlet form as *Primitive Episcopacy: Bishop Cummins' Sermon at the Consecration of Bishop Cheney* (New York: Edward O. Jenkins, 1874). All quotations from Cummins's sermon in these paragraphs are from the transcript published in *The Episcopalian*.

20. "'Bishop' Cheney, The Manner of His 'Consecration' Yesterday," in *Chicago Tribune*, December 15, 1873, p. 1.

21. "Cheney," *Chicago Times*, in Leacock Miscellanies Book, p. 117.

22. "Pictures of the Day," in Leacock Miscellanies Book, p. 125.

23. John Fulton, *Letter to a Presbyter of Illinois on the Reconciliation of Schismatics, and on the Validity of Ordinations by a Deposed Bishop* (Mobile, Ala.: Henry Farrow, 1874), pp. 13–14.

24. "New Religious Movement," *New York Times*, December 3, 1873, p. 5.

25. Cheney, "The Reformed Episcopalian and His Bishop," in *What Do Reformed Episcopalians Believe? Eight Sermons Preached in Christ Church, Chicago* (Philadelphia: Reformed Episcopal Publication Society, 1888), p. 98.

26. Leacock, *Personal Recollections Connected with the Reformed Episcopal Church*, ed. Robert K. Rudolph (Philadelphia: Reformed Episcopal Publication Society, 1976), pp. 74–76.

27. A. Cummins, *Memoir of George David Cummins*, pp. 458, 451.

28. "The New Episcopal Movement, Interesting Services in Peoria," in Leacock Miscellanies Book, p. 112.

29. "Moncton, New Brunswick, The Opening Services, January 11th," in Clippings Book No. 2, pp. 81–82.

30. "Moncton, New Brunswick," in Clippings Book No. 2, pp. 92–93.

31. "Program of the Seventy-Fifth Anniversary of Grace Chapel, April 3, 1949," Archives of the Reformed Episcopal Church.

32. "Reformed Protestant Episcopal Church," in Clippings Book No. 3, Archives of the Reformed Episcopal Church, p. 22.

33. "Emmanuel Church of Louisville, Ky., Withdraws from the Old Organization, and Follows the Lead of its Pastor," in Clippings Book No. 5, Archives of the Reformed Episcopal Church, p. 52.

34. "Kentucky, First Reformed Episcopal Church," from *The Episcopalian*, in Clippings Book No. 5, p. 55.

35. *Journal of the Proceedings of the Third General Council of the Reformed Episcopal Church, Commencing Wednesday, May 12, and ending Tuesday, May 18, 1875* (Philadelphia: James A. Moore, 1875), p. 22.

36. "Bishop Cummins' Visitation to Ottawa," in Clippings Book No. 5, pp. 59-60. See also A. Cummins, *Memoir of George David Cummins*, p. 462.

37. "New Jersey" and "New Jersey, Newark," in Clippings Book No. 5, pp. 75, 76-77.

38. "Opening Services of the Reformed Episcopal Church," in Clippings Book No. 2, p. 55; Leacock, *Personal Recollections*, p. 61; "The New Church, Inaugural Services, Sermon by Bishop Cummins," *New York Times*, January 5, 1874, p. 5.

39. "Religious Movements, Foundations of a New Church," *New York Tribune*, January 5, 1874, p. 2.

40. Stephen R. Graham, "Philip Schaff and the Protestant Mind in the Nineteenth Century: A Critique of Religion and Society," *Fides et Historia* 21 (January 1989): 36.

41. "First Reformed Episcopal Church of New York City," in Clippings Book No. 2, pp. 95-96.

42. "First Reformed Episcopal Church, of New York, Report of the Committee on Organization," in Clippings Book No. 2, p. 98; Leacock, *Personal Recollections*, pp. 61-63.

43. "Bishop Cummins's New Departure," *Church Journal*, March 16, 1874, in Clippings Book No. 5, p. 32.

44. A. Cummins, *Memoirs of George David Cummins*, p. 459.

45. Leacock, *Personal Recollections*, p. 65.

46. "Building the Old Waste Places," *Episcopal Recorder* 96 (December 1919): 7.

47. Vestry Minutes, April 24, 1874, April 30, 1874, April 24, 1875, and May 1, 1876, First Reformed Episcopal Church, New York City.

48. "Illinois," in Clippings Book No. 2, p. 97.

49. Longmire, "Charles Edward Cheney," pp. 39-40.

50. Cheney, "The Evangelical Ideal of a Visible Church," in *Journal of the Proceedings of the Second General Council of the Reformed Episcopal Church . . . Commencing Wednesday, May 13, and ending Tuesday, May 19, 1874* (Philadelphia: James A. Moore, 1874), p. 20.

51. The basic materials on Nicholson's life can be found in *William Rufus Nicholson: Bishop of the Reformed Episcopal Church* (privately printed, 1903), pp. 5-7.

52. Ernest Sandeen, *The Roots of Fundamentalism: British and American Millenarianism, 1800-1930* (Chicago: University of Chicago Press, 1970), p. 149. And yet Sandeen seriously exaggerates the influence of dispensationalism within the Reformed Episcopal Church as a whole when he suggests that dispensationalism had some precipitating role to play in the actual founding of the Reformed Episcopal Church. Cummins never displayed any particular interest in "prophetic" subjects in any of his surviving sermons or papers or in his oft-repeated reasons for the founding of the Reformed Episcopal Church. Cheney was unsympathetic to Nicholson's dispensationalism (or at least to Nicholson's brand of it), and the clergy who espoused dispensationalism never constituted more than an important minority.

53. Cheney, in *William Rufus Nicholson*, pp. 20-21.

54. "New Jersey," in Clippings Book No. 5, p. 72.

55. "Philadelphia" and "Second Reformed Episcopal Church," in Clippings Book No. 5, pp. 32–34, 76.

56. Aycrigg, *Memoirs*, p. 198.

57. "The Late Bishop Edward Cridge," *Episcopal Recorder*, May 22, 1913, p. 3; F. A. Peake, *The Anglican Church in British Columbia* (Vancouver: Mitchell Press, 1959), pp. 78–81; Philip Carrington, *The Anglican Church in Canada: A History* (Toronto: Collins, 1963), p. 150.

58. Price, *History*, p. 244; Peake, *Anglican Church in British Columbia*, pp. 82–84.

59. "British America, Particulars of the Formation of a Reformed Episcopal Church in Victoria, British Columbia," in Clippings Book No. 5, p. 64.

60. Price, *History*, p. 273; Peake, *Anglican Church in British Columbia*, p. 84.

61. Alice Katharine Fallows, *Everybody's Bishop, Being the Life and Times of the Right Reverend Samuel Fallows, D.D.* (New York: J. H. Sears, 1927), pp. 190–191.

62. Carter, *The Spiritual Crisis of the Gilded Age* (Dekalb: Northern Illinois University Press, 1971), p. 184.

63. Howard-Smith, "Divine Inspiration," in *Journal of the Proceedings of the Ninth General Council of the Reformed Episcopal Church, . . . Commencing Wednesday, May 23rd, and ending Monday, May 28th, 1883* (Philadelphia: William Syckelmore, 1883), Appendix, p. 10.

64. Howard-Smith, *The Historic Basis of the Reformed Episcopal Church* (Philadelphia: Reformed Episcopal Publication Society, 1883), p. 5.

65. Cummins, "Sermon," in *Journal of the Third General Council, 1875*, Appendix, p. 14.

66. Ibid., p. 18.

67. Dabney, "Ecclesiastical Equality of Negroes," in *Discussions: Evangelical and Theological* (1891; reprint, Edinburgh: Banner of Truth Trust, 1967), vol. 2, pp. 203–204.

68. Clarence L. Mohr, *On the Threshold of Freedom: Masters and Slaves in Civil War Georgia* (Athens, Ga.: University of Georgia Press, 1986), pp. 251–254.

69. Albert Sidney Thomas, *A Historical Account of the Protestant Episcopal Church in South Carolina, 1820–1957* (Columbia, S.C.: R. L. Bryan, 1957), p. 89.

70. Ibid., p. 448.

71. Ibid., p. 404.

72. Herbert McCarrier, "A History of the Missionary Jurisdiction of the South of the Reformed Episcopal Church," *HMPEC* 41 (1972): 200; Thomas, *Historical Account*, p. 485; Peter F. Stevens to J. W. Treen, October 9, 1892, Archives of the Reformed Episcopal Church.

73. Frank C. Ferguson to J. W. Treen, undated, Archives of the Reformed Episcopal Church.

74. Stevens to Treen, October 9, 1892, Archives of the Reformed Episcopal Church.

75. Ferguson, in McCarrier, "History of the Missionary Jurisdiction," p. 201.

76. Ibid.

77. Ferguson to Treen, in Archives of the Reformed Episcopal Church.

78. A. Cummins, *Memoir of George David Cummins*, p. 483.

79. Johnson, in *Journal of the Proceedings of the Fourth General Council of the Reformed Episcopal Church, . . . Commencing Wednesday, July 12, and ending Monday, July 17, 1876* (Philadelphia: James A. Moore, 1876), p. 55.

80. Ibid., p. 57.

81. "The 'Monthly Record' and Bishop Cummins!" (n.d.), pp. 2–3, in Robert Livingston Rudolph Papers, Archives of the Reformed Episcopal Church.

82. A. Cummins, *Memoir of George David Cummins*, pp. 486–487; McCarrier, "History of the Missionary Jurisdiction," pp. 203–204.

83. Johnson, in *Journal of the Fourth General Council, 1876*, p. 57.

84. McCarrier, "History of the Missionary Jurisdiction," p. 205.

85. Johnson, in *Journal of the Fourth General Council, 1876*, p. 57.

86. Merryweather, in Frank Vaughan, *A History of the Free Church of England* (London: Free Church of England Publications Committee, 1960), pp. 39–40.

87. Ibid., p. 38.

88. Ibid., pp. 40–42.

89. "Correspondence with the Free Church of England," in *Journal of the Second General Council, 1874*, Appendix E, p. 23.

90. Cummins to Aycrigg, June 1, 1875, in Benjamin Aycrigg Papers, Archives of the Reformed Episcopal Church.

91. Marshall Smith to Aycrigg, March 8, 1877, in Aycrigg Papers.

92. Alfred S. Richardson to Aycrigg, February 16, 1877, in Aycrigg Papers.

93. "Correspondence with the Free Church of England," in *Journal of the Second General Council, 1874*, Appendix E, p. 24.

94. Vaughan, *History of the Free Church*, pp. 43–44.

95. Aycrigg, *Memoirs*, pp. 271, 281.

96. Even more unusual was the response offered when it was objected, in the Free Church Convocation, that Price was ineligible to receive episcopal consecration because he had never been episcopally ordained as a deacon or priest. As Cridge reported to the General Council, the objectors yielded to the argument "that Episcopal ordination covered all the ground," a view that implies that the episcopate "contains" all other orders within itself. It is interesting that this was a typically Anglo-Catholic argument, and hardly Evangelical. See *Journal of the Proceedings of the Fifth General Council of the Reformed Episcopal Church, . . . Commencing Wednesday, May 9, and ending Tuesday, May 15, 1877* (Philadelphia: James A. Moore, 1877), p. 23.

97. Alfred S. Richardson to Aycrigg, February 16, 1877, in Aycrigg Papers.

98. Price, *History*, p. 226.

99. Nicholson, in *Journal of the Fourth General Council, 1876*, p. 24.

CHAPTER 6

1. Cummins, in *Journal of the Third General Council of the Reformed Episcopal Church, . . . Commencing Wednesday, May 12, and ending Tuesday, May 18, 1875* (Philadelphia: James A. Moore, 1875), pp. 21–22.

2. Alexandrine Cummins, *Memoir of George David Cummins, First Bishop of the Reformed Episcopal Church* (Philadelphia: E. Claxton, 1878), pp. 520, 522.

3. The lead editorial in *The Appeal* on Cummins's death was probably written by Samuel Fallows. A clipping of the editorial is pasted into Leacock Miscellanies Book, p. 164, Archives of the Reformed Episcopal Church, Philadelphia Theological Seminary, Philadelphia.

4. "Funeral of Bishop Cummins," from *The Appeal*, also in Leacock Miscellanies Book, p. 166.

5. Cheney, "The Preacher Bishop" [July 2, 1876], in *Sermons* (Chicago: Cushing, Thomas & Co., 1880), pp. 234–235.

6. Nicholson, "The Priesthood of the Church of God," in *Journal of the Fourth General Council of the Reformed Episcopal Church, . . . Commencing Wednesday, July 12, and ending Monday, July 17, 1876* (Philadelphia: James A. Moore, 1876), p. 26.

7. "Funeral of Bishop Cummins," from *The Appeal*, in Leacock Miscellanies Book,

p. 166. See also A. Cummins, *Memoir of George David Cummins*, p. 521. Nicholson also reported Cummins's exhortation to the General Council several weeks later as simply "Tell them to go forward" (*Journal of the Fourth General Council, 1876*, p. 25).

8. *Journal of the Proceedings of the Second General Council of the Reformed Episcopal Church, . . . Commencing Wednesday, May 13, and ending Tuesday, May 19, 1874* (Philadelphia: James A. Moore, 1874), p. 16.

9. Ibid., p. 26.

10. Ibid., p. 24.

11. Aycrigg, *Memoirs of the Reformed Episcopal Church* (New York: Edward O. Jenkins, 1880), p. 277.

12. Cheney, "Digging Out Stopped-Up Wells," in *A Neglected Power and Other Sermons* (New York: Fleming H. Revell Co., 1916), p. 169.

13. Cheney to Aycrigg, November 15, 1878, in Aycrigg Papers, Archives of the Reformed Episcopal Church.

14. *Episcopal Recorder and Covenant*, November 5, 1881, p. 4.

15. "The Episcopate: Views of a Layman" (n.d.), pp. 10–11, Archives of the Reformed Episcopal Church.

16. Alexandrine Cummins to Aycrigg, September 28, 1880, in Aycrigg, *Memoirs*, pp. 372–373.

17. George David Cummins, in ibid., p. 278.

18. "The Reformed Episcopalians, the Second General Council," *New York Herald*, May 14, 1874, p. 1. See also "The Reformed Episcopalians, Second Day's Proceedings of the General Council," *New York Herald*, May 15, 1874, p. 1, and "Work of the New Church," *New York Tribune*, May 16, 1874, p. 1.

19. Leacock, *Personal Recollections Connected with the Reformed Episcopal Church*, ed. R. K. Rudolph (Philadelphia: Reformed Episcopal Publication Society, 1976), pp. 72–73.

20. Cummins, "Antioch and Its Warning" (January 11, 1874), in Cummins sermon manuscript Book, Bishop Cummins Memorial Reformed Episcopal Church, Catonsville, Md.

21. "Report of Bishop Nicholson," in *Journal of the Proceedings of the Tenth General Council of the Reformed Episcopal Church, . . . Commencing Wednesday, May 27th, and ending Monday, June 1st, 1885* (Philadelphia: Reformed Episcopal Publication Society, 1885), p. 41.

22. H. Alexander to Aycrigg, December 30, 1874, in Aycrigg Papers, Archives of the Reformed Episcopal Church.

23. Aycrigg, *Memoirs*, p. 277.

24. Cummins to Aycrigg, May 5, 1876, in Aycrigg Papers. See also Aycrigg, *Memoirs*, pp. 278–279.

25. *Journal of the Proceedings of the Fourth General Council, 1876*, p. 34.

26. *Journal of the Fourth General Council, 1876*, pp. 66, 70–71.

27. *Journal of the Sixth General Council of the Reformed Episcopal Church, . . . Commencing Wednesday, May 8, and ending Monday, May 13, 1878* (Philadelphia: James A. Moore, 1878), pp. 56, 62, 67.

28. The editorial from *Church and State* is pasted into the Leacock Miscellanies Book, pp. 135–136. See also Aycrigg, *Memoirs*, pp. 44–45.

29. "The Reformed Episcopal Church in Council," *New York Herald*, May 17, 1874, p. 4.

30. "Reformers at Work," *New York Tribune*, May 20, 1874, p. 4.

31. "An Explanation from Dr. Muhlenberg," *New York Tribune*, May 17, 1874, p. 3.

32. Aycrigg to Joseph Dawson Wilson, July 17, 1882, in Aycrigg Papers. See also Aycrigg, *Memoirs*, pp. 360–362.

33. Cheney, "The Reformed Episcopalian and His Duty to His Own Church," in *What Do Reformed Episcopalians Believe? Eight Sermons Preached in Christ Church, Chicago* (Philadelphia: Reformed Episcopal Publication Society, 1888), p. 62.

34. Douglas W. Frank, *Less Than Conquerors: How Evangelicals Entered the Twentieth Century* (Grand Rapids, Mich.: William B. Eerdmans, 1986), pp. 103–166.

35. *Journal of the Second General Council, 1874*, pp. 20–21, Appendix F, p. 42.

36. Leacock, in Aycrigg, *Memoirs*, p. 199.

37. George Marsden, *Fundamentalism and American Culture: The Shaping of Twentieth-Century Evangelicalism, 1870–1925* (New York: Oxford University Press, 1980), pp. 51–54.

38. Thomas H. Powers to Marshall Smith, May 11, 1878, Archives of the Reformed Episcopal Church.

39. Aycrigg, *Memoirs*, p. 307.

40. *Journal of the Second General Council, 1874*, p. 14.

41. Leacock, *Personal Recollections*, p. 66.

42. Wilson to Aycrigg, July 11, 1882, in Aycrigg Papers.

43. "Articles of Religion of the Reformed Episcopal Church in America, A.D. 1875," in *The Creeds of Christendom, with a History and Critical Notes*, ed. Philip Schaff (1877; reprint, Grand Rapids, Mich.: Baker Book House, 1969), vol. 3, p. 820.

44. Ibid., p. 822.

45. Ibid., pp. 822–823.

46. Ibid., pp. 817–818.

47. Aycrigg to T. H. Gregg, September 10, 1877, in Aycrigg Papers.

48. Aycrigg to Samuel Fallows, January 3, 1879, in Aycrigg Papers.

49. Aycrigg to Joseph Dawson Wilson, July 17, 1882, in Aycrigg Papers.

50. Sabine, in *William Rufus Nicholson, D.D.: Bishop of the Reformed Episcopal Church* (privately printed, 1903), p. 11.

51. Wilson to Aycrigg, July 11, 1882, in Aycrigg Papers.

52. *Journal of the Third General Council, 1875*, p. 53.

53. Wilson to Aycrigg, July 11, 1882, in Aycrigg Papers.

54. *Journal of the Third General Council, 1875*, pp. 20–21.

55. *Journal of the Second General Council, 1874*, p. 5.

56. *Journal of the Fourth General Council, 1876*, pp. 25, 53–54.

57. Ibid., p. 54.

58. Joseph Dawson Wilson to Benjamin Aycrigg, May 8, 1879, in Aycrigg Papers.

59. Gallagher, *Errors and Mistakes of the Reformed Episcopal Church* (Stamford, Conn.: Gillespie Bros., 1886), p. 17.

60. "The Episcopate: The Views of a Presbyter" (n.d.), pp. 1, 4–5, Archives of the Reformed Episcopal Church.

61. Gallagher, *Mistakes and Errors of the Reformed Episcopal Church*, p. 12.

62. "Address of Bishop Cheney, June 4, 1880," *Episcopal Recorder*, in Leacock Miscellanies Book, p. 234.

63. *Journal of the Proceedings of the Fifth General Council of the Reformed Episcopal Church, . . . Commencing Wednesday, May 9, and ending Tuesday, May 15, 1877* (Philadelphia: James A. Moore, 1877), p. 54.

64. "Bishop Nicholson's Report," in *Journal of the Sixth General Council, 1878*, p. 35; "Episcopalians, The Convocation of the Reformed Church," in Leacock Miscellanies Book, p. 177.

65. "Convocation, The New Reformed Episcopal Church," in Leacock Miscellanies, Book, p. 177.

66. *Journal of the Proceedings of the Seventh General Council of the Reformed Episcopal*

Church, . . . Commencing Wednesday, May 28th, and ending Wednesday, June 4th, 1879 (Chicago: Rand, McNally & Co., 1879), p. 64; "Synod of New York," from *Episcopal Recorder,* in Leacock Miscellanies Book, pp. 192–193.

67. "The Synod of New York and Philadelphia," *Episcopal Recorder,* in Leacock Miscellanies Book, pp. 239–240.

68. "The Synod of New York and Philadelphia," *Episcopal Recorder,* in Leacock Miscellanies Book, pp. 225, 230.

69. *Minutes of the Formation of the First Synod of the R.E. Church, Dominion of Canada, . . . Montreal, 26th May, 1880,* in Robert Livingston Rudolph Papers, Archives of the Reformed Episcopal Church.

70. Henry Alexander to Aycrigg, October 12, 1877, in Aycrigg Papers.

71. F. S. Merryweather to Henry Alexander, February 19, 1877, in Aycrigg Papers.

72. Frank Vaughan, *A History of the Free Church of England, Otherwise called the Reformed Episcopal Church* (Bungay, Suffolk: The Free Church of England Publications Committee, 1960), pp. 75–76.

73. Norton to Aycrigg, February 24, 1877, in Aycrigg Papers.

74. "The Right Reverend T. Huband Gregg, D.D., M.D.," *Biographical Magazine* 8 (February 1887): 192–193, 199.

75. Gregg, *The Ridsdale Case and the Bennett Judgment* (London: Marlborough & Co., 1877), p. 7.

76. Gregg to Aycrigg, December 16, 1876, in Aycrigg Papers.

77. Gregg to Alfred Richardson, February 16, 1877, in Aycrigg Papers.

78. Richardson to Benjamin Aycrigg, January 29, 1877, in Aycrigg Papers.

79. On Cheney's opposition, see Edward D. Neill's letter to Charles D. Kellogg, secretary of the General Committee, September 22, 1879, Archives of the Reformed Episcopal Church.

80. *Journal of the Proceedings of the Fifth General Council, 1877,* p. 84.

81. Aycrigg to Thomas Huband Gregg, November 26, 1877, in Aycrigg Papers.

82. Gregg to Marshall Smith, November 6, 1877, Archives of the Reformed Episcopal Church.

83. Aycrigg to Thomas Huband Gregg, November 26, 1877, in Aycrigg Papers.

84. *Journal of the Proceedings of the Sixth General Council, 1879,* p. 93.

85. "America," *Reformed Church Record* 10 (April 1889): 30.

86. *Journal of the Proceedings of the Seventh General Council, 1879,* p. 50.

87. Aycrigg, *Memoirs,* 324; "Consecration of a Bishop of the Reformed Episcopal Church," *Southend Standard,* November 8, 1878, p. 4.

88. Wilson to Benjamin Aycrigg, October 3, 1879, Aycrigg Papers.

89. Norton to Benjamin Aycrigg, December 31, 1878, in Aycrigg Papers.

90. General Committee minutes, January 29, 1879, in General Committee Minute Book, 1879, pp. 6, 8.

91. *Journal of the Proceedings of the Seventh General Council, 1879,* pp. 29, 43.

92. "Report of Bishop Nicholson," in *Journal of the Proceedings of the Eighth General Council of the Reformed Episcopal Church, Commencing Wednesday, May 25th, and ending Monday, May 30th, 1881* (Philadelphia: William Syckelmore, 1881), p. 33.

93. *Journal of the Proceedings of the Seventh General Council, 1879,* pp. 89, 97.

94. J. P. Fleming, Tonbridge, Kent, to Benjamin Aycrigg, January 8, 1879, in Aycrigg Papers.

95. Ussher, March 31, 1879 (privately printed circular letter), in Leacock Miscellanies Book, p. 203.

96. Wilson to Benjamin Aycrigg, May 8, 1879, in Aycrigg Papers.

97. Janet Mayo, *A History of Ecclesiastical Dress* (London: Batsford, 1984), pp. 84–88,

99–100. See also Percy Dearmer, *The Ornaments of the Ministers* (London: A. R. Mowbray, 1908), pp. 127–128, 146–147, 149, 167.

98. See the engraving of Cummins in William Stevens Perry, *The Episcopate in America: Sketches Biographical and Bibliographical* (New York, 1895), and in Alexandrine Cummins, *Memoir of George David Cummins.*

99. James Allen Latane, *A Plea for the Settlement of the Question of Ecclesiastical Vestments in the Reformed Episcopal Church* (n.d.), p. 5.

100. "The Early Use of the Surplice in Connecticut," in *Connecticut Churchmanship: Records and Historical Papers Concerning the Anglican Church in Connecticut in the Eighteenth and Early Nineteenth Centuries,* ed. Kenneth Walter Cameron (Hartford, Conn.: Transcendental Books, 1969), p. 7.

101. James M. Gray, *The Romeward Drift of the Protestant Episcopal Church in 1887* (Boston, n.d.), pp. 3–4.

102. Mayo, *History of Ecclesiastical Dress,* pp. 103–104.

103. Latane, *Plea for Settlement,* p. 4.

104. Leacock, *Personal Recollections,* p. 55.

105. Cheney, *The Surplice and the Bishop's Robes* (n.p., 1895), p. 16.

106. Leacock, *Personal Recollections,* p. 56.

107. Ibid., Appendix p. 10.

108. Cheney, *The Surplice and the Bishop's Robes,* pp. 20–21; Aycrigg, *Memoirs,* p. 258.

109. A. Cummins, *Memoir of George David Cummins,* p. 262.

110. Leacock, *Personal Recollections,* p. 59.

111. Leacock, in *Episcopal Recorder,* November 16, 1894, p. 4.

112. Aycrigg, *Memoirs,* p. 255.

113. Peter F. Stevens, "Church Unity," in *Journal of the Proceedings of the Twelfth General Council of the Reformed Episcopal Church, . . . Commencing Wednesday, May 22nd, and ending Monday, May 27th, 1889* (Philadelphia: Reformed Episcopal Publication Society, 1889), Appendix p. 10.

114. *Questions and Answers About the Protestant Episcopal Church* (n.p., n.d.), pp. 3–4, Archives of the Reformed Episcopal Church.

115. Latane, *A Plea for the Settlement,* p. 97.

116. Leacock, *Personal Recollections,* p. 58.

117. Rodney H. Longmire, "Charles Edward Cheney, Bishop of the Reformed Episcopal Church" (S.T.M. thesis, Lutheran Theological Seminary, Philadelphia, 1965), p. 58.

118. Latane, *A Plea for the Settlement,* p. 5.

119. Ibid., p. 7.

120. Cheney, *The Surplice and the Bishop's Robes,* p. 7.

121. Cheney, "Loyalty to the Reformed Episcopal Church," in *1884–85 Yearbook and Calendar of the Reformed Episcopal Church* (Philadelphia: Reformed Episcopal Publication Society, 1885), p. 19.

122. Latane, *Plea for the Settlement,* p. 19.

123. Ibid., p. 96.

124. Ibid., p. 87.

125. See newspaper accounts of the debates, which reported the speeches on the issue of vestments in greater fullness than the council journal: *New York Sun,* June 11 and 12, 1897; *New York Evening Sun,* June 11, 1897; *New York Herald,* June 11, 1897; *New York Mail and Express,* June 11, 1897; *New York Times,* June 12, 1897.

126. *Journal of the Proceedings of the Fifteenth General Council of the Reformed Episcopal Church, . . . Commencing Wednesday, June 9th, and ending Monday, June 14th, 1897* (Philadelphia: Reformed Episcopal Publication Society, 1897), pp. 87–88.

127. Smith to Benjamin Aycrigg, July 27, 1880, in Aycrigg Papers.

CHAPTER 7

1. E. J. Hobsbawm, *The Age of Empire, 1875–1914* (New York: Pantheon, 1987), pp. 271–272.

2. James R. Moore, "Theodicy and Society: The Crisis of the Intelligentsia," in *Victorian Faith in Crisis: Essays on Continuity and Change in Nineteenth-Century Religious Belief*, ed. R. J. Helmstedter and B. Lightman (London: Macmillan, 1990), p. 154.

3. Paul R. Conkin, *Puritans and Pragmatists: Eight Eminent American Thinkers* (New York: Dodd, Mead, 1968), p. 260; Martin Marty, *Modern American Religion*, vol. 1, *The Irony of It All, 1893–1919* (Chicago: University of Chicago Press, 1986), p. 70; James Hoopes, *Consciousnesss in New England: From Puritanism and Ideas to Psychoanalysis and Semiotic* (Baltimore: Johns Hopkins University Press, 1989), pp. 192–205.

4. James Turner, *Without God, Without Creed: The Origins of Unbelief in America* (Baltimore: Johns Hopkins University Press, 1985), p. 189.

5. D. H. Meyer, "The Victorian Crisis of Faith," in *Victorian America*, ed. D. W. Howe (Philadelphia: University of Pennsylvania Press, 1976), p. 76.

6. T. J. Jackson Lears, *No Place of Grace: Antimodernism and the Transformation of American Culture, 1880–1920* (New York: Pantheon, 1981), p. 301.

7. Ferenc Morton Szasz, *The Divided Mind of Protestant America, 1880–1930* (University, Ala.: University of Alabama Press, 1982), p. 73.

8. Eric Foner, *Politics and Ideology in the Age of the Civil War* (New York: Oxford University Press, 1980), p. 26.

9. Thomas J. Richards to Robert L. Rudolph, March 31, 1930, in Robert Livingston Rudolph Papers, Archives of the Reformed Episcopal Church, Philadelphia Theological Seminary, Philadelphia.

10. William Rufus Nicholson, *The Reformed Episcopal Church: Its Doctrines, Worship and Work* (Philadelphia: Covenant Publishing, 1881), p. 11.

11. William Russell Collins to Robert L. Rudolph, December 6, 1928, in Rudolph Papers.

12. "Social Position," *Episcopal Recorder*, February 19, 1881, p. 1.

13. Sabine, Ms. Visitation Book for 1902, p. 92, Archives of the Reformed Episcopal Church.

14. "Report of the Committee on the State of the Synod," in *Minutes of the Proceedings of the Twenty-Sixth Council of the New York and Philadelphia Synod of the Reformed Episcopal Church* (Philadelphia: James M. Armstrong, 1907), 32.

15. W.A.L. Jett, "The Spirit's Presence the Great Need of the Church," in *Minutes of the Proceedings of the Twenty-Fifth Council of the New York and Philadelphia Synod of the Reformed Episcopal Church* (Philadelphia: James M. Armstrong, 1905), p. 9.

16. Cheney, *What Is the Reformed Episcopal Church?* (Chicago: Evangelical Episcopalian Co., 1911), pp. 15–16.

17. D. O. Kellogg, *Events Leading to the Formation of the Reformed Episcopal Church, Read at the Twentieth Anniversary of the Founding of the Church, in the First R.E. Church, New York City, December 3, 1893* (Philadelphia: Reformed Episcopal Publication Society, 1894), pp. 3, 8.

18. Collins, "The Centenary of the Episcopal Recorder," *Episcopal Recorder*, October 1924, p. 4.

19. Brewing, "The Spirit of the Founders," *Episcopal Recorder*, May 1924, pp. 8–9.

20. D. M. Stearns, *"Salvation Is from the Jews"; or, God's Purpose Concerning Israel* (Harrisburg, Pa.: F. Kelker, 1882), pp. 24–25.

21. "The Board of Trustees of the Looney-Hoffman Fund," in *Minutes of the Proceedings of the Thirty-Fourth Council of the New York and Philadelphia Synod of the Reformed Episcopal Church* (Philadelphia: James M. Armstrong, 1914), p. 51.

22. Robert L. Rudolph to William Freemantle, July 28, 1927, in Rudolph Papers.

23. Robert L. Rudolph to Charles Edward Cheney, June 19, 1914, in Rudolph Papers.

24. Robert L. Rudolph to William Freemantle, July 28, 1927, in Rudolph Papers.

25. Wilson to William Russell Collins, June 12, 1916, in Rudolph Papers.

26. Stearns, "Church News," *Episcopal Recorder*, April 11, 1918, p. 6; Sabine, Ms. Visitation Book, pp. 24, 76, 144.

27. George W. Huntington, in *Minutes of the Proceedings of the Twenty-Sixth Council of the New York and Philadelphia Synod of the Reformed Episcopal Church* (Philadelphia: James M. Armstrong, 1907), p. 46.

28. William Russell Collins to Thomas J. Richards, February 14, 1924, in Rudolph Papers.

29. Wilson, "To Ministers and Church Wardens," *Episcopal Recorder*, January 8, 1914, p. 4.

30. Cooper, "God with Our Church," *Episcopal Recorder*, July 1, 1882, p. 3.

31. Cheney, *What Is the Reformed Episcopal Church?* pp. 13–14.

32. Gallagher, "Anniversary Address," *Episcopal Recorder*, February 17, 1883, p. 11.

33. Turner, "Martin College," *Episcopal Recorder*, December 30, 1882, p. 2.

34. Cheney, "The Martin Gift Again," *Episcopal Recorder*, May 20, 1882, p. 9.

35. Raymond A. Acker, *A History of the Reformed Episcopal Seminary, 1886–1964* (Philadelphia: Theological Seminary of the Reformed Episcopal Church, 1965), p. 35.

36. "Report of the Trustees of the Theological Seminary," *Journal of the Proceedings of the Twelfth General Council of the Reformed Episcopal Church* (Philadelphia: Reformed Episcopal Publication Society, 1889), p. 36.

37. "Report of the Bishop Coadjutor," in *Minutes of the Proceedings of the Thirtieth Council of the New York and Philadelphia Synod of the Reformed Episcopal Church* (Philadelphia: James M. Armstrong, 1910), p. 45.

38. "Report of Bishop Rudolph," in *Journal of the Proceedings of the Twentieth General Council of the Reformed Episcopal Church . . .* (Philadelphia: James M. Armstrong, 1912), p. 116.

39. David George Dabback to Robert L. Rudolph, October 24, 1927, in Rudolph Papers.

40. "Report of the Bishop," in *Minutes of the Proceedings of the Thirty-Eighth Council of the New York and Philadelphia Synod of the Reformed Episcopal Church* (Philadelphia: James M. Armstrong, 1919), p. 23.

41. "Report of the Bishop," in *Minutes of the Proceedings of the New York and Philadelphia Synod of the Reformed Episcopal Church* (Philadelphia: James M. Armstrong, 1920), p. 23.

42. "Report of Bishop Rudolph," in *Minutes of the Proceedings of the Forty-Fourth Council of the New York and Philadelphia Synod* (Philadelphia: James Armstrong, 1925), p. 17.

43. "Bishop Rudolph's Report," in *Journal of the Proceedings of the Twenty-First General Council of the Reformed Episcopal Church . . .* (Philadelphia: James Armstrong, 1915), p. 70.

44. "The Synods," *Episcopal Recorder*, October 9, 1913, pp. 6–7.

45. Charles Mott Cramer [Class of 1928] to the author, July 31, 1984.

46. Rudolph to Fred Mackenzie, June 19, 1928, in Rudolph Papers.

47. Rudolph was able to say this, in spite of the doubts of his Seminary colleague Joseph Dawson Wilson on some of these points, because Wilson was canonically resident in the Synod of Chicago rather than in the New York and Philadelphia Synod; "Report of the Bishop," in *Minutes of the Proceedings of the Forty-Third Council of the New York and Philadelphia Synod of the Reformed Episcopal Church* (Philadelphia: James Armstrong, 1924), p. 43.

48. Walter J. McGettigan to the author, July 7, 1984.

49. Robert K. Rudolph to Willard Brewing, December 6, 1948, in Rudolph Papers.

50. "Report of the Bishop," in *Minutes of the Proceedings of the Thirty-Fourth Council of the New York and Philadelphia Synod of the Reformed Episcopal Church* (Philadelphia: James M. Armstrong, 1914), p. 33.

51. "Report of Bishop Robert L. Rudolph, D.D.," in *Minutes of the Proceedings of the Forty-Seventh Council*, p. 25.

52. Robert L. Rudolph to Norman McCausland, January 19, 1924, in Rudolph Papers; Robert L. Rudolph to Charles Denly, September 21, 1923, in the collection of the Church of the Epiphany (courtesy of the Rev. Roger F. Spence).

53. Rudolph, "Jubilate Deo," *Episcopal Recorder*, May 1924, p. 8.

54. "Church Not Split," *New York Herald*, June 11, 1897.

55. Richard L. Sonne to Robert L. Rudolph, March 20, 1928, in Rudolph Papers.

56. William Russell Collins to Robert L. Rudolph, March 15, 1929, in Rudolph Papers.

57. On the "Special Church Extension Trust," see *Journal of the Twelfth General Council of the Reformed Episcopal Church*, pp. 33–35. See also *New York Times*, June 12, 1897, and *New York Sun*, June 12, 1897, on the withdrawal of the trust.

58. Eugene Pierre Weed, "Class Prophecy," *University Quarterly* 15 (August 1892): 166, 168.

59. J. J. Robinson, "Leaven and Individualism," May 20, 1922 (typescript), in Rudolph Papers.

60. E. G. Porter to Bishop Fallows, April 24, 1908, in Rudolph Papers.

61. "Failed to Tell His Parish of Marriage, Pastor Forced Out," *Philadelphia North American*, July 10, 1915.

62. "Synod Declines to Oust Rector," *Philadelphia Public Ledger*, October 21, 1915.

63. *Concerning This House: A Brief History of Trinity Church, Southend-On-Sea* (n.p., 1938), p. 7.

64. "Organisation," *Reformed Church Record*, 10 (February 1889): 13.

65. Alfred Richardson to Charles Kellogg, May 9, 1889, Archives of the Reformed Episcopal Church.

66. Greenland, "To the Right Reverend the Bishops, Clergy, and Deputies of the Synod of the Reformed Episcopal Church in England, in Synod assembled, 1889" (printed circular, January 1, 1889), Archives of the Reformed Episcopal Church.

67. Cheney to Charles Kellogg, January 28, 1889, Archives of the Reformed Episcopal Church.

68. "Restored Union in Canada," *Reformed Church Record* 9 (June 1888): 46; "Bishop Stevens' Canadian Report" in *Journal of the Twelfth General Council*, pp. 88–89.

69. Latane, "The Next General Council," *Episcopal Recorder*, April 11, 1889, pp. 2–3.

70. Gallagher, "Extract from a paper prepared to be read in the General Committee of the Council of the Reformed Episcopal Church, Boston, May, 1889—presenting reasons why Rev. B.B. Ussher . . . should not be received with the Office, or Title of Bishop, in said Church" (printed circular, n.d.), p. 4, Archives of the Reformed Episcopal Church.

71. Cheney to Charles D. Kellogg, February 28, 1889, Archives of the Reformed Episcopal Church.

72. Cheney to John Sugden, January 31, 1889, Archives of the Reformed Episcopal Church.

73. Sugden to William T. Sabine, February 23, 1889, Archives of the Reformed Episcopal Church.

74. Richardson to Charles Kellogg, March 13, 1889, Archives of the Reformed Episcopal Church.

75. Richardson to Charles Kellogg, May 9, 1889, Archives of the Reformed Episcopal Church.

76. Gregg to Cheney, January 11, 1889, *Reformed Church Record* 10 (February 1889): 15–16.

77. *Episcopal Recorder,* April 11, 1889, p. 3.

78. "Bishop Cheney's Report," in *Journal of the Twelfth General Council,* p. 59.

79. Ibid., p. 24.

80. "Terrible Allegations Against Bishop Gregg," *Southend Standard,* July 16, 1891, p. 5.

81. "An Extraordinary Sermon at Trinity Church, Southend," *Southend Standard,* July 16, 1891, p. 5.

82. "Gregg v. Rowe at the Assize," *Southend Standard,* July 30, 1891, p. 8; "Death of Bishop Gregg," *Southend Standard,* April 2, 1896, p. 5.

83. Frank Vaughan, *A History of the Free Church of England, otherwise called the Reformed Episcopal Church* (Bungay, Suffolk: Free Church of England Publications Committee, 1960), pp. 88–102.

84. *Journal of the Proceedings of the Fifth General Council of the Reformed Episcopal Church* (Philadelphia: James A. Moore, 1877), p. 73.

85. Herman S. Hoffman, "Lalitpur," in *The Missions of the Reformed Episcopal Church* (Chicago: Literature Committee of the Synod of Chicago of the Reformed Episcopal Church, 1909), p. 2.

86. "Report of the Board of Foreign Missions," in *Journal of the Proceedings of the Sixteenth General Council of the Reformed Episcopal Church* (Philadelphia: James M. Armstrong, 1900), p. 135.

87. Hoffman, "Lalitpur," in *Missions of the Reformed Episcopal Church,* p. 3.

88. "Report of the Bishop" (Robert L. Rudolph), in *Minutes of the Thirty-Fourth Council of the New York and Philadelphia Synod of the Reformed Episcopal Church,* p. 31.

89. Hastings to Robert L. Rudolph, August 25, 1915, in Rudolph Papers.

90. Cook, "Triennial Report of the H. S. Benson Memorial Hospital, Lucknow, India, 1912–1915," in Rudolph Papers.

91. "Missionary Held in Bail of $5000," *Philadelphia Public Ledger,* April 2, 1930, p. 2.

92. Deposition of Charles R. Cook, *In re Reformed Episcopal Church v. Cook,* March 19, 1930, in Rudolph Papers. See also John W. Robinson (Methodist Episcopal Church missionary bishop, Delhi, India) to Robert L. Rudolph, April 8, 1929, in Rudolph Papers.

93. Herbert Geer McCarrier Jr., "A History of the Missionary Jurisdiction of the South of the Reformed Episcopal Church, 1874–1970," in *HMPEC* 41 (June 1972): 219.

94. Mrs. Samuel M. Gibson, "The Reformed Episcopal Church in South Carolina" (Chicago: Literature Committee of the Synod of Chicago, n.d.), p. 1, in Rudolph Papers.

95. "Bishop Cheney's Report," in *Journal of the Proceedings of the Synod of Chicago, . . . October 15 and 16, 1913,* p. 26.

96. Warren C. Platt, "The African Orthodox Church: An Analysis of Its First Decade," *Church History* 58 (December 1989): 474–488.

97. "Report of Bishop Stevens," in *Journal of the Proceedings of the Fourteenth General Council* (Philadelphia: Reformed Episcopal Publication Society, 1894), p. 123.

98. Arthur L. Pengelly to Robert L. Rudolph, December 15, 1915, in Rudolph Papers.

EPILOGUE

1. Paul Avis, "In Search of Anglican Identity," in *Anglicanism and the Christian Church: Theological Resources in Historical Perspective* (Edinburgh: T. & T. Clark, 1989), pp. 1–20.

2. Joseph Dawson Wilson, "The Church, the Witness to the Supernatural Life," in *Journal of the Proceedings of the Seventh General Council of the Reformed Episcopal Church* (Chicago: Rand, McNally, 1879), pp. 110–111.

3. Smith to Benjamin Aycrigg, July 27, 1880, in Aycrigg Papers, Archives of the Reformed Episcopal Church, Philadelphia Theological Seminary, Philadelphia.

4. Heman Dyer, *Records of an Active Life* (New York: Thomas Whittaker, 1886), pp. 365–366.

5. Benjamin B. Leacock, *Personals Recollection Connected with the Reformed Episcopal Church*, ed. Robert K. Rudolph (Philadelphia: Reformed Episcopal Publication Society, 1976), pp. 1–2.

6. Charles Edward Cheney, "The Reformed Episcopalian and His Prayer Book," in *What Do Reformed Episcopalians Believe? Eight Sermons Preached in Christ Church, Chicago* (Philadelphia: Reformed Episcopal Publication Society, 1888), p. 110.

7. Henry Benjamin Whipple, *Address to the Seventeenth Annual Convention of the Diocese of Minnesota, June 10th, A.D. 1874* (Minneapolis: Johnson & Smith, 1874), p. 5.

8. Stevens, in *New York Times*, May 22, 1874. See also William Bacon Stevens, *Portions of the Annual Address of the Rt. Rev. Wm. Bacon Stevens, D.D., LL.D., Bishop of the Diocese of Pennsylvania, delivered before the 90th Annual Convention of the Diocese of Pennsylvania* (Philadelphia: McCalla & Stavely, 1874).

9. Samuel H. Kerfoot, *Bishop Kerfoot's Visitation Address to the Congregation of Calvary Church, Pittsburgh, Fifth Sunday in Lent, March 22nd, 1874* (Pittsburgh: Bakewell & Marthens, 1874), p. 4.

10. Morgan Dix, *Sermons Preached in Trinity Church, New-York, on the Feast of the Ascension, May 14, 1874* (New York: John W. Amerman, 1874), pp. 4–5.

11. Warren C. Platt, "Ecumenism and the Reformed Episcopal Church: An Analysis of Its Development from the Late Nineteenth Century Until 1945," *Anglican and Episcopal History* 57 (September 1988): 326–327.

12. William Montgomery Brown, *The Church for Americans* (New York: Thomas Whittaker, 1905), pp. 453–454.

13. Wilson, "Wherein Do We Differ? Results of a Conference with the Reformed Episcopalians," *The Living Church*, September 28, 1938, pp. 291–292.

14. Robert K. Rudolph, "Shall the R.E. Church Be Continued? An Episode in Her History" (1985), manuscript, author's collection.

15. Brown, *Church for Americans*, p. 455.

16. Schaff, in John A. Hutchison, *We Are Not Divided: A Critical and Historical Study of the Federal Council of the Churches of Christ in America* (New York: Round Table Press, 1941), p. 19.

17. "Proposals Looking Toward Church Union," in *The Creeds of Christendom*, ed. Philip Schaff (1877, 1919; reprint, Grand Rapids, Mich.: Baker Book House, 1969), vol. 3, p. 948.

18. Hutchison, *We Are Not Divided*, p. 34.

19. Don Herbert Yoder, "Christian Unity in Nineteenth-Century America," in *A History of the Ecumenical Movement, 1517–1948*, ed. Ruth Rouse and Stephen Charles Neill (Philadelphia: Westminster Press, 1967), p. 251.

20. "Federal Council of Churches of Christ in America: A Statement of Its Plan, Purpose and Work," Bulletin No. 6, December 1, 1913 (New York: National Office, 1913), p. 2.

21. Hutchison, *We Are Not Divided*, p. 42.

22. *Christian Century*, December 21, 1932, quoted in Hutchison, *We Are Not Divided*, pp. 73–74.

23. Samuel McCrea Cavert, *The American Churches in the Ecumenical Movement* (New York: Association Press, 1968), pp. 64–65.

24. Hutchison, *We Are Not Divided*, p. 56.

25. Freemantle, "The General Council of 1918," *Episcopal Recorder*, April 11, 1918, p. 2.

26. "Report of Bishop Sabine," in *Minutes of the Proceedings of the Twenty-Ninth Council of the New York and Philadelphia Synod of the Reformed Episcopal Church* (Philadelphia: James M. Armstrong, 1909), pp. 14–15.

27. *Journal of the Proceedings of the Nineteenth General Council of the Reformed Episcopal Church, . . .* (Philadelphia: James M. Armstrong, 1909), pp. 114, 123.

28. *Journal of the Proceedings of the Twenty-First General Council of the Reformed Episcopal Church, . . .* (Philadelphia: James M. Armstrong, 1915), pp. 114.

29. *Journal of the Proceedings of the Twenty-Second General Council of the Reformed Episcopal Church . . .* (Philadelphia: James M. Armstrong, 1918), pp. 119–120.

30. Frank Vaughan, "The Christian Faith and the Challenge of To-Day," *Episcopal Recorder*, June 1924, p. 10.

31. "The Kikuyu Conference—What Will Come of It?" *Episcopal Recorder*, January 8, 1914, p. 7.

32. *Journal of the Proceedings of the Twentieth General Council of the Reformed Episcopal Church, . . .* (Philadelphia: James M. Armstrong, 1912), p. 166. See also "The General Council," *Episcopal Recorder*, May 23, 1912, p. 8.

33. Peach, "Organic Union of Evangelical Churches in the United States of America," *Episcopal Recorder*, April 10, 1919, pp. 2–3.

34. "Report of the Commission on Church Unity," in *Journal of the Twenty-Second General Council*, p. 149.

35. *Journal of the Proceedings of the Twenty-Third General Council of the Reformed Episcopal Church . . .* (Philadelphia: James Armstrong, 1921), p. 46.

36. "Report of the Commission on Church Unity," in *Journal of the Proceedings of the Twenty-Fourth General Council of the Reformed Episcopal Church . . .* (Philadelphia: James Armstrong, 1924), p. 149.

37. Wilson, "Church Union," *Episcopal Recorder*, July 18, 1918, p. 3.

38. McCormick, "The Inter-Church Movement," *Episcopal Recorder*, July 24, 1919, p. 3.

39. Gray, "The Proposed World Church Union: Is It of God or Man?" *Episcopal Recorder*, May 8, 1919, p. 3.

40. Rudolph to D. M. Stearns, August 13, 1912, Rudolph Papers, Reformed Episcopal Archives, Philadelphia Theological Seminary, Philadelphia.

41. Cheney to Robert L. Rudolph, November 5, 1912, Rudolph Papers.

42. "Church News," *Episcopal Recorder*, May 2, 1912, p. 11.

43. *Minutes of the Proceedings of the Thirty-Second Council of the New York and Philadelphia Synod of the Reformed Episcopal Church* (Philadelphia: James M. Armstrong, 1912), p. 42.

44. *Journal of the Twenty-First General Council*, pp. 153–154.

45. "Bishop Cheney's Report," in *Journal of the Proceedings of the Synod of Chicago, . . . October 16 and 17, 1912*, p. 15; Thomas J. Mason, General Secretary of the Council, in *Journal of the Proceedings of the 40th Annual Council of the Synod of Chicago, October Twentieth and Twenty-First, 1920*, pp. 9–10.

46. Platt, "Ecumenism and the Reformed Episcopal Church," pp. 341–342.

Bibliography

The most important sources for this study were the manuscripts and other materials housed as part of the archival collections of the Reformed Episcopal Church at the Philadelphia Theological Seminary, Philadelphia, Pennsylvania (until 1990 known as the Theological Seminary of the Reformed Episcopal Church). The most important parts of the Reformed Episcopal archives for this book were the Robert Livingston Rudolph Papers, the Benjamin Aycrigg Papers, and the Ashmead Miscellanies Book. The Reformed Episcopal archives also contain four clippings books—blank record books with a mass of newspaper clippings pasted in by unknown hands in the 1880s and 1890s that provide a marvelous chronicle of the growth and conflicts of the Reformed Episcopal Church. The archives also contain a large collection of Charles Edward Cheney's sermon manuscripts, most of which were published in the two anthologies of his sermons that appeared during his lifetime. The archives also contain his parish register, in which Cheney meticulously recorded every service he led and every sermon title (and sermon text) he preached during his long ministry at Christ Church, Chicago. These registers not only chronicle Cheney's comings and goings but also contain an occasional stray comment that Cheney would use to pass judgment on people or situations. Beyond these materials, the archives also contain minute books for the General Committee (although only for a few years in the 1870s) and Bishop William T. Sabine's visitation book, which Bishop Sabine used to record his own personal observations (and not always flattering ones) of parish life in the New York and Philadelphia Synod of the Reformed Episcopal Church. The Kuehner Memorial Library of the seminary also houses a complete set of the *Episcopal Recorder* from 1880 on, at which point its editor, Charles W. Quick, left the Protestant Episcopal Church to join the Reformed Episcopal Church and made the *Recorder* the principal Reformed Episcopal church magazine (a set of the pre-1880 issues of the *Recorder* is housed at General Theological Seminary in New York City). The Philadelphia Theological Seminary itself possesses the minute books of its trustees and the meetings of its faculty from 1887 on, along with a full collection of its catalogs (beginning in 1890) and commencement programs.

Few Reformed Episcopal parishes have the facilities for long-term storage or preservation of their own records, and the early membership lists I had hoped to find and use to construct class and geographical profiles (using nineteenth-century city directories) have largely vanished. Nevertheless, the First Reformed Episcopal Church, New York City, has carefully preserved a continuous set of vestry minutes from 1874 onward. (These minutes make it clear that at First Church the principal laypeoples' concern in joining the Reformed Episcopal Church was not theological but liturgical.) The Bishop Cummins Memorial Reformed Episcopal Church in Catonsville, Maryland, permitted me to use the Leacock Miscellanies Book, a massive folio book of 249 pages containing clippings from various church and national newspapers covering the disruption of the Episcopal Church from 1868 to 1881. The Leacock Book, created by Benjamin B. Leacock, also contains a large number of important papers connected with the founding of the Reformed Episcopal Church. The church also allowed me to use its bound collection of sermon manuscripts belonging to George David Cummins. Both the New York and Maryland diocesan archives (Mr. Gardiner Rainey and George Hernandez, archivists) contain substantial and useful materials on Cummins and the Reformed Episcopal Church, and the Methodist Historical Society in Baltimore provided a number of useful leads on Cummins's brief ministry with the Methodist Episcopal Church. I have also relied heavily on the reports of New York and national newspapers to tell me what the official pronouncements of church officials did not, using primarily the microfilm collections of the Van Pelt Library at the University of Pennsylvania to consult the *New York Herald*, the *New York Tribune*, the *New York Times*, the *Philadelphia Inquirer*, the *Philadelphia North American*, the *Chicago Tribune*, the *Chicago Times*, and the *Louisville Courier-Journal*.

Throughout the notes and in this bibliography, I have abbreviated the *Historical Magazine of the Protestant Episcopal Church* as HMPEC. This quarterly is continuous with *Anglican and Episcopal History*, its new title, which I have abbreviated as *AEH*.

CHURCH CONVENTION AND COUNCIL MINUTES AND PROCEEDINGS

Methodist Episcopal Church

General Minutes of the Annual Conferences of the Methodist Episcopal Church, 1835–1844. New York, 1844.

Journal of the General Conference of the Methodist Episcopal Church held in Baltimore, Md., May 1–31, 1876. New York: Nelson & Philips, 1876.

Protestant Episcopal Church (chronological order)

Journal of the Proceedings of the Bishops, Clergy, and Laity of the Protestant Episcopal Church . . . 1853. Philadelphia: King & Baird, 1854.

Journal of the Proceedings of the Bishops, Clergy, and Laity of the Protestant Episcopal Church . . . 1865. Boston: William A. Hall, 1865.

Journal of the Proceedings of the Bishops, Clergy, and Laity of the Protestant Episcopal Church . . . 1868. Hartford, Conn., 1869.

Forty-Fourth Annual Convention of the Protestant Episcopal Church, Diocese of Kentucky. Louisville, Ky., 1872.

Forty-Fifth Annual Convention of the Protestant Episcopal Church in the Diocese of Kentucky. Louisville, Ky., 1873.

Reformed Episcopal Church (chronological by General Council and synod)

Journal of the First General Council of the Reformed Episcopal Church, . . . December 2d, 1873. New York: Edward O. Jenkins, 1874.

Journal of the Proceedings of the Second General Council of the Reformed Episcopal Church, . . . Commencing Wednesday, May 13, and ending Tuesday, May 19, 1874. Philadelphia: James A. Moore, 1874.

Journal of the Proceedings of the Third General Council of the Reformed Episcopal Church, . . . Commencing Wednesday, May 12, and ending Tuesday, May 18, 1875. Philadelphia: James A. Moore, 1875.

Journal of the Proceedings of the Fourth General Council of the Reformed Episcopal Church, . . . Commencing Wednesday, July 12, and ending Monday, July 17, 1876. Philadelphia: James A. Moore, 1876.

Journal of the Proceedings of the Fifth General Council of the Reformed Episcopal Church, . . . Commencing Wednesday, May 9, and ending Tuesday, May 15, 1877. Philadelphia: James A. Moore, 1877.

Journal of the Proceedings of the Sixth General Council of the Reformed Episcopal Church, . . . Commencing Wednesday, May 8, and ending Monday, May 13, 1878. Philadelphia: James A. Moore, 1878.

Journal of the Proceedings of the Seventh General Council of the Reformed Episcopal Church, . . . Commencing Wednesday, May 28th, and ending Wednesday, June 4th, 1879. Chicago: Rand, McNally & Co., 1879.

Journal of the Proceedings of the Eighth General Council of the Reformed Episcopal Church, . . . Commencing Wednesday, May 25th, and ending Monday, May 30th, 1881. Philadelphia: William Syckelmore, 1881.

Journal of the Proceedings of the Ninth General Council of the Reformed Episcopal Church, . . . Commencing Wednesday, May 23rd, and ending Monday, May 28th, 1883. Philadelphia: William Syckelmore, 1883.

Journal of the Proceedings of the Tenth General Council of the Reformed Episcopal Church, . . . Commencing Wednesday, May 27th, and ending Monday, June 1st, 1885. Philadelphia: Reformed Episcopal Publication Society, 1885.

Journal of the Proceedings of the Twelfth General Council of the Reformed Episcopal Church, . . . Commencing Wednesday, May 22nd, and ending Monday, May 27th, 1889. Philadelphia: Reformed Episcopal Publication Society, 1889.

Journal of the Proceedings of the Fourteenth General Council. Philadelphia: Reformed Episcopal Publication Society, 1894.

Journal of the Proceedings of the Fifteenth General Council of the Reformed Episcopal Church, . . . Commencing Wednesday June 9th, and ending Monday, June 14th, 1897. Philadelphia: Reformed Episcopal Publication Society, 1897.

Journal of the Proceedings of the Sixteenth General Council of the Reformed Episcopal Church. Philadelphia: James M. Armstrong, 1900.

Journal of the Proceedings of the Nineteenth General Council of the Reformed Episcopal Church. . . . Philadelphia: James M. Armstrong, 1909.

Journal of the Proceedings of the Twentieth General Council of the Reformed Episcopal Church. . . . Philadelphia: James M. Armstrong, 1912.

Journal of the Proceedings of the Twenty-First General Council of the Reformed Episcopal Church. . . . Philadelphia: James M. Armstrong, 1915.

Journal of the Proceedings of the Twenty-Second General Council. . . . Philadelphia: James M. Armstrong, 1918.

Journal of the Proceedings of the Twenty-Third General Council of the Reformed Episcopal Church . . . . Philadelphia: James M. Armstrong, 1921.

Journal of the Proceedings of the Twenty-Fourth General Council of the Reformed Episcopal Church. Philadelphia: James M. Armstrong, 1924.

Journal of the Proceedings of the Synod of Chicago, . . . October 16 and 17, 1912. N.p., n.d.

Journal of the Proceedings of the Synod of Chicago, . . . October 15 and 16, 1913. N.p., n.d.

Journal of the Proceedings of the 40th Annual Council of the Synod of Chicago, October Twentieth and Twenty-First, 1920. Chicago: n.p., n.d.

Minutes of the Formation of the First Synod of the R.E. Church, Dominion of Canada, . . . at Montreal, 16th May, 1880. N.p., n.d.

Minutes of the Proceedings of the Fifteenth Council of the New York and Philadelphia Synod of the Reformed Episcopal Church. Philadelphia: Reformed Episcopal Publication Society, 1895.

Minutes of the Proceedings of the Twenty-Fifth Council of the New York and Philadelphia Synod of the Reformed Episcopal Church. Philadelphia: James M. Armstrong, 1905.

Minutes of the Proceedings of the Twenty-Sixth Council of the New York and Philadelphia Synod of the Reformed Episcopal Church. Philadelphia: James M. Armstrong, 1907.

Minutes of the Proceedings of the Twenty-Ninth Council of the New York and Philadelphia Synod of the Reformed Episcopal Church. Philadelphia: James M. Armstrong, 1909.

Minutes of the Proceedings of the Thirtieth Council of the New York and Philadelphia Synod of the Reformed Episcopal Church. Philadelphia: James M. Armstrong, 1910.

Minutes of the Proceedings of the Thirty-Second Council of the New York and Philadelphia Synod of the Reformed Episcopal Church. Philadelphia: James M. Armstrong, 1912.

Minutes of the Proceedings of the Thirty-Fourth Council of the New York and Philadelphia Synod of the Reformed Episcopal Church. Philadelphia: James M. Armstrong, 1914.

Minutes of the Proceedings of the Thirty-Eighth Council of the New York and Philadelphia Synod of the Reformed Episcopal Church. Philadelphia: James M. Armstrong, 1919.

Minutes of the Proceedings of the Forty-Third Council of the New York and Phila-delphia Synod of the Reformed Episcopal Church. Philadelphia: James M. Armstrong, 1924.

Minutes of the Proceedings of the New York and Philadelphia Synod of the Reformed Episcopal Church. Philadelphia: James M. Armstrong, 1920.

Minutes of the Proceedings of the Forty-Fourth Council of the New York and Phila-delphia Synod of the Reformed Episcopal Church. Philadelphia: James M. Armstrong, 1925.

1884–85 Yearbook and Calendar of the Reformed Episcopal Church. Philadelphia: Reformed Episcopal Publication Society, 1885.

PRIMARY SOURCES

Alfred Lee, First Bishop of Delaware. Philadelphia: James B. Rodgers, 1888.

Andrews, Charles Wesley. *Baptismal Regeneration: A Review of the Controversy, with Thoughts on the Duty of the Evangelical Portion of the Episcopal Church at the Present Time, Touching on the Toleration of Ritualism.* Alexandria, Va.: J. & W. J. Entwisle, 1869.

————. *Notes on the State of the Church and also on the Question of Revision.* Philadelphia: J. B. Lippincott, 1874.

An Apology: The Protestant Episcopal Society for the Promotion of Evangelical Knowledge: Its Origin, Constitution, Tendencies, and Work. New York: J. Gray, 1854.

An Appeal from Grace Church, Galesburg, to the Diocesan Convention of Illinois, sitting September 13th, 1865, Against the Course of the Bishop towards that Parish. Galesburg: D. Myers, Book & Job Printers, 1865.

Arnold, Thomas. *The Miscellaneous Works of Thomas Arnold, D.D.* New York: D. Appleton, 1845.

Aycrigg, Benjamin. *Memoirs of the Reformed Episcopal Church and of the Protestant Episcopal Church.* 5th ed. New York: Edward O. Jenkins, 1880.

Baird, Robert. *Religion in America; or, An Account of the Origin, Relation to the State, and Present Condition of the Evangelical Churches in the United States.* New York: Harper & Brothers, 1856.

Barnes, Albert. *The Position of the Evangelical Party in the Episcopal Church.* 1844. Reprint. Philadelphia: James A. Moore, 1875.

————. *Reply to a Review of the Tract on the Position of the Evangelical Party.* 1844. Reprint. Philadelphia: James A. Moore, 1875.

Bricknell, W. Simcox, ed. *The Judgement of the Bishops Upon Tractarian Theology.* Oxford, 1845.

Brooke, J. T. *Union: How Far Consistent or Justifiable in view of the Present Differences between Churchmen.* Cincinnati, Ohio: Moore, Wilstack, Kerp & Co., 1859.

Brown, William Montgomery. *The Church for Americans.* New York: Thomas Whittaker, 1905.

Canfield, Eli H. *Review of "A Pastoral Letter to the Clergy of the Diocese of New York, from the Bishop."* New York, July 1865.

Cheney, Charles Edward. *A Neglected Power and Other Sermons.* New York: Fleming H. Revell, 1916.

————. *Personal Reminiscences of the Founding of the Reformed Episcopal Church.* Philadelphia: Reformed Episcopal Publication Society, 1913.

————. *The Reformed Episcopal Church: A Sermon Preached in Christ Church, Chicago.* Chicago: Perry, Morris & Sultzer, 1874.

------. *Sermons*. Chicago: Cushing, Thomas & Co., 1880.

------. *The Surplice and the Bishop's Robes*. N.p., 1895.

------. *What Do Reformed Episcopalians Believe? Eight Sermons Preached in Christ Church, Chicago*. Philadelphia: Reformed Episcopal Publication Society, 1888.

------. *What Is the Reformed Episcopal Church?* Chicago: Evangelical Episcopalian Co., 1911.

Church, R. W. *The Oxford Movement: Twelve Years, 1833–1845*, ed. Geoffrey Best. Chicago: University of Chicago Press, 1970.

Clark, John Alonzo. *Letters on the Church*. Philadelphia: Stavely, 1839.

------. *A Walk About Zion*. New York: Robert Carter, 1869.

Colton, Calvin. *The Genius and Mission of the Protestant Episcopal Church in the United States*. New York: Stanford & Swords, 1853.

Cummins, Alexandrine M.B. *Memoir of George David Cummins, D.D., First Bishop of the Reformed Episcopal Church*. Philadelphia: E. Claxton, 1878.

Cummins, George David. "Address." In *Fifth Annual Report of the Board of Managers of the Evangelical Educational Society of the Protestant Episcopal Church . . . October 12, 1871*. Philadelphia: McCalla & Stavely, 1871.

------. *The African a Trust from God to the American*. Baltimore: John D. Toy, 1861.

------. *The Christian, in time of National Peril, Trembling for the Ark of God: A Sermon Delivered on Thanksgiving Day in St. Peter's Church, Baltimore, November 29, 1860*. Baltimore: John D. Toy, 1860.

------. *The Claims of the Prayer Book Upon Protestant Christendom: A Sermon Preached at the Anniversary of the Bishop White Prayer Book Society*. Philadelphia: King & Baird, 1861.

------. *Following the Light: A Statement of the Author's Experiences Resulting in a Change of Views Respecting the Prayer-Book of the Protestant Episcopal Church, and of the Reasons for Changing the Direction of Ministerial Labors in the Gospel of Christ*. Philadelphia: James A. Moore, 1876.

------. *Old and New St. Paul's Church, Louisville: A Sermon Preached at the Re-Opening, September 4, 1873*. Louisville, Ky.: Maxwell & Co., 1873.

------. *The Prayer Book a Basis of Unity*. Louisville, Ky.: Louisville Courier Steam & Job Print, 1867.

------. *Primitive Episcopacy: Bishop Cummins' Sermon at the Consecration of Bishop Cheney*. New York: Edward O. Jenkins, 1874.

------. *The Protestantism of the Episcopal Church*. New York: Protestant Episcopal Society for the Promotion of Evangelical Knowledge, 1868.

------. "Roman and Reformed Doctrines of Justification Contrasted." In *History, Essays, Orations, and other Documents of the Sixth General Conference of the Evangelical Alliance Held in New York, October 2–12, 1873*. New York: Harper & Brothers, 1874.

------. *Sermons By Bishop Cummins*. Philadelphia: Reformed Episcopal Publication Society, 1884.

------. "Witnessing to Evangelical Truth a Perpetual Duty," *The Episcopalian*, July 13, 1870, p. 1.

Dabney, Robert Lewis. *Discussions: Evangelical and Theological*. 1891. Reprint. Edinburgh: The Banner of Truth Trust, 1967.

Digest of the Canons for the Government of the Protestant Episcopal Church in the United States of America. Boston: William A. Hall, 1865.

Dix, Morgan. *Sermons Preached in Trinity Church, New-York, on the Feast of the Ascension, May 14, 1874.* New York: John W. Amerman, 1874.

Drumm, John H. *The Cummins Controversy.* Bristol, Pa., 1874.

Dyer, Heman. *Records of an Active Life.* New York: Thomas Whittaker, 1886.

Eastburn, Manton. *The Moderation of the Protestant Episcopal Church.* Boston, 1849.

Eli Trembling for the Ark; or, The Action of the Late General Convention and its Lessons. New York: Sutton & Bowne, 1869.

Fulton, John. *Letter to a Presbyter of Illinois on the Reconciliation of Schismatics, and on the Validity of Ordinations by a Deposed Bishop.* Mobile, Ala.: Henry Farrow, 1874.

Gallagher, Mason. *Mistakes and Errors of the Reformed Episcopal Church.* Stamford, Conn.: Gillespie Brothers, 1886.

———. *An Open Letter to Bishop James S. Johnston, D.D., of the Protestant Episcopal Diocese of Western Texas, concerning his address on Cahenslyism.* Philadelphia: James M. Armstrong, 1893.

Graham, Andrew J., ed. *The Debates of the House of Clerical and Lay Deputies in the General Convention of the Protestant Episcopal Church held in New York City, 1868.* Hartford, Conn., 1868.

Gray, James M. *The Romeward Drift of the Protestant Episcopal Church in 1887.* Boston, 1887.

Gregg, Thomas Huband. *The Ridsdale Case and the Bennett Judgment.* London: Marlborough & Co., 1877.

Harris, R. W. *Christian Worship Not Symbolical: A Sermon Preached in St. George's Church, Astoria, L.I.* New York: Hallet & Breen, 1868.

Henshaw, J.P.K. *Memoir of the Life of the Rt. Rev. Richard Channing Moore, D.D.* Philadelphia: William Stavely, 1842.

Hobart, John Henry. *Apology for Apostolic Order and its advocates.* New York: T. & J. Swords, 1807.

———. *The Churchman: The Principles of the Churchman stated and explained.* New York: T. Swords, 1819.

———. *A Companion for the Festivals and Fasts of the Protestant Episcopal Church.* New York: Stanford & Delisser, 1858.

———. *The High Churchman Vindicated.* New York: T. & J. Swords, 1826.

Hodge, Charles. *Systematic Theology.* 1871–1873. Reprint. Grand Rapids, Mich.: William B. Eerdmans, 1979.

Hopkins, John Henry. *The Novelties Which Disturb Our Peace: Letters Addressed to the Bishops, Clergy, and Laity of the Protestant Episcopal Church.* Philadelphia: John M. Campbell, 1844.

———. *A Tract for the Church in Jerusalem . . . considered in a Friendly Remonstrance to the editors of the Church Journal.* Burlington, Vt., 1854.

Howard-Smith, John. *The Historic Basis of the Reformed Episcopal Church.* Philadelphia: Reformed Episcopal Publication Society, 1883.

———. *The Protestant Episcopal and the Reformed Episcopal Churches: Is the Organization of the Reformed Episcopal Church Justifiable?* Philadelphia: James A. Moore, 1877.

Johns, Henry Van Dyke. *The Protestant Episcopal Pastor Teaching the People Committed to His Charge.* Baltimore, Md.: N. Hickman, 1842.

Johns, John. *Address delivered at the Seventy-Eighth Annual Council of the Protestant Episcopal Church in Virginia.* Richmond, Va., 1873.

———. *A Memoir of the Life of the Rt. Rev. William Meade, D.D., Bishop of the*

Protestant Episcopal Church in the Diocese of Virginia. Baltimore, Md.: Innes & Co., 1867.

——. *A Sermon on the Lord's Supper*. New York, 1858.

——. *A Valedictory Discourse: By the Rev. J. Johns, D.D., Delivered in Christ Church, Baltimore, October 3, 1842*. Baltimore: N. Hickman, 1842.

Kellogg, D. O. *Events Leading to the Formation of the Reformed Episcopal Church, Read at the Twentieth Anniversary of the Founding of the Church, in the First R.E. Church, New York City, December 3, 1893*. Philadelphia: Reformed Episcopal Publication Society, 1894.

Kerfoot, John Barrett. *Bishop Kerfoot's Visitation Address to the Congregation of Calvary Church, Pittsburgh, Fifth Sunday in Lent, March 22nd, 1874*. Pittsburgh: Bakewell & Marthens, 1874.

Kerfoot, Samuel H. *Bishop Whitehouse and the Diocese of Illinois*. Chicago, 1860.

Latane, James Allen. *Letter of the Rev. James A. Latane, Rector of St. Matthew's Church, Wheeling, West Virginia to Bishop Johns, Resigning the Ministry of the Protestant Episcopal Church*. Philadelphia: James A. Moore, 1877.

——. *A Plea for the Settlement of the Question of Ecclesiastical Vestments in the Reformed Episcopal Church*. N.p., n.d.

Leacock, Benjamin B. *Personal Recollections Connected with the Reformed Episcopal Church*, ed. Robert K. Rudolph. Philadelphia: Reformed Episcopal Publication Society, 1976.

Lee, Alfred. *The Right and Responsibility of Private Judgment*. New York: Protestant Episcopal Society for the Promotion of Evangelical Knowledge, 1856.

——. *The Sermon delivered at the Opening of the General Convention of the Protestant Episcopal Church . . . Wednesday, Oct. 7th, 1868*. New York: Protestant Episcopal Society for the Promotion of Evangelical Knowledge, 1868.

Lee, Henry Washington. *Sanctification: The Primary Charge to the Clergy of the Protestant Episcopal Church in the Diocese of Iowa*. Davenport, Iowa: N.p., 1857.

Locke, James DeWitt Clinton. *Personal Reminiscences of the Diocese of Illinois, 1856–1892*, ed. R. B. Dibbert. Chicago, Ill.: Grace Church, 1976.

May, James. *The Advantages of Church Membership with reference to some errors, historically considered*. Philadelphia, 1847.

McIlvaine, Charles Pettit. *The Chief Danger of the Church in These Times: A Charge delivered to the Clergy of the Diocese of Ohio at the Twenty-sixth Annual Convention of the Same, in Rosse Chapel, Gambier, September 8th, 1843*. New York: Harper & Brothers, 1843.

——. *Oxford Divinity Compared with that of the Romish and Anglican Churches: With a special view to the Illustration of the Doctrine of Justification by Faith*. Philadelphia: Whethan & Son, 1841.

——. *Rome and Geneva; or, False Protestantism Exposed*. New York: Protestant Episcopal Society for the Promotion of Evangelical Knowledge, 1841.

Meade, William. *Companion to the Font and Pulpit*. Washington: J. & G. S. Gideon, 1846.

——. *Lectures on the Pastoral Office Delivered to the Students of the Theological Seminary at Alexandria, Va.* New York: Standford & Swords, 1849.

——. *The Wisdom, Moderation, and Charity of the English Reformers, and of the Fathers of the Protestant Episcopal Church in the United States: A Sermon Preached before the Students of the Theological Seminary of the Diocese of Virginia*. Washington, D.C.: J. Gideon, 1840.

The Missions of the Reformed Episcopal Church. N.p.: Literature Committee of the Synod of Chicago of the Reformed Episcopal Church, 1909.

Muhlenberg, William A. *Evangelical and Catholic Papers: A Collection of Essays, Letters and Tractates from the Writings of Rev. William Augustus Muhlenberg, D.D.*, ed. Anne Ayres. New York: Thomas Whittaker, 1875.

——. *Suggestions for the Formation of an Evangelic and Catholic Union: A Paper Read at the Evangelical Conference in Philadelphia, November 9, 1869.* New York: Thomas Whittaker, 1870.

Murphy, D. F., ed. *Debates in the House of Deputies in the General Convention of the Protestant Episcopal Church.* Hartford, Conn., 1871.

Newman, John Henry. *Apologia Pro Vita Sua*, ed. D. J. DeLaura. New York: W. W. Norton, 1968.

Newman, John Henry, et al. *Tracts for the Times.* London: J. G. & F. Rivington, 1838.

Nichols, Effingham H. *A Letter to the Right Rev'd Horatio Potter, D.D., LL.D. . . . relating to the Proceedings against the Rev. Stephen H. Tyng, Jr.* Washington, D.C.: Gibson Brothers, 1868.

Nicholson, William Rufus. *Reasons Why I Became a Reformed Episcopalian.* Philadelphia: James A. Moore, 1875.

——. *The Reformed Episcopal Church: Its Doctrines, Worship and Work.* Philadelphia: Covenant Publishing, 1881.

[Potter, Alonzo]. *Memorial Papers: The Memorial with Circular & Questions of the Episcopal Commission.* Philadelphia: E. H. Butler, 1857.

Potter, Henry Codman. *Reminiscences of Bishops and Archbishops.* New York: G. P. Putnam's Sons, 1906.

Potter, Horatio. *A Pastoral Letter to the Clergy of the Diocese of New-York, From the Bishop.* New York, May 1865.

Prayer Book Vs. Prayer Book. Philadelphia: James A. Moore, 1875.

Rising, Franklin. *Are There Romanizing Germs in the Prayer-Book?* New York, August 1868.

Ryle, John Charles. *Knots Untied, being plain Statements on disputed points in Religion from the standpoint of an Evangelical Churchman.* 1877. Reprint. Cambridge: James Clarke, 1977.

Schaff, Philip, ed. *The Creeds of Christendom, with a History and Critical Notes.* 1877. Reprint. Grand Rapids, Mich.: Baker Book House, 1969.

Schenck, Noah. *The Preaching of Jesus: A Sermon Preached at the Consecration of Trinity Church, Chicago, Ill., on Sunday, April 24, 1864.* Chicago: Tribune Book & Job Office Print, 1864.

Shiras, Alexander. *Life and Letters of Rev. James May, D.D.* Philadelphia: Protestant Episcopal Book Society, n.d.

Simeon, Charles. *Expository Outlines on the Whole Bible.* 1847 (originally published as *Horae Homileticae*). 22 vols. Reprint. Grand Rapids, Mich.: Baker Book House, 1966.

Smith, John Cotton. *The Church's Law of Development; or, Different Schools of Opinion in the Church.* New York: T. Whittaker, 1872.

——. *A Plea for Liberty in the Church: A Letter to the Rt. Rev. Horatio Potter, D.D., D.C.L.* Cambridge: Riverside Press, 1865.

Smith, Marshall. *A Letter to the Rt. Rev. William Henry Odenheimer, D.D.* New York, 1874.

Sparrow, William. *The Christian Ministry: An Address delivered at the Annual Commencement of the Theological Seminary of the Protestant Episcopal Church of the Diocese of Virginia, June 24, 1869.* New York: American Church Press, 1869.

————. *Sermons by the Rev. William Sparrow, D.D.* New York: Thomas Whittaker, 1877.

Stearns, Daniel Miner. *"Salvation Is From the Jews"; or, God's Purpose Concerning Israel.* Harrisburg, Pa.: F. Kelker, 1882.

Stevens, William Bacon. *The Past and the Present at St. Andrew's: Two Discourses preached in St. Andrew's Church, Philadelphia, on the 12th and 19th of September, 1858.* Philadelphia: C. Sherman & Son, 1858.

————. *Portions of the Annual Address of the Rt. Rev. Wm. Bacon Stevens, D.D., LL.D., Bishop of the Diocese of Pennsylvania, delivered before the 90th Annual Convention of the Diocese of Pennsylvania.* Philadelphia: McCalla & Stavely, 1874.

Stone, John Seely. *A Memoir of the Life of James Milnor.* New York: American Tract Society, 1848.

Strong, George Templeton. *The Diary of George Templeton Strong,* ed. Allan Nevins and Milton Halsey Thomas. New York: Macmillan, 1952.

Tyng, Stephen H., Jr. *The Liberty of Preaching: Its Warrant and Relations.* New York: John A. Gray & Green, 1867.

Tyng, Stephen H., Sr. *Letter to Rt. Rev. Horatio Potter, D.D.* New York: John A. Gray & Green, 1865.

————. *Memoir of the Rev. Gregory T. Bedell, D.D.* New York: Protestant Episcopal Society for the Promotion of Evangelical Knowledge, 1859.

The Tyng Case: A Narrative Together with the Judgement of the Court, and the Admonition by the Bishop of New York. New York: Pott & Amery, 1868.

The Voice of Experience; or, Thoughts on the Best Method of Conducting Missions in the Protestant Episcopal Church. New York: Stanford & Swords, 1852.

Walworth, Clarence. *The Oxford Movement in America; or, Glimpses of Life in an Anglican Seminary.* 1895. Reprint. New York: Johnson Reprint Co., 1974.

Whipple, Henry Benjamin. *Lights and Shadows of a Long Episcopate.* New York: Macmillan, 1899.

White, William. *The Case of the Episcopal Church in the United States Considered.* Philadelphia: David C. Claypoole, 1782.

————. *Commentaries Suited to Occasions of Ordination.* New York: Stanford & Swords, 1848.

————. *Comparative Views of the Controversy between the Calvinists and Arminians.* Philadelphia: M. Thomas, 1817.

Wilberforce, Robert I. *The Doctrine of the Incarnation of Our Lord Jesus Christ in its Relation to Mankind and to the Church.* New York: E. & J. B. Young, 1885.

William Rufus Nicholson: Bishop of the Reformed Episcopal Church. N.p., 1903.

Wilmer, William. *The Episcopal Manual, Being Intended as a Summary Explanation of the Doctrine, Discipline, and Worship of the Protestant Episcopal Church.* Baltimore: E. J. Coale, 1829.

SECONDARY SOURCES

Acker, Raymond A. *A History of the Reformed Episcopal Seminary, 1886–1964.* Philadelphia: Theological Seminary of the Reformed Episcopal Church, 1965.

Addison, James Thayer. *The Episcopal Church in the United States, 1789–1931*. New York: Charles Scribner's Sons, 1951.

Ahlstrom, Sidney. *A Religious History of the American People*. New Haven: Yale University Press, 1972.

Albright, Raymond W. *Focus on Infinity: A Life of Phillips Brooks*. New York: Macmillan, 1961.

———. *A History of the Protestant Episcopal Church*. New York: Macmillan, 1964.

Allen, Alexander V. G. *Life and Letters of Phillips Brooks*. New York: E. P. Dutton, 1900.

Avis, Paul. *Anglicanism and the Christian Church: Theological Resources in Historical Perspective*. Edinburgh: T. & T. Clark, 1989.

Ayres, Anne. *The Life and Work of William Augustus Muhlenberg, Doctor in Divinity*. New York: Thomas Whittaker, 1889.

Balleine, G. R. *A History of the Evangelical Party in the Church of England*. London: Longmans, Green, 1908.

Barclay, Ian. *The Call to Seriousness: The Evangelical Impact on the Victorians*. New York: Macmillan, 1976.

Barratt, Norris Stanley. *Outline of the History of Old St. Paul's Church, Philadelphia, Pennsylvania*. Lancaster, Pa.: Colonial Society of Pennsylvania, 1917.

Beardsley, Eben Edwards. *The History of the Episcopal Church in Connecticut*. New York: Hurd & Houghton, 1865.

———. *Life and Correspondence of the Right Reverend Samuel Seabury*. Boston, 1881.

Bennett, Gareth. *To the Church of England: Essays and Papers*, ed. Geoffrey Rowell. Worth, W. Sussex: Churchman Press, 1988.

Bonomi, Patricia U. *Under the Cope of Heaven: Religion, Society, and Politics in Colonial America*. New York: Oxford University Press, 1986.

Booty, John, and Stephen Sykes, eds. *The Study of Anglicanism*. London: SPCK, 1988.

Bozeman, Theodore Dwight. *Protestants in an Age of Science: The Baconian Ideal and Antebellum Religious Thought*. Chapel Hill: University of North Carolina Press, 1977.

Bradley, Ian. *The Call to Seriousness: The Evangelical Impact on the Victorians*. New York: Macmillan, 1976.

Brand, William Francis. *The Life of William Rollinson Whittingham, Fourth Bishop of Maryland*. New York: E. & J. B. Young, 1883.

Bridenbaugh, Carl. *Mitre and Sceptre: Transatlantic Faiths, Ideas, Personalities, and Politics, 1689–1775*. New York: Oxford University Press, 1962.

Brown, Bruce T. "Grace Church, Galesburg, Illinois, 1865–1866: The Supposed Neutrality of the Episcopal Church During the Years of the Civil War," in *HMPEC* 46 (June 1977):187–208.

Bryant, M. Darrol, ed. *The Future of Anglican Theology*. Toronto Studies in Theology. New York: Edwin Mellen Press, 1984.

Butler, Diana Hochstedt. "Standing Against the Whirlwind: The Evangelical Party in the Nineteenth Century Protestant Episcopal Church." Ph.D. dissertation, Duke University, 1991.

Butler, Jon. *Awash in a Sea of Faith: Christianizing the American People*. Cambridge, Mass.: Harvard University Press, 1990.

Cameron, J. M. "John Henry Newman." In *Nineteenth Century Religious*

Thought in the West, ed. Ninian Smart et al. Cambridge: Cambridge University Press, 1985.

Cameron, Kenneth Walter, ed. *Anglican Climate in Connecticut*. Hartford, Conn.: Transcendental Books, 1974.

————, ed. *The Anglican Episcopate in Connecticut*. Hartford, Conn.: Transcendental Books, 1970.

————, ed. *Connecticut Churchmanship: Records and Historical Papers Concerning the Anglican Church in Connecticut in the Eighteenth and Early Nineteenth Centuries*. Hartford, Conn.: Transcendental Books, 1969.

Carey, Kenneth M., ed. *The Historic Episcopate in the Fullness of the Church*. London: Dacre Press, 1954.

Carpenter, Edward. *Cantuar: The Archbishops in Their Office*. 1971. Reprint. Oxford: A. R. Mowbray, 1988.

Carrington, Philip. *The Anglican Church in Canada: A History*. Toronto: Collins, 1963.

Carter, Paul A. *The Spiritual Crisis of the Gilded Age*. Dekalb: Northern Illinois University Press, 1971.

Cavert, Samuel McCrea. *The American Churches in the Ecumenical Movement*. New York: Association Press, 1968.

Chadwick, Owen, ed. *The Mind of the Oxford Movement*. Stanford, Calif.: Stanford University Press, 1960.

————. *The Victorian Church: Part One*. New York: Oxford University Press, 1966.

Chatfield, Mark. *Churches the Victorians Forgot*. Ashbourne, Derbys: Moorland Publishing, 1989.

Chorley, E. Clowes. *Men and Movements in the American Episcopal Church*. New York: Charles Scribner's Sons, 1950.

————. *The New American Prayer Book: Its History and Contents*. New York: Macmillan, 1929.

————. "The Oxford Movement in the General Theological Seminary," *HMPEC* 5 (1936): 177–201.

Clarke, C.P.S. *The Oxford Movement and After*. London: A. R. Mowbray, 1932.

Clarke, W. K. Lowther, ed. *Liturgy and Worship: A Companion to the Prayer Books of the Anglican Communion*. London: SPCK, 1954.

Conkin, Paul R. *Puritans and Pragmatists: Eight Eminent American Thinkers*. New York: Dodd, Mead Co., 1968.

Conser, Walter H., Jr. *Church and Confession: Conservative Theologians in Germany, England, and America*. Macon, Ga.: Mercer University Press, 1984.

Cook, Olive, Graham Hutton, and Edwin Smith. *English Parish Churches*. New York: Thames & Hudson, 1976.

Crowther, M. A. *Church Embattled: Religious Controversy in Mid-Victorian England*. Newton Abbot, Devon: David & Charles, 1970.

Davis, James. *Historical Sketch of the Origin and Operations of the Evangelical Alliance*. London: W. J. Johnson, 1874.

Dearmer, Percy. *The Ornaments of the Ministers*. London: A. R. Mowbray, 1908.

Demille, George E. *The Catholic Movement in the American Episcopal Church*. Philadelphia: Church Historical Society, 1950.

Douglas, Ann. *The Feminization of American Culture*. New York: Alfred A. Knopf, 1977.

Ellis, Joseph. *The New England Mind in Transition: Samuel Johnson of Connecticut, 1696–1772*. New Haven: Yale University Press, 1973.

Fairweather, Eugene R., ed. *The Oxford Movement*. New York: Oxford University Press, 1964.

Fallows, Alice Katharine. *Everybody's Bishop, Being the Life and Times of The Right Reverend Samuel Fallows, D.D.* New York: J. H. Sears, 1927.

Foner, Eric. *Politics and Ideology in the Age of the Civil War*. New York: Oxford University Press, 1980.

Foster, Ross A. "The Origin and Development of the Reformed Episcopal Church in America, 1873–1973." Ph.D. dissertation, Clarksville School of Theology, 1978.

Frank, Douglas W. *Less Than Conquerors: How Evangelicals Entered the Twentieth Century*. Grand Rapids, Mich.: William B. Eerdmans, 1986.

Gaustad, Edwin Scott. *Historical Atlas of Religion in America*. New York: Harper & Row, 1962.

Goen, Clarence C. *Broken Churches, Broken Nation: Denominational Schisms and the Coming of the Civil War*. Macon, Ga.: Mercer University Press, 1985.

Goodwin, W.A.R., ed. *History of the Theological Seminary in Virginia and Its Historical Background*. New York: Edwin S. Gorham, 1923.

Graham, Stephen R. "Philip Schaff and the Protestant Mind in the Nineteenth Century: A Critique of Religion and Society." *Fides et Historia* 21 (January 1989): 32–49.

Guiney, L. I. *Hurrel Froude: Memoranda and Comments*. London: Methuen, 1904.

Hardman, Keith J. *Charles Grandison Finney, 1792–1875: Revivalist and Reformer*. Syracuse, N.Y.: Syracuse University Press, 1987.

Hardy, E. R. "Evangelical Catholicism: W. A. Muhlenberg and the Memorial Movement," *HMPEC* 13 (1944): 155–192.

Harrison, Hall. *Life of the Right Reverend John Barrett Kerfoot*. New York: James Pott, 1886.

Hatchett, Marion. *The Making of the First American Book of Common Prayer*. New York: Seabury Press, 1982.

Helmstedter, R. J., and B. Lightman, eds. *Victorian Faith in Crisis: Essays on Continuity and Change in Nineteenth-Century Religious Belief*. London: Macmillan, 1990.

Hobsbawm, E. J. *The Age of Empire, 1875–1914*. New York: Pantheon, 1987.

Hogue, William M. "The Religious Conspiracy Theory of the American Revolution: Anglican Motive." *Church History* 45 (September 1976): 277–292.

Holmes, David. "The Episcopal Church and the American Revolution." *HMPEC* 47 (1978): 261–291.

———. "William Holland Wilmer: A Newly Discovered Memoir." *Maryland Historical Magazine* 81 (Summer 1986): 160–164.

Hoopes, James. *Consciousness in New England: From Puritanism and Ideas to Psychoanalysis and Semiotic*. Baltimore: Johns Hopkins University Press, 1989.

Hopkins, Hugh Evans. *Charles Simeon of Cambridge*. Sevenoaks, Kent: Hodder & Stoughton, 1977.

Hovenkamp, Herman. *Science and Religion in America, 1800–1860*. Philadelphia: University of Pennsylvania Press, 1978.

Howe, Daniel Walker. "The Evangelical Movement and Political Cultures in the North During the Second Party System." *Journal of American History* 77 (March 1991): 1216–1239.

———. *The Political Culture of the American Whigs*. Chicago: University of Chicago Press, 1979.

————. *The Unitarian Conscience: Harvard Moral Philosophy, 1805–1861.* Cambridge, Mass.: Harvard University Press, 1970.

————, ed. *Victorian America.* Philadelphia: University of Pennsylvania Press, 1976.

Hutchison, John A. *We Are Not Divided: A Critical and Historical Study of the Federal Council of the Churches of Christ in America.* New York: Round Table Press, 1941.

Isaac, Rhys. *The Transformation of Virginia, 1740–1790.* Chapel Hill: University of North Carolina Press, 1982.

Jarvis, Lucy Cushing, *Sketches of Church Life in Colonial Connecticut.* New Haven: Tuttle, Morehouse & Taylor, 1902.

Jones, Cheslyn, G. Wainwright, and E. Yarnold. *The Study of Liturgy.* New York: Oxford University Press, 1978.

Ker, Ian. *John Henry Newman: A Biography.* Oxford: Clarendon Press, 1988.

Konolige, Kit, and Frederica Konolige. *The Power of Their Glory: America's Ruling Class, the Episcopalians.* New York: Wyden Books, 1978.

Kuklick, Bruce. *Churchmen and Philosophers: From Jonathan Edwards to John Dewey.* New Haven: Yale University Press, 1985.

Lears, Thomas Jonathan Jackson. *No Place of Grace: Anti-Modernism and the Transformation of American Culture, 1880–1920.* New York: Pantheon, 1981.

Loetscher, Lefferts A. *Between the Enlightenment and Pietism: Archibald Alexander and the Founding of Princeton Theological Seminary.* Westport, Conn.: Greenwood Press, 1983.

Longmire, Rodney Howat. "Charles Edward Cheney, Bishop of the Reformed Episcopal Church." S.T.M. thesis, Lutheran Theological Seminary, Philadelphia, 1965.

Loveland, Clara O. *The Critical Years: The Reconstitution of the Anglican Church in the United States of America.* Greenwich, Conn.: Seabury Press, 1956.

Manross, William W. *A History of the American Episcopal Church.* New York: Morehouse-Gorham Co., 1950.

Marsden, George M. *Fundamentalism and American Culture: The Shaping of Twentieth-Century Evangelicalism, 1870–1925.* New York: Oxford University Press, 1980.

Marty, Martin E. *Modern American Religion,* vol. 1, *The Irony of It All, 1893–1919.* Chicago: University of Chicago Press, 1986.

————. *Pilgrims in Their Own Land: 500 Years of Religion in America.* Boston: Little, Brown, 1984.

May, Henry F. *The Enlightenment in America.* New York: Oxford University Press, 1976.

Mayo, Janet. *A History of Ecclesiastical Dress.* London: Batsford, 1984.

McCarrier, Herbert. "A History of the Missionary Jurisdiction of the South of the Reformed Episcopal Church." *HMPEC* 41 (June/September 1972): 197–220, 287–323.

McLoughlin, William G. *The Meaning of Henry Ward Beecher: An Essay on the Shifting Values of Mid-Victorian America, 1840–1870.* New York: Alfred Knopf, 1970.

Mills, Frederick V. *Bishops by Ballot: An Eighteenth Century Ecclesiastical Revolution.* New York: Oxford University Press, 1978.

————. "The Protestant Episcopal Churches in the United States, 1783–1789: Suspended Animation or Remarkable Recovery." *HMPEC* 46 (1977): 151–170.

Mohr, Clarence L. *On the Threshold of Freedom: Masters and Slaves in Civil War Georgia*. Athens: University of Georgia Press, 1986.

Mullin, Robert Bruce. *Episcopal Vision/American Reality: High Church Theology and Social Thought in Evangelical America*. New Haven: Yale University Press, 1986.

Neill, Stephen. *Anglicanism*. 4th ed. New York: Oxford University Press, 1977.

Newton, William Wilberforce. *Dr. Muhlenberg*. Boston: Houghton & Mifflin, 1890.

Noll, Mark A. *Princeton and the Republic, 1768–1822: The Search for a Christian Enlightenment*. Princeton: Princeton University Press, 1989.

Oldfield, J. R. "The Protestant Episcopal Church, Black Nationalists and Expansion of the West African Mission Field, 1851–1871," *Church History* 57 (March 1988): 31–45.

Ousley, David. "Unity and Authority." *Churchman* 104 (1990): 147–152.

Peake, F. A. *The Anglican Church in British Columbia*. Vancouver: Mitchell Press, 1959.

Peck, Kenneth M. "The Oxford Controversy in America: 1839." *HMPEC* 33 (1964): 49–63.

Penhale, Francis. *The Anglican Church Today: Catholics in Crisis*. London: A. R. Mowbrays, 1987.

Perry, William Stevens. *The Episcopate in America: Sketches Biographical and Bibliographical*. New York, 1895.

———. *The History of the American Episcopal Church, 1587–1883*, 2 vols. Boston: James R. Osgood, 1885.

Pickering, W.S.F. *Anglo-Catholicism: A Study in Religious Ambiguity*. London: Routledge, 1989.

Platt, Warren C. "The African Orthodox Church: An Analysis of Its First Decade." *Church History* 58 (December 1989): 474–488.

———. "Ecumenism and the Reformed Episcopal Church: An Analysis of Its Development from the Late Nineteenth Century Until 1945." *AEH* 57 (September 1988): 320–344.

———. "The Reformed Episcopal Church: The Origins and Early Development of Its Ideological Expression." *HMPEC* 51 (1983): 245–273.

Price, Annie Darling. *A History of the Formation and Growth of the Reformed Episcopal Church, 1873–1902*. Philadelphia: James M. Armstrong, 1902.

Prichard, Robert W. *A History of the Episcopal Church*. Harrisburg, Pa.: Morehouse, 1991.

———. "Nineteenth-Century Episcopal Attitudes on Predestination and Election." *HMPEC* 51 (1982): 23–51.

Prothers, Rowland E. *The Life and Correspondence of Arthur Penrhyn Stanley*. 2 vols. New York: Charles Scribner's Sons, 1893.

Rahner, Karl, ed. *Sacramentum Mundi: An Encyclopedia of Theology*. New York: Herder & Herder, 1970.

Rouse, Ruth, and Stephen Charles Neill, eds. *A History of the Ecumenical Movement, 1517–1948*. Philadelphia: Westminster Press, 1967.

Samuel, David N., ed. *The Evangelical Succession in the Church of England*. Cambridge: James Clarke, 1979.

Sandeen, Ernest. *The Roots of Fundamentalism: British and American Millenarianism, 1800–1930*. Chicago: University of Chicago Press, 1970.

Schneider, Carol, and Herbert Schneider. *Samuel Johnson, President of King's*

College: His Career and Writings. New York: Columbia University Press, 1929.

Schroeder, John Frederick. *Memorial of Bishop Hobart*. New York: T. Swords, 1831.

Seiler, William H. "The Anglican Parish in Virginia." In *Seventeenth-Century America: Essays in Colonial History*, ed. James Morton Smith. Chapel Hill: University of North Carolina Press, 1959.

Sellers, Charles. *The Market Revolution: Jacksonian America, 1815–1846*. New York: Oxford University Press, 1991.

Shepherd, Massey H. *The Oxford American Prayer Book Commentary*. New York: Oxford University Press, 1950.

Simpson, W. J. Sparrow. *The History of the Anglo-Catholic Revival from 1845*. London: George Allen & Unwin, 1924.

Skardon, Alvin W. *Church Leader in the Cities: William Augustus Muhlenberg*. Philadelphia: University of Pennsylvania Press, 1971.

Sprague, William Butler, ed. *Annals of the American Pulpit*. Vol. 5, *Episcopalians*. New York: Carter & Brothers, 1858.

Stanley, Arthur Penryhn. *The Life and Correspondence of Thomas Arnold, D.D.* Boston: Ticknor & Fields, 1860.

Steiner, Bruce. *Samuel Seabury, 1729–1796: A Study in the High Church Tradition*. Athens: Ohio State University Press, 1972.

Stowe, Walter Herbert, ed. *The Life and Letters of Bishop William White*. New York: Morehouse Publishing Co., 1937.

Swinford, Frances Keller, and Rebecca Smith Lee. *The Great Elm Tree: Heritage of the Episcopal Diocese of Lexington*. Lexington, Ky.: Faith House Press, 1969.

Sykes, Stephen. *The Integrity of Anglicanism*. London: A. R. Mowbrays, 1978.

Szasz, Ferenc Morton. *The Divided Mind of Protestant America*. University: University of Alabama Press, 1982.

Temple, Sydney A., ed. *The Common Sense Theology of Bishop White: Selected Essays from the Writings of William White*. New York: King's Crown Press, 1946.

Thomas, Albert Sidney. *A Historical Account of the Protestant Episcopal Church in South Carolina, 1820–1957*. Columbia, S.C.: R. L. Bryan, 1957.

Thomas, George M. *Revivalism and Cultural Change: Christianity, Nation-Building, and the Market in the Nineteenth-Century United States*. Chicago: University of Chicago Press, 1989.

Tiffany, Charles C. *A History of the Protestant Episcopal Church in the United States of America*. New York: Christian Literature Co., 1895.

Toon, Peter. *Evangelical Theology, 1833–1856: A Response to Tractarianism*. Atlanta: John Knox Press, 1979.

Towle, Eleanor. *John Mason Neale, D.D.: A Memoir*. London: Longmans, Green, 1906.

Turner, James. *Without God, Without Creed: The Origins of Unbelief in America*. Baltimore: Johns Hopkins University Press, 1985.

Tyng, Charles Rockland. *Record of the Life and Work of the Rev. Stephen Higginson Tyng, D.D.* New York: E. P. Dutton, 1890.

Vaughan, Frank. *A History of the Free Church of England, otherwise called the Reformed Episcopal Church*. Bungay, Suffolk: Free Church of England Publications Committee, 1960.

Vidler, Alec R. *The Church in an Age of Revolution: 1789 to the Present Day*. 1961. Reprint. New York: Viking Penguin, 1985.

Voll, Dieter. *Catholic Evangelicalism: The Acceptance of Evangelical Traditions by the Oxford Movement During the Second Half of the Nineteenth Century.* London: Faith Press, 1963.

Walker, Cornelius. *The Life and Correspondence of Rev. William Sparrow, D.D.* Philadelphia: James Hammond, 1876.

Ward, Julius H. *The Life and Times of Bishop White.* New York: Dodd, Mead & Co., 1892.

Warner, Oliver. *William Wilberforce and His Times.* London: Batsford, 1962.

Whale, John. "Comprehensive Church: Anglican Readiness to Receive All Believers." *Church Times,* April 15, 1988.

Wilson, George Herbert. *The History of the Universities' Mission to Central Africa.* London: UMCA, 1936.

Woolverton, John F. *Colonial Anglicanism in North America.* Detroit: Wayne State University Press, 1984.

———. "Philadelphia's William White: Episcopalian Distinctiveness and Accommodation in the Post-Revolutionary Period." *HMPEC* 43 (1974): 279–296.

Zabriskie, Alexander C., ed. *Anglican Evangelicalism.* Philadelphia: Church Historical Society, 1943.

Index

Birth and death dates for Reformed Episcopal clergy, where such information has been available, have been noted beside their names.